THE IRAQI WAR DEBRIEF

To Those Who did Not Come Back From Two Gulf Wars:

> They shall not grow old, as we that are left grow old:
> Age shall not weary them, nor the years condemn.
> At the going down of the sun and in the morning
> We will remember them.

Extract from *The Fallen* (1914) by Laurence Binyon (1869-1943)

To the People of Iraq: Inheritors of a Great Historical Tradition:

> 'She is the abode of peace and the capital of Islam.'

Comment about Baghdad by the 14th Century Arab traveler Ibn Battuta

To People Everywhere: A Warning:

> *And every nation has its appointed term: when*
> *their term comes, neither can they delay it nor can*
> *they advance it an hour (or a moment)*

The Holy Qur'an 7:34

BY THE SAME AUTHOR

The Terror Fighters: Purnell (1969)
Underwater Africa: Purnell (1971)
Report on Portugal's War in Guiné-Bissau: California Institute of Technology, Pasadena (1973)
Underwater Seychelles: Victoria, Seychelles (1973)
Portugal's Guerrilla War: Malherbe (1973)
Under the Indian Ocean: Harraps, London (1973)
Africa At War: Devin Adair, Connecticut, USA (1974)
The Zambezi Salient: Devin Adair (1974)
Coloured: A Profile of Two Million South Africans: Human & Rousseau (1974)
The Black Leaders of Southern Africa: Siesta (1976)
Africa Today: Macmillan (1977)
Vorster's Africa: Keartlands, Johannesburg (1977)
South African Handbook for Divers: Ashanti Publishing (1987)
Challenge: South Africa in the African Revolutionary Context: (Ed) Ashanti Publishing (1988)
South Africa's Second Underwater Handbook: Ashanti Publishing (1988)
Underwater Mauritius: Ashanti Publishing (1989)
Where to Dive: In Southern Africa and Off the Islands: Ashanti Publishing (1991)
War in Angola: Concorde Publishing, Hong Kong (1992)
The Chopper Boys: Helicopter Warfare in Africa: Stackpole Books, US: Greenhill Books, UK (1994)
War Dog: Fighting Other Peoples' Wars, Due out in 2004

NOVELS

Soldier of Fortune: W.H. Allen, London (1980)

THE
IRAQI WAR
DEBRIEF

WHY SADDAM HUSSEIN WAS TOPPLED

BY
AL J VENTER

**EARTHBOUND
PUBLICATIONS**

To Madelon

PUBLISHED IN THE REPUBLIC OF SOUTH AFRICA
BY
Earthbound Publications cc
Registered Address: 20 High Street, Hermanus, South Africa 7200

DISTRIBUTED IN THE UNITED STATES
BY
Casemate Publishers
2114 Darby Road, Havertown. PA 19083
Tel: +1.610.853-9131
Fax: +1.610.853-9146
e-mail: casemate@casematepublishing.com

DISTRIBUTED IN THE UNITED KINGDOM
BY
Verulam Publishing
152A Park Street Lane, Park Street, St Albans AL2 2AU
Tel +44.1727 872770
Fax +44.1727 873866
e-mail: verulampub@yahoo.co.uk

ISBN 0-620-30735-8 (Cloth)
0-620-30724-2 (Paper)

PRINTED IN THE REPUBLIC OF SOUTH AFRICA
BY
PAARL PRINT
22 Oosterland Street, Dal Josafat, PO Box 248, Paarl 7620

Selfishness, my brother, is the cause of blind superiority, and superiority creates clanship, and clanship creates authority, which leads to discord and subjugation.

The soul believes in the power of knowledge and justice over dark ignorance; it denies the authority that supplies the swords to defend and strengthen ignorance and oppression – that authority which destroyed Babylon and shook the foundation of Jerusalem and left Rome in ruins.

It is that which made people call criminals great men; made writers respect their names; made historians relate the stories of their inhumanity in manner of praise.

Kahlil Gibran

ARMENIA AZERBAIJAN

TURKEY

AZER.

Caspian
Sea

SYRIA

IRAN

7 Al Jesira

Al
Hadre

Ash Sharqat

Al Qaim

Salladine

5 Al Tarmiya

Al Ameen
Al Radwan

4 Rashdiya

Akashat

Al Amir
Al Atheer

★ BAGHDAD

Daura

2

1 Al Tuwaitha

3

Al Hateen

6

Al Qa Qaa

Al Furat

IRAQ

SAUDI
ARABIA

KUWAIT

Persian
Gulf

0   200
Miles

CONTENTS

ACKNOWLEDGMENTS

This book is not the work of one man. For more than a decade many individuals and organizations have contributed to projects in which I was involved while covering some of the events then unfolding in the Near East.

Serious issues came to light, especially after the first Gulf War, which we knew as 'Operation Desert Storm' or Gulf War 1. Not long after the conclusion of hostilities, it became apparent that Saddam Hussein was racing ahead with the development of weapons of mass destruction (WMD). Having got into the business of reporting contemporary events in Iraq, I felt that if I were to properly cover these issues, I'd have to familiarize myself with some of the disciplines involved. It was a bit like going back to school.

This being open-handed America, it wasn't long before I found many people who were prepared to help. Several of the more prominent players had to take me almost literally by the hand through a succession of minefields that eventually led to an understanding of chemical and biological weapons. Iraq's nuclear weapons program followed. It was a tough road: when I started, it was almost like not knowing the difference between a bacillus and a baccalaureate.

My first vote of thanks goes to Eric Croddy, author of two major works on chemical and biological weapons. Over the years Eric has been a rock of support and he has offered unstintingly of both experience and time.

So too, with Dr Jonathan Tucker who unlocked the arcane secrets of chemical and biological weaponry. He was also instrumental in making some of the facilities of the Center for Nonproliferation Studies at the Monterey Institute of International Affairs available to me. That organization remains one of the pivots of WMD research.

My thanks to Colonel David Franz who hosted me at the US Army germ warfare facility at USAMRIID, Fort Detrick, Maryland, when he was head honcho there; also Colonel Jerry Parker and the always-helpful Stacy Vanderlinde. Dr Terry Wilson has done some remarkable work there and he came up with good stuff from time to time.

While exploring the realm of nuclear physics, David Albright, President of Washington's Institute for Science and International Security (ISIS) and always a good friend, was among the most supportive of the professionals. With his help, I would go on to learn more about what was going on not only in Iraq but also Iran, Syria, Israel, Egypt, The Sudan, Pakistan, Libya and elsewhere. It is notable that ISIS warned about nuclear developments in North Korea - and kept on warning - long before that became the haunting issue that it is today. Check the ISIS website at www.isis-online.org.

It is not only I that regards ISIS as one of the most instructive of Washington's think-tanks. Albright was one of the first outsiders to spend time with Dr Khidir Hamza following his defection from Iraq and after the CIA had had their measure of the man. Following his own debrief, David was good enough to pass on transcripts of his interviews with Hamza, more than a hundred pages in all and fascinating stuff.

There were more stalwarts at the Pacific Northwest National Laboratory (PNNL) where I went on to cover some of the nuclear proliferation problems faced by the Former Soviet Union (FSU). While there, I spent time with Mike Foley, with whom I still talk when the mood takes us. His colleague, Don Bradley, as well as Bill Cliff, an international specialist on border security of renown, were all helpful.

Others in the game include Dr Richard Spertzel, formerly UNSCOM head weapons inspector in Iraq (Biological) and Dr David Kay, head of UNSCOM's nuclear inspection team. Both men gave me solid support. They also made significant international contributions to some of the clandestine developments that took place in Iraq both before and after the first Gulf War.

Then there was Judith Miller of *The New York Times*. Familiar with the machinations of Al Qaeda long before the word obtained common purpose, we've swopped notes for a while now. Even among her colleagues, few people are aware that Judy was one of the first to blow the whistle on Pakistan's slide towards Islamic fundamentalism. Indeed, she might very well have been instrumental in the US coming to Islamabad's rescue at a critical time in South Asia. We can only speculate what might have happened had Washington not done so. Typically, she was also among the first of the foreign writers to enter Baghdad after Saddam had been toppled. And, before that, one of the last to conduct an interview with the rebel Afghan guerrilla Massoud before he was assassinated by the Taliban. To reach him, she had to trek on foot through Afghanistan's ongoing civil war to reach him deep in the Hindu Kush.

I am most grateful to the editors with whom I have worked at Britain's Jane's Information Group, among them Peter Felstead who was running *Jane's Intelligence Review* when I returned to the fold. Clifford Beal too, was of inestimable help while editing Jane's *International Defense Review* and, thereafter, *Jane's Defence Weekly*. Mark Daly took over from Clifford on *IDR* and, as a consequence, my relationship with Jane's persists. Alfred Rolington had the vision to make Jane's into the international news gathering organization that it has become and he has let me use excerpts from material that I did for the company over many years.

But of them all, I have to thank Stephen Ulph, a classic Arabist, polymath and founding editor of Jane's *Islamic Affairs Analyst* for so many insights to the sometimes fascinating, always frustrating yet astonishing world of The Prophet, Peace be upon Him. Fluent in Arabic and on first name terms with many of the region's intelligentsia, you only need to read his award winning Special Report 'Arab Progress In Reverse Gear' in the February 2003 issue of Jane's *Islamic Affairs Analyst* to understand his grasp of some of the problems that beset the Moslem world. You can read his full report in Appendix A.

David Isenberg was to have been a contributor to this volume, but the invasion overtook developments: his was a piece leading up to 'Operation Iraqi Freedom'. Thank you, also, Anne Joyce, editor of Washington DC's *Middle East Policy*. Some of the work that I have done for her group over the years was expanded into a few of the chapters you see before you.

An expert without whose input much of what I have used would not have materialized was Ewen Buchanan of UNSCOM, the first of the UN weapons monitoring bodies in Iraq (it was superseded by Hans Blix's UNMOVIC and what a disaster that was). Ewen dealt with what were invariably difficult issues with a skill that was both consummate and perspicacious.

A measure of appreciation also, to two CIA old-timers, Jim Woolsey (now, it seems, on the comeback trail) and Doug MacEachin (he was at Harvard when we communicated) for their input, as well as the prolific Michael O'Hanlon at the Brookings Institution, Washington DC.

Harvard's Professor Matt Messelson helped me understand the intricacies of anthrax to the extent that I can hardly do him justice with a simple thank you. Always a scholar and gentleman, he provided me with valuable insight at a time when anthrax was regarded as something of little more than curiosity value to the world community. My, how things have changed.

Personal support has come from many quarters. Jim Morris was always at hand with his web connections when I needed him. So was my old friend Floyd Holcolm who was matching wits with one of the Iraqi Republican Guard divisions around Baghdad during the latter part of this book's completion. And David Batt of The Bank of the Pacific, Naselle: he kept the wolf from the door. This book wouldn't have happened without all these good people. There are a handful of others that I should mention, including some individuals at the DIA who, for now, must remain nameless. There are also the editors of the *Journal of the American Medical Association*, and Captain Hussein Ghaddar who escorted me through Lebanon in difficult times. A notable thank you too, to his boss, then head of the Lebanese Armed Forces - now President of Lebanon - Emile Lahoud, who made it possible for me to visit his country in the first place.

Over the years there have been innumerable other contacts at UNIFIL headquarters at Naqoura, South Lebanon, where I spent many a night recuperating after 'taking in the countryside'. Arab watchers should never underestimate the influence of tiny Lebanon in the Middle East: it has powerful links to many of the players, as has Hizbollah, umbilically tied, almost, to Tehran, Syria (now under duress, following the fall of Baghdad) and Saudi Arabia included.

I have met a lot of spooks in my day, but Robert Baer must rate near the top of the list for no other reason, than his love of the unconventional and his ability to sense skullduggery before it happens. This former ski bum and graduate of Georgetown University, excelled in another direction. He studied Arabic at the behest of the CIA in Tunis and was able to go unchallenged in an embattled Lebanon at a time when there was a hefty price on the head of any American national that the zealots might bring in. Langley is certainly that much poorer for having let him go just as he reached his prime as an unconventional intelligence operator. But then the CIA has done so many stupid things of late.

Scott Ritter too, has suffered the wrath of Langley and, subsequently, of the entire Bush Administration. Pity he didn't stick to doing what he knows best rather than throw in his lot with a despot.

Dr John Pike warrants most sincere thanks for his input. So does Dr Seth Carus for what eventually became several comprehensive briefings that started when I visited his offices at the National Defense University in Washington. He spoke on the prospect of weapons of mass destruction being used by terrorists in the future. Seth has since moved on to greater things and I wish him well. Pat Grant at the Lawrence Livermore Laboratory provided help in another direction; thanks also to Dr Bogdan Maglich of HiEnergy Technology for explaining the intricacies of using a fast neutron activator in the non-intrusive detection of explosives and anthrax. A born teacher, he was able to present his theories in a way that even I could understand. I am also indebted to associates at *The Bulletin of the Atomic Scientists* and the *Middle East Quarterly* and also the Washington Institute for Near East Policy.

The Stockholm International Peace Research Institute deserves special mention: that organization was kind enough to give me access to several SIPRI papers relating to the complex Middle East equation. And not to forget that old germ warfare expert Dr Ken Alibek, who never failed to unravel the most knotty issues. As for Stratfor: I'll do some work for you folks yet: your briefings are always outstanding. Ray Lauer of the FBI office in Seattle explained some of the problems associated with tracking international terrorism.

The Jaffee Center for Strategic Studies and the Moshe Dayan Institute, both at Tel Aviv University, were most helpful, and I should not forget the always-invaluable Barry Rubin and the university's Haim Gal Documentation Center. Only Barry could have produced, in short shrift, such a marvelous compendium as his *Crisis in the Contemporary Persian*

Gulf (Frank Cass, London and Portland; 2002). His timing was superb.

Bruce Gonneau did a marvelous job of designing both the book and the cover, but then he also did well with my next book out of this stable: *War Dog: Fighting Other Peoples' Wars*, which has at its theme the modern mercenary. The man is a brilliant innovator of artistry and style.

The biggest thanks of all to my old friend and mentor Jack Shepherd Smith who, as editor of this book rightly demonstrates, is the best wordsmith in the business. Jack grabbed my lucubrations and made sense of it all.

And what would I have done without support from the indomitable Richard Davis with whom I've observed a spot or two of mine and UXO clearing in Croatia? Richard founded Second Chance, today one of the world's biggest body armor manufacturers. It was he who originally built the first bullet proof vests that are worn by police departments on every continent. I never went into action without him having provided me with the necessary. A big thank you Richard, and to the good folks at Central Lake, Michigan.

A few other notables deserve thanks. The first of these are the publishers David Farnsworth of Casemate Publishing in Philadelphia and David Collins of Verulam Publishers in St Albans, England for going that extra unsolicited mile.

Les Grau, today one of the foremost authorities on the nature of unconventional warfare in Afghanistan (you need to read his book *The Bear Came Over the Mountain* on why the Soviets lost their war to understand why) opened new vistas. Worthy of mention too, is former Navy SEALS Captain Larry Bailey: it was he who blazed a path to John Weisman's door. Thanks, too, to Steve Forester with whom I've trudged the hills above Fort Columbia in the Pacific Northwest. My photograph came from his newspaper, Oregon's *The Daily Astorian*. There are good friends in Chinook, Washington who offered support while I was writing: the always-effervescent Joyce Otterson, my two lovely 'guardians' Don and Joyce Stone and Larry Wolff, my incorrigible old trekking buddy.

Closer to home, dear friend Johann Strauss upped the anté: he made possible what would not otherwise have happened. So too, with my children Johan and Madie in Zambia. Naomi Musica, as usual, did an excellent job of the index.

Madelon, my lovely wife stood by me through it all, even when things looked hopeless. These were some of the most difficult days of our lives but we came out of it on top.

Here's to the next thirty years, darling one.

Al J. Venter, London, January 2004

INTRODUCTION

Tyranny truly is a horror: an immense, endlessly bloody, endlessly painful, endlessly varied, endless crime against not humanity in the abstract but a lot of humans in the flesh. It is, as Orwell wrote, a jackboot forever stomping on a human face.

Michael Kelly, killed in action while 'embedded' with the US Army's 3rd Infantry Division. He was the *Atlantic Monthly* editor-at-large and a *Washington Post* columnist who abandoned the security of his editorial offices to be involved in the war in Iraq.

Those of us who report on conflict thought we'd seen it all in 'Operation Desert Storm', the world's first live televised conflict, 'courtesy of your friendly sponsors'. But 'Operation Iraqi Freedom', America's second invasion of Iraq or what some like to call 'the defanging of Saddam Hussein' was different.

There was good reason: more than six hundred members of the media - print, television and radio - were allowed, strictly as observers, to take an active part in hostilities. Huddled in trenches, tanks, armored personnel carriers and elsewhere, they were 'embedded' with Coalition units. A dozen of them were killed in action and, as we go to press, two more are still missing. This was the highest tally of media KIA for a war of barely five weeks' duration, which I suppose, says it all.

For all that, there were some vocal critics of 'embedding' members of the media with active units on the battlefield, and those who were loudest in voicing dissension, tended to forget that this sort of thing has been going on a while. Remember, thousands of journalists covered World War 2 with Allied Forces, most times when the fighting was at its worst: the Hemingways, the Martha Gelhorns, the Ernie Pyles. Would Hitler have given them permission to go in with the *Wehrmacht*? Or perhaps the Japanese High Command to join their battalions deployed in New Guinea, the Pacific Islands or Burma? Hardly!

Exactly the same situation held for Iraq more than half a century later, which underscores the old aphorism that probably dates back, appropriately, to before the Sumarian epoch: one war is as filthy as the next.

Which leads to the next question: was a single Western reporter permitted to report from the Iraqi side of the front? My sources tell me that there were many that asked and, with the benefit of hindsight, it is fortunate that none of these requests were granted. Consequently, it was work with friendly forces or stay home: easy choice. It is an anomaly perhaps worth remembering for next time. That said, with the West now firmly ensconced in Baghdad, we've been treated to a plethora of reports, discussions, opinions, exposés, assessments and the occasional scoop, as well as a good deal of propaganda and misinformation from all sides. In this regard, the Right has been every bit as offensive and devious as the Left.

Looking at the broader picture, it is clear that the Bush Administration seems to have cocked a mighty snoot at its detractors. But then as the aphorism goes: 'to the victor the spoils'. In Iraq's case all vestiges of control are strictly symbolic, even that country's oil. As Washington keeps telling us, it belongs to the Iraqi people and, the way things are happening right now, so it shall.

The British press, in turn – often with some justification – took an often-jaundiced view of events as they unraveled. Some reputations were made, others, such as that of Piers Morgan, editor of London's *Daily Mirror*, were tarnished, often irrevocably. Morgan's efforts lost his newspaper forty-five thousand readers in the first two or three weeks of the war. That too, must be regarded as a remarkable first.

Another casualty was British journalist Robert Fisk, arch critic of all things American. Fisk was guilty, culpably at times, of letting emotion rather than the reality of the day dictate the thrust of his reports. But then, as I was to see for myself during shootouts between Muslims and Christians in Beirut in the Eighties, he was always an outspoken apologist for all things Islamic and, in particular, the frightful regime of Saddam Hussein.

It was Fisk who went into print, wondering how the Americans would ever penetrate Iraqi defenses south of Baghdad. How, one must ask - with so much American air power passing over his head each day - could any thinking person be so naïve? As the British media guru Stephen Glover commented afterwards, much of it stemmed from the *Independent*'s 'near total reliance' on him.

Fisk, said Glover 'allowed his anti-Americanism to get the better of him, and (he) has had a pretty dreadful war'. Like Saddam, hubris prevailed and this British journalist eventually seemed impervious to any kind of criticism.

Politicians appeared to fare the worst of all. Very much tongue-in-cheek, the *Wall Street Journal's* 'Best of the Web Today' carried this report on May 1, 2003:

'Seventy-nine-year-old Peter Scholl-Latour, "who is regarded as Germany's top Mideast expert", asserted on March 29 that not even five hundred thousand US soldiers fighting in Vietnam could prevent the debacle there, and that the Iraq war would "last for a very long time".'

Curiously, this brusque little diatribe came from Germany's top expert on the Middle East. As the *Journal* asks, 'imagine how wrong Germany's *lesser* Mideast experts got things.' One cannot help feeling that Herr Peter Scholl-Latour's projection would have been much more appropriately delivered on April 1. Or try this one for size, also from 'Best of the Web': German Environmental Minister, Juergen Trittin of the Green Party, the junior partner in Chancellor Gerhard Schroeder's Coalition, grandly declared on February 26:

'The German government possesses various studies expecting up to 200,000 victims of military operations in Iraq. And it is feared that another 200,000 persons will die from indirect results of the war.'

One needs to look back a little to get the bigger picture of how things developed in Iraq immediately prior to 'Operation Iraqi Freedom', launched on March 20, 2003.

About the time the Bush campaign for toppling Saddam Hussein got into gear, some pointers to the man's seemingly dual personality emerged from the mouth of his long-time mistress who, with the help of friends, managed to escape to the West in the summer of 2002. No obfuscation this; the tidbits provided by the fifty-four-year-old tyrant's moll, Parisoula Lampsos, showed another side to the man who set himself and his country apart from the international community.

Ms Lampsos had some interesting things to tell ABC's *Primetime*, including the fact that she had been Saddam's lover for thirty years and was one of a string of women who shared his bed. While he enjoyed watching videos of his enemies being tortured, often to death, he also had a human side, she revealed, like dyeing his hair, eating desert gazelle for dinner and enjoying a tipple, usually Scotch. His favorite movie, she said, was *The Godfather*, which makes you wonder because there are only so many times you can view any film and still enjoy the, by now, horribly predictable outcome.

She also mentioned that Saddam used Viagra and enjoyed dancing to Frank Sinatra, all innocent enough for a man who used deadly sarin and VX nerve gases to destroy his enemies. His victims included members of Iraq's Kurdish population and thousands of Iranians during the eight-year war of the Eighties that left more than a million mothers' sons dead on both sides of an ever-vacillating front.

This is a book not only about the actions of a man who we now know had a predilection for extreme actions, but also of the consequences thereof. British Prime Minister Tony Blair made some revelations of his own about

Saddam Hussein in his controversial Iraqi dossier published in September 2002. The Iraqi despot, he disclosed, was responsible for a large number of executions. The details are bizarre:

- 4,000 prisoners executed at Abu Ghraib Prison in 1984.
- 3,000 prisoners executed at the Mahjar Prison between 1993 and 1998.
- About 2,500 prisoners executed between 1997 and 1999 in a 'prison cleansing' campaign.
- 122 male prisoners executed at Abu Ghraib prison in February/March 2000. A further 23 political prisoners were executed there in October 2001.
- In October 2000 dozens of women accused of prostitution were beheaded without any judicial process. Some were executed for purely political reasons.
- Their guards routinely rape women prisoners at Mahjar.
- Methods of torture used in Iraqi jails include using electric drills to mutilate hands, pulling out fingernails, knife cuts, sexual attacks and 'official rape'.
- Prisoners at the Qurtiyya Prison in Baghdad and elsewhere kept in metal boxes the size of tea chests. If they did not confess they were left to die.

Since the overthrow of the Iraqi dictator, the world has been fed even more horrific detail. Each day sees individual Iraqis come forward with their own stories of terror at the hands of Saddam's security bosses or members of the Iraqi Ba'ath Party. These were the ones that survived and sadly, they're in the minority.

Mr Blair detailed some of the activities of Saddam's late son Uday who, he declared, maintained a private torture chamber known as the Red Room in a building on the banks of the Tigris disguised as an electricity installation. In 1994 he created a militia that used swords to execute victims outside their homes; he personally beheaded dissidents, notably in the Shi'ite uprising at Basra which followed Gulf War 1.

Nobody was immune to persecution: not even members of Saddam's family. A cousin of Saddam, Ala Abd al-Qadir al-Majid, fled to Jordan from Iraq citing disagreements with the regime over business matters. He returned to Iraq after the Iraqi Ambassador in Jordan declared publicly that his life was not in danger. Met at the border by Tahir Habbush, Head of the Directorate of General Intelligence (the *Mukhabarat*), he was taken to a farm owned by Ali Hasan al-Majid. There Ala was tied to a tree and executed by members of his immediate family who, following orders from

Saddam, took turns to fire bullets at him. In total, some forty of Saddam's relatives, including women and children, were killed during the course of Saddam's rule. His sons-in-law Hussein and Saddam Kamel – both of whom defected in 1995 - returned to Iraq from Jordan after the Iraqi government announced amnesties for them. They were executed in February 1996, within hours of arriving back in Baghdad. Though the details are obscure and there is some talk of a 'shoot-out', it appears that Udayy shot both men in the face at point blank range.

Nor should we forget the Iraqi leader's human rights transgressions, which make some modern-day oppressors look beneficial by comparison. There is a fair selection of these as well in Chapter 5, courtesy of Prime Minister Blair.

Though most of this book was written in the United States, it was completed abroad after the war was over, which is possibly just as well because the political overview from the other side of the pond presents a very different picture from what one hears and sees in America these days.

In Europe, the appeasement charge prior to engagement was (and is still) led largely by the media, very much as it was in 1939. Then there was a powerful lobby that urged the Free World to ignore what was going on in Germany. As a consequence, there was a considerable body of opinion – even in America - to let Hitler get on with whatever he was doing.

We were faced with this selfsame syndrome prior to Coalition Forces going into Iraq. What is notable about this development is that much of the criticism of American actions to protect itself from international terrorism came from those who obviously knew least about the esoterics of the nuclear, biological and chemical (NBC) disciplines. They also showed little regard for history. In many instances emotions were driven by ignorance of what was taking place behind the shutters in this country of about twenty-five million people.

For a start, the appeasers tended to ignore recent history: there had already been two major invasions by Iraq as well as the bombing of both Saddam's own citizens and those of a neighbor, either with chemical or biological weapons - and Iran's case, both.

None of this is rumor or speculation. The man had a history of pathological violence and we now have substantial evidence to that effect. But even today, with the war behind us, how many critics of American military pre-emptive action are even prepared to glance at the dossiers now unfolding before the civilized world?

One of the immediate side effects is that all key health workers in Britain were inoculated against smallpox in the period immediately preceding hostilities. 'If deemed necessary, millions more doses will be distributed to protect the whole fifty-eight million population,' Reuters reported on October 10, 2002.

Overreaction? Not if you consider a CIA report that emerged weeks after Coalition Forces had taken Baghdad. A complex plot was uncovered to kill thousands of Americans with a suitcase full of anthrax.

The way it was pieced together, an Egyptian merchant seaman, Ibrahim Saved Soliman Ibraham had apparently been contacted in Cairo by an Egyptian shipping company to fly to Brazil to join the *Wabi Alaras*, a ship then being loaded with bauxite and bound for Canada. Shortly before he was due to fly out, a stranger offered him 'a large sum of money' to take a suitcase for someone who would fetch it once he had reached his Canadian destination.

Ibrahim concurred and the plot would have been successful had curiosity not got the better of him. In his Brazilian hotel room prior to boarding, he opened the case and died shortly afterwards from vomiting, internal bleeding and multiple organ failure. Five Brazilian health workers who dealt with his body at the hotel before the pathogen had been identified also went down with anthrax symptoms. Prompt treatment by the health authorities saved their lives.

It was left to Tomas Castro of the Brazilian Federal Police to comment that the dead man 'was a victim of anthrax…we imagine this is about bioterrorism and that Brazil was used as a point of transfer'.

Since then, there has been obfuscation galore. The Brazilians have denied that Ibrahim died of anthrax, or even that he had anthrax in his suitcase. You can hardly get anybody in Brazilia, the capital, to venture comment on the event, which is strange considering the international implications. Something to do with tourism, somebody commented.

That said, it's perhaps worth reminding critics of American actions in Iraq what most likely would have happened at about the time that I was born had the world done nothing about another monster with grandiose aspirations. His name was Hitler and we all know what happened there.

Adolf Hitler's scientists then, were only slowly coming round to accepting the notion of nuclear fission, even though there were some German physicists who sensed the possibility of harnessing such a force, including the controversial Heisenburg. Richard Rhodes spells it out in one of the most remarkable books of our time, his Pulitzer Prize, National Book Award and National Book Critics Circle Award-winning *The Making of the Atomic Bomb*[1]. Read it, because it is like an adventure story and appropriate to the times we live in.

As far as Nazi Germany was concerned, we were indeed fortunate that the mad corporal had to divert so many of his resources elsewhere to cope with the vicissitudes of a two-front war. Consequently a German nuclear weapon never materialized.

It wasn't lost on Rhodes either, that a disproportionate number of the scientists engaged on America's Manhattan Project in Los Alamos at the time were of German extraction. One shudders to think what might have happened had they remained in Europe. Then - had he gone ahead and beaten Britain and the United States to the punch - we'd probably all be flying the German flag today and for two very good reasons.

The first is that London would probably have been the first recipient of a German atomic bomb. Second, Germany was way ahead of everybody else in developing the world's first jet fighter. One can only speculate what would have happened had Hitler been given the luxury of more time and the facilities to equip the *Luftwaffe* with jets. His pilots would have cleared Europe's skies of Allied planes within months. It's axiomatic that Churchill, Stalin and Truman would have sued for peace. They would really have had no other option.

Also, a resurgent Germany with Hitler at the helm would have left very few Jews alive. Nor would the word Israel have been integral to contemporary lexicography.

With Iraq, time was again of critical consequence. While Saddam Hussein had neither the human nor economic resources to even remotely threaten the world in the way that the Third Reich did, his weapons of mass destruction at his peak were more potent than anything Germany fielded in World War 2. Being the ultimate manipulator and having deployed them before, he could probably have done so again. And, as before, he would have protested his innocence, volubly.

That too, has precedent. Is there anybody who can provide real evidence as to who bombed the USS *Cole*? Or blew up the two American embassies in East Africa with horrific loss of life? Or who motivated the first bombing of New York's World Trade Center? Or blew up the Khobar Towers killing dozens of American servicemen and women? Or killed forty people in a succession of bomb blasts in the lovely North African city of Casablanca, Morocco? We have a pretty good idea, but, as they say, there ain't no smoking gun. Not yet, anyway.

The question begs: was the West really expected to wait for an Iraqi-engineered smallpox attack to ravish American cities, or for one of Saddam's atom bombs to blow half of Chicago away before his tyranny was tackled? That concept is not as far-fetched as some would like to make it. Loaded onto a freighter, a nuclear device could – using the St Lawrence River and

Great Lakes – arrive in America's heartland long before any customs inspector gets anywhere near the ship.

Europe might have looked at all these issues a little differently had it been Paris or Frankfurt in Saddam's sights. Sixty-five years ago the appeasers also did nothing and we can now appreciate the dreadful consequences.

Had the Iraqi leader been another President Mubarak or King Abdullah, there would have been no need for anything like an invasion of Iraq. Saddam Hussein, we are now aware, had in his armory a modest but deadly arsenal of weapons of mass destruction.

Eric Croddy tells us in his most recent book *Chemical and Biological Warfare: A Comprehensive Survey for the Concerned Citizen*[2], that the term 'weapons of mass destruction' was probably coined by the Soviet Red Army Marshal Georgi Konstantinovich Zhukov (yes, the same illustrious Zhukov who snatched Stalingrad back from the Nazis). He also makes the point that like any defining word, it has its shortcomings.

The former Soviet biological warfare scientist Ken Alibek - he changed his name from Kanatjan Alibekov after defecting to America in the early Nineties - was of the opinion that more appropriate terminology might be 'mass casualty weapons', since, as Croddy explains, their object is to inflict human injury but not to destroy buildings or property. The same applies to germ or biological warfare.

Which brings us back to the often-overlooked fact that the man actually used some of these weapons against his enemies. Why else would he have manufactured hundreds of tons of nerve agents, including tabun, sarin, cyclosarin (GF) and VX? Those are the ones we know about: there could be others. I deal with all these aspects in Chapter 12.

In a submission before the House Armed Services Committee on September 10, 2002, biowarfare expert Dr Richard Spertzel (he spent years trying to uncover Saddam's secrets while heading the biological wing of UNSCOM in Iraq after 'Operation Desert Storm') told members present that there was some evidence that the Iraqis might also have had the deadliest nerve gas of all, Novichok. A product of the Cold War, Novichok is a dozen times more potent than any other agent. Worse, it easily penetrates all known gas masks produced in the West, Israel's included.

In fact, submissions made before Congress by Spertzel and Dr David Kay, UNSCOM's Chief Weapons Inspector (Nuclear), in those final months before the invasion was launched are instructive. Both men dealt with the effects of an enemy deploying WMD, one chemical, another nuclear. Significantly, Saddam was known to have had both in his clandestine arsenal and though it might take time, some of these assets will eventually surface. He had four years in which to hide them in a country as big as California. As they say, you can hide some of the stuff some of the time, but not all of it forever.

Asked what the effect would be should the Iraqi leader have unleashed smallpox, Dr Spertzel disclosed that relative to the possibility that such an attack might actually have taken place, a war game was conducted four months before September 11. It all happened at the Andrews Air Force Base outside Washington in May 2001. Called 'Dark Winter', the exercise envisioned a deliberate outbreak of three cases of smallpox: three individual cases in each of three states, Pennsylvania, Alabama and Arkansas. Within two weeks there were two million Americans afflicted with smallpox, he declared.

For his part, Dr Kay answered questions about the nature and extent of fatalities from an atomic bomb should Saddam have launched that fateful mission. It was his view that it would have taken the Iraqi dictator about six months to field a nuclear weapon once he had managed to acquire the necessary fissile material, possibly from the Former Soviet Union (FSU).

And the damage? Accepting that there were a number of variables, Kay reckoned that using an unmanned aerial vehicle (UAV) which Iraq had acquired in numbers (and some of which were captured in Gulf War 2) - an atom bomb detonated at an altitude of, say, a thousand feet over the Israeli city of Tel Aviv, 'would probably cause fifty thousand reasonably prompt deaths'. He added that 'it could also be much larger depending on several factors including the altitude at which the bomb was detonated.

'But fifty thousand Israelis basically?' asked US Republican Representative for Illinois, Mark Steven Kirk.

'Yes.'

Dr Kay told the House Armed Services Committee that with forty kgs (eighty-eight lbs) of highly enriched uranium, the Iraqis 'could probably have two devices that would work'. Each would have the power - depending on how it was all configured - roughly equivalent to the atom bombs dropped at Hiroshima and Nagasaki. Earlier, Kay reminded the House that in September 2000, Saddam Hussein made a speech in which he called on what he termed his 'nuclear mujahadeen' to 'defeat the West'.

Rarely, since the United Nations was forced to withdraw its weapons inspectors from Iraq in 1998 have so many revelations about that country's illegal weapons industry emerged as before this distinguished committee. Preceded by a closed session earlier in that day, Dr Kay stated in his introduction that Saddam's nuclear program had gone on for longer than a decade.

At its best, he declared, it employed over twenty thousand people in two dozen major sites, most of which were not known before 'Operation Desert

Storm'. Nor were these sites bombed during the course of the first Gulf War.

The size of this project, he suggested, could be gauged from the fact that Saddam spent in excess of $10 billion to develop his nuclear weapons program 'and if the bulk of it hadn't been uncovered by UN weapons inspectors, then one can only speculate what he's been able to achieve in the meantime without the world body monitoring his activities.

'The briefings that we received from the national intelligence services - both in the West and the Middle East prior to our going in - did not point to any large Iraqi nuclear program, (which) should warn you how much you can know from the intelligence from the outside. It also describes the task of understanding and unmasking such a program.

'Further, that nuclear program was not a list of facilities that you could simply destroy. Iraq had learnt to understand, had conquered the secrets of building a nuclear weapon. They perfectly understood enrichment technology and they were very well on their way to very large enrichment facilities.

'What we can say with a great deal of certainty is that Baghdad had solved all the intellectual problems of producing nuclear weapons. They had unraveled all of the science, from enriching to fabricating the device to getting a workable design completed that was not terribly different from the first nuclear weapons design that emerged from the Manhattan Project of World War 2.'

With that, Dr Kay offered Congress a memorable aside: 'I will never forget, on my second mission, arriving at a facility called Al Ferat, which, had war not intervened, could have been the largest centrifuge facility in the entire European theater. It was bigger than any one in Western Europe,' he declared, adding that only the Soviet Union had larger centrifuge facilities.

'And what made it even more serious was that we were not even aware that it existed before the Gulf War.'

It was the view of both Drs Kay and Spertzel that information about where clandestine weapons of mass destruction programs were at any one time were inherently difficult to unravel. In Iraq's case, they disclosed that UNSCOM weapons inspectors 'faced a serious, organized world class deception, denial and clandestine hiding of programs'. This, they said, had started long before the war and it certainly got worse during UN inspections 'as Baghdad played against UNSCOM inspectors', Dr Kay stated.

'Even when we penetrated the deception and clandestine nature of what was going on, we would be frustrated in carrying out our inspection, physical access would be blocked or we'd be invited to spend four days in a parking lot or outside a facility.' And though more secret weapons programs were coming to light all the time, UNSCOM never had more than about a hundred inspectors available to do a job that should have included thousands more. And for all that, 'the group had at its disposal only two helicopters to move inspectors around the whole country: and that in a country twice the size of Idaho,' Dr Kay declared.

More points made on the Hill by these two former UNSCOM weapons inspectors include the following:

Many (weapons inspectors) felt that by 1997, UNSCOM had almost become a shielding force for Iraq's weapons of mass destruction development 'because we were so emasculated and unable to carry out the operation'. (Kay).

One of the worst things that I can recall happening was when they (the UN) restrictively allowed the declaration of sensitive sites. And for a sensitive site, only three inspectors were allowed to go into a facility (that was) roughly the size of the Rayburn Building. And then expect them to find anything? It's not going to happen and yet these conditions were imposed on us. (Spertzel).

My experience in the Middle East is that nothing succeeds as much as success...I mean, we're really lucky to have an opponent that outraged most of his neighbors. (Kay).

Iraq had no problem getting critical items (into the country) even while the inspectors were there...they were imported clandestinely across the border from Jordan and Syria. (Spertzel).

(On actual weapons inspections): If the Iraqis knew where you were going next, you could bet that when you got there what you were looking for was not going to be there. They were able to perfect over eleven years, a deception, denial, and concealment program that was based on mobility, prior knowledge and quick movement. (Kay).

If you look at what Iraq was doing with their biological weapons, some of which were stored in a hole in the ground at the end of a dirt runway, buried, covered with tarpaulin...and others buried in pits along the Tigris Canal and more in railroad tunnels no longer used by trains, the likelihood of inspectors finding (this stuff) with good intelligence is somewhere between zero and nil. (Spertzel).

One of the most egregious violations was when we caught the Iraqis receiving not once, not twice, but three times, accelerometers and gyroscopes needed for Saddam's WMD programs. And what did the (previous) administration do about it at the time? Pretend that we didn't see (the stuff)? We never imposed the requisite sanctions and that was in 1997. (Kay).

In dry form...in powdered form, smallpox is relatively stable, so getting it into the United States is not an issue...and the amount needed - about one pint or 200 grams - could easily be contained in the standard ziploc bag. (Spertzel).

Though it is going to take a while to find at least some of the weapons uncovered in Iraq following 'Operation Iraqi Freedom', and since there is a substantial body of evidence to indicate that both Iran and, to a lesser extent Syria, are following a similar route, one needs to ask how it is possible that countries like these could acquire such deadly weapons?

One disturbing truth emerged with the firing some years ago of General Anatoly Kuntsevich, personal advisor on chemical disarmament to former President Yeltsin. He was given his marching orders after it was discovered that he had been instrumental in smuggling nerve gas precursors to Syria in 1995. This activity followed the visit to Damascus in the early 1990s by the then commander of the Russian Chemical Corps, General Pikalov.

Cosy relationship between Presidents Bush and Putin notwithstanding, there are still people in the Former Soviet Union who don't wish us well. Imparting sensitive information about the manufacture of WMD is only one of many ways they choose to express their dislike.

While most of this activity has stopped, it is also a sad truth that everybody appears to have his price. In the case of Pikalov, as long as it's not his sons who are in the firing line, why not make a few bucks on the side? It gets more serious if the man's actions were dictated by ideology: since anti-Semitism is as old as Mother Russia herself, that puts a very different gloss on some of the issues discussed here.

How serious then was Saddam's threat? There aren't many people who aren't aware that the Iraqi leader used chemical weapons against the Kurds in the north of his country. Nor does everybody know the full extent of its deployment in the war with Iran, or that Baghdad also used biological weapons in that struggle.

In a fact sheet issued by Stockholm's International Peace Research Institute (SIPRI) in May 1984, the authors Julian Perry Robinson and Jozef Goldblat list these atrocities in detail[3]. This development was all the more bizarre since both Iraq and Iran are supposed to be signatories to the Geneva Protocol which prohibits the use of 'asphyxiating, poisonous or other gases, and of all analogous liquids, materials or devices, as well as the use of bacteriological methods of warfare'.

Their study came after consistent reports by Tehran Radio of the use of chemical weapons by the Iraqi Army on the Southern Front. Shortly afterwards, the Iranian Foreign Minister told the Conference on

Disarmament in Geneva that there had been at least forty-nine instances of Iraqi chemical attacks in forty border regions.

A week later Baghdad launched a major counter offensive in the border marshlands to the immediate north of Basra where, at Majnoon Islands, Iraq has vast untapped oil resources. Majnoon was a strategic military location where a large artillery battery enabled the Iranians to keep both defensive and offensive control of the Iran-Iraq frontier. I quote:

...Iraq used chemical weapons on at least 14 further occasions, adding more than 2,000 to the total number of people wounded by poison gas.

On the question of verification, SIPRI commented:

One of the chemical warfare instances reported by Iran, at Hoor-ul-Huzwaizeh on March 13, 1984 has since been conclusively verified by an international team of specialists dispatched to Iran by the United Nations Secretary General. The evidence adduced in the report by the UN team lends substantial credence to Iranian allegations of Iraqi chemical warfare on at least six other occasions during the period February 26 to March 17.

Another report published a decade ago attracted almost no attention at the time but has recently been reprinted. It appeared in the April 1991 issue of *Military Medicine* (Vol. 156) and provides a thorough review of a biological (and chemical) weapons attack by Iraq in the war with Iran.

A bombing took place in March 1984, on 5,000 Iranian troops stationed off the southwest corner of Iraq with the initiation of the Kheibar Offensive. The authors, Texan doctors Hooshang Kadivar and Stephen Adams say that Iraqi planes dropped a number of bombs over Iranian troop concentrations:

'These exploded silently in mid-air, giving no indication of their lethal content. Among the biological agents dispersed were Trichothecene Mycotoxins; toxins that affect multiple organs systems in the body simultaneously. They were used in conjunction with conventional chemical agents including mustard gas, tabun and lewisite. The Iranians suffered a 15 per cent mortality rate as a consequence of this action. By all accounts Tehran's forces were caught completely by surprise and the incident apparently had a severe effect on Iranian troop morale.'

So, in answer to the most obvious question being asked in the streets of London, San Francisco, Paris, New York and elsewhere as to whether Saddam Hussein would actually have used weapons of mass destruction had he had the time and ability to deploy them before America unleashed its most crippling bombardment ever, you only have to look at some of the preparations that he made prior to 'Operation Desert Storm' twelve years before to bomb Coalition Forces with nerve and bacterial agents (including anthrax).

More to the point, since he already showed himself capable of killing his own countrymen in nerve gas attacks, what makes one think he wouldn't have relished the opportunity to strike to best advantage against American troops? Such actions would certainly have polished the few marbles that he had left in the Arab world.

As Dr David Kay told me shortly after returning from Iraq (where he headed UNSCOM's nuclear inspection team): 'Never underestimate Saddam Hussein.'

That much was powerfully underscored by Britain's International Institute for Strategic Studies in September 2002 when it released its think-tank dossier, *Iraq's Weapons of Mass Destruction: A Net Assessment*[4].

The most important revelation, according to the Institute, was that Saddam Hussein could have had nuclear weapons within months were he successful in acquiring weapons grade uranium, or in the argot, fissile material. The dossier also stated that Saddam, based on his record and the extraordinary array of unconventional weapons that he had secreted from the international community prior to the Gulf War in 1991, remained engaged in developing nuclear, biological and chemical warheads.

It is worth remembering that for all his posturing, Saddam wouldn't have taken himself and his country to the brink if he didn't believe that he had at least a sporting chance to achieve some kind of a victory at the end of it all.

He blundered in his tactical planning in 1991 but, prior to 'Operation Iraqi Freedom' it couldn't simply be taken for granted that he would do so again. Until his overthrow, nobody was certain what this tyrant had up his proverbial sleeve.

What was critical at that time was that Western intelligence agents were aware that he still needed fissile material with which to arm the three atomic bombs. They knew too, that his weaponization team had assembled: he again called this group together in 2000 and he certainly wouldn't have done so had he not already acquired the wherewithal to make waging war a viable option. How he set about trying to build his atom bombs is comprehensively covered in Chapter 1.

All this is sobering stuff, if only because such a device - whether manufactured by Iraq, Iran, Pakistan or North Korea - doesn't have to be dropped on any city from aircraft or unmanned aerial vehicles (UAVs).

It could be detonated in the approaches to Haifa harbor or after it reaches one of the container depots in Baltimore. There are no rules to this horrendous game.

More of Saddam's WMD program was highlighted in Britain's *Observer* late September 2002. This was a special report by Peter Beaumont in London and Nick Paton Walsh in Moscow[5].

The two journalists spelt out the lengths to which Baghdad was prepared to go to acquire fissile material for Iraq's nuclear program. They also detailed contacts with companies in Belarus where, they maintained, Iraq acquired a variety of technical equipment such as high-specification machine tools including diamond cutters, a powder-metal production line and a plasma spray machine, all of which would have had potential nuclear usage. Much of this was subsequently smuggled into Iraq through the Jordanian port of Aqaba.

Iraq's contacts in Minsk were still viable in the summer of 2002 when its deputy Prime Minister and Minister for Military Industrialization, Abdul Tawab Mulla Howeish was in that city to sign a new protocol authorizing scientific and technical exchanges between the two countries.

At the end of this deeply clandestine and duplicitous activity, it is one of the unsettling truisms of the era in which we live - highlighted by Messrs Spertzel and Kay before Congress - that the only time we would have known (prior to the invasion) whether or not Iraq had a nuclear capability - was when Saddam used this weapon for the first time. The same with chemical and biological weapons.

In trying to achieve his objectives, Saddam sought bedfellows in some rather unusual quarters and clearly, Minsk was not the only transgressor in beating the arms embargo.

The *Middle East Intelligence Bulletin* issued a related report[6] late 2002, that the Iraqi dictator had been heavily resupplied with weapons and spares through Syria. It mentioned a report published the previous July by the liberal Israeli daily *Ha'aretz* that Syria had transferred to Baghdad T-55 tank engines and replacement parts for T-72 tanks from Bulgaria and Belarus, military trucks from Russia, eighty MiG-29 engines and radar systems from the Ukraine[7].

Also delivered were spare parts of unknown origin for Iraqi Air Force MiG-21s, 23s and 25s. Western intelligence sources - cited by the London *Times* a month earlier[8] - confirmed the allegations. According to this report, Czech arms shipments as well as tanks imported by Syria from Bulgaria several years ago were smuggled overland into Iraq via the Aleppo-Mosul railway, which connects to the Iraqi capital. But more of that later.

Arguably the most worrying development during the period leading up to war was the appointment of a Swede, Mr Hans Blix, to head the newly constituted United Nations arms inspectorate UNMOVIC. As with its predecessor, the United Nations Special Commission (UNSCOM), this body was charged with searching for, finding and ultimately destroying Saddam's weapons of mass destruction.

By all accounts - as subsequently emerged - Blix was hardly the ideal choice of UNMOVIC team leader. A London *Times* report[9] on March 10, 2003, disclosed that for reasons best known to himself, the Swedish arms inspector had deliberately withheld information from Britain and America that his inspectors had found a large Iraqi unmanned aircraft which violated the UN arms mandate. Only later did Blix concede that he had done so to avoid war.

Days later[10] the American chairman of Accuracy in Media, Reed Irvine wrote a column which he titled 'Hans Blix is Saddam's Man'.

Reed quoted a piece in the *Wall Street Journal* (November 26, 2002) where Gary Milhollin, director of the Wisconsin Project on Nuclear Arms Control pointed out that Blix 'had no intention of demanding that Saddam comply with the provision in UN Resolution 1441 that authorized UN inspectors to demand that Iraqi scientists be allowed to go outside Iraq with their families to be interviewed about weapons of mass destruction.' Blix, he said, had dismissed this maneuver as having 'practical difficulties'.

According to an erstwhile colleague, former Swedish Deputy Prime Minister Per Ahlmark, he described Blix as probably the most inept choice of all. Ahlmark recalls (Chapter 9) that Blix was the man who 'blithely assured the world - after several inspections - that nothing alarming was happening in Iraq'.

In a savage indictment of the choice of chief UN weapons inspector, Ahlmark recalled that after 'Operation Desert Storm' (when Blix led the disarmament team for the first time), 'he totally failed to realize that the Iraqis were lying when they said they were hiding nothing'.

Ahlmark: 'David Kay, perhaps the most effective of the arms inspectors, insisted that he did not trust the Iraqis. But Blix reproached Kay for his attitude. "You must believe in official information," the Swede told him.

'The turning point came when Kay initiated inspections of suspect buildings without notifying the Iraqis of his intentions. This new and aggressive strategy had dramatic consequences: Kay went on to uncover material that confirmed that Iraq was only twelve to eighteen months away from producing a nuclear device.

'That historic discovery ended up in a confrontation in a parking lot in Baghdad. UN cars were surrounded by two hundred Iraqi soldiers and a mob, ordered out to the scene by Iraqi officials. For four days and nights the siege continued as Kay and his colleagues used satellite telephones to fax crucial documents to the West.'

According to this former Swedish deputy Prime Minister, Blix bitterly opposed the raid, which is one of the reasons why the Americans remained skeptical about the efficacy of an organization that was then led by a man who appeared to be thoroughly manipulated by the Iraqis the first time round.

Relevant too perhaps, is that Blix is no Richard Butler, former head of the now-defunct UNSCOM, a body that successfully uncovered many of Saddam's arms caches. Diplomat or not, Butler is an Aussie fighter in the true Wallaby tradition. In retrospect, he was admirably suited for the job, but possibly because he's the kind of man who is not afraid to get in anybody's face if it means doing the necessary, he didn't get it.

As Dr David Kay declared since: 'with Blix in charge, you could not really expect any dramatic results in the new search for arms. Blix being Blix, there was nothing to show that he would not take the limp wrist approach again. And that was one of our fears.

'Another was that by the time the West eventually got around to checking Saddam's WMD programs the second time round, it might have been too late.'

In the end, an invasion by Coalition Forces removed that part of the equation. What we do have to ask is what exactly it was that the United Nations secretary-general Kofi Annan was thinking when he appointed Hans Blix, a man with a notorious history of bungling to one of the world's most sensitive positions?

1   Richard Rhodes: *The Making of the Atomic Bomb.* Interestingly, Nobel Laureate for Physics in 1944, I.I. Rabi is on record as saying that the work '…is an epic worthy of Milton. Nowhere else have I seen the whole story put down with such elegance and gusto and in such revealing detail and simple language, which carries the reader through wonderful and profound scientific discoveries and their application.' If you're interested in how maverick states are trying to acquire nuclear weapons today, this book is a must because they are using many of the same systems in their bids to achieve parity

2   *Chemical and Biological Warfare: A Comprehensive Survey for the Concerned Citizen* by Eric Croddy with Clarisa Armendariz and John Hart, Copernicus Books, New York, 2002

3   http://projects.sipri.se/cbw/research/factsheet-1984.html

4   London, September 2002: http://www.iiss.org

5   *The Observer,* London, September 22, 2002

6   *The Middle East Intelligence Bulletin*: http://www.meib.org/articles/0209_s2.htm

7   *Ha'aretz,* Israel, July 15, 2002

8   *The Times,* London, June 10, 2002

9   *The Times,* London, March 10, 2003

10   *Accuracy in Media* 'Weekly Column'; 'Hans Blix is Saddam's Man' by Reed Irvine, March 13, 2003

1

HOW SADDAM ALMOST BUILT HIS BOMB

After President Saddam Hussein stopped a United Nations strip-search of his country for real or imagined stocks of weapons of mass destruction, nobody really knew what he had been doing in the interim. For its part, Tehran was also alarmed at the lack of any kind of monitoring process in place. The story behind Baghdad's bid to build a nuclear weapon makes for a remarkable mix of deception, intrigue, political power play as well as downright greed on the part of some of those in both East and West who gave him a hand. This was to have been the first Arab bomb: Iraq's atom bomb.

What the aftermath of 'Operation Desert Storm' did for those involved in the Middle East was to stir the recurrent nightmare of a major Israeli-Arab conflict involving nuclear weapons. This dreadful scenario continues to haunt strategists on both sides of the Atlantic. Looking back, there are quite a few arms specialists who concede that the prospect of Saddam getting a bomb of his own was a pretty close-run thing.

The boffins reckon that while Iraq had serious problems with some of the more arcane disciplines associated with building a nuclear weapon, Baghdad, using indigenous facilities, might have been as little as two or three years from producing the first Arab atom bomb. Others talk about six or eight months. And while it was Pakistan that built the first *Islamic* bomb, there was a brief window when Islamabad began to share some of its secrets associated with weapons of mass destruction with Baghdad.

Some specialists also maintain that had the Iraqi dictator taken the short cut (which is what his Iranian neighbors are suspected of doing right now, with plutonium and weapons grade uranium bought on the Former Soviet Union [FSU] black market) that objective might have been achieved even sooner.

It is worth noting that it was Saddam Hussein's original intention, once it became clear that the invasion of Kuwait would be fiercely opposed, to use his safeguarded highly enriched uranium (HEU) - covered by the Nuclear Nonproliferation Treaty (NPT) - for the construction of a single nuclear device. Had he succeeded, he might well have had his bomb within a year. And while he would still have lacked the means to deliver it to target, he was spending a lot of money and effort on working on that as well.

United States National Intelligence estimates said at the time: 'Iraq (with a supply of HEU) could build such a device in six months to a year.' At the same time, it concluded that the final product was fraught with problems and, in any event, it would have been 'too big to deliver by missile'.

Vienna's International Atomic Energy Agency (IAEA), and by inference, the major powers, were very much aware that when the Coalition Forces launched 'Desert Storm', Iraq had in stock a total of more than thirty lbs of fresh Russian-supplied 80 per cent-enriched uranium as well as twenty-six lbs of lightly irradiated 93 per cent uranium together with about a pound of 93 HEU, the last two bought from France.

All had been subject to IAEA scrutinies which, according to Dr David Kay (chief inspector of the three early UN nuclear weapons inspection programs in post-Gulf War Iraq), had been cleverly manipulated by Baghdad. The point made here by several observers is the fact that Saddam was in possession of HEU and that gave him a certain amount of leverage.

During the course of subsequent weapons' searches, the Iraqis were obliged to admit to UN inspectors that after the IAEA made their routine inspection of this material in November 1990 (following the invasion of Kuwait, but before the Allies started bombing), they intended to divert all their HEU and further enrich a portion of it[1]. Indeed, they were planning to convert it to metal 'buttons' for the final weaponization process, which should have taken place by April 1991. The intention was to present the world with a fait accompli: that Iraq had its bomb.

Israeli sources in Washington have suggested to this author that in order to do this, Saddam Hussein might have exercised one of two options:

- He could have test fired his bomb in the desert at a site to be built near the Saudi Arabian border. This would have demonstrated to the world that Iraq had nuclear capability (and thus, possibly, bring about a stalemate in the Kuwaiti issue with his forces still ensconced at the head of the Gulf). As it was, he was pre-empted by the invasion.

- Alternatively, there is a school of thought that believed he might have considered trying to transport such a bomb to Israel, possibly by boat, for detonation in the roadstead to Haifa harbor. This is a premise that did the rounds in Beirut during the mid-Nineties and is thought to have originally been mooted by Iran's Pasdaran or Revolutionary Guards (author's visit to Lebanon, August 1997).

Significantly, people involved in such things have maintained all along that it is not necessary to *physically* land a nuclear weapon on American soil in order to cause destruction. Such a device could be detonated while still onboard ship in New York (or any other) harbor.

It is clear that the biggest shock of post-war IAEA inspections was the discovery that Iraq had a very substantial electromagnetic isotope separation (EMIS) program for the envisaged production of an A-bomb. It was vast. Numerous buildings were constructed at Al Tuwaitha, about twenty miles south of Baghdad. These housed the research and development phases of both the EMIS and gaseous diffusion enrichment programs.

The diffusion program (which lasted from 1982 until mid-1987) occupied three large buildings. Interestingly, the EMIS project was located in other structures at Al Tuwaitha, which disconcerted a lot of the staff working there. They were only too aware of what had happened at Osiraq in June 1981 when the Israelis bombed that reactor. They knew, too, that Israel had already complained about the huge conglomeration of buildings at the complex. When Saddam added still more structures, it did little for morale.

In the meantime, though, his EMIS program had a home. EMIS is such a large and energy-intensive technology that intelligence agencies have always assumed that with modern electronic and satellite-surveillance techniques they would easily be able to detect such a development, even in its infancy.

More significant, neither Russia nor America believed that any nation would pursue 'obsolete' calutron technology in a bomb program. It was outdated, World War 2 stuff, the pundits argued. In any event, the US abandoned that route soon after Japan capitulated. Yet the detail is there, in print, among documentation that was declassified years ago. For decades it has been available for public inspection by anybody who knows where to look. (In the US, old timers recalled that the magnets were so strong that they could feel their shoes affected by the magnetic field, due to the customary tiny metal tacks in the soles.)

After Iraq lost the war and the first of the international inspectors arrived, they uncovered what was termed at the time 'a remarkable clandestine nuclear materials production and weapons design of unexpected size and sophistication[2].' The total value of the program was initially estimated at about $5 billion. Later considerations put it at double that. Dr David Kay, in his testimony before the US Senate Foreign Relations

Committee in October 1991 reckoned that there were about seven thousand scientists and twenty thousand workers involved on the nuclear side alone, never mind all those still working on chemical and biological programs as well as missile delivery systems.

One of the most comprehensive reports on how the Iraqis managed to befuddle the West is contained in a report that Kay wrote for the Center for Strategic and International Studies at Boston's Massachusetts Institute of Technology. Another was authored by Dr Khidir Hamza, at the time the most senior Iraqi nuclear physicist to defect to the West. He detailed the extent of his (and others') work in a report published in *The Bulletin of the Atomic Scientists*[3] and, subsequently, in his book *Saddam's Bomb Maker*. Dr Hamza now lives in the US with his family, all of whom the CIA successfully smuggled out of Iraq.

Kay pointed out that in terms of Security Council Resolution 687, Iraq was required to give the UN precise details of the quantities and locations of all its nuclear, chemical, biological and ballistic missile stockpiles. These listings were designed to provide a touchstone for subsequent inspection activities and were to lead to the dismantling of Iraq's WMD.

'What really happened was that just about every detail that emanated from Baghdad thereafter was misleading,' Dr Kay subsequently stated.

'On the nuclear front,' declares Kay, 'the scale of deception was even greater. Iraq's initial declaration on April 19, 1991 was that it had no proscribed nuclear materials This was amended eight days later to acknowledge that it had only what was reported to the IAEA before the war, as well as a peaceful research program centered on the Al Tuwaitha Nuclear Research Center.'

Subsequent inspections found something altogether different. It soon became clear that Iraq had been involved in a massive nuclear weapons program (certainly the largest in any Third World country) for some years. Kay writes: 'At the time of the invasion of Kuwait, (Iraq) had begun the start-up for industrial-scale enrichment using calutrons and had acquired the material, designs and much of the equipment for perhaps as many as twenty thousand modern centrifuges. Design, component testing and construction of manufacturing facilities for actual bomb production were well advanced.'

UN inspectors reckoned about that time that the electromagnetic isotope separation program had put Iraq just eighteen to thirty months from having enough material for between one and three atom bombs. (It is worth noting that prior to going pro-Iraq in the early years of this millennium, former UNSCOM inspector Scott Ritter confirmed to this writer that there were three or four. Indeed, he was about to uncover them in September 1998, when the State Department halted his vigorous inspection program.)

The UN Action Team also found a great deal of sophisticated European centrifuge technology. This seemed to indicate a leak of substantial - as yet unspecified - proportions from the triple-nation (Germany, the Netherlands and Britain) Uranium Enrichment Company better known as Urenco.

What quickly became apparent was that there were detailed plans for building an 'implosion' nuclear device which can use either HEU or plutonium. This type of weapon contains a mass of nuclear material, in this case, HEU, at its core. Iraqi scientists envisioned building an implosion device with conventional explosives around the central mass detonating simultaneously: it has the effect of compressing fissile material into a supercritical mass. At that instant, neutrons are injected into the material to initiate a chain reaction and explosion. (China uses something similar in their warheads with HEU.)

The appropriately-named 'Fat Man', an American atom bomb dropped on the city of Nagasaki that caused about twenty thousand immediate deaths, (and another seventy thousand over the next twelve months or so) was such a weapon. It had a yield of less than 20 kT.

All this was no easy task. Vienna's IAEA discovered early on that the Iraqis appeared to be just starting to comprehend the extremely complex principles associated with spherical geography linked to this kind of weapons' research.

Another IAEA inspector told this writer that Iraqi scientists were planning a device with a solid core of about forty lbs of weapons grade uranium. It would have included a reflector of natural uranium metal about an inch thick and a tamper of hardened iron. An atom bomb of this type would weigh about a ton with an outer diameter of about thirty-six inches (just less than a meter), making it significantly smaller and lighter than the devices developed by Robert Oppenheimer and his Los Alamos club in the mid-forties. The circumference would still have precluded it from being fitted to Scuds, the only missile available to Baghdad.

Astonishment has always been expressed at the 'true breadth of Saddam's nuclear weapons enterprise', as well as the amount of maneuvering - both adroit and malfeasant - that was needed to keep it hidden from prying eyes both on the ground and above it, says David Albright. He spent time with the IAEA Action Team in Iraq and is president of Washington's Institute of Science and International Security (ISIS). These discoveries shook the international nonproliferation regime and the tremors persist since there are now other nations getting into the act, North Korea and Iran included.

What was revealed were critical weaknesses in inspection routines, export controls and in intelligence gathering and the sharing of these assets. Albright reckons that the reality of those first disclosures, and the well-founded suspicion that more lay ahead, led to the initial assumption that Saddam was 'on the brink' of putting his own atomic weapon on the international table. Yet while the Iraqi nuclear program involved tens of thousands of people, no one in the West was aware until long afterwards of the numbers of Iraqi students that had been sent abroad to acquire the necessary expertise.

These youngsters - and some not-so-young academics - were rarely sent to the same universities or countries, which made it difficult for any single authority to appreciate the breadth of technical skills being acquired by Baghdad. It also presented problems for the world community to keep track of individual Iraqi scientists. The two exceptions, peculiarly, were France and Italy, who together hosted about four hundred Iraqis; yet none were officially approached about the subjects or courses that they were actually following. Dr Hamza told me that nearly all the current leaders of the program were drawn from those batches of trainees.

Dr Kay highlighted all this with a disturbing observation. While in Iraq, he said, he dealt for months with a senior Iraqi scientist whose entire university training - from undergraduate level, all the way through to his doctorate - had been in America. His first real job was at a US nuclear power plant. Yet, declared Kay, all basic data on or pictures of this key individual could not be found at any of the academic institutions where he had spent time. In retrospect, the issue has a something of Dr Strangelove resonance about it.

It is interesting that the Iraqi experience (together with developments that followed September 11) has since led to a significant tightening up of IAEA inspection procedures which, essentially, is to prevent such things from happening again. You only need to look at developments in Iran towards the close of the millennium and it would appear that history is repeating itself[4].

There have been other anomalies. It is no longer a secret that prior to 'Desert Storm' the Iraqis received generous amounts of tactical aid from what later became their chief antagonists, the Americans. During the Iran-Iraq War, while Washington was providing arms to Iran in the hope of getting their hostages in Lebanon freed, it was also rushing classified satellite intelligence to Baghdad almost as soon as it came in. This gave Baghdad a good idea what the Americans were able to see, and, by inference, how they could be fooled. With time, they would use this knowledge to good advantage[5].

Before that, Baghdad managed to gain acceptance by Vienna's IAEA by placing Abdul-Wahid Al-Saji, a mild-mannered Iraqi physicist, in a position to serve his country as a bona fide IAEA inspector. Gradually, the Iraqis came to understand the machinations of the agency: this knowledge ultimately proved useful to Baghdad's weapons program in obtaining nuclear technology.

According to Dr Hamza, the agency accepted Iraq's importation of HEU for its research reactor without ever evaluating the possibility that it might be diverted for military use. Most important, Iraqis were able to gain a complete understanding of IAEA inspection procedures and processes. Iraqi officials were also alerted to the success of satellite remote sensing in uncovering clandestine and, especially, underground activities. For this reason, Saddam with few exceptions, built almost no underground facilities.

Kay makes instructive comments about the way the Iraqis demonstrated their ability to understand the limitations of US technical collection systems, and of how data gathered by such systems were interpreted by the experts.

'The catalogue of these techniques is long. It includes the erection of buildings within buildings (Tuwaitha); deliberately constructing buildings designed to the same plans and for the same purposes to look different (Ash Sharqat and Tarmiya); hiding power and water feeds to mislead as to facility use (Tarmiya); disguising operational state (Al Atheer); diminishing the value of a facility by apparent low security and lack of defenses (Tarmiya); severely reducing off-site emissions (Tuwaitha and Tarmiya); moving critical pieces of equipment as well as dispersing and placing some facilities below ground level.'

Hamza points out that even though Al Tuwaitha had hundred-foot high berms (which from the start should have attracted suspicion that the plant was being used for other purposes) good effort went into carefully escorting IAEA inspectors each time they arrived. Customarily they were shunted along pre-designated paths that exposed none of the buildings where secret research was being conducted. Also, answers to possible difficult questions would be endlessly rehearsed for days beforehand.

It was only after the first invasion, 'Desert Storm', when Vienna received aerial photos of the site, that the IAEA learned about many other buildings that they had never been allowed to enter.

When the bombings were done, the Pentagon had to concede that while Iraq had suffered through the most sophisticated aerial bombardment in history, the country emerged, in the words of former US Air Force Chief of Staff Merrill A. McPeak, with enough nascent nuclear capability to produce weapons early in the new millennium.

Now that there have been two invasions of Iraq, there is sentiment among some of the major powers at UN Headquarters in New York that Iraq might have gone nuclear if UN sanctions had been prematurely lifted. Partly, the rationale was based on reports that reached the world outside through defectors (and from sources close to the IAEA) that Iraq remained on the nuclear path for many years following 'Operation Desert Storm'. There was a lot of other evidence too.

For a start, the fundamental scientific and industrial infrastructure to build a nuclear weapon remained firmly in place. More pertinent, the staff responsible - there were hundreds of them - were on permanent standby. They and their families were supported by the state as if they were employed full-time. And while it is acknowledged that some of the material intended for use to construct such a bomb had been either uncovered or destroyed, there was good evidence that much remained hidden.

There were also unsettling indications in late 1998, that some kind of 'technical cooperation' between Iraq and its former blood enemy, Syria, was in place. Israeli intelligence sources indicated that this could have included a joint development program of WMD. Certainly, Damascus has been proved to be involved with both chemical and biowarfare agents and while it is too early to speculate about any kind of nuclear link, it could have been a feasible scenario for the next decade, especially if UN sanctions on Iraq remained rooted.

Remember too that Saddam was always been keen to make use of his assets in what he termed 'the interests of Islamic hegemony', especially if the ultimate target was to have been the Jewish homeland. We know too that after the first Gulf War, he managed to get some of his WMD assets to Libya. These were then forwarded overland to The Sudan[6].

Meanwhile, in the decade that followed 'Operation Desert Storm' Syria continued to demonstrate an interest in acquiring WMD of its own. By early 1997, Israeli reports said that Damascus had tipped some of its Scud-C missiles deployed along the southern (Israeli) front with sarin and the even more deadly VX nerve gas. This prompted an IDF spokesman to declare that if such weapons were used against the Israeli state, it would automatically be followed by nuclear retaliation; harsh words in an already tough environment.

According to Paul Stokes, a former UNSCOM Action Team deputy leader, frequent inspections prevented Iraq from conducting nuclear weapons development work at declared sites after the end of the war. There was evidence - including a good deal from defectors who had come across to the West - that this did not prevent Saddam's people from going ahead elsewhere in clear violation of a variety of Security Council resolutions.

Dr Kay provided explicit evidence of such deceptions in his MIT report; it was often a nightmare of duplicity, he said.

What became clear with time is that Iraq was devious throughout the inspection period. As one observer stated: 'The Iraqis lied fluently from day one.'

He told this correspondent that, among those who had originally worked with the UN in the region (before they were ignominiously kicked out) it was common knowledge that the Iraqis had stalled, obfuscated, covered up or confused wherever and whomever they could. They did everything possible to hide what had been going on.

For instance, he declared, one of the conclusions already reached in 1997, was that while the Iraqis claimed to have had little success with the centrifuge enrichment program, there was a mismatch between the sophistication of the materials that they admitted to having imported and those that were actually turned over to UN inspection[7]. This gap raised real concerns that a hidden centrifuge facility still remained to be found. There are other examples.

It took the defection of Saddam's son-in-law, General Hussein Kamel, former head of the Ministry of Industry and Military Industrialization (MIMI), to expose the full extent of what Iraq had achieved after 'Desert Storm'. Once he was safely ensconced in Jordan, Iraq had no option but to hand over to the IAEA half a million pages of secreted documents (from the 'chicken farm') as well as almost twenty tons of high-strength maraging steel and stocks of carbon fiber for more than a thousand gas centrifuges, all of which (and much more) Kamel had detailed in his debrief. Some of these items, according to Ritter on his return to the US, were directly linked to what was believed to be still hidden.

There was good reason for this supposition. Iraq is known to have since tried to acquire hydrofluoric acid - a chemical used in the production of uranium hexafluoride feedstock. Scientists use it in gas centrifuge and other enrichment processes and as a purging agent to remove industrial residues from centrifuges and calutron parts. According to Michael Eisenstadt, a Military Affairs Fellow at the Washington Institute for Near East Policy, it raised questions - notwithstanding the current IAEA monitoring process - about the status of the Iraqi nuclear program[8].

In the simplest terms, the Iraqi nuclear program comprehensively covers the years from 1976 (when construction on the French-supplied Tammuz 1RR/PPR reactor began) to about mid-1991, when all major nuclear work was halted by the first Gulf War. In between, the most significant highlights were:

- 1981: Destruction of the nearly completed Tammuz reactor at Osiraq by Israeli warplanes
- 1982: Research concerning various gas enrichment methods gets into full swing
- 1987: Lab-scale quantities of LEU produced by calutrons, now referred to as 'Baghdadtrons'
- 1987/88?: Construction of the Sharqat calutron enrichment plant begins
- 1989: Construction begins at the Al Furat centrifuge production facility
- 1990: Initiation of crash program using diverted reactor fuel
- 1991: Work halted by war as the IAEA and UNSCOM weapon strip-search began
- 1999: Abrupt ending of both UNSCOM and IAEA monitoring of Iraq's weapons and nuclear programs

The Israeli Air Force bombing of the facilities at the Osiraq reactor (and subsequent developments) highlighted at a very early stage the fact that Iraq was fostering a nuclear weapons interest.

Saddam Hussein had bought two nuclear reactors from France: a 40 megawatt thermal research reactor which was destroyed, a fuel manufacturing plant together with nuclear fuel-reprocessing facilities, all under cover of acquiring the expertise needed to eventually build and operate nuclear power plants and recycle nuclear fuel.

What is amazing is that nobody in the West questioned the logic of these programs, coming, as they were, from Iraq, the country with the second largest oil reserves in the world (as is the case with Iran today, with equally formidable resources). These are the last two nations on earth that need to generate electricity by burning uranium.

These deals were followed by further purchases from Italy of a radiochemistry laboratory in 1978, that included three 'hot cells' used for the reprocessing of plutonium. Until destroyed in the Gulf War, they were operating at Al Tuwaitha. Meanwhile, Iraq signed the Nuclear Nonproliferation Treaty. Iran is also an NPT signatory.

Dr Jafer dhia Jafar, leader of Iraq's nuclear-weapons effort (even though his curriculum vitae includes the notation that he was jailed for twenty months by Saddam for 'political crimes') claims it was the Israeli bombing of Osiraq that had originally prompted his government to proceed with a secret enrichment program. Educated at the University of Manchester and Imperial College, London, he spent four years thereafter working at CERN, the European accelerator center in Switzerland.

Of note here, is the fact that this man was among the first of Saddam's 'most wanted' who cut a deal with the Americans to come in from the cold after Baghdad had fallen in April 2003.

It was Jafar's view that the Israeli bombing of the Osiraq nuclear facility cost his country almost a billion dollars. Yet, he says, the world community never punished Israel for what was clearly an act of war. This was one of the factors, he maintains, that caused his nation to resort to subterfuge. As he described it during the inspection phase to UN inspectors: 'Let Israel believe it destroyed our nuclear capacity. Accept the sympathy being offered for this aggression and then proceed in secret with the bomb program: which is what we did.'

Already in 1982, the Iraqis had begun to explore electromagnetic isotope separation at Al Tuwaitha, which eventually became the principal focus of nuclear research in the country. Baghdad was said to be confident that its scientific establishment had the necessary skills and technology to master this extremely difficult process. They also reached out in other directions: gas centrifuge, gaseous diffusion, chemical enrichment and laser isotope separation.

To begin with, time, money and effort went into gaseous diffusion. This route was abandoned when some technical problems proved insurmountable. Also, Saddam's agents were having trouble getting their hands on essential equipment on the open market, much of which had been embargoed by the West. Looking at the lists, they appear, nonetheless, to have been remarkably successful.

Starting in the late 1980s, Iraqi scientists began working on centrifuge enrichment as a possible alternative, or as a source of LEU or Low Enriched Uranium (containing more than 0.71 and less than 20 per cent ^{235}U) for EMIS. They had hoped to achieve a production output of about thirty lbs of 93 per cent weapons grade uranium a year at each of the EMIS production units that they intended to build.

'Originally, the gaseous diffusion elements would have provided low-enriched uranium as a feedstock for the EMIS plants, dramatically increasing HEU production,' Jafar explained during an interview.

The Tarmiya complex on the Tigris River (built by a Yugoslavian firm, Federal Directorate of Supply and Procurement) and its 'twin' at Ash Sharqat (a few hundred miles to the north of Baghdad) were designated to support industrial-scale EMIS production. While there were numerous problems of a technical nature, both plants together, ultimately, could have produced between sixty and two hundred lbs of weapons grade HEU a year had they operated successfully. This would have given Iraq the capacity to build up to four atomic bombs a year.

A small plutonium separation program was started in the mid-1970s. Following contact with SNIA-Techint of Italy, a facility was established in Baghdad for research on fuel processing under IAEA safeguards. This laboratory was eventually able to separate small quantities of plutonium; again contrary to the NPT safeguards agreement.

Kay's observations about some of the deception techniques employed by Baghdad are interesting. Iraq, he maintains, was able to use the strong desire of Western providers of technology to make sales in order to effectively conceal the true purposes of its efforts. Thus, they were able to extract a considerable amount of proprietary information from these firms without compensation. He gives the classic example that lay at the heart of Iraq's efforts to obtain technology for the chemical enrichment (Chemex) of uranium:

At the time there were two suppliers in the world of chemical enrichment technology; one is Japanese, the other French. In the mid-1980s Iraq initiated preliminary discussions with both and indicated a desire to acquire this capability. In the end they concentrated on France.

Iraq engaged the European company in lengthy negotiations, which would soon take a familiar pattern. Each time Iraq would say that it needed 'only a little more data' to make a decision. The French would reveal more. The cycle would begin again later and this went on for several years. Finally, after the suppliers had disclosed just about all the technology involved, Baghdad announced that it was too expensive and was abandoning all interest in pursuing it. Iraqi scientists were then able to begin the clandestine development of Chemex on their own.

Years later, Washington's ISIS chief David Albright stressed that in the evaluation of enrichment technologies, the Iraqis saw many advantages in EMIS technology, the first being that the procedure involves large and static pieces of equipment[9].

Baghdad regarded this as preferable to gas centrifuge programs which required advanced engineering technology and was perhaps ill suited to a developing country with a limited industrial base, he told me. For example, the rotors on gas centrifuges move at seven or eight times the speed of sound and the slightest instability can, in an instant, cause bearings to fail and rotors to crash. It is common knowledge that Pakistan battled with this technique for years; an intelligence source has indicated to this writer that for all their success in exploding a bomb, they never quite mastered it.

The advantages of following the antiquated EMIS route are important, especially since they might well apply to other developing countries intent on following this path:

These include: (a) EMIS is well-documented in the open literature; (b) the basic scientific and technical problems associated with the operation of EMIS separators are relatively straightforward to master; (c) the computational software and main equipment are often not on international export control lists, making procurement easy; (d) the design and manufacture of the main equipment for prototypes can be accomplished indigenously; (e) the feed material is relatively easy to produce and handle; (f) final enrichment can be handled in two stages in machines that act independently of each other (one or more separator failures do not affect the operation of other separators); and (g) a LEU feed can be used for a substantial increase in productivity.

Now, as recent disclosures have indicated, Iran appears to be heading the same way. Like Iraq, Tehran likes to keep its options open with regard to gas centrifuge technology, laser as well as chemical separation. This is not at all unusual, because British Intelligence sources inform us that there are more than twenty countries - all of them Third World - intent on acquiring this kind of expertise[10].

In Iraq, meanwhile, atom bomb design (weaponization) was the responsibility of scientists and technicians at Al Atheer, which the minister said - when he opened the plant about thirty miles south of the capital - was to be 'like Los Alamos'.

By the time David Kay and his IAEA Action Team associates visited the site - which was bombed by the Allies during the first Gulf War - the Iraqis had managed to acquire a variety of advanced equipment, much of it on Western export control (and thus embargoed) lists. Included were such items as high-speed streak cameras (from Hamamatsu Photonics of Japan) and maraging steel (which was found elsewhere in Iraq) from European suppliers.

Al Atheer was also involved in sophisticated work in metallurgy, chemistry and detonation engineering. Here, the Swiss company Asea Brown Boveri provided a state-of-the-art, cold isostatic press which could be used to shape explosive charges. More Swiss firms that supplied equipment to Iraq included Acomel SA of Neuchatel (five high frequency inverters suitable for centrifuge cascades) and, among other shipments, seven hundred uranium hexafluoride-resistant bellows-valves from Balzer AG and VAT AG (together with the American company Nupro).

There is little doubt that in pursuing his objective to acquire a bomb, Saddam relied heavily on foreign technical resources for much of it. The bulk, curiously, came from not from his old allies the Soviets or their cohorts, but from free Europe. David Albright and Mark Hibbs stated in their reports that Iraq's 'Petrochemical Project Three' - the code name for the secret program (conducted under the auspices of MIMI) - received massive infusions of money and resources. Like America's redundant Manhattan Project, Iraq sought a number of different technical avenues to the bomb[11].

The Iraqi leader sent out a minor army of secret agents to establish an elaborate procurement network that had operatives throughout the developed world. Even Africa was covered; South Africa (through Armscor) had much potential.

By then the Apartheid regime had supplied Iraq with the vaunted G-5 gun, a 155mm artillery piece which, until silenced in the first Gulf War, was used to good effect against Coalition Forces in 'Operation Desert Storm'. The entire program was subject to the most stringent secrecy. There wasn't an Iraqi legation abroad that was not involved. Curiously, Gerald Bull (the Canadian maverick arms developer who was involved in Saddam's 'Super Gun' when Israel's Mossad killed him in Belgium) also had a hand in developing the G-5. He was assassinated outside his Belgian apartment, itself a remarkable story of intrigue and betrayal.

Ostensibly, everything that was acquired for Saddam's nuclear program was intended for what his agents liked to term civil or peaceful use. Purchases were hidden behind such innocuous pursuits as dairy production, car and truck manufacture as well as oil refining. But it did not take the major powers long to click: Iraq was covering up its real activities and, what was even more disconcerting, it was happening on a breathtaking scale and pace.

Many of the bulky calutron pole magnets used to enrich uranium were produced in Austria by a state-owned firm that shipped the finished products to Iraq - half by truck through Turkey and the rest through Hamburg. The Austrians never asked the purpose of this equipment while the Iraqis volunteered nothing. Much the same story applies to the high-quality copper that was used to wrap these magnets. It was produced in Finland to Iraqi specifications[12].

Hundreds of tons of HMX high explosives - in the trade, regarded by specialist demolition experts as the 'big brother' of the better-known RDX (some of which would be used in the A-bomb program) - was imported from Carlos Cardoen of Chile, well known to members of the old South African Apartheid regime. This man eventually built a plant in Iraq to manufacture cluster bombs. Cardoen came under investigation by the US Justice Department immediately afterwards.

Germany (both pre- and post-unification) featured prominently in almost every phase of the Iraqi nuclear program, so much so that it is impossible that Bonn could *not* have been aware of the extent of it.

German companies included international conglomerates like Siemens AG (a workshop for 'tube processing'); H&H Metalform (flow-forming machines to make steel maraging steel rotor tubes for centrifuges); Neue Magdeburger Werkzeugmachinen GmbH (aluminum forgings and a CNC machine to machine casings); Rhein-Bayern Fahrzeugbau GmbH (almost a quarter-million magnetizable ferrite spacers for centrifuges); oxidation furnaces from Degussa AG and Leybold Heraeus (electron beam welder); centrifuge balancing machines from Reutlinger und Sohne KG; Arthur Pfeiffer Vakuum Tecknik GmbH (vacuum induction furnace) and a host of other companies and products. It has been suggested by Western intelligence agencies that some companies doing work of a similar nature might now have shifted their focus towards Iran.

H&H was contracted by Baghdad for centrifuge assistance and served, while doing so, as a conduit for advanced technical expertise, material and equipment for the Iraqi nuclear effort. Much of the finance for the project was handled by the scandal-ridden Bank of Credit and Commerce International (BCCI) before it folded. Subsequently, the Atlanta-based branch of an Italian bank, Banco Nationale da Lavore (BNL) was placed under investigation in the US.

British companies were involved too and some remained under a cloud of suspicion for years afterwards. These included Endshire Export Marketing, a company that met an order for ring magnets which had come from Inwako GmbH, a firm directed by the German arms dealer Simon Heiner.

Britain's Special Intelligence Service (SIS), aware by now that the magnets were for a nuclear program, let the shipment proceed in order to try to establish what technical route the Iraqis were taking. London tends to work closely with Langley on such matters.

It transpired too that the Technology Development Group, a company co-directed by an Iraqi intelligence agent, Safa Al-Haboudi, was an associate of some of the German firms involved in the transactions. Al-Haboudi eventually implicated the British firm Matrix Churchill; he was on that company's senior management too. Matrix Churchill offered a lucrative, long-term contract for a tool shop (ostensibly for automobile parts manufacturing) to the Swiss metal-working combine Schmiedemeccanica SA.

The records show that some of these exports never got through. Once the West had been alerted, they came down hard. Swiss and German customs officials halted a shipment of special computer numerically-controlled (CNC) machines for making the endcaps and baffles of centrifuges. Earlier, Iraqi operators were caught trying to smuggle detonation capacitators from CSI Technologies of California. This material would have been incorporated in an implosion-type bomb.

For all the help that Baghdad received from abroad, there were some serious technological gaps. Iraqi electronics expertise, for instance, did not warrant close scrutiny. The Iraqis, it was discovered later, were having difficulty developing adequate capacitators and bridge wire detonators. Rolf Ekeus, the former head of UNSCOM, said that while Iraq had blueprints and considerable knowledge, they tended to lag a bit in the engineering aspect. Also, Baghdad had been noticeably slowed by their inability to obtain what they needed from overseas as Western government controls began to stymie deliveries[13].

It is important to observe that during its subterfuge stage, Iraq was not alone in this sort of skullduggery. The newsletter *Nuclear Fuel* reported on June 20, 1994, that several shipments of preformed tubes for scoops in gas centrifuges from the German metalworking firm Team GmbH were shipped to Pakistan after being declared in customs documents as bodies for ball-point pens. There are other examples, a few of them still under wraps.

Looking at the broader canvas, it is clear that this targeted Arab nation was able to demonstrate an astonishing level of enterprise by getting as far as it did. It is also worrying that there are other nations that might wish to emulate.

Basic items - factories, electrical supply, power equipment - were easy to buy. But, as Albright explained, 'the more specific the equipment Iraq sought, the more export controls began to bite. Crucial transfers of components were thus effectively blocked'.

Orders were subdivided into sub-components that, on paper, looked innocuous. Or machines were bought to manufacture something back home. Middlemen and unethical companies in their hundreds were bribed to disguise final destinations or to falsify end-user certificates in much the same way as South Africa (under UN sanctions) stocked its arsenal with embargoed items of choice.

German technicians were secretly hired to work on the Arab enrichment project. Once the IAEA went to work and uncovered names, some of these people were charged with treason as, ultimately, will South African scientists who have been helping Tehran build WMD.

In Iraq's case, several were jailed. Among these individuals were Bruno Stemmler, Walter Busse and Karl-Heinz Schaab. It was Schaab and

Stemmler who provided Saddam with classified centrifuge blueprints. The three men had worked on the centrifuge program at MAN Technologie AG of Munich and came to Iraq under the sponsorship of the German company H&H Metalform.

Together, they operated efficiently as a team and met many of Iraq's technical requirements. They also assisted in locating international suppliers. Some were companies with whom they had previously been associated.

In the end, says Albright, their assistance greatly accelerated Iraq's gas centrifuge-design process. 'It sped the acquisition of necessary materials, know-how and equipment for manufacture.' During an earlier period, some Iraqis had already spent time in Urenco training programs in order to familiarize themselves with complex centrifuge-related procedures.

What then does all this tell us? While the Iraqi nuclear program was effectively halted in the end, Iran, according to some sources, might right now be further ahead than Saddam was by the time that UNSCOM began their search. Worse, should Tehran have managed to acquire a supply of weapons grade uranium on the Russian or Ukrainian black market - and there is a lot of conjecture right now (television sensationalism apart) that the mullahs might have done exactly that - it is not impossible that they are on the brink of their own atomic revolution. The implications are chilling.

As Dr David Kay observed, 'the failed efforts of both IAEA safeguards inspectors and national intelligence authorities to detect - prior to the Gulf War - a nuclear weapons program of the magnitude and advanced character of Iraq's, should stand as a monument to the fallibility of on-site inspection and national intelligence when faced by a determined opponent[14]'.

He maintained that those words should be cast in concrete and embedded into the floor of Washington's Capitol.

Kay: 'The Iraqi military build-up, as well as the multiple failures of its timely detection is an experience rich in lessons that, if correctly understood, may help in detecting other covert weapons programs and, equally important, US understanding of the limits of its ability to guarantee timely detection[15].'

This followed a statement by John Deutch, the erstwhile and since discredited US Director of Intelligence, in *Foreign Affairs* in 1992[16]:

As he stated, 'the point is not how wrong the United States was about Iraq's timetable for acquiring a bomb, but rather how greatly the US underestimated the magnitude of the Iraqi covert effort. As it stands, such a massive miscalculation of a nation's ability, high or low, can surely happen again'.

1   'Has Iraq Come Clean at Last?' by David Albright and Robert Kelley (*Bulletin of the Atomic Scientists:* Nov/Dec, 1995)

2   'Iraq's Secret Nuclear Weapons Program' by Jay C. Davis and David A. Kay: (*Physics Today*, July, 1992)

3   September/October 1998

4   Until Iranian opposition groups pinpointed several sites – among them, the one at Natanz, where they claimed Tehran was involved with nuclear work (small centrifuges were found for enriching uranium), the Iranians prevented IAEA staff from setting up environmental monitoring units in some areas where the Atomic Energy Organization of Iran was active. They were particularly restrictive at some newly established uranium processing plants: See 'Inspectors in Iran Examine Machines to Enrich Uranium': *New York Times,* February 23, 2003

5   *Critical Mass* by William Burrows & Robert Windrem (Simon & Schuster, New York, 1994) Davis & Kay (*Ibid*)

6   Davis & Kay (*Ibid*)

7   *Pointer,* supplement to *Jane's Intelligence Review,* London, March, 1998

8   *Like a Phoenix from the Ashes? The Future of Iraqi Military Power* by Michael Eisenstadt (The Washington Institute of Near East Policy, 1993)

9   *Plutonium and Highly Enriched Uranium 1996:* by David Albright, Frans Berkhout and William Walker (OUP 1997)

10 *International Defense Review:* (Jane's Information Group) London, Sept, 1997

11 'Iraq's Shop-Till-You-Drop Nuclear Program' by David Albright and Mark Hibbs; (*Bulletin of the Atomic Scientists*; April, 1992)

12 'Denial and Deception Practices of WMD Proliferators: Iraq and Beyond' by Dr David Kay (The Center for Strategic and International Studies & Massachusetts Institute for Technology: *The Washington Quarterly:* Winter, 1995)

13 *Iraq's Shop-Till-You-Drop Nuclear Program* by David Albright and Mark Hibbs: (*Ibid*)

14 *Denial and Deception Practices of WMD Proliferators: Iraq and Beyond* by Dr David Kay (The Center for Strategic and International Studies & Massachusetts Institute for Technology: *The Washington Quarterly:* Winter, 1995)

15 Note also Iraqi attempts to acquire krytons: In March, 1991, Iraq attempted to illegally import Krytons from CIS Technologies Inc. of the US. Several years earlier, Iraq had imported weapons-quality capacitors from other American concerns. IAEA investigators have also found about 230 metric tons of high-energy explosive HMX in Iraq that may have been purchased from Czechoslovakia: Monterey Institute, CNS, Iraqi Nuclear Abstracts: 1992 http://cns.miis.edu/research/iraq/iraqnu92.htm

16 'The New Nuclear Threat' by John M. Deutch (*Foreign Affairs:* 71: Fall, 1992)

2

THE IRAN-IRAQ WAR: A PRECEDENT[1]

Like Hitler before him, Saddam Hussein appointed himself supreme military commander (field marshal) and commander-in-chief of all Iraqi armed forces: and that for a man with no military service whatever. At the same time he was the country's head of state, in charge of all its security services, chairman of both the Ba'ath Party and the national ruling body, the Revolutionary Command Council. It might consequently have been expected that poor military judgment and lack of resolve very often hindered the Iran-Iraq war conflict.

Of the many conflicts in progress around the world in early 1988, the Iran-Iraq War was by far the bloodiest and the costliest. It was a war that was multifaceted and included religious schisms, border disputes as well as political differences.

Differences contributing to the outbreak of hostilities ranged from centuries-old Sunni-versus-Shi'ite and Arab-versus-Persian religious and ethnic disputes, to a personal animosity between Saddam Hussein and Ayatollah Sayyid Ruhollah Khomeini, Iran's supreme religious leader. Above all, Iraq launched the war in an effort to consolidate its rising power in the Arab world and to replace Iran as the dominant state at the head of the oil-rich Persian Gulf.

Phebe Marr, a noted analyst of Baghdad's affairs, stated that 'the war was more immediately the result of poor political judgment and miscalculation on the part of Saddam Hussein'. Moreover, she declared after it was all over, 'the decision to invade, taken at a moment of Iranian weakness, was Saddam's'. Tehran, just then, was in turmoil.

For many years the two countries had engaged in border clashes. By 1979 they had also revived the dormant Shatt al Arab waterway dispute with Iraq claiming the hundred-and-twenty-mile channel (which extended right up to the Iranian shore) as its territory. For its part, Tehran insisted that the *thalweg* - a line running down the middle of the waterway - negotiated last in 1975, was the official border. The Iraqis, especially Iraq's Ba'ath leadership, regarded the 1975 treaty as merely a truce, not a definitive settlement.

More significant, considering developments just then in its neighboring country, the Iraqis also perceived revolutionary Iran's Islamic agenda as threatening to their pan-Arabism. Ayatollah Khomeini, already bitter over his expulsion from Iraq in 1977 after 15 years in exile in An Najaf, vowed to avenge Shi'ite victims of Ba'athist repression.

Baghdad became progressively more confident, however, as it watched the once invincible Imperial Iranian Army disintegrate while most of its highest-ranking officers were being executed for real or imagined crimes against Islam and the state. In Khuzestan (Arabistan to the Iraqis), Iraqi intelligence officers incited riots over labor disputes. Similarly, in Iran's Kurdish regions, a new rebellion caused the Khomeini government still more problems.

As the Ba'athists planned their intended military campaign, they had every reason to be confident. Not only did the Iranians lack cohesive leadership, but the Iranian armed forces (according to Iraqi intelligence estimates) also lacked spare parts for their American-made equipment. Baghdad, in contrast, possessed fully equipped and trained forces, morale was running high and the portents looked favorable. Against Iran's armed forces, including the Pasdaran (Revolutionary Guard) troops, led by Islamic zealots with little or no military experience, the Iraqis could muster twelve complete mechanized divisions equipped with the latest Soviet materiel.

In addition, the area across the Shatt al Arab posed no major obstacles, particularly for an army equipped with Soviet river-crossing equipment. Western analysts are aware now that Iraqi commanders correctly assumed that transit sites on the Khardeh and Karun rivers were lightly defended against their mechanized divisions. Moreover, Iraqi intelligence sources reported that Iranian forces in Khuzestan - which had formerly included two divisions distributed among Ahvaz, Dezful, and Abadan - now consisted of only a number of ill-equipped battalion-sized formations.

Tehran was further disadvantaged because the area was controlled by the Regional 1st Corps with headquarters at Bakhtaran (formerly Kermanshah), whereas almost all operational control had to come from the capital.

In the year following the overthrow of the Shah of Iran, only a handful of company-sized tank units had been operative. The rest of Iran's armor had been poorly maintained.

For Iraqi planners, the only uncertainty was the combat ability of the Iranian Air Force, equipped mainly with American-made aircraft. Despite the execution of key air force commanders and pilots, the Iranian Air Force had made a good showing during local riots and demonstrations. It was also active following the failed US attempt to rescue American hostages in April 1980.

This show of force had impressed Iraqi decision makers to such an extent that they decided to follow the Israeli lead of the June 1967 Arab-Israeli War and launch a massive pre-emptive air strike on Iranian air bases.

For much of Iraqi history, the Shi'ites have been both politically impotent and economically depressed. Beginning in the 16th Century, when the Ottoman Sunnis favored their Iraqi coreligionists in the matter of educational and employment opportunities, the Shi'ites were consistently denied political power. Thus, although this branch of Islam constituted more than half the population, they occupied a relatively insignificant number of government posts. Similarly, on the economic level, aside from a small number of wealthy landowners and merchants, the descendants of Ali were historically exploited as sharecropping peasants or menially employed slum dwellers.

Come the oil boom of the 1970s and much of the prosperity that followed was denied the Shi'ite community. Things did begin to change in the late Seventies with Saddam's populist economic policies having a favorable impact on all, enabling many of them to join the ranks of a new Iraqi middle class.

That didn't prevent widespread Shi'ite demonstrations taking place when the government, suspecting a bomb, closed Karbala to pilgrimage at the height of a religious ceremony in 1977. Violent clashes between police and Shi'ite pilgrims spread from Karbala to An Najaf and lasted for days before army troops were called in to quell the unrest.

It was the 1979 Islamic Revolution in Iran, however, that transformed Shi'ite dissatisfaction with Baghdad's Ba'ath-led government into an organized religion-based opposition. Following some prompting from Iran, more riots broke out in An Najaf and in Karbala after the government refused Ayatollah Muhammad Baqir as Sadr's request to lead a procession to Iran to congratulate Ayatollah Khomeini.

Even more worrisome was Iraqi intelligence's uncovering of a clandestine Shi'ite group headed by religious leaders that had ties to Tehran. Baqir as Sadr was the inspirational leader of the group, named Ad Dawah al Islamiyah (the Islamic Call), and commonly referred to as Ad Dawah. Espousing a program similar to Khomeini's, he urged a return to fundamental Islamic precepts of government and for universal social justice.

It is worth noting that despite Iraqi concern, the eruption of the 1979 Islamic Revolution in Iran did not immediately destroy the Iraqi-Iranian rapprochement that had prevailed since the 1975 Algiers Agreement. As a sign of Iraq's desire to maintain good relations with the new government in Tehran, President Bakr sent a personal message to Khomeini offering 'his best wishes for the friendly Iranian people on the occasion of the establishment of the Islamic Republic'.

In addition, by August 1979, Baghdad extended an invitation to Mehdi Bazargan, first president of the Islamic Republic of Iran, to visit Iraq with the aim of improving bilateral relations. The fall of the moderate Bazargan government in late 1979, and the rise of Islamic militants preaching an expansionist foreign policy finally soured issues between the two countries.

Several events touched off the rapid deterioration in relations during the spring of 1980. In April of that year, the Iranian-supported Ad Dawah attempted to assassinate the long-serving Iraqi foreign minister Tariq Aziz, who, incidentally, is a Christian. Shortly after this failed grenade attack, Ad Dawah was suspected of attempting to assassinate the Iraqi Minister of Culture and Information, Latif Nayyif Jasim.

In response, Baghdad immediately rounded up members and supporters of the movement and deported thousands of Shi'ites of Iranian origin back to their home country. In the summer of 1980, Saddam Hussein ordered the executions of presumed Ad Dawah leader Ayatollah Sayyid Muhammad Baqr as Sadr and his sister.

In September 1980, skirmishes along the Iran-Iraq border erupted in the central sector near Qasr-e Shirin, with an exchange of artillery fire by both sides. A few weeks later, Saddam Hussein officially abrogated the 1975 treaty between the two countries and announced that the Shatt al Arab was returning to Iraqi sovereignty. Only weeks later did Iraqi troops march into Iranian territory.

Iraqi Offensives, 1980-82

On September 22, 1980, formations of Iraqi MiG-23s and MiG-21s attacked Iran's air bases at Mehrabad and Doshen-Tappen (both near Tehran), as well as Tabriz, Bakhtaran, Ahvaz, Dezful, Urmia (sometimes cited as Urumiyeh), Hamadan, Sanandaj, and Abadan.

Though Iranian defenses were caught off guard, the raids failed because Iranian jets were protected in specially strengthened hangars and also because bombs designed to destroy runways did not totally incapacitate Iran's very large airfields. Within hours, Tehran retaliated. Iranian F-4 Phantoms took off from these same air bases, successfully attacked strategically important targets close to several major Iraqi cities and returned home with few losses.

Concurrently with its air attack, Iraq ordered six of its divisions across the border into Iran, where they drove five miles inland and occupied about five hundred square miles of Iranian territory. As a diversionary measure, an

Iraqi mechanized division overwhelmed the border garrison at Qasr-e Shirin, while five more armored and mechanized divisions invaded Khuzestan on two axes. They first crossed the Shatt al Arab near Basra, which led to the siege and eventual occupation of Khorramshahr, with the second heading for Susangerd. This objective had Ahvaz, the major military base in Khuzestan, in its sights.

In addition, Dehloran and several other towns were targeted. They were rapidly occupied to prevent reinforcements from Bakhtaran and Tehran reaching them. By mid-October, a full Iraqi division was able to advance through Khuzestan on its way to Khorramshahr and Abadan, with the strategic oil fields nearby.

Iraq's blitz-like assaults against scattered and demoralized Iranian forces led many observers to believe that Baghdad was on the cusp of victory and that the war would be over within weeks. Indeed, Iraqi troops did capture the Shatt al Arab and they were able to gain control of a thirty-mile-wide strip of Iranian territory.

For all its losses, Tehran rejected any kind of settlement offer and managed to hold the line against the militarily-superior Iraqi force. With that, Iran began a series of slow counter-offensives in January 1981. First it stopped Iraqi forces on the Karun River and, with limited military stocks, unveiled its 'human wave' assaults, which used thousands of *Basij* (Popular Mobilization Army or People's Army) volunteers.

The recapture of the oil port of Abadan, Iran's first major victory came in September 1981.

Interestingly, the expected 'popular' Shi'ite uprising in Iraq - solemnly predicted by Tehran's Mullahs - did not happen. If anything, the war initially cemented relations between the two main Islamic factions and the huge majority of Iraqi Shi'ites rallied to Saddam's call to arms. Their contribution to hostilities and numbers killed and wounded in action testify to an expected national pride and determination within the largest single religious group in the country[2].

Iraqi Retreats, 1982-84

In March 1982, Tehran launched its 'Operation Undeniable Victory'. That event marked a major turning point in the Iranian military onslaught as the Ayatollah's forces were able to gain access to Iraq's so-called 'impenetrable' lines. The immediate effect was to split the opposing military structure and force the Iraqis to retreat.

By late June 1982, Baghdad stated its willingness to negotiate a settlement of the war. It would withdraw its forces from Iran, was the offer.

Iran refused, and in July 1982 Tehran launched its well-timed 'Operation Ramadan' on Iraqi territory, near Basra.

The Iranian Army, with heavy air support, used Pasdaran (Republican Guard) forces and *Basij* volunteers in one of the biggest land battles since the end of 1945. With the combatants ranging in age from nine years to more than fifty, these eager but relatively untrained soldiers swept over minefields and fortifications to clear safe passageways for their tanks. In doing so, the Iranians sustained immense casualties, but their efforts did enable Iran to recover some territory before the Iraqis could be brought into action in a bid to repulse the invaders.

By the end of 1982, Iraq had been substantially resupplied with Soviet hardware and the ground war entered a new and definitive phase.

Using newly-acquired T-55 and T-62 tanks, BM-21 Stalin Organ rocket launchers together with large numbers of Mi-24 (Hind) helicopter gunships, the Iraqis prepared a Soviet-type three-line defense, replete with obstacles, minefields, and fortified positions. At the same time, Iraq's Combat Engineer Corps played a distinctive role in constructing a variety of bridges across water obstacles. They also laid minefields and prepared new defense lines and fortifications.

By 1983, Iran prepared to launch three major but unsuccessful human wave offensives: again the losses were catastrophic along almost the entire length of the front.

Launched on February 6, Tehran sent in two-hundred-thousand of its 'last reserve' Pasdaran troops in an attack line that was spread out along a strategic twenty-five-mile stretch of territory near Al Amarah, roughly a hundred miles southeast of Baghdad. Backed by air, armor and artillery support, Iran's six-division thrust was powerful enough to create a break in Iraqi lines.

In response, Baghdad sent in its air force. There were more than two hundred sorties, many of them flown by attack helicopters. More than six thousand Iranians were killed that day, while achieving only miniscule ground gains.

Two months later, the Mandali-Baghdad north-central sector witnessed some bitter fighting as Iraqi mechanized and infantry divisions stopped repeated Iranian attacks.

Casualties were high throughout, and by the end of 1983 an estimated hundred-and-twenty thousand Iranians and sixty thousand Iraqis had been killed on these battlefields. Despite heavy losses, Tehran in 1983 held a distinct advantage in its attempt to wage and eventually win the war of attrition.

The War of Attrition, 1984-87

On available information filtering through from the Middle East, most foreign military analysts believe that until then, neither Iraq nor Iran had made proper use of their modern equipment. Frequently, sophisticated military materiel was ignored and sidelined on the edge of a battlefield when its use would almost certainly have swung events in favor of either side. For example, instead of being maneuvered to lead or support an assault, main battle tanks and armored vehicles were dug in and used as static artillery pieces.

William O. Staudenmaeir, a seasoned military analyst, reported that 'the land-computing sights on the Iraqi tanks (were) seldom used. This reduced the accuracy of modern T-62 tanks to World War 2 standards'. In addition, both sides frequently abandoned their equipment out in the field because they lacked the skilled technical personnel needed to carry out minor repairs.

Observers of the war also assert that the armies of both countries very often showed little or poor coordination and that some units were left to fight the war largely on their own. In a protracted war of attrition, soldiers and officers sometimes failed to display initiative or any of the kind of professional expertise in combat that might have been expected of experienced soldiers. Section commanders referred difficult decisions, which, on occasion, should have had immediate attention, to their respective capitals for action. Meanwhile, they would wait and do nothing until orders arrived.

Except for the predictable bursts on important anniversaries, the war, by the mid-1980s, was stalemated.

In early 1984, Iran had begun 'Operation Dawn V', which was intended to split the Iraqi 3rd and 4th Army Corps near Basra. An estimated half-million Pasdaran and *Basij* forces - using either shallow boats or moving on foot - moved to get to within a few miles of the strategic Basra-Baghdad waterway between February 29 and March 1, in one of the largest battles of the war. Without large-scale armor and air support of their own, the Iranians faced Iraqi tanks, mortars, and helicopter gunships. By the time it was over, the two armies had inflicted twenty-five-thousand fatalities on each other.

Within weeks, Tehran opened another front in the shallow lakes of Iran's Hawizah Marshes, just east of Al Qurnah. Near the confluence of the Tigris and Euphrates rivers, Iraqi forces - again using Soviet- and French-built helicopter gunships - inflicted huge casualties on five Iranian defending brigades in what became known as the Battle of Majnoon.

Lacking the equipment to open secure passages through Iraqi minefields, and, by then, having too few tanks at their disposal, Tehran again resorted to classic human-wave tactics. In March 1984 an East European journalist claimed that he 'saw tens of thousands of children, roped together in sections of about twenty - to prevent the faint-hearted from deserting - make such an attack'.

The Iranians made little if any progress despite these sacrifices. Perhaps as a result of this performance, Tehran, for the first time, used a regular army unit, the 92nd Armored Division, at the Battle of the Marshes a few weeks later.

Within a month-long period in early 1984, the Iraqis reportedly killed forty thousand Iranians for the loss of only nine thousand of their own. But even this was deemed an unacceptable ratio and in February that year, the Iraqi supreme command ordered the deployment of chemical weapons. Despite repeated denials from Baghdad, Iran claimed more than forty instances of Iraqi use of chemical weapons between May 1981 and March 1984.

The year 1984 ended with sections of the strategic Majnoon Islands - together with a few pockets of Iraqi territory - still in Iranian hands. Casualties notwithstanding, Tehran maintained its military posture. Baghdad meanwhile was re-evaluating its overall strategy.

The major development in 1985 was the increased targeting by both sides of major urban centers and their adjacent industrial suburbs. That May saw Iraq begin a succession of aerial bombardments and ground offensives on Tehran and other major Iranian cities involving long-range artillery and surface-to-surface missiles. There were forty-four raids on Iran's Khark Islands between August and November of that year in futile attempts to destroy its installations. Iran responded with its air raids of its own. Missile attacks on Baghdad and other Iraqi towns followed.

In addition, Tehran systematized its periodic maritime stop-and-search patrols. These were conducted to verify the cargoes of ships in the Persian Gulf and to seize war materiel destined for Iraq.

The only major ground offensive - involving an estimated sixty thousand Iranian troops - took place near Basra in March 1985. Again the assault proved inconclusive except for heavy casualties.

In 1986, however, Iraq suffered a major loss in the southern region. On February 9, Iran launched a successful surprise amphibious assault across the Shatt al Arab and captured the abandoned Iraqi oil port of Al Faw. The occupation of this harbor was a major logistical feat and involved thirty thousand regular Iranian soldiers who were able to quickly entrench themselves. Saddam vowed to eliminate the bridgehead 'at all costs'.

Unable to dislodge the Iranians from Al Faw in 1986, the Iraqis went on the offensive capturing first the city of Mehran in May, only to lose it again two months later. The rest of that year witnessed small hit-and-run attacks by both sides, while the Iranians massed almost half-a-million troops for another promised 'final offensive', which never happened.

In retaliation the Iraqis began a series of a concerted air strikes that July.

Heavy attacks on Khark Island forced Iran to rely on makeshift installations farther south in the Gulf at Sirri Island and Larak Island. Iraqi jets, refueling in midair or using a Saudi military base, then turned on Sirri and Larak. During the course of 1986 the two belligerents between them also attacked more than a hundred neutral ships in the Gulf.

Meanwhile, to help with its defense, Iraq managed to build some impressive fortifications along the eight-hundred-mile war front. Baghdad devoted particular attention to the southern city of Basra, where concrete-roofed bunkers, tank- and artillery-firing positions, minefields, and stretches of barbed wire - all of them shielded by an artificially flooded lake almost twenty miles long and more than a mile wide - were constructed. Most visitors to the area acknowledged Iraq's astonishingly effective use of combat engineering to erect these defensive barriers.

On Christmas Eve 1986, Iran launched one more assault on the Basra region. Three weeks later, that annual 'final offensive' resulted in more than forty thousand dead. Although Tehran's push came close to breaking Iraq's last line of defense east of Basra, the forces of the Ayatollah were unable to score the necessary breakthrough that was required to win outright victory.

The Tanker War, 1984-87

By early 1981 naval operations between the belligerents came to a halt, presumably because Iraq and Iran had lost many of their ships. That lull lasted for two years. In March 1984, Iraq again initiated sustained naval strikes in its self-declared seventy-mile maritime exclusion zone, extending from the mouth of the Shatt al Arab to Iran's port of Bushehr, presently the site of Iran's first nuclear reactor being built by the Russians.

Earlier, in 1981, Baghdad had attacked Iranian ports and oil complexes as well as neutral tankers and ships sailing to and from Iran; by 1984 Iraq had expanded the so-called 'Tanker War' by using French Super-Etendard combat aircraft armed with Exocet missiles. Neutral-flag merchant ships became favorite targets while the long-range Super-Etendards flew sorties farther south. Altogether seventy-one merchant ships were attacked in 1984 alone, compared with forty-eight in the first three years of the war. Iraq's motives in increasing the tempo were prompted by a desire to break the stalemate, presumably by cutting off Iran's oil exports and forcing the Mullahs to the negotiating table. However, repeated Iraqi efforts failed to put Iran's main oil exporting terminal at Khark Island out of commission.

Iran retaliated by attacking first a Kuwaiti oil tanker near Bahrain in May 1984 followed by a Saudi tanker in Saudi waters five days later, making it clear that if Iraq continued to interfere with Iran's shipping, no Gulf state would be safe.

These sustained attacks cut Iranian oil exports by half, reduced shipping in the Gulf by a quarter, forced Lloyd's of London to increase insurance rates and slowed Gulf oil supplies to the rest of the world. Further, the Saudi decision in 1984 to shoot down an Iranian Phantom jet intruding in Saudi territorial waters played an important role in ending both belligerents' attempts to internationalize the tanker war.

Iraq and Iran finally accepted a 1984 UN-sponsored moratorium on the shelling of civilian targets. Tehran later proposed an extension of the moratorium to include Gulf shipping, a proposal that Baghdad rejected unless it included its own Gulf ports.

Iraq began ignoring the moratorium soon after it went into effect and stepped up its air raids on tankers serving Iran and Iranian oil-exporting facilities in 1986 and 1987. Its aircraft attacked even vessels belonging to conservative Arab states of the Persian Gulf. Iran responded by escalating its attacks on shipping serving Arab ports in the Gulf.

As Kuwaiti vessels made up a large portion of the targets in these retaliatory raids, the Kuwaiti government sought protection from the international community in the fall of 1986. The Soviet Union responded first, agreeing to charter several Soviet tankers to Kuwait in early 1987. Washington, which had been first approached by Kuwait (but initially postponed its decision) eventually followed Moscow's lead.

United States involvement was sealed by the May 17, 1987, Iraqi missile attack on the USS *Stark*, in which thirty-seven crew members were killed.

Baghdad apologized and claimed that the attack was a mistake. Ironically, Washington used the *Stark* incident to blame Iran for escalating the war and sent its own ships to the Gulf to escort eleven Kuwaiti tankers that were 'reflagged' with the American flag and had American crews manning them.

Iran refrained from attacking the United States naval force directly, but it did use various forms of harassment, including mines, hit-and-run attacks by small patrol boats, and periodic stop-and-search operations.

On several occasions, Tehran fired its Chinese-made Silkworm missiles on Kuwait from the Al Faw Peninsula.

When Iranian forces hit the reflagged tanker *Sea Isle City* in October 1987, Washington retaliated by destroying an oil platform in the Rostam field and by using the United States Navy SEAL commandos to blow up a second one nearby.

Within a few weeks of the *Stark* incident, Iraq resumed its raids on tankers but moved its attacks farther south, near the Strait of Hormuz. Washington played a central role in framing UN Security Council Resolution 598 on the Gulf War, passed unanimously on July 20 of that year. However, Western attempts to isolate Iran were frustrated when Tehran rejected the resolution because it did not meet its requirement that Iraq should be punished for initiating the conflict.

In early 1988, the Gulf had become an extremely crowded theater of conflict. At least ten Western navies and eight regional maritime forces patrolled the area.

The Arab Ship Repair Yard in Bahrain and its counterpart in Dubai in the United Arab Emirates were unable to keep up with demands for repairs of ships damaged in these attacks.

The fighting stopped shortly afterwards.

1   These reports on the seven-year war between Iran and Iraq were originally part of a series prepared by the Federal Research Division of the Library of Congress under the Country Studies/Area Handbook Program. The US Department of the Army sponsored the studies. *Data as of May 1988*

2   With Saddam ruthlessly suppressing the Shi'ite rebellion after the US-led 'Operation Desert Storm' of the early Nineties, large numbers were driven out of their southern traditional areas. Tens of thousands of Shi'ites died in these government-sponsored purges.

3

CHEMICAL WARFARE IN THE IRAN-IRAQ WAR

Extract from a SIPRI Fact Sheet (1984, updated October 1, 1998) by Julian Perry Robinson and Jozef Goldblat: Courtesy: The Stockholm International Peace Research Institute, Sweden.

Allegations of the use of chemical weapons have been frequent during the Iraq-Iran War. An international team dispatched to Iran by the UN secretary general has conclusively verified one of the instances reported by Iran.

Both Iran (1929) and Iraq (1931) are parties to the Geneva Protocol, which prohibits the use of asphyxiating, poisonous or other gases, and of all analogous liquids, materials or devices, as well as the use of bacteriological methods of warfare.

The UN Security Council has issued a statement condemning the use of chemical weapons during the Gulf War. It remains uncertain whether the sources of supply were indigenous or external. Export controls have been placed on certain chemicals that could be used in the production of mustard and nerve gases.

In this Fact Sheet, SIPRI provides background information on the international law that has been violated, the two poison gases which the UN team identified in its samples, and the possible origins of the chemical weapons used in the Iraq-Iran War.

INTRODUCTION

Allegations

There have been reports of chemical warfare from the Gulf War since the early months of Iraq's invasion of Iran. In November 1980 Tehran Radio was broadcasting allegations of Iraqi chemical bombing at Susangerd. (Less than four years) later, the Iranian Foreign Minister told the Conference on Disarmament in Geneva that there had been at least forty-nine instances of Iraqi chemical warfare attack in forty border regions and that the documented dead totaled a hundred-and-nine people, with hundreds more wounded.

He made this statement on February 16, 1984, the day on which Iran launched a major offensive on the central front, and one week before the start of offensives and counter-offensives further south, in the border marshlands to the immediate north of Basra where, at Majnoon Islands, Iraq has vast untapped oil reserves. According to official Iranian statements during the thirty-one days following the Foreign Minister's allegations, Iraq used chemical weapons on at least fourteen further occasions, adding more than two-thousand-two hundred to the total number of people wounded by poison gas.

Verification

One of the chemical-warfare instances reported by Iran, at Hoor-ul-Huzwaizeh on 13 March, 1984, has since been conclusively verified by an international team of specialists dispatched to Iran by the United Nations sécretary general. The evidence adduced in the report by the UN team lends substantial credence to Iranian allegations of Iraqi chemical warfare on at least six other occasions during the period February 26 to March 17.

The efficiency and dispatch with which this UN verification operation was mounted stands greatly to the credit of the secretary general. His hand was presumably strengthened by the announcement on March 7 by the International Committee of the Red Cross (ICRC) that a hundred-and-sixty cases of wounded combatants visited in Tehran hospitals by an ICRC team 'presented a clinical picture whose nature leads to the presumption of the recent use of substances prohibited by international law'. The casualties visited were reportedly all victims of an incident on February 27. The ICRC statement came two days after the US State Department announced that 'the US Government concluded that the available evidence indicates that Iraq has used lethal chemical weapons'.

Iraq denounced the Washington statement as 'political hypocrisy', 'full of lies', a 'fabrication by the CIA', and suggested that the hospital patients - examined by the ICRC - 'sustained the effects of these substances in places other than the war front'.

On March 17, at almost the same time that the UN team acquired its most damning evidence, the general commanding the Iraqi 3rd Corps (then counter-attacking in the battle for the Majnoon Islands) spoke as follows to foreign reporters: 'We have not used chemical weapons so far and I swear by God's Word I have not seen any such weapons. But if I had to finish off the enemy,' he declared, 'and if I am allowed to use them, I will not hesitate to do so.'

Some Consequences

On March 30, the UN Security Council issued a statement condemning the use of chemical weapons during the Gulf War. Evidently none of the five permanent members used veto power to block the condemnation. At the same time the US government announced that it was instituting special licensing requirements for exports to Iraq and Iran of particular chemicals that could be used in the manufacture of chemical weapons, and that it had urged other governments to do likewise. Other governments took similar steps.

Reports of Iraqi chemical warfare dwindled following the UN statement, but they (did) not stop altogether. A British television team filming on the Iranian side of the Majnoon Islands front encountered evidence of a mustard gas attack (a few weeks later). Iranian media were no longer publicizing such reports, perhaps mindful of a potential negative impact on the country's domestic audience.

VIOLATION OF INTERNATIONAL LAW

The use in war of poisonous as well as asphyxiating or other gases, and of all analogous liquids, materials or devices was originally prohibited - along with the use of bacteriological methods of warfare - in the June 1925 Geneva Protocol, which entered into force on February 8, 1928.

The agreement was prompted by the experience of World War 1, during which the battlefield use of chemical agents caused an estimated 1.3 million casualties, including ninety thousand deaths. In fact, the Protocol only re-affirmed a constraint on acts that were held in abhorrence and which had been condemned by the general opinion of the civilized world.

In the part dealing with chemical weapons, the Protocol reiterated a prohibition already contained in previously signed international documents. These included the 1899 Hague Declaration IV 2, under which the contracting powers agreed to abstain from the use of projectiles for the diffusion of asphyxiating or deleterious gases, as well as the 1907 Hague Convention IV, which prohibited the use of poison or poisonous weapons.

Since 1925, chemical weapons had been used on several occasions, but on each time, the extent of international indignation and censure testified to the immutability of the standard of international law as embodied in the Geneva Protocol. It is, in great part, due to this international instrument that the history of chemical warfare since World War 1 has been one of relative restraint. The Protocol is now binding on more than a hundred parties, including all states that are militarily important.

Iran acceded to the Protocol on November 5, 1929, while Iraq acceded on September 8, 1931. The latter did so with the express reservation that its government would not be bound by the prohibitions in question towards any state whose armed forces did not respect the provisions of the Protocol. Over forty parties, including the great powers formulated such a requirement of reciprocity. Iran did not attach any condition to its accession, but since the reservations made by others have, in essence, turned the Protocol into a no-first-use treaty, it (eventually) considered itself free from its obligations towards Iraq.

Neither the UN group of experts that established the use of chemical weapons in the war between Iraq and Iran, nor the UN Security Council, which condemned such use, specified which party was guilty of violation. However, the Geneva Protocol does not require that violators be internationally identified.

Iran could thus claim the right to reprisal in kind, on the basis of its own findings. In other words, there is a danger of an escalating chemical warfare. Indeed, there can be no guarantee that the weapons banned by the Geneva Protocol will not be resorted to as long as there is no absolute prohibition on their very possession, subject to international control.

Significantly, at the Committee on Disarmament at Geneva, Iran declared that, due to humanitarian considerations, it would not embark on retaliatory action with chemical weapons against Iraq.

THE POISON GASES IDENTIFIED BY THE UN TEAM

Mustard gas

From an unexploded bomb found at an Iraqi-attack site, the UN team drew a sample that its analysts in Sweden and Switzerland later found to be high-quality mustard gas.

What is mustard gas?

Mustard is bis (2-chloroethyl) sulfide, an oily liquid with a garlic-like smell. Even in warm weather it evaporates slowly enough for an area over which it has been scattered to remain dangerous for many hours, even days, yet fast enough for the imperceptible vapor that it gives off also to cause casualties. Both in vapor and in liquid form, its effect is to burn any body-tissue it touches. Taken into the body, it can act as systemic poison, deadlier, weight for weight, than hydrogen cyanide.

Its burning effects are not normally apparent for some hours after exposure, whereupon they build up into a hideous combination of blindness, blistering and lung damage such as was displayed by the patients sent from Iran to hospitals in Austria, Belgium, Britain, France, (West) Germany, Japan, the Netherlands, Sweden and Switzerland.

Mustard gas was first used as a chemical warfare agent during World War 1, when it was responsible for about seventy per cent of the million-plus gas casualties. Its most prominent use after that was by Italy in Ethiopia during 1936.

During World War 2, Britain, Canada, France, Germany, Hungary, Italy, Japan, the Netherlands, Poland, South Africa, the USA and the USSR produced it. It was the CW agent that during the course of that conflict was stockpiled in the greatest quantity – to the order of hundreds of thousands of tons overall. Ultimately, mustard gas during World War 2 was used as a weapon only by Japan's forces in China. It is probably still the most heavily stockpiled CW agent today. The established use of mustard gas by Cairo appears to have been when Egyptian forces intervened in the (North) Yemeni civil war of the mid-Sixties.

Effectiveness of mustard gas

Mustard gas can be spread from munitions deliverable by virtually any type of weapon, including mortars, artillery and aircraft. Iraqi forces are reported to have used all these means.

Among many air-deliverable mustard munitions that Britain produced during World War 2, one report judged the most cost-effective was a five-gallon oil drum filled with mustard gas and fitted with a simple burster charge. The munition from which the UN team retrieved its sample in Iran appears to have been a light-case two-hundred-and-fifty-lb white-phosphorus bomb, such as might otherwise be used for smoke-screening or incendiary purpose. Published eyewitness accounts suggest that the Iraqi practice was for eight such bombs to be fitted to each ground-attack jet aircraft. They were dropped from a height of roughly between six hundred and eight hundred feet.

There may well be an international trade in such munitions. It would be relatively easy (though hazardous) to exchange the phosphorus payload (or perhaps any other high explosive fill) for mustard gas.

Manufacture

Mustard gas may be made in different ways according to whether ethylene, vinyl chloride or thiodiglycol is chosen as the precursor. Published UN findings suggest that Iraqi mustard gas was made from the last of these. Thiodiglycol is quite widely used as an industrial commodity: as an antioxidant, a vulcanizing agent, an intermediate for other commodities or as a solvent for dyes that are employed by the textile industry. Its conversion to mustard gas is a simple matter: the only technological problem is to prevent those making it from themselves becoming casualties. This is a serious problem: When Britain first manufactured mustard gas in 1918, there were 1.27 cases of mustard illness per person employed in a six-month period.

The quantity of thiodiglycol needed to produce enough mustard gas to fill eight of the kind of bombs sampled by the UN would be about seven-hundred-and-fifty lbs. A hundred tons could yield sufficient mustard gas to arm maybe three hundred aircraft sorties or to possibly keep a medium-artillery battalion firing nothing but mustard shell for something like two weeks.

Tabun

The second poison gas identified by the UN team was the nerve gas tabun. This was found in a sample, which, the team was assured by Iranian authorities, had been taken from a dud Iraqi bomb by an Iranian soldier. The device was said to have had the same appearance as the one from which the UN team had earlier taken mustard gas.

Iranian authorities told the UN team that chemical weapons had affected about four hundred people during the attack from which the tabun sample was said to have originated. The attack purportedly happened on March 17, while the UN team was in Tehran, and was said to have been delivered by four Iraqi aircraft. Forty of the casualties were in a field hospital that the UN team visited the following day. The signs and symptoms in the six cases which the UN team had time to examine were quite different from those linked to mustard gas. The UN team concluded from them that the patients had been exposed to an anticholinesterase agent.

What is tabun?

Tabun, or ethyl NN-dimethylphosphoramidocyanidate - otherwise known by its US army code name GA - is such an agent. It is a liquid that evaporates only half as fast as mustard gas, but is so powerful a poison that even a short exposure to small concentrations of its vapor will result in almost immediate symptoms. These are felt first in the eyes (as a persistent contraction of the pupil) followed by the chest (as a tightness or asthma-like constriction). If a lethal dosage has been received - either from inhalation or by absorption through the skin - a characteristic sequence of toxic manifestations ensues. This can range from a running nose, sweating, involuntary urination and defecation to vomiting, twitching, convulsions, paralysis and, finally, unconsciousness. Prior to observations made by the UN team at the field hospital, such signs had apparently not before been seen in hospitalized chemical-warfare casualties, although one or two of the earlier Iranian communiqués (as from the northern front in October 1983) referred briefly to 'nervous system' effects. At about the same time Iranian publications stated that nerve gas had been used on at least ten occasions during the period 1980-83.

Effectiveness of tabun

Because tabun acts much more rapidly than mustard gas, it might be capable of stopping massed infantry assaults on the move, at least when dropped in large air-burst bombs. In static, warm weather conditions, it would probably not be significantly more effective than mustard gas as a weapon of attrition.

The chief significance of the tabun reports was twofold. First, if true, the reports may well have described the first ever use of nerve gas in combat operations, thus providing lessons which military authorities around the world would have been eager to absorb. Second, if Iraq's resorting to tabun was motivated by the kind of military considerations just outlined, there may well have been powerful incentives for the potential for rapid mass-destruction: nerve agents such as sarin and VX are stockpiled by the USA. Under optimal atmospheric conditions, about a metric ton of sarin is required to inflict fifty per cent casualties over an area of about a square kilometer. So the amount to inflict a few hundred thousand casualties in an urban environment would require literally hundreds of aircraft[1].

Manufacture

Tabun, like sarin, was a secret discovery of Germany's at the time of World War 2. Germany manufactured about twelve thousand tons of it during 1943-44. In 1944 it also manufactured sarin on a small pilot plant scale. Soman, in contrast, was discovered in 1944 by German chemist Richard Kuhn but was produced only in laboratory quantities before the end of World War 2.

For use with conventional munitions - artillery shell and bombs - German tabun was diluted with up to twenty per cent of the solvent that had been used during its synthesis, namely chlorobenzene. The sample analyzed by the UN team contained a comparable proportion of chlorobenzene, suggesting it had been made by the original German method.

The method (employed by the Iraqis to manufacture tabun) was based on using phosphoryl chloride in a two-stage chemical process, of which both were conducted within the same reactor. Advanced containment measures were used to protect plant workers from the agent, but even they were insufficient to prevent at least ten deaths and innumerable lesser exposures.

The quantity of undiluted phosphoryl chloride needed to produce enough tabun to fill eight of the bombs examined by the UN team would be about twelve hundred lbs. Also needed would be about two-hundred-and-fifty lbs of sodium cyanide, three hundred lbs of ethyl alcohol and a hundred-and-forty lbs of dimethylamine (synthesizable from ammonia and methyl alcohol). A hundred tons of phosphoryl chloride could yield sufficient tabun to arm maybe two hundred sorties by MiG, Mirage or Sukhoi jet aircraft.

ORIGIN OF THE CHEMICAL WEAPONS

The UN report provided only negative evidence of the origin of the mustard gas sample. The absence in the sample analyzed in Sweden and Switzerland of polysulphides - and of more than a trace of sulfur - indicates that it was not of US-government manufacture: all US mustard gas was originally produced by the Levinstein process from ethylene and mixed sulfur chlorides. The same process is said to have been employed by the USSR. For the same reasons, British-made mustard can probably also be ruled out, even though substantial stocks were once held at British depots in the Middle East.

For more positive evidence, other sources of information need to be consulted. Over the years (since the mid-Sixties) a lot of information has been published purporting to describe Iraqi chemical weapons, but much of it is contradictory and all is of a reliability which SIPRI has been in no position to judge.

A major caveat: Chemical warfare is such an emotive subject that it lends itself very readily to campaigns of disinformation and black propaganda, campaigns which the politics both of the Gulf War and of the current chemical weapons negotiations have unquestionably stimulated to no small degree.

First it is necessary to look at the nature of the chemical weapons technology which Iraq has been reported to have acquired.

In addition to bulk-filled free-fall aircraft bombs, at least two other categories of chemical munitions have reportedly been employed: Artillery shell and air-to-ground rockets.

Iranians sent for hospital treatment in London suffering from what must almost certainly have been mustard-gas burns, have attributed their injuries to all three categories of munitions.

There was no evidence that Western countries were stockpiling mustard-filled air-to-ground rockets. The rockets (whose use was described by one of the Iranians) apparently had submunition warheads, a relatively sophisticated design.

Other agents reported to have been used

Tear gas: In August 1982, US officials were quoted in the press as being 'confident' that the Iraqis did not possess any 'deadly chemical weapons', only tear gas.

Choking gas: Chlorine, the archetypal war gas, is included in at least one of the lists of Iraqi chemical warfare agents published (during the Iran-Iraq war) by the Iranian authorities.

Arsenicals: Iran informed the UN secretary general (during the course of the war) that 'compounds containing arsenic' had been used in Iraqi chemical weapons. Speaking to reporters, one of the Swedish specialists treating Iranian gas casualties said he thought it probable that the latter had been exposed to a mixture of mustard gas and lewisite. Such mixtures were standard munition-fills in the arsenals of Japan, the USSR and probably other states too, during World War 2.

Nitrogen mustard: Official Iranian sources have several times stated that an agent of this type had been identified by Iranian military experts in samples from Iraqi chemical munitions. 'Knowledgeable' but unidentified US officials have also been reported as speaking of Iraqi nitrogen mustard.

Germ-warfare agents: Israeli intelligence sources have been cited for reports that anthrax had been found in hospitalized Iranians. Iranian sources have referred to Iraqi use of 'microbic' and 'bacteriological' weapons.

Mycotoxins: A Belgian forensic toxicologist with a dubious professional reputation has claimed that his laboratory found mycotoxins (T2, HT2, nivalenol and verrucarol) in addition to mustard gas in samples of blood, urine and faeces taken from Iranian gas victims hospitalized in Vienna, but (at the time the report was published) this claim remained unverified and open to question. There were reports of similar findings from patients hospitalized in Belgium, France, Germany, Sweden and Switzerland, but these too remained open to doubt, especially since, in the Swedish case, the Swedish authorities concerned expressly repudiated the report. The UN team inspected cadavers returned to Tehran from Swedish and Austrian hospitals, but its report made no mention of any post-mortem tissue samples having been taken for analysis. Mycotoxins were sought but not found in the chemical samples analyzed by the UN team. The search method used, had a detection limit of 0.00005 per cent: i.e. capable of finding mycotoxins at loadings greater than a third of a gram per two-hundred-and-fifty-lb bomb.

Novel unidentified agent: There had been speculation in the press about Iraqi use of a toxic agent unknown in the West. This was underscored by reports from the Gzaiel sector, just to the north of Basra, of groups of Iranian corpses having been seen that were said to bear no external trace of injury, looking as though they had fallen asleep in their foxholes.

Indigenous or external sources of supply?

With the exceptions, perhaps, of the last two of these categories of putative Iraqi agents, sources of supply might (be both) indigenous and external to Iraq, given the technology implied. Involvement of the last three categories would, in some circles, implicate the USSR as supplier, for reason that Moscow is said (to have weaponized) all three in recent years. For its part, the USSR has expressly denied supplying Iraq with toxic weapons. Reports of Soviet supply attributed to US and other intelligence sources nonetheless recurred. The earliest such information available predates reports of Iraqi use of chemical weapons in the Gulf War.

Official Iranian commentaries have also pointed to the USSR as a supplier of the Iraqi weapons. These sources also accused Brazil, France and, most conspicuously, Britain of supplying weapons. No basis for any of these Iranian accusations was disclosed. France, alongside Czechoslovakia and both Germanies, is reportedly rumored to be among 'foreign military and diplomatic sources' in Baghdad, to have supplied Iraq with chemical precursors needed for an indigenous production effort. Unofficial published sources have cited Egypt as a possible supplier of actual chemical weapons. In the mid-Sixties, sources of supply were reported in the Western press.

Production capability in Iraq *(This part of SIPRI's report has been overtaken by events: see Chapter 10)*

Technological capacity

Other than the need for elaborate safety measures, there seems to be nothing that the technology of producing mustard gas or tabun - or lewisite or nitrogen mustard - that would obviously be beyond the capacities of the Iraqi chemical industry. It is an industry that has been growing rapidly in size and sophistication since the early Seventies. However, if nerve gases of a type whose production would necessitate the technically demanding and comparatively specialized processes of phosphorus-fluorination and/or phosphorus-alkylation, that is, nerve gases such as sarin, soman and VX, then foreign technology might very well have to be imported. There is strong public evidence (but by no means conclusive yet) that Iraq has been endeavoring to acquire these or related technologies from private corporations in the USA, Britain, (West) Germany and Italy since 1975; and that it has been dissembling these endeavors under the guise of acquiring production capacity for organophosphorus pesticides.

The search for materials

Any need to import special chemical-process plant and associated know-how could be lessened by importing, instead, some of the chemical intermediates needed to produce chemical warfare agents. This would be preferable to trying to manufacture those intermediates from indigenous raw materials (of which the Iraqi mining, petroleum and related industries appear to provide the full range needed for mustard and nerve gases, with the possible exception of some of the latter of fluoride minerals).

To which Croddy adds, 'it seems to me that fluoride can be mined from phosphates, or at least from bi-products during leach process mining of phosphates: And Iraq is sitting on a rather abundant supply of phosphates[2].'

Certain intermediates can be identified that could reduce the requirements for chemical plant to processing equipment of standard off-the-shelf or easily improvised types. Iraq had not concealed the fact that it was in the market for chemicals that did indeed fall within this category. This was most conspicuous in Iraq's search in America for supplies of methylphosphonous dichloride and dimethyl methyl-phosphonate. These two chemicals do however, have certain civil applications. But at least in the former case they were not ones which, in the normal course of events, Iraq might obviously have been expected to exploit.

Export controls

On March 30, the US government announced the imposition of 'foreign policy controls' on the export to the Gulf War belligerents of five chemicals that could be used in the production of mustard and nerve gases. US officials told the press that this had been done in response to an unexpected volume of recent orders from Iraq for those chemicals.

They said that Japan, Federal Republic of Germany and other unspecified European countries had been exporting the chemicals contrary to the export control list. Since then, other European governments also announced embargoes of varying scope. (That was followed) by Foreign Ministers of the EU agreeing in principle on a common and complementary policy. There were also Western press reports of suspicions in Western diplomatic circles in the Middle East that the USSR was shipping intermediates to Iraq through Jordan.

---

1   Personal comments made by Eric Croddy
2   Croddy: *Ibid*

4

IRAQ: THE COUNTRY
AND ITS PEOPLE

**I understand why some dislike the idea, and fear the
ramifications of America as a liberator. But I do not
understand why they do not see that anything is better
than life with your face under the boot. And that any rescue
of a people under the boot (be they Afghan, Kuwaiti or
Iraqi) is something to be desired. Even if the rescue is less
than perfectly realized. Even if the rescuer is a great,
overmuscled, bossy, selfish oaf. Or would you, for yourself,
choose the boot?**

Michael Kelly

America's Central Intelligence Agency in its customary simplistic public
style possibly best encapsulates Iraq's early history in a single paragraph that
heads its World Factbook[1] file.

The report reads: 'formerly part of the Ottoman Empire, Iraq became
an independent kingdom in 1932. A "republic" was proclaimed in 1958,
but in actuality a series of military strongmen have ruled the country since
then, the latest being Saddam Hussein.'

It goes on to talk about territorial disputes with Iran that led to an
inconclusive and costly eight-year war (1980-1988). In August 1990 Iraq
seized Kuwait, but was expelled by US-led, UN Coalition Forces during
January-February 1991. The victors did not occupy Iraq however, thus
allowing the regime to stay in control. Following Kuwait's liberation, the
UN Security Council required Iraq to scrap all weapons of mass destruction
(WMD) and long-range missiles and to allow UN verification inspections.
UN trade sanctions remain in effect due to incomplete Iraqi compliance
with relevant UNSC resolutions.

There is much more to Iraq. In fact, if there is such a thing as the 'cradle of
civilization', then academics would have us believe that it is quite possible
that it lies - among more than ten thousand archeological sites - between
the twin basins of the great Tigris and Euphrates Rivers. These two
waterways snake down to the Gulf through Iraq from Turkey and what has
become apparent to scholars of all persuasions and beliefs through the ages

is that there has been a human presence in the region from the earliest period. This is a part of the globe that contains not only the world's richest known archeological sites, but almost all of the origins of mankind's first recorded history.

Much of this was evident in Iraq's magnificent museums, some of which were trashed by dissidents and looters following 'Operation Iraqi Freedom'. While the damage was not as serious as first thought, there are irreplaceable icons of man's birthright that are gone forever. And though some of these treasures have been recovered, those willfully smashed are gone forever. The looting of Iraq's museums will always be one of the great catastrophes of our epoch.

At the same time, be reminded that it was not all that long ago that Iraq pillaged Kuwait's historic treasures. Iraqi troops - not looters - systematically trashed Kuwait's museums. One needs to get this issue into perspective because though there were promises out of Baghdad by the bucketful, not all of the artifacts stolen - many of them priceless - were returned.

What is clear to those who have made a serious study of Iraq's history is that a thousand centuries ago, families of Paleolithic-age man gathered in this region. It was these same waters that provided vegetation and fish for these nomadic hunter-gatherers.

For almost a hundred millennia, early tribes moved their camps seasonally to hunt wild animals and to collect seeds, fruit, nuts, wild wheat, barley and rye. Remains from their encampments indicate the slow progression and development of the culture of man. In fact, Mesopotamian man left artifacts in Shanidar Caves about fifty thousand years ago, showing numerous elements of their life. It is known that they were advanced enough to leave flowers on the graves of their dead, a touching tribute to these predecessors of our present generation.

By 10,000 BC, small settled groups at Shanidar and Karim Shahir had domesticated herds of sheep: these they took into the mountains in spring and fall to graze on the sweet grasses that emerged from under the snow.

Four thousand years later, in the Neolithic Age, there were permanent villages formed where man slowly learnt the skills of farming, animal husbandry, house building, weaving, pottery and even the creation of art objects through painting and sculpture[2].

Once known as Mesopotamia (land between the rivers), Iraq gradually developed to become the site of several flourishing ancient civilizations, including the Sumerian, Babylonian, and Parthian cultures. The age-old cities of Sumer, Babylon and Assyria, among the oldest on earth, were all located in what is now modern Iraq. It was the dual nature of the two rivers that led to some of the great cultures of the past: the role played by their potential to be both productive and destructive. As a consequence, two distinct legacies were founded. On the one hand, Mesopotamia's plentiful water resources and lush valleys allowed for the production of surplus food that served as the basis for the civilizing trend begun at Sumer and preserved by rulers such as Hammurabi (1792-1750 BC), Cyrus (550-530 BC), Darius (520-485 BC), Alexander (336-323 BC) and the Abbasids (AD 750-1258).

Mesopotamia could also be an extremely threatening environment, driving its people to seek security from the vicissitudes of nature.

Throughout recorded Iraqi history, various groups formed autonomous, self-contained social units. These sought allegiances to ancient religious deities at Ur and Eridu, membership in the Shi'ite Ali (or party of Ali, the small group of followers that supported Ali ibn Abu Talib as rightful leader of the Islamic community in the 7th Century), residence in the *asnaf* (guilds) or the *mahallat* (city quarters) of Baghdad under the Ottoman Turks.

Others resorted to strengthening tribal or village ties; in exactly the same way that Saddam Hussein, at the height of his power, elevated his own Tikriti community to unprecedented prominence. Such efforts to build autonomous, security-providing structures exerted a powerful centrifugal force on Iraqi culture.

It was Islam that took the country into the modern period after Muslims conquered Iraq in the 7th Century AD. In the 8th Century, the Abassid caliphate established its capital at Baghdad, which became a frontier outpost of the Ottoman Empire. At the end of the Great War, Iraq became a British-mandated territory. When it was declared independent in 1932, the Hashemite family (which also ruled Jordan) ruled as a constitutional monarchy. This has always been one of the criticisms of the modern period: that as a country (and like so much of contemporary Africa, for that matter), Iraq was created on the drawing boards of Europe.

In 1945, Iraq joined the United Nations and became a founding member of the Arab League. Little more than a decade later the Baghdad Pact allied Iraq, Turkey, Iran, Pakistan, and the United Kingdom. It established its headquarters in Baghdad. Some dramatic changes followed, the consequences of which are still felt throughout Iraqi society today.

In a bloody coup in July 1958, Army General Abdul Karim Qasim took power. During that transition, King Faisal II and Prime Minister Nuri as-Said were murdered, Qasim ended Iraq's membership in the Baghdad Pact in 1959 and he himself was assassinated in February 1963, when the Arab Socialist Renaissance Party (it now calls itself the Ba'ath Party) took power under the leadership of Gen. Ahmad Hasan al-Bakr as prime minister and Col. Abdul Salam Arif as president. Nine months later, Arif led a coup ousting the Ba'ath government.

In April 1966, Arif was killed in a plane crash and was succeeded by his brother, Gen. Abdul Rahman Mohammad Arif. On July 17, 1968, a group of Ba'athists and military elements overthrew the Arif regime. Ahmad Hasan al-Bakr re-emerged as the President of Iraq and Chairman of the Revolutionary Command Council (RCC). Bakr resigned in July 1979 and his chosen successor, Saddam Hussein, emerged to assume both offices.

The Iran-Iraq war (1980-88) followed, devastating the economy of both countries. Always the innovator, Saddam declared victory in 1988, but actually, all he did achieve was a weary return to the status quo antebellum.

The war left Iraq with the largest military establishment in the Gulf region but with huge debts and an ongoing rebellion by Kurdish elements in the northern mountains. Baghdad suppressed the rebellion by using weapons of mass destruction on civilian targets, including a mass chemical weapons attack on the city of Halabja that killed several thousand civilians.

The invasion of Kuwait followed in August 1990, and an American-led coalition acting under United Nations resolutions expelled all Iraqi forces from the tiny kingdom in February 1991.

After the war, UN-mandated sanctions based on Security Council resolutions called for the regime to surrender its WMD and submit to mandated United Nations inspections: Saddam's regime refused to fully cooperate with UN inspections.

From 1998 until the start of the second Gulf War, Iraq did not allow weapons inspectors into the country, giving rise to fears that he might again have been engaged in developing chemical and biological weapons and, worse, possibly the atom bomb. As these chapters show, he had people working on all these disciplines: at its peak, his nuclear program employed close to twenty thousand people.

While the impasse continued - prior to March 2003 - Iraq was allowed under the UN Oil-For-Food program to export limited quantities of oil with which to purchase food, medicine, and other humanitarian relief equipment and infrastructure support necessary to sustain the civilian population. The UN Coalition, meanwhile, enforced no-fly zones in southern and northern Iraq to protect Iraqi citizens from attack by the regime. There was also a no-drive zone in southern Iraq to prevent the regime from massing forces to threaten or again invade Kuwait.

Despite many changes, Iraq's Ba'ath Party seemed to have survived the tumult of the earlier years. It was Saddam who cemented its place at the head of the ruling hierarchy with a nine-member Revolutionary Command Council (RCC). Little more than a rubber-stamp grouping, it enacted Saddam's legislation by decree.

The RCC's president (chief of state and supreme commander of the armed forces) was an elected member by a two-thirds majority of the RCC. The same with the Iraqi Council of Ministers (cabinet), appointed by the RCC. It had administrative and some legislative responsibilities, but in fact, it did what it was told by Saddam Hussein.

The country also boasted a two-hundred-and-fifty-member National Assembly but throughout, this body endorsed the whims of its leader. The last one, consisting of two-hundred-and-two members 'elected by popular vote' and who served a four-year term (together with another thirty appointed by the president to represent the three northern provinces), was last elected in March 2000.

Iraq under Saddam was divided into eighteen provinces, each headed by a governor with extensive administrative powers. As long as these demagogues answered to the supreme leader they were largely left to their own devices.

The country's judicial system (then and now, following 'Operation Iraqi Freedom') is based on the French model introduced during Ottoman rule. It has three types of lower courts. These are civil, religious, and special. Special courts try broadly-defined national security cases. An appellate court system and the court of cassation (court of last recourse) completed the judicial structure.

Iraq's economy has always been dominated by the oil sector, which has traditionally provided more than ninety per cent of all foreign exchange earnings.

In the 1980s, financial problems - caused by massive expenditures in the eight-year war with Iran and damage to oil export facilities by Iran - led the government to implement austerity measures, borrow at an unprecedented rate and later reschedule foreign debt payments. By now Iraq had suffered economic losses of at least $100 billion from the war.

Iraq's seizure of Kuwait in August 1990, subsequent international economic sanctions, together with damage from military action by the international Coalition Forces in January 1991, drastically reduced economic activity throughout the country.

Subsequent Iraqi government policies were disjointed. They supported a large number of military and internal security forces, at the same time allocating untold resources to key supporters of the regime. It was to be expected therefor that with time, such handouts would begin to hurt the economy. And while the implementation of a United Nations Oil-For-Food program in December 1996 did help to improve conditions for the average Iraqi citizen, it was not by much.

The truth is that a good deal of money received for this oil was diverted by Saddam to build grandiose palaces. There were also monuments, statues and effigies in his honor in every single city and town in Iraq, including a massive outstretched hand - Saddam's - in Baghdad. It was grandiloquent megalomania on a crazy scale, perhaps matched only by what is taking place in an equally cock-eyed North Korea today.

In December 1999, the UN Security Council authorized Iraq to export as much oil as required to meet humanitarian needs. Oil exports rose to more than three-quarters their pre-war level. Per capita food imports increased significantly, while medical supplies and health care services improved. Per capita output and living standards, though, were still well below the pre-war level, but estimates allowed for a wide range of error. The country's economic well-being or otherwise was characterized by an exceptionally heavy dependence on oil exports together with emphasis on development through central planning.

Prior to the outbreak of the war with Iran in September 1980, Iraq's economic prospects looked good. Oil production had reached a level of 3.5 million barrels per day and oil revenues were $21 billion in 1979 and $27 billion in 1980. By the outbreak of the war, Iraq had amassed an estimated $35 billion in foreign exchange reserves.

The Iran-Iraq War changed all that. Hostilities depleted Iraq's foreign exchange reserves, devastated its economy and left the country saddled with a foreign debt of more than $40 billion.

After the war ended in 1988, oil exports gradually increased with the construction of new pipelines and the restoration of damaged facilities. But the Iraqi invasion of Kuwait, subsequent international sanctions, all of it coupled to damage from military action by an international coalition beginning in January 1991, drastically curtailed it all.

Government policies of diverting income to key supporters of the regime (while sustaining a large military and internal security force) further impaired finances. This left the average Iraqi citizen facing desperate hardships. Implementation of the UN Oil-For-Food program in December 1996 improved conditions a bit, but clever fiddling of the books and selected deprivation by Saddam caused much unnecessary hardship, especially among the very young and the old.

In 1999, Iraq was authorized to export unlimited quantities of oil to finance humanitarian needs including food, medicine, and infrastructure repair and spare parts. But this new development also resulted in abuse. Oil exports fluctuated as the regime alternately started and halted exports at Saddam's whim. In general, by the time of the second Gulf War, oil exports had reached three-quarters of their pre-Gulf War levels.

Similarly, per capita output and living standards remained well below pre-war levels, though it is also true, as observed by Stephen Ulph, editor of Jane's *Islamic Affairs Analyst* in the summer of 2002, that the average Iraqi was still better off than the average Egyptian.

Saddam's principal focus throughout these travails was to build up the Iraqi armed forces to an unprecedented level. The war with Iran ended with Iraq retaining the largest military structure in the Middle East. It had more than seventy divisions in its army and an air force of over seven hundred modern aircraft. Losses during the invasion of Kuwait and subsequent ejection of Iraqi forces from Kuwait in the brief but bloody (for Iraqis) 'Operation Desert Storm' resulted in the reduction of Iraq's ground forces to twenty-three divisions and air force to less than three hundred aircraft.

At one stage Saddam gave orders for his air force to fly many of his best aircraft across the border into Iran, hoping to be able to get them back after the war. Tehran had other ideas. The mullahs seized the lot, claiming this sophisticated booty as part of war reparations from the earlier war with Iraq.

Military and economic sanctions prevented Iraq from properly rebuilding its military strength to previous levels, though by the time of the second Gulf War, it still maintained standing military forces of almost four-hundred-thousand men.

Politically, things were not much better. Iraqi-Iranian relations, for example, have always remained cool, very much as had been the case since the end of the Iraq-Iran War.

Outstanding issues from that conflict, including prisoner of war exchanges and support of armed opposition parties operating in each other's territory remained to be solved. Interestingly, it was only after the last war, in May 2003, that the last of the Iraqi POWs (together with the remains of many others who died in captivity) were handed back by the Tehran government.

Iraq's relations with the Arab world have always been varied. Some of Iraq's neighbors might have resented Washington having taken the initiative and toppled Saddam in 2003, but what did become apparent afterwards was that the entire Islamic world breathed a collective sigh of relief when the tyrant was finally ousted.

The man was a monster. And though it rankled within the minds of the average Muslim to have to admit that one of their own could be so evil, there was little argument at grass-roots level that in the end he simply had to go. That event sparked furious debate in newspapers throughout the Arab world but in most cases, sense prevailed. Which, let it be said, certainly does not mean that the Islamic world likes America any the more for what it has done.

Politically, things were never easy with Iraq. Egypt broke off relations with Iraq in 1977 following Iraq's criticism of President Anwar Sadat's peace initiatives with Israel. A year later Baghdad hosted an Arab League summit that condemned and ostracized Egypt for accepting the Camp David Accords. Subsequently, Egypt's strong material and diplomatic support for Iraq in the war with Iran led to warmer relations and numerous contacts between senior officials, despite the continued absence of ambassadorial-level representation. During 1983, Iraq repeatedly called for the restoration of Egypt's 'natural role' among Arab countries and in January 1984 successfully led Arab efforts within the OIC to restore Egypt's membership.

However, Iraqi-Egyptian relations split again in 1990. That was after Egypt joined the UN Coalition that forced Iraq out of Kuwait. Relations did improve afterwards, to the point where, shortly before 'Operation Iraqi Freedom', Egypt was one of Iraq's main trade partners under the Oil-For-Food program.

The same applied to Iraq's links with Syria. These were constantly marred by traditional rivalry for pre-eminence in Arab affairs, especially since both countries were Ba'athist. Almost as long as anybody can remember there have been allegations of involvement in each other's internal affairs and disputes over the waters of the Euphrates River, oil transit fees, and the 'requisite stance' toward Israel.

Syria broke ties with Baghdad after Iraq invaded Kuwait in 1990 and joined other Arab countries in sending its military forces to the coalition that forced Saddam's forces out of Kuwait. Thus, relations remained cool until Bashar Assad succeeded his late father to become President of Syria in 2000 and that, in turn, led to a strengthening of economic ties based largely on the smuggling of oil.

Politically the relationship seemed to remain distant, but this could have been a ploy on the part of both leaders as there has been evidence of a great deal of collusion in high places. Many of Iraq's hierarchy fled to Syria after US forces entered Baghdad and it was only a bit of strong-arm stuff from US secretary of state Colin Powell during his visit to Damascus early May 2003 that partially stopped the rot.

With Jordan, Iraq's ties improved significantly after 1980 when Amman declared its support for Iraq at the onset of the Iran-Iraq war. The late King Hussein's support for Iraq during the Gulf War resulted in further warming.

Since his son, King Abdullah, took office in 2000 relations have cooled again and the Gulf War 2 made further adjustment unnecessary.

Iraq's invasion of Kuwait also resulted in Kuwait, Saudi Arabia, and most Gulf states severing relations with Baghdad and joining the UN Coalition. Iraq's refusal to implement UN Security Council Resolutions and continued threats toward Kuwait resulted in relations remaining cool throughout.

It is interesting that this should have been so because Iraq was a significant participant in the Arab-Israeli wars of 1948, 1967 and 1973. Traditionally Baghdad also opposed all attempts to reach a peaceful settlement between Israel and the Arab States and this suited the Pan Arabic approach.

After Israel attacked Iraq's nuclear research reactor under construction near Baghdad in July 1981 Saddam became a blood enemy of the Jewish State, though during the Iran-Iraq war Saddam did moderate his anti-Israel stance somewhat. In August 1982, President Hussein told a visiting US Congressman that 'a secure state is necessary for both Israel and the Palestinians'.

While the Iraqi dictator did not oppose President Reagan's Arab-Israeli peace initiative of September 1982, and it supported the moderate Arab position at the Fez summit that same month, Saddam Hussein repeatedly stated that he would support whatever settlement was acceptable to the Palestinians. However, after the Iran-Iraq war, he and his ministers reverted to more strident anti-Israel statements. This is underscored by the fact that some weapons being developed by Baghdad in the Eighties could only have had Israel in their sights. One of these was the mysterious 'Super Gun' developed by Canadian inventor Gerald Bull who was later assassinated by the Mossad (See Chapter 12 under the heading 'Super Gun').

Throughout, the destruction of Israel was behind most of what Saddam did. During the Gulf War, his forces fired Scud missiles at Israeli civilian targets in an attempt to divide the US Coalition. Following that war, Iraq embraced a most extreme hard-line position, including periodically calling for the total elimination of Israel.

For the last decade or more, Iraq had no diplomatic relations with the United States. An American Interests Section operated in Baghdad with the Government of Poland as the Protecting Power, while there was an Iraqi Interests Section in the Algerian Embassy in Washington DC.

The population make-up in Iraq is interesting. Turkey, Iran, Kuwait, Saudi Arabia, Jordan, Syria and the Persian Gulf surround it and its population of around about twenty-three million is ethnically and religiously diverse.

Approximately three-quarters of the people are Arabs, though just about everybody uses the Arabic language in their day-to-day activities. Altogether, the Sunni Muslim community forms around a fifth of Iraq's Arab population and under the tyrant, dominated the government: Saddam Hussein was Sunni.

Shi'ite Iraqis are in the majority (about sixty per cent in Iraq compared to about fifteen per cent of all Muslims worldwide) and this worries many Western Arabists, including those on The Hill. There are theorists who fear that despite the paucity of numbers, nobody can rule out the creation of another mullah-dominated state along Iranian lines. They point to the revolutionary Hizbollah movement in Lebanon, today a powerful political and military entity that despite its size, commands respect in the Arab world because of what it has done to the Israeli Defense Force.

Notably, Hizbollah was also spawned by revolt more than twenty years ago. Among its first acts was to send suicide bombers to destroy the US Embassy in Beirut as well as a US Marines barracks near the airport: that fundamentalist Islamic grouping set the scene for a lot of what is happening in Israel today. In those singular acts, Hizbollah achieved terrible loss of American lives. Certainly, if the Shi'ite clergy were to get obstreperous in Iraq, they might also cause intractable problems for the new US-led Iraqi Administration. And while it would be impossible, in the long term at any rate, to prevent Iraq becoming a preponderantly Shi'ite state, it is not something to which the US will quickly acquiesce, especially while Washington continues to hold the balance of power in the Gulf.

There is much more to Iraqi society. Altogether about a fifth of the population is of Kurdish extraction, though some dispute these statistics, saying that that tally is too high. Nobody can argue because it has been impossible to hold a census there for decades.

The remaining three per cent of Iraqis consists of Assyrians, Turkomans, Armenians, Christians and Yazidis. There was a large Jewish community prior to 1948, but just about all of them relocated to Israel following the wars that accompanied that state's independence.

It is the Shi'ites who hold the key to the future of Iraq not only because they are the majority 'tribe' but because Washington has made a big play of installing a democratic regime there once the dreaded Saddam had gone.

Terribly repressed by just about every sector of Iraqi society - by Saddam's stooges, by the ruling Ba'athist Party, by the overwhelming security apparatus and by many non-Shi'ites who believed they could score points with the authorities by putting them down - there are Shi'ite leaders who moved swiftly to fill the power vacuum once the Americans had crossed the Euphrates. Certainly, there is a huge community of Shi'ite Iraqis who aspire to claim political dominance for the first time in modern Iraqi history.

As London's *Times*[3] commented shortly after Saddam had fled, 'the spectacle of a million Shi'a Muslims beating their chests, chanting and flagellating themselves in a frenzy of religious fervor as they performed the first mass pilgrimage to Karbala for twenty-five years was astonishing, heartening yet ominous. That so many were able to perform this ritual so soon after the end of the war is testimony to the resilience of a downtrodden community and the strength of its organization…

'For some, who watched from afar the processions, the blood and the anti-American slogans, this eruption of religious feeling came as a shock. To the State Department, it was hideously familiar: Iraq was swept by a revolution in which religious extremism was harnessed to a burning resentment of Western, and especially American, influence. Already nervous, State Department officials speak about being "unprepared" for such demonstrations, while more hawkish members of the Administration are giving warning that they will not tolerate any attempt to hijack Iraq's nascent democracy or set up a theocratic state…'

The only good news in this extremely volatile politico-religious conundrum is that as a single Islamic entity, the Shi'ites, for all their professions of single-mindedness, are not quite as united as some of them would have us believe.

There are fissures that plague Iraq's Shi'ite adherents, demonstrated by a mob that early in the war murdered a cleric loyal to Saddam and widely hated by Shi'ites.

Nor has anybody in Iraq forgotten that Mohammed Hamza al-Zubaydi, the man who was labeled 'Shi'ite Thug' by his own people, was probably responsible for more sectarian deaths than just about any other Iraqi. He was actually proud to be serving Saddam by murdering members of his own clan. It doesn't make sense.

Roger Hardy, a BBC Middle East analyst[4] has his own opinion about this community. For all their sense of communal solidarity, he wrote, (the Shi'ites) are not homogenous: one divide is between the religious and the secular. Another is between the political activists and those who favor keeping out of politics.

In the second category is Iraq's Ayatollah Ali Sistani, the most senior religious figure in the holy Shi'ite city of Najaf. It was Sistani, always the pragmatist - following his release from house arrest as the American forces were pushing north towards Baghdad - who broadcast to his followers that 'the Shi'ite community should not back the intruders.' He added a rider:

'Nor should they oppose the invasion,' Ayatollah Sistani declared in a Friday sermon at mosque.

Hardy mentions three main Shi'ite groups that should be watched, all of them activists. There is the Daawa Party, The Sadr Group and SCIRI, the Supreme Council for the Islamic Revolution of Iraq.

The first of these is the oldest of the Shi'ite Islamist movement and was founded in the Fifties. After a series of attempts to assassinate Saddam Hussein and some of his ministers, it was harshly suppressed and eventually split into several factions.

The Sadr group represents a radical, home-grown trend that some see as a force to be reckoned with. Named after a popular religious figure, the Ayatollah Mohammed Sadeq al-Sadr who was assassinated by agents of the Saddam regime, it is popular in Najaf and in Baghdad's Shi'ite suburbs, the biggest of which was formerly Saddam City and has now been renamed 'Sadr City'.

Nobody is certain what role SCIRI will eventually play in Iraqi Shi'ite politics, except that it takes some of its orders from Tehran (but then, as somebody else observed, so do quite a lot of Iraqi Shi'ites). About all that is different is that whereas Iraqi SCIRI were ecstatic twenty years ago about the Iranian revolution and the its leader the Ayatollah Khomeini, Hardy reckons that the ideal has since 'lost much of its fizz'.

As Associated Press writer Steven Gutkin[5] observed in his syndicated assessment, there is also a split between Shi'ites who stayed in Iraq and those who fled the Saddam years. In addition, he wrote, 'there is at least a quiet competition between the Shi'ites of Karbala and the Shi'ites of Najaf', quoting R.K. Ramazani, a renowned expert on Shi'ites at the University of Virginia.

Nor can a Sunni backlash be discounted, especially if they get some support from the victors. Sunni political dominance of Iraq goes back to the birth of Iraq as a state. As Gutkin comments, 'Sunnis have dominated education, the army and the economy, using military force to repress rivals. They are unlikely to surrender quickly.'

And support from Iran? Obviously, that could happen, as it did with Hizbollah in Lebanon. The truth is that the confessional ties shared by many Iraqi Shi'ites with Tehran are, at best, tentative.

'Many Iraqi Shi'ites share Arab suspicions of Iran and may have a different outlook and agenda,' said the *Times*.

Part of the strength and resilience of Shi'ites everywhere, is perhaps to be found in this community's remarkable capacity to cope with adversity. The Israeli Defense Force (IDF) used everything that came to hand to hammer

Shi'ite communities in South Lebanon but to little effect. This attrition included a civil war that took thousands of lives and went on for decades.

To the surprise of all, instead of humbling these Muslims, Hizbollah used these exact same obstacles as building blocks to create a tough new society from which it today draws the bulk of its fighters. It was these same Shi'ites - not Sunnis or Christians from the central or northern reaches of Lebanon - that eventually forced Jerusalem to withdraw its forces behind its own national borders.

I was to see a little of it at first hand while flying combat in Sierra Leone in the summer of 2000. Reporting for Jane's, I spent five weeks going out intermittently with a South African mercenary pilot Neall Ellis in a rickety old Mi-24 helicopter gunship that leaked when it rained. The Hind was kept aloft by a bunch of Ethiopian technicians who were Russian-trained.

Unofficially, our crew was drawn from a mixed bag of foreigners who were in West Africa at the time including a French secret service agent. Among our side gunners was Hassan, originally from Lebanon and also a Shi'ite.

'Our tame Shi'te,' the crew called him, very much aware that he was a devoted follower of Hizbollah and the revolutionary movement's leader, Hassan Nasrallah (See Chapter 15). Tough as old boots but still a youngster in his twenties, Hassan was not only resourceful, he was also strong and brave. The previous time the rebels banged at the gates of Freetown, he single-handedly rescued scores of Lebanese civilians - many of them children - who were trapped behind the lines.

Onboard our helicopter he relished a scrap, even when the odds were stacked against a single helicopter that was ranged against perhaps several hundred rebels, some of them with 12.7mm and, occasionally, 14.5mm anti-aircraft weapons. That story still needs to be told[6].

Laptop in one hand and cellular phone in the other - with an AK tucked, not too discreetly under his arm - Hassan graphically illustrated the face of the up and coming young Shi'ite of the New Millennium. Should Tehran be allowed to proselytize its followers across the borders, such actions would not bode well for the New Iraq of tomorrow.

1   Central Intelligence Agency *CIA's World Factbook File - Iraq*: Langley, Virginia (Appendix B)
2   For historical detail about these and more recent periods, as well as more relevant information about early Iraq see website http://www.iraq-mission.org/historical.htm
3   Editorial: *The Times*, London, April 26, 2003
4   'Analysis: Shi'a Role in New Iraq' Roger Hardy on BBC News, London, published April 22, 2003
5   'Who are Iraqi Shi'ites and What do they Want?' Steven Gutkin, Associated Press Writer, April 17, 2003
6   *War Dog: Fighting Other Peoples' Wars* by Al J. Venter, Casemate Publishing, Philadelphia, USA, to be published early 2004

SADDAM HUSSEIN: THE MAN

'When it comes to demonizing Saddam Hussein, nothing captures the popular imagination in America better than the statement that he "gassed his own people". This is an allusion to the deployment of chemical weapons by Iraq's military in the Iraqi Kurdistan town of Halabja in March 1988...'

Dilip Hiro: 'When US Turned a Blind Eye to Poison Gas', *The Observer,*
London, September 1, 2002

John F. Burns of *The New York Times* painted a chilling picture of Saddam Hussein's final hours from Baghdad[1]. In his article 'Last, Desperate Days of a Brutal Reign' he says that in the twenty-six days of American warfare that it took to bring that era down, the hallmark of Mr Hussein's rule was 'revealed not as one of grandeur but of gangsterism and thuggery'.

Burns, hardly a propagandist, tends to shoot from the lip. The gist of his article reflected both surprise and revulsion. He talks of the gilded marble tablets posted at the gateways of a score of presidential palaces that depicted the previous quarter century as 'The Era of Saddam Hussein'.

He adds, as American troops closed in: '...but there were no Churchillian scenes of Mr Hussein visiting the wounded, or clambering atop rubble left by airstrikes. Instead, the sixty-five-year-old leader appeared on television, until cruise missiles knocked it off the air, in videotapes recorded from a small, low-ceilinged room, white sheet against the wall, like a leader of an underground group taunting those hunting him down.'

Burns goes on: 'If any one moment marked the end of Mr Hussein's rule, it was the sight of one his statues, legs cracking, its torso tumbling and the severed head and body being pelted with garbage and shoes - the ultimate Arab insult - by the hundreds of Iraqis who had gathered to celebrate their freedom.'

We now also know that in the days immediately before the collapse, his son had crept into the national bank in the dark hours and removed a billion dollars or more. The cash was towed away by tractors in a convoy of three trailers and was last seen crossing the Syrian border. So much then for being concerned about the welfare of his people.

But then, as another sclerotic hack - British, and not exactly known for pro-American pronouncements - observed shortly before leaving the Palestine Hotel on the long overland haul to Amman, 'that was his style. Only he came down so hard on his own people once he'd achieved power, that nobody could do a damn thing about it.'

Iraq's story over the past two decades or more is also the story of Saddam Hussein. All real authority in what was to become one of the most authoritarian states on the globe rested with the President and his immediate circle. Saddam's family, tribe and a small number of associates - the majority of them Tikritis (from the northern town of Tikrit) remained his most loyal supporters and he had little compunction in using them, often ruthlessly. They would convey his orders, including those to members of the government to effect any law that pleased him.

Look under the covers and the observer will quickly recognize the hallmarks of utter totalitarianism.

Saddam employed patronage and violence to motivate his supporters. Likewise, he either controlled or eliminated the actual or perceived opposition. At the same time, potential rewards included a treasure house of social status for Saddam's fairly extensive coterie, money and access to the kind of goods denied the majority of the population. Sound familiar? There are some astonishing parallels with conditions in the former Soviet Union, or for that matter, with Kim Jong Il's equally repressive North Korea.

Also, it is not surprising that Moscow has always been close to Baghdad, a fact demonstrated not unexpectedly, by President Putin's determined opposition to America's invasion of Iraq in March 2003.

Saddam's extensive security apparatus and Ba'ath Party network was all but omnipotent. With informants in every village and town, at all social levels of the community leadership included, it covered every possible section of Iraqi society.

The system was subject to dreadful abuse. If one had a grudge against a neighbor, or possibly coveted his wife (there are numerous instances now coming to light of this happening) that person would tip off the *Mukhabarat*. Only there wasn't one such security body, there were many, their priorities overlapping to keep the nation on its toes.

In his dossier justifying possible future British military action against the Baghdad Government and published in the last quarter of 2002, Prime Minister Tony Blair was unequivocal about the fact that Saddam Hussein routinely practised torture, execution and other forms of coercion against his enemies - real or suspected.

'His targets are not only those who have offended him, but also their families, friends or colleagues,' said Blair about six months before the invasion. He added that Saddam acted vigorously to ensure that there were no other centers of power that might have threatened his hegemony.

Indeed, 'he has crushed parties and ethnic groups, such as the communists and the Kurds, which might have been trying to assert themselves. Members of the opposition abroad became targets of assassination attempts invariably conducted by Iraqi security services.'

Explaining Iraq's domestic political infrastructure, Mr Blair said that army officers were an important part of the government's network of informers. Suspicion that officers might have ambitions other than the service of the President, he said, often led to immediate execution.

'It is routine for Saddam to take pre-emptive action against those who he believes might conspire against him,' the Prime Minister declared.

There is some debate as to whether Saddam Hussein was born, as he claimed, on April 28, 1937 in a mud hut in Tikrit, seat of Iraq's Saladdin Province to the north of Baghdad. Others have said, judging by his hands, that he was older. The April date was official.

His father, Saddam al-Majid died shortly afterwards, and his mother was taken as one of the wives of a shepherd, Ibrahim Hassan, who apparently severely abused the young Saddam. At the age of ten the future dictator left for Baghdad to live with his uncle, Khayrallah Tulfah, a passionately anti-Western army officer who was dismissed for supporting a failed coup. Studying his early background, it becomes evident that much of Saddam's subsequent political career was shaped during this period, enough to move him to appoint his uncle mayor of Baghdad in later years.

Having left school at the age of sixteen, he applied and failed to make the grade at the Baghdad Military Academy: that was when he immersed himself in politics. A year later he became a member of the Ba'ath Socialist Party, having already been involved in a failed coup against the young King Faisal II. The Baghdad grapevine maintains that he killed his first adversary at the age of seventeen and often boasted that he had started his political career inordinately young.

Not long afterwards he was arrested and detained for six months for political activities against the regime - he was still at secondary school. Before finishing his studies, he was again involved in a plot, this time in an attempt to topple the dictator Abdel-Karim Kassem who had initiated a decade of mass killings, attempted assassinations and violent changes of government. The country has a history of tyrants.

For all his troubles Saddam was shot in the leg and sentenced to death in absentia on February 25, 1960, immediately enhancing his status among his peers.

Always on the move, the youthful Saddam - he had not started to shave properly - escaped to Syria. From there he went to Egypt where he completed his secondary school studies in 1962. He was able to return home from self-imposed exile only after the 14th of Ramadhan Revolution (which unseated the then presidential incumbent) had occurred in February 1963.

By this time Saddam had already been admitted to the College of Law in Cairo, but these studies were discontinued when he returned to Baghdad in another bid to topple the government. By the end of that year - still in his twenties - he was elected as a member of the Ba'ath Party Leadership.

Once more he was forced into hiding after the Ba'ath Party fell from power later that year. Shortly afterwards Saddam was captured and imprisoned, but in 1967 escaped and took over responsibility for Ba'ath security. With that, he set about imposing his will on the Party and establishing himself at the center of power.

The Ba'ath Party returned to power in 1968. A year later Saddam became Vice-Chairman of the Revolutionary Command Council, deputy to the president, and deputy secretary general of the Regional Command of the Ba'ath. In 1970 he joined the party's National Command and in 1977 was elected assistant secretary general.

Finally, in July 1979, Saddam Hussein took over the Presidency of Iraq. Within days, five fellow members of the Revolutionary Command Council were accused of involvement in a coup attempt and together with seventeen others were taken behind the Ba'athist headquarters and summarily shot.

From that day on, the Iraqi dictator set in motion a remarkably efficient and complex security apparatus. The main aspects were:

- The Special Security Organization oversaw Saddam's personal security and monitored the loyalty of other security services. Its recruits were predominantly drawn from the Tikriti tribe and hailed from his hometown, Tikrit in the north of the country.
- The much vaunted (and, as we now recognize, artificially bolstered) Special Republican Guard was supplied with the best available military equipment. Its members were selected on the basis of loyalty first to the president, and then to the regime.
- The Directorate of General Security was primarily responsible for countering threats from the civilian population.
- The Directorate of General Intelligence monitored and suppressed dissident activities at home and abroad.
- The Directorate of Military Intelligence's role included the investigation of military personnel.

- The Saddam Fidayeen, under the control of Saddam's son Uday, was used to deal with civil disturbances but had blanket authority to examine any organization or individual (military included) in the country.

For all the years that Saddam remained at the helm, the Iraqi Ba'ath Party was the only legal political party in the country.

As with the equally oppressive Syrian Ba'ath Party of President Bashar Assad, it totally pervaded Iraqi life to the point where children were encouraged to spy on their parents. Membership, at around seven hundred thousand was a prerequisite for self-advancement and, as we have seen, conferred benefits from the regime.

Did the United States play a role in bringing Saddam to power? The conclusion, in a Reuters article written by David Morgan and datelined Philadelphia, is a very definite yes.

He mentions Roger Morris, a former State Department service officer who was on the National Security Council staff during the Johnson and Nixon Administrations and who claims that the CIA had a hand in two coups in Iraq, including a 1968 putsch 'that set Saddam Hussein firmly on the path to power'.

> 'In 1963, two years after the ill-fated US attempt at overthrow in Cuba known as the Bay of Pigs, Morris says the CIA helped organize a bloody coup in Iraq that deposed the Soviet-leaning government of Gen. Abdel-Karim Kassem. As in Iran in 1953, it was mostly American money and even American involvement on the ground, said Morris, referring to a US-backed coup that had brought the return of the Shah to neighboring Iran. Kassem, who had allowed communists to hold positions of responsibility in his government, was machine-gunned to death. Consequently, the country wound up in the hands of the Ba'ath Party.'

At the time, says Morris, Saddam was a Ba'ath Party operative studying law in Cairo, one of the venues that the CIA chose to plan the coup. In fact, he claims the former Iraqi ruler...was actually on the CIA payroll in those days.

'There's no question,' Morris told Reuters. 'It was there in Cairo that (Saddam) and others were first contacted by the agency.'

He goes on: 'Five years later, in 1968, Morris says the CIA encouraged a palace revolt among Ba'ath Party elements led by long-time Saddam mentor Ahmed Hassan al-Bakr, who would turn over the reins of power to his ambitious protégé in 1979. It's a regime that was unquestionably midwived by the United States, and the (CIA's) involvement there was really primary,' Morris said.

A spokesman for the Central Intelligence Agency declined to comment on Morris' claims of CIA involvement in the Iraqi coups but said his assertion that Saddam once received payments from the CIA was 'utterly ridiculous'. Morris's credentials bear examination. Reuters says he resigned from the NSC staff over the 1970 US invasion of Cambodia, and told them that he learned the details of American covert involvement in Iraq from ranking CIA officials of the day including President Teddy Roosevelt's grandson Archibald Roosevelt.

In his report, David Morgan also quotes David Wise, a Washington-based author who has written extensively about Cold War espionage. Wise maintains that he is only aware of records showing that a CIA group known as the 'Health Alteration Committee' tried to assassinate Kassem in 1960 by sending him a poisoned monogrammed handkerchief. Clearly, they felt that Kassem was somebody (in Iraq) who had to be eliminated, Wise said.

'Saddam stories' emerge all the time. While some were embellished with time, one nevertheless gets the message.

The majority relate to his ruthlessness in dealing with those under him. No man - in uniform or out - was allowed to become either too prominent or too popular. Anyone even perceived by Saddam to be a threat to his leadership or to the state was jailed or murdered. All were tortured. Iraq, in essence, became the ultimate totalitarian state where individuals or their families did not have to commit crimes to be executed.

Following his accession to power, Saddam's enemies documented how, in his early days, he had four-hundred-and-fifty army officers, deputy prime ministers and other 'unfaithfuls' rounded up and killed. That was the same year that Islamic fundamentalists overthrew the Shah of Iran.

Saddam, it appears, feared that such radical ideas might spread to members of his own Shi'ite community. Notably, the war with Iran followed soon afterwards.

John Sweeney of London's *Observer* provided British readers[2] with an insight to conditions within Iraq in an article published about a year before 'Operation Iraqi Freedom'. On a different tack to the customary British liberal approach to what was going on in Iraq at the time, Sweeney, completely debunked Iraqi claims that children were 'dying in their thousands because of the West's trade embargoes'. His story centered on evidence that the Iraqi president was actually faking baby funerals that led, it is said, to Osama bin Laden justifying his September 11 attack of New York's Twin Towers by referring 'to a million dead Iraqi children killed by sanctions'. Sweeney reckons that even among Iraqis there was the belief that the dictator invented the numbers.

One critic mentioned by Sweeney - 'Ali', whose daughter became a victim of Saddam's lunacy - spoke openly about how the regime's propaganda had faked mass baby funerals. This was an attempt to support 'evidence' of the seven thousand children under the age of five that Baghdad claims are being killed each month by sanctions, he wrote.

'Small coffins, decorated with grisly photographs of dead babies and their ages - "three days", "four days", usefully written for the English speaking media - are paraded through the streets of Baghdad on the roofs of taxis, the procession led by a throng of official mourners.'

There was only one problem, recalled the journalist: Because there were not enough dead babies around, the regime prevented parents from burying their infants immediately, a strict Muslim tradition. They did so solely 'to create more powerful propaganda'.

Also, the taxi drivers did exactly what they were told, 'as everybody does in Saddam's Iraq - to their evident disgust'.

Before 'Ali' defected to the north, a taxi driver friend of his explained how it worked: 'I went to Najaf (a religious center about a hundred miles south of Baghdad) a couple of days ago and brought back two bodies of children for one of the mass burials. The smell was very strong.'

Ali continued: 'The taxi driver didn't know how long they had been in the freezers, perhaps six or seven months. The drivers would collect them from the regions and would be told when a mass funeral was arranged so they would be ready.'

A second, Western source visited a Baghdad hospital and during one of those rare moments when the official Iraqi 'minder' was absent, he was taken to the mortuary. The doctor opened the doors of the freezers and showed the newcomer numerous dead babies lying stacked, waiting for the next official procession.

Tony Blair made issue of the fact that Saddam Hussein pursued a long-term program of persecution of the Iraqi Kurds, including the use of chemical weapons.

In his dossier, he recounts how during the Iran-Iraq war, Saddam appointed his cousin, Ali Hasan al-Majid as his deputy in the north (this was the appropriately-named 'Chemical Ali' who was killed in a British bomb attack in Basra early during the second invasion).

It was al-Majid who, in the winter of 1987/88, led what the media now refers to as the *Anfal* campaign, a series of nerve gas attacks on Kurdish villages. Amnesty International estimated afterwards that more than a hundred thousand Kurds were killed or disappeared during this period.

Nor was that the end of it. After the first Gulf War in 1991, Kurdish communities in the north of the country again rose up against Baghdad's rule. Saddam's response was to kill or imprison many thousands of Kurds. That prompted a humanitarian crisis and was instrumental in Washington shortly afterwards instituting no-fly zones over parts of Iraq. Over a million Kurds fled into the mountains or tried to escape the country.

Saddam's persecution of his Kurd citizens continued until the end, although the Northern No-Fly Zone offered some protection from the Iraqi military, curbing some of the worst excesses. Outside this military area, however, Baghdad continued a policy of persecution and intimidation.

As Blair reminded us, we are today also aware that Saddam's regime used chemical weapons against the Kurds, most notably in an attack on the town of Halabja in 1988. It was the first instance in history of a leader using chemical weapons against his own people.

One program on which Saddam Hussein embarked in later years, was to try to displace traditional Kurdish and Turkoman populations in areas under his control, primarily in order to weaken Kurdish claims to the oil-rich area around the northern city of Kirkuk. Kurds and other non-Arabs were consequently forcibly ejected to the three northern Iraqi governorates, Dohuk, Arbil and Suleimaniyah, all of which were to come under de facto Kurdish control. According to the United Nations Commission on Human Rights (UNCHR) Special Rapporteur for Iraq, almost a hundred thousand Kurds had been expelled since 1991. Similarly, agricultural land owned by these people was confiscated and redistributed to Iraqi Arabs. That was followed by incentives offered to Arabs from southern Iraq to move into the Kirkuk region.

So, too, with the Shi'ites (See Chapter 4). On March 1, 1991 in the wake of 'Operation Desert Storm', riots broke out in the southern city of Basra. Disturbances spread quickly to other cities in the largely Shi'ite-dominated southern parts of the country. The regime, in turn - sensing that Washington was preoccupied with other issues - responded by killing thousands of dissidents. Many Shi'ites tried to escape to Iran and Saudi Arabia. Some, hostile to the regime, sought refuge in the marshlands of southern Iraq.

Then came another of Saddam's mindless follies. In a bid to bring the entire community of what historians have always referred to as Marsh Arabs to heel, Saddam embarked on a mammoth program to drain these pristine waterways, and that in a region as big as Scotland. It was primarily done to allow Iraqi ground forces to eliminate all opposition there.

The rural population had no option but to flee.

Having flouted international opinion for so long and got away with it, a lot of evidence gradually started to emerge of Saddam's role in other anti-Western (in particular anti-American) escapades.

Following contact with an Iraqi dissident in the northern town of Suleimaniyeh, Scott Peterson, a staff writer of the *Christian Science Monitor*[3] told of how Baghdad was involved in plots to blow up American warships in the Persian Gulf, early 2000. His informant said he was given the assignment by ranking members of the dictator's inner circle.

'The alleged plan involved loading at least one trade ship with half a ton of explosives and - sailing under the Iranian flag to disguise Baghdad's role - together with a crew of suicide bombers, the idea was to blow up a US ship in the Gulf,' wrote Peterson.

The operative, who claimed to have 'smuggled weapons for Saddam through Iran for Al Qaeda during the late 1990s', said he was told that $16 million had been put aside for the assignment - 'the first of "nine new operations" which he said the Iraqis wanted him to carry out'. Some of these were to include missions in Kuwait.

Peterson stated that the first of these is remarkably similar to the onslaught in the port of Aden on the American destroyer USS *Cole* on October 12, 2000. It was, however, never carried out. The status of the other eight is unclear.

Now in the custody of the Kurds, the smuggler - Mohamed Mansour Shalab - told his interrogators that he was first informed of the role that he was intended to play in February 2000. This was a month after an apparently unrelated attempt was made to target another US destroyer, the USS *The Sullivans*, also in the Yemeni Republic.

This was not Iraq's first overt act of terrorism against the US. Ten years before, Saddam's agents tried to assassinate former President George Bush, the incumbent President's father during a visit to Kuwait. This has led some critics of 'Dubya' to aver that 'Operation Iraqi Freedom' had absolutely nothing to do with Saddam's human rights excesses and that it was 'pay back time'. They might just be right.

Israeli sources have told this writer that Saddam took interest in everything to do with the Palestinian issue. He rewarded suicide bombers against Israeli targets with dollar rewards that were often as much as $20,000 per hit. The cash was paid to the bomber's family, usually by Iraqi agents.

In December 2003, Laurie Mylroie, who has taught at Harvard and at the US Naval War College and is currently publisher of *Iraq News*[4], devoted an entire issue to what she termed 'Baghdad's Renewed Hostility Towards Israel'. Recalling that Baghdad launched thirty-nine Scud missiles on Israel during the 1991 Gulf War, the continued Iraqi threat was largely ignored by the Jewish State in the aftermath of that conflict. A resurgence of domestic violence together with a succession of Intifada campaigns also deflected attention from some of the noises coming from Israel's immediate east, including a vicious anti-Semitic diatribe that Saddam launched on his July 17 national day in 1997.

While there is little of practical assistance that Saddam can offer Palestinian dissidents - apart from money - Saddam was known to watch every development inside Israel. He was obsessed with the Jewish State and spent long hours with his advisors in trying to devise ways of damaging the country. This became apparent when violence in the West Bank and Gaza escalated in October 2000: both Israeli and American intelligence observed the movement of Iraqi troops towards a key crossroads less than a hundred miles from the Jordanian border[5].

Initially the deployments were dismissed by the CIA as a training exercise, until it emerged that the force was composed of four Republican Guard divisions, plus a mechanized infantry division, among them some of Iraq's best units (though in retrospect, that's not saying much). Even then the Clinton Administration remained dismissive. Its argument (correctly, as we know now) was that the force lacked air cover.

Mylroie makes the point here that relations between Iraq and Syria just then were quite good. It was not impossible that the Syrian Air Force might have been the instrument for air cover on that occasion, she suggested.

Since much of it is speculation, it doesn't really rate comment. What does, is that the Iraqi Army, throughout the period under review, remained a viable and potent military force. Also, it was not the first time that Saddam - like the Grand Old Duke of York - had moved his troops about to try to intimidate his neighbors. He had done so at least three times since 'Operation Desert Storm' shifting large concentrations of troops and armor southwards, almost within sight of the Kuwaiti frontier, once again immediately prior to the second invasion.

While a lot of Saddam's actions were bluster, it is worth noting that it always took some kind of a firm reaction from Washington to counter any possibility of Saddam doing anything pre-emptive, especially if he were stupid enough to believe he might have got away with it. Most Middle East watchers agree, that half the trouble was that the man was unpredictable. But then so was Hitler.

The most shocking section in Mr Blair's report was left till last. It drew on reports of human rights abuses from authoritative international organizations, including Amnesty International and Human Rights Watch. He made no bones about the fact that the abuses continued. We know too, that they went on until the very end.

Blair: 'People continue to be arrested and detained on suspicion of political or religious activities or often because they are related to members of the opposition. Executions are carried out without due process of law. Relatives are often prevented from burying the victims in accordance with Islamic practice. Thousands of prisoners have been executed.'

Meanwhile, Saddam issued a series of decrees establishing severe penalties for criminal offenses. These included amputation, branding, the cutting off of ears (for troops who had perhaps been AWOL) and other forms of mutilation. Anyone found guilty of slandering the President had his or her tongue removed.

Take the case of Abdallah, a member of the Ba'ath Party whose loyalty became suspect. He was imprisoned for four years at Abu Ghraib in the 1980s. On the second day of his incarceration, he and other prisoners were forced to walk between two rows of five guards each in order to receive their containers of food.

While walking to get the food, they were beaten by the guards with plastic telephone cables. They had to return to their cells the same way, so that an amble to get breakfast resulted in twenty or more lashes. According to Abdallah, 'It wasn't that bad getting to the food, but coming back it was spilled when we were beaten. The same procedure happened when the men went to the bathroom.

On the third day, the torture continued. 'We were removed from our cells and beaten with plastic pipes. This surprised us because we were asked no questions. Possibly it was being done to break our morale,' Abdallah speculated. Throughout, he was held in solitary in a room that measured about three yards by two and which opened on to a corridor.

Eventually, he says, we were subjected to as many as sixteen torture sessions daily and, as Abdallah remembers, this slice of inhumanity was both organized and systematic.

'We were allowed to go to the toilet three times a day. Then they reduced our visits to once a day and then only for only a minute: I went for four years without a shower or a wash.' He learned to cope with horrific periods of deprivation and the hunger that accompanied his detention:

'I taught myself to drink a minimum amount of water because there was no place to urinate. They used wooden sticks to beat us and sometimes the sticks would break. I found a piece of a stick, covered with blood, and managed to bring it back to my room. I ate it for three days: a person who is hungry can eat anything.

'Pieces of our bodies started falling off from the thrashings and for some of us, our skin was so dry that it began to fall off. I ate pieces of my own body.

'No one, not Pushkin, not Mahfouz, can describe what happened to us. It is impossible to describe what living this day to day was like,' he declared.

'I was totally naked the entire time. Half of the original group (of about thirty men) died. It was a slow type of continuous physical and psychological torture. Sometimes, it seemed that orders would come to kill one of us. Whoever was chosen would be beaten to death.' (*Source: Human Rights Watch.*)

'...I saw a friend of mine, al-Shaikh Nasser Taresh al-Sa'idi, naked. He was handcuffed and a piece of wood was placed between his elbows and his knees.

'Two ends of the wood were placed on two high chairs and al-Shaikh Nasser was suspended like a chicken. This method of torture is known as *al-Khaygania* (a reference to a former security director, the ultimate sadist, known to all as al-Khaygani).

'An electric wire was attached to al-Shaikh Nasser's penis and another attached to one of his toes. He was asked if he could identify me and he said "this is al-Shaikh Yahya".

'They took me to another room and after about ten minutes they stripped me of my clothes and a security officer said "the person you saw has confessed against you".

He said to me: "You followers of (Ayatollah) al-Sadr have carried out acts harmful to the security of the country and have been distributing anti-government statements coming from abroad."

'He asked if I had any contact with an Iraqi religious scholar based in Iran who has been signing these statements.

'I said "I do not have any contacts with him"...I was then left suspended in the same manner as al-Shaikh al-Sa'idi. My face was looking upward. They also attached an electric wire on my penis and the other end of the wire was linked to an electric motor.

'One security man was hitting my feet with a cable. Electric shocks were applied every few minutes and were increased. I must have been suspended for more than an hour. During some of this time I lost consciousness. They took me to another room and made me walk even though my feet were swollen from beating... They repeated this method a few times[6].'

The final case history in Mr Blair's dossier involved a Kurdish businessman from Baghdad who was arrested outside his house by plainclothes security men in December 1996.

Initially his family did not know his whereabouts and went from one police station to another inquiring about him. Then they found out that he was being held in the headquarters of the General Security Directorate in Baghdad. The family was not allowed to visit him.

Eleven months later the family was told by the authorities that he had been executed and that they should go and collect his body. There were evident signs of torture on his body: his eyes were gouged out and the sockets filled with paper. His right wrist and left leg had been broken.

The family was not given any reason for his arrest and subsequent execution. They did suspect that he was possibly killed because of his friendship with a retired army general who had links with the Iraqi opposition outside the country. That man had been arrested just before and was also executed. (*Source: Amnesty International*).

1   John F. Burns 'Last, Desperate Days of a Brutal Reign': *The New York Times*, April 20, 2003

2   John Sweeney, 'How Saddam "Staged" Fake Baby Funerals': *The Observer*, London, June 23, 2002

3   Scott Peterson: 'Ex-Smuggler Describes Iraqi Plot to Blow up US Warship', *Christian Science Monitor*, April 3, 2002

4   Laurie Mylroie: *Middle East Intelligence Bulletin;* Vol 2, #11, December, 2000

5   Israeli Television, October 22, 2000; *Yedi'ot Aharanot*, October 25, 2000

6   Amnesty International, testimony from an Iraqi theology student from Saddam City- since renamed Sadr City, in memory of the much revered Shi'ite mullah who was brutally put to death by Saddam

6

ENTER THE UNITED NATIONS AND UNSCOM[1]

Salman Zweir worked for thirteen years as an engineer for the Iraqi Atomic Energy Commission before defecting to the West, late in 1998. He was involved with Iraq's centrifuge uranium enrichment program and claimed that Saddam recalled him and many other technical personnel to the nuclear-weapons program in the fall of 1998. Zweir refused. He was imprisoned, tortured, and eventually escaped to the West.

Weapons inspectors - whether working for the United Nations or their respective governments - are a breed of specialists apart. They have to be in order to do the sometimes dangerous, meticulous and often clandestine detective work that is expected of them. Especially in an environment as volatile as Iraq's.

That was one of the conclusions reached by Scott Ritter when I first spoke to him following his return to the United States in the late Nineties. Since then, this former UNSCOM weapons inspector switched steeds. But the sentiment that inspired him tends to persist, borne out by some of the inspectors who briefly went to Baghdad prior to the second Iraqi invasion of 2003.

Their numbers are small. In the past they have included the likes of Dr Jonathan B. Tucker, today head of the Chemical and Biological Weapons Nonproliferation Program at the Monterey Institute of International Studies in California and author of the definitive work on smallpox titled *Scourge: The Once and Future Threat of Smallpox*[2].

According to Tucker, it was perhaps no accident that scientists working for Saddam Hussein were experimenting with camelpox virus (a close relative of the smallpox virus that does not produce significant illness in humans). Another American biowarfare specialist, Dr Richard Spertzel reckoned that the Iraqis may have used camelpox as a 'surrogate' for smallpox in developing production, weaponization, and delivery techniques for the latter virus[3].

The most recent batch of weapons inspectors – attached to Hans Blix's UNSCOM's successor, the UN Monitoring, Verification and Inspection Commission (UNMOVIC) was a relatively small force: there were just over two hundred experts from forty-four countries on UN books. They were all extricated before Gulf War 2.

Like UNSCOM before them, these people came from diverse backgrounds and from many countries. Quite a number had nuclear, missile, biological and chemical expertise. Still more were linguists. There were even a few with experience in customs and trade of the illicit kind. A spokesman for the UN said at the time that most were deployed in and around Baghdad. The rest fanned out countrywide. They were assisted by a tiny support group of doctors, aviators, drivers, interpreters and the rest. In addition there were hundreds more UN staff in a dozen countries on standby to analyze and assess the information that UNMOVIC staff was hoping to send out of Iraq.

At the end of it - this round of searches lasted only months - the effort was dismally understaffed in a country about the size of California. But the Iraqis were resolute: the inspectors were not welcome and what they were doing was illegal anyway, was the official Baghdad line.

What should have made UNMOVIC's job easier was that they - and American inspectors who came after them, following 'Operation Iraqi Freedom' - had access to a new generation of equipment that was denied UNSCOM more than a decade ago. Some of this gadgetry was electronic and included items capable of detecting gamma radiation, which would indicate past and present nuclear activity. It was also likely to include remote chemical and explosives detectors such as those developed by HiEnergy of Irvine, California, which uses fast neutrons and reflected-back gamma rays to 'see' through half an inch of steel or through a brick wall.

For all that, the work is exacting. Saddam Hussein had a history of obfuscation when dealing with United Nations weapons inspections teams. As one observer pointed out, 'even under the best circumstances, if Saddam were to come clean and hand over all his banned weapons, there would have been no way of telling how much more he might have had hidden away.'

Dr Richard Spertzel made the insightful point before the House Armed Services Committee in Washington DC on September 10, 2002 that with Iraq being such a huge area to cover, a proper search for secreted weapons could take years, even if the UN deployed thousands more inspectors.

'That's been his game all along because it is time that the man is playing for,' he added.

An interesting observation made after some UNSCOM weapons inspectors had inspected Saddam Hussein's palaces was that 'very little was achieved' by these actions, even though they lasted several weeks. Following his return to America after his usual spell in Iraq, Dr Spertzel disclosed - echoing the words of Charles Wuelfer - that the palaces had literally been 'wiped clean' by Iraqi goons long before the inspectors got anywhere near them.

'In room after room into which we were allowed we found nothing but bare walls. Everything had been removed, and it had been done only a short while before,' he disclosed.

'It was obvious that many of the rooms that we examined had been stacked with equipment, files, packing cases and a good deal besides. All of it was gone. Some of these palaces had been used to store equipment, but we don't know what it is.' Another report spoke of much of it having been moved, en bloc, in all probability according to several Washington reports, to Syria and Libya.

It was Spertzel's opinion that it was 'a serious blunder to give Saddam four or five months' breathing space to hide whatever was going on there and then sanitize the entire cleaning operation as if nothing had taken place.' Eventually, he said, they would get to the bottom of it, but by then it might be too late.

What was significant, he added, was evidence that chemicals had been used in the sanitization, or, as others would phrase it, the decontamination process.

Another source indicated that UNSCOM was seriously hampered all along in doing an effective job because it lacked the most modern hi-tech equipment for use in detecting chemical or biological agents. While Dr Spertzel subsequently disputed this, the monitoring body was never short of cash: money came not from the UN but from Iraq's frozen assets.

In a confidential briefing, the source compared the US military build-up prior to UNSCOM's final visit with the UN body's rather limited resources. Billions of dollars would be spent each time a major task force was assembled. Then all those assets were wasted when, Saddam playing his cards close to his chest, would back down and yield just enough to avoid a full military confrontation.

'If a fraction of the money they wasted getting battle groups to the Gulf was spent equipping us with the sort of sensors that are now available, it would be a different story altogether,' he declared.

He also disclosed that one of the gaps that UNSCOM had faced was not being able to make 'non-intrusive' surveys of buildings, warehouses, structures, underground bunkers and tunnels, some of which might have had double walls or false floors or ceilings. It is instructive that after Coalition Forces grabbed Baghdad, Allied troops discovered a conglomerate of underground tunnels under the city, some big enough to drive a vehicle through. They even found a complex tunnel system running beneath Baghdad Airport.

'These were all ploys that Saddam's people had used in the past to keep their assets hidden.' Also, he added, there were sensors available that were not supplied to UNSCOM: some could tell in an instant (by reading air samples in ratios of parts-per-trillion) whether there had been chemical or biological agents stored there in the past.

As a weapons inspector, Jonathan Tucker made a lot of observations during his posting in Baghdad. He kept a diary and this excerpt marginally lifts the veil of obscurity that surrounded so many of the activities in which UNSCOM was involved while its members were guests of Saddam Hussein. Hardly the stuff of a thriller, it nevertheless provides a brief but fascinating insight to a day in the life of a weapons inspector.

It is worth mentioning that Dr Rihab Taha, the Iraqi biologist originally responsible for Tucker and his group, was later placed on the 'most wanted' list following the collapse of the Saddam regime.

Jonathan B. Tucker — Iraq Diary, excerpt (February 5, 1995)

After a morning inspection team meeting at UNSCOM's Baghdad Monitoring and Verification Center in the former Canal Hotel, we get on the bus and drive for an hour and half to the Al Hakam Factory for our first inspection. On the way, we pass sand-colored urban blocks and then sparser suburbs consisting of mud-walled shacks with corrugated metal roofs, bordering dirt streets where ragged children play. We pass the outskirts of the city and continue into a barren desert landscape, punctuated occasionally by anti-aircraft batteries mounted on earth beams, pointed at the sky.

I am reminded of Churchill's description of Soviet Russia as 'a riddle wrapped in an enigma'. This country is equally baffling. The soldiers wearing variously colored berets, the strangely shaped bunkers, mysterious military compounds behind high walls – it is like trying to decipher an encrypted message without knowing the code. Iraqi officials are equally hard to read. Their superficial friendliness seems to mask an underlying resentment and anger, and their seemingly helpful answers are disingenuous or misleading.

After we have driven for a while across the desert plain, the Al Hakam factory, a complex of light brown warehouse-like buildings rises up ominously along the right side of the road. The biological fermentation facility sprawls over about ten square miles and is surrounded by a barbed wire fence and watchtowers. Although the Iraqis claim the site is strictly civilian, its remote location, oddly dispersed layout, sand-filled bunkers, and unusual level of security have aroused suspicions.

The bus pulls up to the front of the gate, where we are greeted by a smiling portrait of Saddam. At the nearby administration building, Dr Rihab Taha, the plant director together with a group of Iraq 'minders' are waiting for us. We troop into a conference room decorated with another framed portrait of Saddam and some propaganda posters. One shows a stylized image of an Iraqi Scud being launched. Another depicts a small child being strangled by an evil-looking serpent bearing the Arab word for 'embargo'.

We sit around a table and ask questions about the site. As usual, the two Russian microbiologists on the team ask most of the technical questions. Thanks to our excellent interpreters, the questions asked are translated smoothly from Russian to English to Arabic. And then back again.

After the briefing, the team - accompanied by Iraqi minders with video cameras - tours three of the production halls. The first building is a cavernous warehouse that is partially filled with a Swiss-made pilot production line for the biological pesticide Bacillus thuringiensis *(BT, a bacterium that kills insect pests when sprayed on crops) and a much larger BT production line that is not yet operational. Two-storey steel scaffolding holds several stainless-steel fermentor tanks and mixing vessels and a large spray drier, linked together by a profusion of snaking metal pipes. There are also electronic controllers for the pH, temperature, and foam sensors needed to regulate the fermentation process.*

The quality of the welding is poor and the piping is of several different shapes and sizes, suggesting that much of it has been cannibalized from other equipment. Overall, the facility looks jury-rigged and not up to Western standards of cleanliness.

Dr Taha explains that Al Hakam has been unable to scale up BT production because the trade embargo has prevented Iraq from importing some essential pieces of equipment, such as a variable-speed agitator for the five cubic-meter fermentor. The Iraqis plan to import and install the missing items as soon as the embargo is lifted, and then start production.

We tour another building - also not operational - devoted to production of single-cell protein (SCP) as a chicken-feed supplement. Several Italian-made fermentor tanks are arrayed along the wall, in a poor state of cleanliness. Finally we visit a large empty industrial hall where a 50 cubic-meter fermentor for SCP production, currently being manufactured in Iraq, will eventually be installed.

All of the equipment we have seen is 'dual use', meaning that it could potentially be diverted to the illicit production of biowarfare agents such as anthrax and botulinum toxin. Yet none of the production halls have any biocontainment systems such as high-efficiency particulate air filters.

The French and Russian experts on the team contend that the Iraqis had little more than a research program, that their technical capabilities in industrial biotechnology are limited, and that allegations that Iraq produced and weaponized biological warfare agents before the Gulf War are little more than disinformation from US intelligence agencies.

Other team members counter that given Saddam's cavalier attitude toward human life, the Iraq government would be prepared to cut corners on worker health and safety to help disguise a clandestine bioweapons facility. I personally lean to the latter position because of the murderous nature of Saddam's regime. Given the lack of hard evidence either way, however, it's hard to make a strong case.

Jonathan Tucker's Epilogue

During the first half of the 1990s, although UNSCOM never discovered any filled biological munitions in Iraq, it had obtained compelling circumstantial evidence for the large-scale production of BW agents before the Gulf War.

For example, by tracking Iraqi imports of culture media - the nutrient mixture needed to grow bacteria in stainless-steel vats - UNSCOM determined that Baghdad had imported a total of thirty-nine tons of culture medium in 1987 and 1988, or enough to produce roughly four tons of bacteria. Of that amount of imported media, the Iraqi authorities were unable to account for seventeen tons, strongly suggesting that large-scale production of anthrax and other deadly agents had taken place.

In addition, microscopic examination of samples taken from the BT production line at Al Hakam in December 1994 revealed two anomalies: the bacterial cells did not contain the toxin crystals required for insecticidal activity, and the dried product at the end of the production line was too fine for spraying on crops but consisted of particles so small and light that they would float a long distance downwind, a characteristic best suited for disseminating a biowarfare agent such as anthrax as a respirable aerosol. These findings suggested that Iraq was using the BT production line to train technicians for the future production of dried anthrax spores - under the very noses of UNSCOM inspectors.

In August 1995, six months after my inspection team's visit to Al Hakam, Lt. Gen. Hussein Kamel, the son-in-law of Saddam Hussein and the mastermind behind the Iraqi bioweapons program, defected to Jordan and revealed that Iraq had in fact manufactured large quantities of anthrax and botulinum toxin at Al Hakam in late 1990. After production, the agents were filled into at least one-hundred-fifty-seven aerial bombs and twenty-five Scud missile warheads at Al Muthanna State Establishment in

Samarra, north of Baghdad. Finally, the filled munitions were deployed in January 1991 in the vicinity of Iraq air and missile bases, where they remained throughout the Gulf War.

Based on this and other evidence, UNSCOM razed the entire Al Hakam complex to the ground in June 1996. The moral of this story: persistent weapons inspections can work.

UNSCOM's official report, published shortly before the UN weapons inspections teams were pushed out of Iraq in 1998 makes a number of interesting observations. For a start, the document stresses, Iraq is an extremely difficult and harsh country in which to work. One also needs to examine Iraq's socio-political backdrop to understand why Iraq's leaders eventually decided to develop weapons of mass destruction.

Politically, Iraq seems always to have been embroiled in turmoil of one kind or another. Part of the reason for this state of affairs is that the country is composed of a complex amalgam of many different ethnic tribes, clans, sub-groups and political affiliations. Nor can one discount a huge community of Kurds numbering several millions in the north, the ruling Sunni Muslims (under Saddam) in the central regions and more than twelve million Shi'ite Muslims - about sixty per cent of the total population, the majority concentrated in the south.

Iraq also has a history of troubled relations with its neighbors, a diverse lot that includes Iran, Jordan, Kuwait, Saudi Arabia, Syria and Turkey. Possibly the only saving grace - and a powerfully significant one at that - is what the Russians like to term 'black gold': Iraq has some of the largest oil reserves on earth.

Look also at recent history to understand much of the violence that has characterized Iraqi history: this is a difficult country to rule. British colonial rule in the first half of the last century didn't help matters.

Matters were compounded in 1968 when the Ba'ath Party seized control of Iraq. One of the more powerful office bearers to emerge from that putsch was Saddam Hussein, who controlled the party's internal security apparatus. It wasn't long before he effectively became the number two man in the ruling hierarchy. Long before he formally assumed the presidency in July 1979, Saddam was planning a takeover of government of his own.

History has pointed to several developments since then, the most important being Saddam's quest for what he always termed 'Greater Iraq'. Since he viewed some of his neighbors with suspicion and, in turn, fell out with them all, it was to be expected that he would ultimately attempt coercion by force. Indeed, Kuwait wasn't the first country invaded by Iraqi troops.

The Iraq-Iran War began on September 22, 1980 when Iraq sent six divisions of its army across the border into Iran. What should have been a clever move - Saddam had hoped to take advantage of great internal disarray caused by Iran's revolution - eventually became a disaster. His original intention was to revamp the existing political relationship between the two countries, which included abrogating the border deal that Saddam had signed with the Shah.

While the fighting began well for Iraq it quickly turned into a bitter war of attrition, which pitted Iran's superior manpower (at least in terms of raw numbers) against Iraq's technological edge. Important is the fact that Iraq received a considerable amount of support from other Arab states in the Persian Gulf as well as some prominent members of the international community, including Britain and America. At the time, all were fearful of Iran's Mullah-led fundamentalist revolution and Iraq was considered very much the lesser of the two evils.

One of the most important aspects of the war was the use of chemical weapons (CW). This action (the first attacks used mustard gas) was initiated by Iraq in 1982 in violation of its commitments as a signatory to the 1925 Geneva Protocol, a treaty banning the use of CW against another contracting party. The lack of any kind of formal international condemnation emboldened the Iraqi leadership further and Saddam soon put deadly nerve gases on the agenda. Whereas the early use of CW served defensive purposes, by the time offensive operations of the final campaigns of 1988 were set in motion, they had been fully integrated into Iraq's extensive military planning. By then he had also sprayed biological weapons on to some Iranian troop concentrations (See Chapter 3).

Although both sides reportedly used CW during the war, most observers accept that Iraq began the practice first. Baghdad also made far greater use of chemical agents than Iran - also a signatory of the Geneva Protocol.

It was these early successes that probably prompted Saddam to use chemical weapons against his own people. In 1987, a succession of reports of CW attacks on Kurdish villages and guerrilla fighters became frequent and detailed. Clinical evidence as well as soil samples confirmed the use of mustard gas and the nerve agent tabun against the Kurdish population.

In March 1988, Iraq launched a major attack with CW against the Kurdish town of Halabja and its surroundings: Iranian forces a short while before had occupied the region. Although the exact number of casualties is uncertain, it is believed that several thousand Kurdish civilians and Iranian soldiers in the area were killed. There were several thousands more injured, with hundreds still debilitated by the effects of nerve gas today. By summer of that year, more CW agents were sprayed on Kurdish settlements in the north on a massive scale, forcing tens of thousands to flee to Iran and Turkey.

It's worth noting that the UN Security Council (which was provided all the evidence that it would need to make a determined stand) still refused to name Iraq explicitly as the main perpetrator of CW attacks. Members could reach no consensus, very much as the Security Council continues to prevaricate today over a variety of sensitive issues, Iraq and nuclear issues in North Korea included.

By the time the war ended and a ceasefire signed on August 8, 1988, Saddam – for all his efforts and terrible loss of life - had achieved almost nothing. By then the war had lasted eight years and there were more than a million soldiers and civilians dead on both sides of the front. Moreover, Iraq was crippled by debt: it owed money to just about every Arab state on the Persian Gulf and the majority insisted on repayment.

Another issue that remained contentious and surfaced more often than Saddam would have liked, was that his neighbors tended to back Kuwait in its territorial disputes with Iraq. Baghdad claimed that Kuwait was illegally pumping Iraqi oil from oil fields along the Iraq-Kuwait border which, Saddam insisted, led to serious losses of revenues for his country. This, said the Iraqi leader, made repayment of war debts even more difficult. With this, Saddam came out strongly with several demands, including restitution, relief from war loans and a renegotiating of his country's border with Kuwait.

As might have been expected, the Kuwaitis rejected these demands. Days later, on August 2, 1990 Iraq invaded the tiny Sheikhdom and declared that henceforth, Kuwait would be a part of Iraq. It was another bad mistake. A broad international coalition, mandated by the United Nations and led by the USA, was formed to eject Iraq's forces from Kuwait. This was achieved in February 1991.

Iraq's capabilities in non-conventional (nuclear, biological and chemical - NBC) weapons were now of particular interest to the international community. There had been real fear that Saddam might use what were then suspected to be extensive CB warfare stockpiles against Coalition troops and, in fact, there is a considerable body of evidence to show that he had the intention of doing just that immediately 'Operation Desert Storm' was launched.

With the benefit of hindsight, we now know that Coalition bombers and strike planes knocked out all Iraqi aircraft and equipment in short order including those that Saddam had intended to use to drop nerve agents. One or two of the specially modified Mirage jets with tanks of CW instead of bombs were shot down soon after taking off (See Chapter 10).

While the worst didn't happen, Iraq did use its long-range missile capability against both Coalition Forces and Israel in an unsuccessful attempt to broaden the war and break the alliance between the Arab world and the West.

These factors, combined with revelations after the war about the extent of Iraq's nuclear weapons program (despite that country having signed the 1968 Nonproliferation Treaty) elicited a tough response from the international community.

The major component of this response was UN Security Council Resolution 687 of April 3, 1991, which created UNSCOM, the acronym for United Nations Special Commission (on Iraq).

The UNSCOM Regime

UN Security Council Resolution 687, in effect, was a conditional ceasefire, outlining an extensive plan for the disarmament of Iraq.

Part C of the Resolution, covering non-conventional weapons, required Iraq unconditionally to destroy and to undertake never to use, develop, construct or acquire non-conventional weapons or ballistic missiles with a range greater than about 100 miles (160 kms). The Resolution also dealt with the return of stolen property, accounting for Kuwaiti troops and civilians missing in action, a border settlement, reparations, terrorist acts and sanctions against Iraq for non-compliance. On April 19, 1991 the Security Council set up UNSCOM. The new body was charged with verifying Iraq's compliance with Resolution 687 in respect of its non-conventional weapons programs.

UNSCOM had two basic functions: to inspect and oversee the destruction or elimination of Iraq's chemical and biological weapons as well as its ballistic missile capabilities and their production and storage facilities; and to monitor Iraq over the longer term to ensure continued compliance. The task of inspecting, destroying and removing all Iraq's nuclear weapon capabilities was assigned to Vienna's International Atomic Energy Agency (IAEA). At that stage, the international community had no idea that Saddam had a huge body of scientists engaged in trying to build an atom bomb.

Included in UNSCOM's mandate was the obligation to assist and cooperate with the IAEA in its work in Iraq. Such assistance comprised transport and communication services and logistic support. In practice, the aim of UNSCOM's second priority, its monitoring work, was to ensure that Iraq did not seek to rebuild these capabilities once the UN body had certified that they had been destroyed.

Particular attention was paid to all dual-use items to ensure that such materials and facilities were not put to use in prohibited military activities. A system for monitoring exports and imports was established by UN Security Council Resolution 1051 of March 27, 1996. It required all sales of dual-use items to Iraq to be notified to both UNSCOM and the IAEA. These items had to be inspected upon arrival in Iraq and at the destination site.

Dual-use items are defined as those which could be applied both to the development of non-conventional weapons and to legitimate civilian purposes such as medicines. UNSCOM's strategy for ongoing monitoring included, but was not limited to, unannounced on-site inspections, aerial surveillance and camera monitoring.

The Main Findings of UNSCOM

By the time that UNSCOM was disbanded - roughly a decade after it had been established – the UN organization was still unable to certify that it knew the full extent of Iraq's chemical and biological weapons programs. It was also unable to determine that all agents, munitions and facilities had been declared and therefore destroyed.

However, its inspectors had been busy. Slowly, carefully and systematically, specialists like Drs Kay, Sterzel and Tucker had been at work inside Iraq collecting hard evidence as well as circumstantial information suggesting that Saddam's programs were either much more advanced or far wider in scope than it was previously thought.

It is now known that Iraq was developing elements of the entire range of non-conventional weapons together with their means of delivery. These included ballistic missiles, prior to the Iraq-Iran War, beginning with some that could transport chemical weapons.

Chemical Weapons (CW)

While Western intelligence agencies were aware that Iraq was producing large quantities of CW ever since the start of the Iran-Iraq war, the actual scope and breadth of its nerve gas programs only became clear with ongoing UNSCOM inspections.

Saddam's CW programs were begun in the 1970s and accelerated during the war. Iraq chose to develop both the World War 1 generation of CW agents, including possibly phosgene as well as mustard agent, and the more sophisticated nerve agents tabun and sarin. The use of several of these agents was confirmed during the war with Iran. Iraq also developed and began producing the more potent VX nerve gas, one of the more toxic agents in military arsenals.

There were a number of problems facing the Iraqis in producing these weapons. Iraqi CW agents, for instance, weren't comparable in quality to those stored in the arsenals of the USA and the former USSR. Impurities meant that the toxic compounds lacked basic stability and consequently decomposed easily. As a result, Iraq started to develop a crude type of binary munition whereby the final mixing of the two precursors to the agent was done inside the shell or container immediately prior to delivery. All this had something of an impact on the logistics of and preparations for chemical warfare, which may partly explain how overwhelming Coalition air superiority prevented the use of CW during the first Gulf War.

Under UNSCOM supervision altogether 38,537 filled and unfilled munitions, 690 tons of agents, 3,000 tons of precursor chemicals to manufacture CW agents, and thousands of pieces of production equipment and analytical instruments were destroyed. Yet despite these achievements, no final and complete accounting of the CW program was ever possible. For three reasons:

- Iraq removed CW, equipment and materials from the main site of the Al Muthanna State Establishment before the first UNSCOM inspection team arrived. Consequently no full accounting of these materials was forthcoming.
- Iraq claimed that it had destroyed 15,620 chemical munitions unilaterally, a fact and total that was never verified. Similarly, it provided no supporting documentation for 16,038 chemical munitions it claimed to have discarded.
- UNSCOM inspectors were reportedly closing in on a program for the production of VX when the standoff between Iraq and the UN Security Council began in the autumn of 1997. In November 1997 UNSCOM found new evidence that Iraq had developed a production capability for VX: Saddam's scientists had obtained at least 750 tons of VX precursor chemicals. (Evidence of VX production was first revealed in 1995.)

Biological Weapons (BW)
Iraq may have produced up to ten billion doses of anthrax, botulinum toxin and aflatoxin, something else that only emerged long after the first Gulf War.

So too with anthrax, a highly infectious bacterium, and botulinum toxin, one of the most toxic substances known to man, are among the most likely candidates for biological weapons agents. Little was known about the development of the BW program up to 1991. In the 1980s, Western intelligence sources were cited as reporting that anthrax had been found among some hospitalized Iranians at the time that Iranian sources were referring to the Iraqi use of microbic and bacteriological weapons. According to a Belgian forensic toxicologist, mycotoxins were said to have been found in samples of body fluids taken from Iranian gas victims. This was never verified, however.

Research and development (R&D) facilities, such as those at Salman Pak and Al Muthanna, were known to intelligence services, but the largest R&D and production site at Al Hakam remained secret and was not bombed during the Gulf War. Although UNSCOM inspectors visited the site, its significance did not become apparent until General Hussein al-Kamel, Saddam Hussein's son-in-law, defected in 1995. It was Kamel who provided the West with major new insights into the extent of Iraq's BW program for which he was executed by one of Saddam's agents within hours of returning to Baghdad. This, in spite of a personal assurance from Saddam himself that all was forgiven.

The discovery that Iraq was researching aflatoxin, not a traditional BW candidate, at first caused considerable surprise among UNSCOM biowarfare specialists. It is a carcinogen, the effects of which manifest themselves only after many years. Several Western experts have rationalized this Iraqi program only in terms of genocidal goals: If aflatoxin were used against the Kurds, for instance, it would be impossible definitively to prove the use of BW once symptoms emerged.

Another possible explanation is its potential use as an immune suppressant, making victims more susceptible to other agents. However, the aflatoxin declaration may also hide other aspects of Iraq's BW program. According to Iraq's depositions, the production program never encountered any mishap (as other parts of the BW program had) and, to judge from the declared time frame for the total amount produced, production could never have stopped, even for cleaning of the equipment. This raised the suspicion that Iraq declared an excessive amount of aflatoxin in order to disguise the fact that other, more destructive agents had been produced in greater quantities.

Finally, as Croddy explains, it could be that aflatoxin was produced because of its rather high acute toxicity, about 1.3mg/kg in laboratory rats - and/or Iraqi scientists produced it because they could - eager to show their superiors in the Ba'ath party that they were making progress. This aflatoxin could have resulted from bureaucratic incentives.

The Iraqi research program focused on other agents as well. These included camelpox, gas gangrene and bubonic plague. There was also some animal testing and, on the basis of circumstantial evidence collected by UNSCOM, possibly even human testing. This is still a significant issue that requires clarification. It is not difficult to imagine that Iraq kept back hidden quantities of freeze-dried organisms from its BW program or, prior to Saddam having been ousted, that his boffins might have been able to resurrect that research and production program quickly.

There were also a variety of BW delivery systems developed by Iraq. These included 155-mm artillery shells, 122-mm rockets, a hundred-and-sixty-six aircraft bombs, twenty-five warheads for the Al Hussein ballistic missile which were intended for use with the three main BW agents (noted above). All were uncovered by UNSCOM, together with an experimental spray tank converted from drop tanks that could have held two thousand liters of anthrax.

The delivery systems may have been primitive and therefore ineffective, but it is only UNSCOM and, before its establishment, the Persian Gulf War that halted further development of Iraq's delivery systems.

Export controls

Iraq had an advanced technological and industrial base for a developing country but was forced to rely heavily on imports to build the production facilities and obtain the materials for its CW and BW.

Here, Western companies were significantly involved in the design and construction of plants and in the sale of relevant equipment and precursor chemicals (See Chapters 1 and 10).

Some of these companies continued to deal with Iraq after certain supplier countries set in place export controls in 1984. This followed the first reports of Iraqi use of chemical weapons, and those involved were subsequently convicted in court.

There were also former Warsaw Treaty Organization countries involved in the training of troops in an NBC environment: They also supplied medical and other protective equipment. Iraq's ability to acquire these goods was undoubtedly facilitated by widespread prejudice against the Tehran government, considered by many in the West as a greater long-term international security threat.

Disclosure and access

After October 1997, fresh conflict began to emerge between UNSCOM and the Iraqi government. It was also felt that developments (which included a distinct lack of enthusiasm on the part of the Baghdad government) might be escalating towards a new round of military violence.

Under Resolution 687, Iraq was required to provide UNSCOM with a full, final and complete disclosure (FFCD) of all aspects of its programs to develop non-conventional weapons. It also needed to include such factors as locations, facilities, components and any other information necessary to account for these programs.

Further, in terms of the resolution, UNSCOM was to be allowed 'unconditional and unrestricted access to all areas, facilities, equipment and records'; that is, not only to the facilities and locations declared by the Iraqi government, but also to facilities and locations designated by UNSCOM itself. Economic sanctions were also intended to force Iraq to comply with the terms of the ceasefire, of which the UNSCOM mandate is a part.

With some obstruction and difficulties at particular sites, UNSCOM succeeded in gaining access to the sites it wished to inspect. In the autumn of 1997, however, in contravention of the UN resolutions and as a challenge to UNSCOM's mandate, Iraqi officials began to insist that some areas of Iraq should be placed off-limits to UNSCOM inspectors.

In October of that year, after denying the inspectors access to suspected sites for several months - and generally refusing to cooperate with the United Nations sponsored operations - Baghdad expelled all seven US members of an UNSCOM inspection team. It branded them as spies working in Iraq under false pretexts.

After Russian assurances and diplomatic intervention together with a reconfiguration of the weapons inspection team, Iraq then agreed to the continuation of UNSCOM's work. But even this arrangement was not to last. In December 1997, another crisis developed when inspectors were denied access to eight of Saddam's presidential sites on the basis that these were 'sovereign territory' and thus beyond the prerogative of the UN. The presidential sites were suspected of hiding evidence of the non-conventional weapons programs.

In a final effort to avoid another military confrontation, UN secretary general Kofi Annan received a mandate from the UN Security Council to seek a diplomatic settlement on the issue of inspection of the presidential sites.

A Memorandum of Understanding (MOU) between the UN and the Republic of Iraq, signed in Baghdad on February 23, 1998 reaffirmed the commitments made by the Iraqi government to cooperate fully with UNSCOM and the IAEA and to accord their inspection teams 'immediate, unconditional and unrestricted access'. UNSCOM was nevertheless required under the MOU 'to respect the legitimate concerns of Iraq relating to national security, sovereignty and dignity' in the performance of its mandated tasks.

Eight presidential sites were explicitly placed under a specific regime agreed upon in the MOU - the Republican Palace site, the Radwaniyah and Sijood presidential sites (all in Baghdad), and the Tikrit, Thartar, Jabal

Mahhul, Mosul and Basra presidential sites. (The perimeters of these sites were surveyed and recorded immediately before Annan's visit to Iraq.) Under the special procedures for the eight sites, a Special Group consisting of experts from UNSCOM and the IAEA together with senior diplomats appointed by the UN secretary general was set up. It was to operate under established UNSCOM and IAEA procedures, but additional procedures (as outlined under the MOU) were to be observed.

The UN head was also charged with submitting the inspections report received from the Executive Chairman of UNSCOM to the Security Council.

The MOU averted the use of military force, the risks being especially serious because precise information concerning the storage location of residual stores of CBW, precursors and related equipment was lacking. The highest Iraqi authorities confirmed and re-established the principle of unrestricted access and agreed that the presidential sites could be thoroughly investigated.

However, since the beginning of the crisis in October 1997, Iraq would have had ample time to remove any suspected stores of CBW, precursors and related equipment from the locations - the presidential sites in particular - which UNSCOM had planned to investigate.

At the presidential sites, the principle of unannounced and surprise inspections was probably lost as the arrival of senior diplomats tended to operate as an early warning to Iraq. Problems began to emerge again when UNSCOM teams closed in on undeclared sites or facilities, as Iraqi cooperation was only forthcoming for declared sites and capabilities.

Obstruction mainly occurred when UNSCOM teams sought access to undeclared locations and capabilities. Finally, the authority of UNSCOM may have been undermined by the opening of a parallel diplomatic channel to the Iraqi leadership and the possibilities it offered to exploit the political divisions inside the Security Council.

By the summer of 1998, the MOU had unraveled. In June, fragments of missiles unilaterally destroyed by Iraq and discovered by UNSCOM inspectors were suspected to bear traces of the nerve agent VX.

On July 18 Iraq reportedly refused to turn over to UNSCOM inspectors a document believed to contain vital information about Iraq's non-conventional weapon program during the Iraq-Iran War. Three days later, Iraq issued a warning to the effect that it would no longer accept what it termed 'excuses or pretexts' for prolonging the sanctions regime.

Finally, on August 7, talks between Richard Butler, the Australian Executive Chairman of UNSCOM, and Iraqi officials collapsed following Iraqi allegations that the inspections were really a ploy by the USA to oust the Iraqi regime. In response to UNSCOM's desire to establish a 'road map', which would set out a four- or five-week timetable for completing the task of destroying Iraq's remaining non-conventional weapon capabilities, Iraq raised strong objections and refused to cooperate further. That was followed by Iraq demanding an immediate end to the inspections and the lifting of sanctions, stating that it had fulfilled its obligations and had nothing further to reveal to UNSCOM. Cooperation between the two parties was thus frozen on Iraq's initiative. Following a week-long suspension of inspections, the Security Council, on August 17, authorized the UNSCOM inspectors to resume work in Iraq regardless.

On August 26 the resignation of Scott Ritter, an experienced weapons inspector from UNSCOM, was announced. Ritter stated his reason for resigning as a lack of determination on the part of the USA and the UN Security Council to enforce UN resolutions to disarm Iraq. He also noted the support that China, France and Russia had expressed for an easing of UNSCOM inspection demands. (Both France and Russia would benefit from an end to sanctions on Iraq: it owed France $5 billion and Russia $7 billion. Such debts could not be repaid until sanctions were lifted and Iraq regained a share of its oil revenue.)

After Ritter's resignation, Iraq demanded a review of the sanctions issue and continued to refuse to cooperate with UNSCOM inspectors, although it stated that monitoring of previously inspected sites would be permitted. With that, Baghdad called for a restructuring of UNSCOM and requested that its headquarters be moved from New York to Geneva.

Only weeks later, on September 10, the UN Security Council suspended its regular reviews of the sanctions against Iraq, citing as the reason Iraq's failure to cooperate with UNSCOM inspectors. In turn, after meeting in an emergency session on September 15, the Iraqi Parliament voted to end all association with the UN inspectors unless the world body renewed its regular reviews of sanctions.

On September 28 Iraq finally made it clear that it had no intention of resuming full status with UNSCOM inspectors in the near future. Iraqi Deputy Prime Minister Tariq Aziz and Kofi Annan met to discuss proposals for resuming the sanctions reviews. Aziz went on to dismiss the inspections as 'provocations'.

The VX Issue

VX is an extremely toxic nerve agent. First synthesized in the 1950s, it belongs to the second generation of nerve agents. Following successful production of the first-generation nerve agents tabun and sarin, Iraq launched a large-scale effort to produce VX in the late 1980s: R&D began in 1985 and production is known to have taken place in 1987-88 and possibly up to 1990.

Iraq only admitted to large-scale VX activities in 1995 when UNSCOM presented Iraqi officials with substantive evidence of it. As with many other aspects of Iraq's CBW-related activities, no comprehensive picture of this program exists.

Iraq declared 3.9 tons of VX as having been produced and destroyed unilaterally (without UNSCOM supervision). The UN believed this to be a gross understatement as it uncovered evidence of the import of precursors sufficient for the production of two hundred tons of the nerve gas.

UNSCOM was able to verify production only for the years 1987-88, but found evidence that the manufacture of precursors continued into 1989, after the production of VX had, according to Iraq's declarations, already stopped. Furthermore, Iraq stated that its program was unsuccessful because it had not resolved the inherent instability of the nerve agent. However, UNSCOM found traces of a VX stabilizer through sampling, observing that Iraq had also acquired some very sophisticated technology for VX production, which undermined its claim of failure.

In a bid to resolve the discrepancies, UNSCOM conducted a five-day technical evaluation meeting with Iraqi officials from February 2, 1998. The outcome, as described by UNSCOM officials, was 'highly unsatisfactory' as Iraq continued to misrepresent the VX program. It also withheld vital information and continued to rely on unsupported individual statements. UNSCOM experts concluded that before the invasion of Kuwait, Iraq had been able to produce fifty to a hundred tons of VX.

Up to June 1998, UNSCOM had found no evidence that Iraq had weaponized its VX nerve agents. Iraq also continued to insist that it had not done so. However, later that month, a US laboratory reported to UNSCOM that it had detected the presence of degradation products of VX and a stabilizer in some samples of missile warhead pieces recovered by UNSCOM inspectors. Although subsequent tests by French and Swiss laboratories on other pieces of warheads failed to confirm these results, this new evidence of Iraqi deception had a major impact on the discussions about lifting economic sanctions and contributed significantly to the stand-off between the Security Council and Iraq.

Economic Sanctions

The UNSCOM experience was indubitably unique in the history of arms control and disarmament. The Security Council mandate, which included the comprehensive destruction of Iraq's NBC weapons and related infrastructure and the establishment of a long-term monitoring system to prevent prohibited activities in future, created the most thorough verification regime ever. However, no guarantee could be given that the full extent of Iraq's CBW programs was uncovered before the activities of the UN body were terminated. This inability to certify Iraq as free from non-conventional weapons and weapon capability remained a key issue in the continuance of economic sanctions against the country.

During the rule of Saddam Hussein, economic sanctions in Iraq took the form of an embargo on the sale of its oil. The import of food and medicines were permitted for humanitarian reasons: Iraq was allowed to export oil up to a value of $5.2 billion every six months and to use the proceeds to purchase humanitarian goods. Sanctions would be lifted only when a United Nations body such as UNMOVIC could certify that the Iraqi NBC weapon programs and their component agents and equipment had been destroyed.

Meanwhile, until the start of the second Gulf War, Iraq continued to push for a comprehensive review of the sanctions, maintaining that it had complied with all UN resolutions since 1991. Iraq consistently demanded this review to demonstrate that some aspects of inspections, such as nuclear weapons, should be moved from an active inspection phase to a monitoring phase. The UK and the USA, in turn, feared that this would create a dangerous precedent for the continued inspection of chemical and biological weapons.

In retrospect, perhaps the most important consequence of the UNSCOM experience was that it reinforced the old lesson that it is difficult to stop a determined proliferator of banned weapons from doing illegal work in the absence of a strong international will to do so.

This, said the Stockholm International Peace Research Institute (SIPRI), was likely to become even more the case because the technologies upon which proliferation depended were becoming more accessible around the world. Moreover, the international community was moving into an era when sub-state actors would be able to acquire these technologies if they were determined enough.

In the face of such realities, declared Stockholm, the need for united action is ever greater. But, it added, unanimity seemed to be more and more difficult to achieve as individual nations sought either to profit from these situations or to take unilateral steps which they hoped would assure their own security. Even if such actions were to result in a weakening of the international nonproliferation regime and created greater insecurity for others.

At the same time, stressed SIPRI, the world should not be blind to the real achievements of UNSCOM. The international community, and in particular the UN, had learned a great deal about how to set up and run an effective intrusive inspection and monitoring regime. Saddam Hussein had provoked the crises precisely because UNSCOM was uncovering ever larger pieces of evidence that his weapons programs did exist, despite considerable and elaborate efforts to prevent such disclosures.

Looking at the broader picture, there is little doubt that the Iraqi leader would hardly have gone to the brink of war if UNSCOM had not been as good as it was at the job it was doing.

The costs of such multilateral intervention may be high, *but the costs of not intervening may be higher,* stated the Swedish-based watchdog organization in conclusion.

1   Excerpts from the Fact Sheet, which forms part of this document, were prepared by SIPRI researchers Gunilla Flodén (Sweden), Elisabeth French (USA), Peter Jones (Canada), project leader, Natalie Pauwels (Canada) and Jean Pascal Zanders (Belgium), project leader, and editor Eve Johansson. It reported on the state of affairs as of late September 1998

2   *Scourge: The Once and Future Threat of Smallpox:* Dr Jonathan Tucker, Atlantic Monthly Press, New York, 2001

3   Personal interview by the author

7

A TIMELY REASSESSMENT OF IRAQ'S NUCLEAR PROGRAM

'Iraq is a special case. It is the only country forbidden to possess separated plutonium and highly enriched uranium (HEU). Under UN Security Council Resolution 687 of April 3, 1991, Iraq was required to pledge not to acquire or develop nuclear weapons. But right now, there is every indication that it is doing so.'

David Albright, President of Washington's Institute for Science and International Security (ISIS) who, after the defection of Dr Khidir Hamza to the US, spent months debriefing the Iraqi nuclear physicist on Saddam's nuclear program

As long as Saddam Hussein remained in power, the race was on in the Middle East to produce the Arab world's first atomic bomb. The two major contenders were Iraq and Iran, though as a matter of pride, no self-respecting Persian would refer to himself as an Arab. With Saddam gone, that leaves Iran.

There might be one or two other contenders, though I doubt it, even if Israeli Prime Minister Ariel Sharon opined[1] in September 2002 that Libya might be 'the first Arab state with nukes'.

In several briefings before Congress in recent years, America's CIA has stated categorically that Iran was driven to build nuclear weapons largely because it feared that its bellicose neighbor might be doing the same. Interestingly, asked whether Iran might be heading towards nuclear capability, Langley has never had a ready answer, though it is common knowledge that the CIA is hardly likely to go public on such sensitive issues.

What Langley did tell American lawmakers was that if Tehran managed to acquire sufficient weapons grade uranium or plutonium, possibly clandestinely, from contacts in the Former Soviet Union (FSU) then it might be able to build a nuclear device. It could do so within about two years or thereabouts, said the Director of Intelligence.

This was not the first time that fears had been voiced in the West about Tehran's 'need' to build an atomic bomb. The country's bitter eight-year war with Iraq, with consequent horrific losses, still looms large in the minds of the majority of the populace. A lot of Iranians lost family in that conflict and in any event, there has always been a powerful groundswell of distrust between the two nations. David Albright takes it a bit further. Until Coalition Forces overran Iraq, he felt that the Iranians were being driven to produce the weapon for no better reason than to prevent them being annihilated as a nation.

Albright: 'Tehran is alarmed at what they know is taking place just across the border. They don't want to be caught short a second time,' he told me[2]. He also suggested that if Iran's war with Iraq hadn't ended when it did, there was a very good chance that Tehran, and not Israel, would have been at the receiving end of Iraq's first atom bomb.

That said, there are not many Middle East strategists who did not believe until very recently that there was real cause for concern at what was happening in Iraq: it was the very *raison d'être* for 'Operation Iraqi Freedom'. According to Ambassador Richard Butler, former head of UNSCOM, the UN inspection team in Iraq, Saddam was so far ahead that he actually mustered his nuclear weapons design team again early in the New Millennium. Until the end, Saddam kept the core of about a thousand nuclear scientists on his payroll.

Butler was not alone in his warnings. Steven Dolley, research director at Washington's Nuclear Control Institute, maintained that the issue was critical.

'Only kilogram quantities of highly enriched uranium (HEU) or plutonium stand between Saddam Hussein and a working nuclear bomb. Further, Vienna's International Atomic Energy Agency acknowledged that even if Iraq allowed inspectors to return, it would have been almost impossible to detect such small amounts of nuclear material being smuggled into Iraq.'

Dolley was of the opinion that Iraq's nuclear bomb program remained on track almost until to the end. Other sources indicate that it was only once war became inevitable that Iraqi scientists started destroying, secreting or exporting the more sensitive items, some of it they claim, to Syria. That, plus the fact that Iraq never surrendered its bomb design information to the IAEA (even though it was pressured by the UN to do so) nor did Baghdad ever present evidence to support its claim that all nuclear bomb components had been destroyed. For a long time, that worried a lot of people.

'Still missing are the explosive lenses needed to trigger a nuclear explosion. Also, Baghdad never turned over a full-scale mock-up of the bomb that was constructed by Iraqi nuclear scientists before the Gulf War,' Dolley declared in one of his reports.

Earlier, in testimony before the Senate Foreign Relations Committee, Paul Leventhal, President of America's Nuclear Control Institute, said that 'the threat from Iraq's nuclear capability could very well be greater than its chemical, biological and missile efforts together'.

'Vital elements of Iraq's nuclear weapons program remain in place. Over two hundred PhDs have continued their work on unknown projects with no supervision by UN inspectors for almost four years now that there is no UN control over what is happening in Baghdad. Iraq operates a worldwide network to procure foreign technology and most trucks entering Iraq from Turkey are not even stopped for inspection.'

Leventhal's report painted a savage picture of unconscionable neglect of a major security issue by the international community. It included the fact that almost all Iraq needed for the project to reach fruition was 'cores of enriched uranium' to make twenty-kiloton nuclear weapons. Meanwhile, Iraqi agents were known to Western intelligence to have been implicated in several attempts to smuggle fissile material out of FSU countries[3].

California's Center for Nonproliferation Studies at the Monterey Institute of International Studies[4] produced a paper that has a substantial bearing on some of the questions surrounding the illegal movement of nuclear material. The Institute observes that almost all these substances originated in FSU states.

Focusing on Turkey in the years 1993 to 1999, the Center maintained that there was not a single FSU state (or any country bordering on what was once the Soviet Union) that during the past decade had *not* reported instances of such illegal activity. Turkey was highlighted, and rightly so, because it borders on several countries known to be interested in weapons of mass destruction, specifically Iraq, Syria and Iran.

There are other countries that have borders with Turkey – notably the FSU countries of Armenia, Georgia and Azerbaijan.

Almost routinely there are reports coming in of smuggled fissile material passing through their borders. Also, the report declared that 'the concentration and types of incidents reported in Istanbul, and the lack of reported incidents on Turkey's borders with the three FSU states mentioned, are somewhat surprising.' (See below: *Reported Nuclear Trafficking Incidents Involving Turkey: Monterey Institute of International Studies, California.*)

Notably, the instances cited are only those that the West knows about. These involve groups or individuals that were actually caught trying to smuggle fissile material. Other, more sophisticated attempts, says the Institute, could very well have escaped attention and got through.

Meanwhile, the IAEA acknowledged that throughout the inspection period there were vital gaps in its information about the Iraqi nuclear program. It was unable to verify what the Baghdad government had managed to accomplish in its efforts to devise a working nuclear weapons design because several of the drawings that should have been handed over to one of the IAEA Action Teams, but never were.

Shortly afterwards there were reports from several sources, including UNSCOM weapons inspector Scott Ritter, that Saddam had most of the components (though not weapons grade uranium) for several completed atom bombs. It should be stressed that Ritter went public with that statement before he had his inexplicable memory loss and did a remarkable tactical about-face regarding Iraq's nuclear ability (See Chapter 16).

In another development, the IAEA wrote that Iraq at first denied that it had built molds for the manufacture of explosive lenses. Then it admitted that it had, but said that 'it couldn't find them'. Similarly, Baghdad at first denied casting explosive lenses, though it subsequently admitted casting one 120mm cylindrical charge that was tested for velocity and pressure.

Further, the US admitted not initially knowing about the existence of the principal nuclear weapons design center at Al Atheer, which was why it survived the Allied bombing of 'Operation Desert Storm'. The facility was subsequently destroyed under UNSCOM auspices.

Prior to its partial destruction after the Gulf War, Saddam's nuclear program was the largest undertaken by any Arab state. By the time the Allies moved in, there were about twelve thousand people in its employ.

To fully understand the implications of this escalation, it is essential to examine what Saddam had achieved by the time he expelled UNSCOM weapons inspectors in 1998. He also severely restricted the activities of the IAEA at about the time of 'Operation Desert Fox' in December 1998[5].

Details below are to be found in a US Government White Paper titled 'Iraq Weapons of Mass Destruction Programs'.

Iraq had a comprehensive nuclear weapons development program before the Gulf War, primarily focused on building an implosion-type weapon, and was linked to a ballistic missile project that was the intended delivery system. This was the same type of weapon that the US Air Force dropped on the Japanese city of Nagasaki and which caused tens of thousands of fatalities [the only difference between Nagasaki and the Iraqi design being the material: plutonium versus ^{235}U in the Iraqi plan].

Iraq admitted experimenting with seven uranium enrichment techniques and was most active in pursuing electromagnetic isotope separation, gas centrifuge and gas diffusion.

Baghdad planned to build a nuclear device after the start of the first Gulf War, illegally using IAEA-safeguarded highly enriched uranium from its Soviet-supplied nuclear reactors.

107

UNSCOM and IAEA inspections hindered Iraq's nuclear weapons program but Baghdad's interest in acquiring them never wavered. Inspectors from IAEA walked right past Tuwaitha and Iraq's ongoing nuclear program while Iraq was 'in compliance' with NPT reporting.

Iraq continued, until Saddam's last gasp as leader, to retain a large cadre of nuclear engineers, scientists and technicians who were at the foundation of its nuclear program. Throughout, the US Government had concerns that while the impasse went on, Iraqi physicists were free to pursue theoretical nuclear research that would ultimately reduce the time required to produce a weapon should Saddam have acquired sufficient illegal fissile material.

Until UNSCOM was expelled, Iraq continued to withhold information about enrichment techniques, foreign procurement, weapons design, weapons hardening (for delivery by aircraft or missile) as well as the role of Iraq's security and intelligence services in obtaining foreign assistance and concerning postwar concealment.

Baghdad never fully explained the interaction between its nuclear program and its ballistic missile program.

It is worth mentioning why Iraq approached the problem of bomb manufacturing the way it did. While none of these multifarious disciplines are easy, highly enriched uranium or ^{235}U does offer some advantages[6]. There are proven and very successful ^{235}U enrichment processes using centrifuges in the developing world: witness Pakistan and now North Korea.

The use of plutonium in an atom bomb (as an alternative) means 'cooking' ^{238}U and that involves substantial energy/heat signatures. It was Sieg Hecker who told Eric Croddy how 'amazingly wacky and difficult are the metallurgic properties of plutonium'. He added: 'I still don't know how anybody can figure out how to get plutonium into the shape of a ball, considering that its physical properties tend to change depending on what day of the week it is!'[7].

Dr Khidir Hamza's tell-almost-all book, *Saddam's Bombmaker* subtitled *The Terrifying Inside Story of the Iraqi Nuclear and Biological Weapons Agenda* (co-authored with Jeff Stein: Simon & Schuster, New York, 2000) has obviously played a part in spurring rounds of conjecture about developments in Iraq prior to the second invasion of Iraq. As one of Saddam's top nuclear physicists, he is regarded by some as having been seminal to the development of almost all these weapons programs, though Albright and others are a little more skeptical[8].

Hamza's case is not unique. Over the decades, many students from Arab states were trained in the United States, Britain, Europe and elsewhere. Some of these people subsequently turned their skills to weapons production. What has changed is that the current generation of foreign students at Western educational establishments are now much more restricted in their access to classified material than before. They do not have unfettered access to the kind of sensitive stuff that might have been viewed by their predecessors.

Dr Hamza arrived in the United States in the 1960s, attended the Massachusetts Institute of Technology and thereafter, Florida State University. He ended up with a doctorate in nuclear physics. After teaching at American academic institutions he returned to Baghdad in 1970. Almost immediately he was ordered to apply his knowledge to what were then the building blocks of Saddam Hussein's nuclear weapons program.

It was a crucial time for the Iraqis, Hamza recalled. The Arab community was aware that the Israelis were producing nuclear weapons. They were also frustrated that there was so little that they or anybody else could do to stop them: Certainly, he commented, Washington wasn't helping the Arab cause.

He disclosed that about then some Palestinian informants spoke of the Jewish state having built fourteen bombs, including some that were thermonuclear. He was aware, too, that their final production target was about two hundred nuclear weapons, though he failed to explain how these figures were arrived at.

Saddam's first step in trying to achieve nuclear parity was to send Hamza to Paris in 1974 to buy a 40-MWth[9] materials test reactor called the Tammuz-1. The French at Osiraq, near Baghdad, constructed it as a prelude to building a plutonium bomb.

Hamza: 'It was a long-range project because the reactor was subject to inspection by IAEA. The French would be there as well. But by then we told Saddam that we would be able to cheat on both parties.'

Then, just prior to the reactor's initial operation, Jerusalem made what Hamza refers to as 'a bad mistake'. The Israeli Air Force , in one of the most daring raids of the era, destroyed the Osiraq reactor in June 1981 because the Mossad believed – correctly, as it has since transpired – that it would be used to provide plutonium for nuclear weapons.

Subsequent disclosures in this regard are significant: Iraq declared that Osiraq had the potential of producing about four-and-a-half lbs of *unsafeguarded* plutonium a year: French estimates subsequently put it at about double that while Israeli intelligence figures were roughly four times higher, but that is to be expected.

The most important consequences were twofold: First, it relieved Saddam of any problems that he might have had with any Nonproliferation Treaty restraints. More salient, almost overnight the secret bomb program became more ambitious. This is directly reflected in staffing levels. Before Osiraq, there were about five hundred people working in nuclear research in Iraq. The program eventually involved seven thousand people and the increase was made in the first five years.

In his Washington press conference at the launch of his book, Hamza said that he believed there might have been as many as twelve thousand people involved in the nuclear program towards the end. This begged an immediate question: Why? Part of the answer, Hamza suggested, was that the sentiment in Iraq at the time was that Israel was a tiny country and could consequently be threatened or destroyed with just two or three atom bombs.

'So, when we started, we believed that the plutonium that we would acquire from Osiraq would give us enough bomb power for about five or ten years. But with that facility suddenly destroyed, Saddam demanded that we achieve the ability of producing two-hundred lbs of highly enriched weapons grade uranium a year, which is an enormous amount of this kind of fuel.'

The Iraqi leader, Dr Hamza stated, 'wanted Baghdad's position to be the center of high power and unity in the Middle East'.

Things went quickly after that. By 1985 Dr Hamza, as advisor to Iraq's nuclear energy program, had begun advance planning for an atom bomb. 'We believed that we had a sense of direction in designing and building it. Two years later I was appointed head of the Iraqi nuclear weapons program.' Then, gradually, things started to unravel.

'We did not understand exactly how Saddam intended to use the weapons we were supposed to produce, or how we were going to test them, or even which testing site would be used. Not long afterwards a nuclear center for atomic weapons was established about fifty miles south-west of Baghdad and matters seemed to be in hand again. Then, overnight, came the invasion of Kuwait.'

Dr Hamza: 'A new vision became apparent when we entered Kuwait. Saddam had begun to regard an atomic bomb as an integral part of his arsenal of war. He wanted a device that could be mounted on mobile rockets, yet we did not yet have a complete weapon and that placed us in great difficulty. For several reasons.'

First, he said, his people had only enough nuclear fuel for a single bomb but they still had no concept of how to finalize it all. Then, once more, things started going off track. Internally, Iraq's scientists began to face other, more serious problems, some of them personal. While Saddam's security services ensured that many professionals who had studied abroad were returning home, many of those already in the country were subjected to different and oft-times discriminatory levels of security.

'That made us look more like hostages: With our families - hostages in our own country. Gradually the whole program shifted into a kind of terror system. We were told: "if you do not work, then you go to jail".' One example: the man who was in charge of the plutonium level was jailed for eleven years for refusing to answer a question from Saddam on plutonium.

Dr Hamza categorized developments as something that had begun well enough, fueled as it was by national pride, but that had subsequently turned sour. As he explained, it was a sort of 'forced confining of scientists'. One of the immediate consequences was that some people who were sent abroad on assignment simply didn't bother to come back.

'We just never heard from them any more...most of them feared for their families.'

Then, when the Chief of Purchasing was suspected of having bank accounts abroad and somebody thought that he might defect, he was murdered on his farm. His body was thrown into a ditch, and that was how they found him.

'That was right next door to where I had my place. I knew then that I had to get out.'

Following the defection of Dr Hamza to the United States in 1995, David Albright and other ISIS staff, including Kevin O'Neill, spent months debriefing the Iraqi nuclear physicist about the clandestine methods that Iraq had used to obtain classified material in the West. During the course of these sessions, Hamza admitted that one of the strongest factors working for him and his staff in their efforts to create a secret nuclear weapons program, was that many of the items involved had dual-use application.

CIA director George Tenet in an address before Congress went some way towards explaining it in June 2000:

'Our efforts to halt (nuclear) proliferation are complicated by the fact that most WMD programs are based on technologies that have civil as well as military use.' He went on: 'Though US intelligence is increasing its emphasis and resources on many of these issues, there is continued and growing risk of surprise. We focus much of our intelligence collection and analysis on ten states (including Iraq) but even concerning those countries, there are important gaps in our knowledge.

'Moreover, we have identified well over fifty countries that are of concern as suppliers, conduits or potential proliferants.'

Backing Hamza's statements, he added that Iraq or Iran could quickly advance their nuclear aspirations through covert acquisition of fissile material or the relevant technology.

'Acquisition of any of the critical components of a nuclear weapons development program - weapons technology, engineering know-how and weapons-usable material - would seriously shorten the time needed to produce a viable weapon.'

Focusing on surprise and the risk that it entailed, Mr Tenet said there were four main reasons and all had a bearing on countries like Iraq and Iran eventually producing nuclear bombs:

The first and most important, he said, was that proliferators were showing greater proficiency in the use of denial and deception. Second, there was a greater availability of dual-use technologies in making it easier for proliferators to obtain the materials they sought

Third, 'the potential for surprise is exacerbated by the growing capacity of countries seeking WMD to import talent that can help them make dramatic leaps on things like new chemical and biological agents and delivery systems. In short, they can buy the expertise that confers the advantage of technological surprise'. Scientists with transferable know-how continued to leave the Former Soviet Union, 'some potentially for destinations of proliferation concern'. Plugging that brain drain, he disclosed, was a key US goal.

'Finally, the accelerating pace of technological progress makes information and technology easier to obtain in more advanced forms than when the weapons were initially developed.'

During his debrief, Dr Hamza disclosed that the first and most comprehensive help he received in his bid to build an atom bomb was 'a gift from the US Atomic Energy Project - library copies on the 1940s Manhattan Project'.

He says he found the reports at Iraq's atomic energy library 'in a corner with piles of dust on them...sitting there telling me exactly what I needed to do'. At the time, in the 1970s, he was one of only three or four nuclear physicists in Iraq.

The Manhattan Project, it will be recalled, was the crash US government program in which scientists developed the atom bombs that were dropped on the Japanese cities of Hiroshima and Nagasaki to end World War 2. He did not know how the Iraqi library got the reports, which, like so much other nuclear information, is readily available almost everywhere now. Significantly, it is also on the web.

One of the prime tasks that Hamza initially set himself and his staff was searching for open literature and getting close to people in the US who had classified information. Specifically, Iraqi students in America combed university libraries for bomb-making information while Iraqi agents and scientists collected data at scientific conferences and elsewhere.

Following the UN embargo on Iraq, there have been a lot of questions raised about whether Saddam actually had the resources to tackle another bomb program. The expense involved was among the first of the considerations.

For several years, the Iraqi leader made a very public issue of his country having being bankrupted. Starving and emaciated children – and the graphic TV images of these victims – were used in arguments against sanctions. That campaign has had something of an effect, especially among journalists who were regarded either as anti-American or sympathetic to the Iraqi cause, often for what appeared to be humanitarian reasons.

The popular view was that there was no way that any leader would allow such suffering if it could be avoided. Suggestions that Saddam might have been involved in such work again were regarded by the disaffected as infamous Western propaganda. After all, nuclear weapons cost billions of dollars to develop and Iraq was destitute, ran the argument. As it now continues to emerges, all that is fiction.

In a submission to the US Senate Armed Services Committee, Under Secretary of Defense for Policy, Walter Slocombe suggested two years before 'Operation Iraqi Freedom', that Saddam Hussein had made a lot more money from his oil sales than anybody could imagine.

In 1989, the last full year before the invasion of Kuwait, he told a Washington gathering, Iraq earned $15 billion from its oil exports. Of that, Slocombe disclosed, Saddam spent $13 billion on his military. We are now also aware that a good proportion of what was left went towards building a succession of sumptuous palaces, each one decorated at great expense and that while Iraqi children starved or were deprived of medicines. There were gold-plated faucets in all of his bathrooms.

'In the year 2000, Iraq is projected to earn $20 billion from its oil exports authorized under the Oil-For-Food program,' Slocombe stated. And while he cautioned that these resources could not be used for military purposes, many more billions of dollars were being funneled into Iraq's coffers from some very sophisticated illegal smuggling operations. Not all of it was secret: Those involved with monitoring such matters intimated often enough that most of Iraq's neighbors, Saudi Arabia and Iraq's old enemy Iran included, were involved in this subterfuge.

One of the observations made by Stephen Ulph, editor of Jane's *Islamic Affairs Analyst*, following a visit to Cairo before the second invasion of Iraq, was that for all the rhetoric about UN-imposed penury, the average Iraqi was a lot wealthier than the average Egyptian. This was proved as huge amounts of money surfaced after the Americans had taken Baghdad. He was never short of cash, usually greenbacks.

For all this, there continues to be a conflicting variance of opinion among UN experts and a number of American organizations responsible for monitoring developments about the ability of Iraq to build a weapon of mass destruction. The most troubling is whether Saddam Hussein actually posed a nuclear threat to the West. That revelation emerged a few years ago as the IAEA moved frighteningly close, as one observer stated, 'to declaring Iraq free of nuclear weapons'.

In fact they didn't quite get that far: they just could not come up with the evidence that Iraq was noncompliant with regard to its *declared* facilities. Had Vienna known about Saddam's secret nuclear program, it would have been another matter. That said, one of the consequences of implying a clean bill of health was that Western weapons experts on both sides of the Atlantic charged Vienna's experts with complacency.

ISIS President David Albright argued prior to the Americans going in a second time that Saddam Hussein, left on his own to proceed with the development of the A-bomb, might very well have been able to build a nuclear weapon in less than a year.

'He has the know-how and he has the resources, all of it hidden,' he said at the time. Qualifying his statement, he reckoned that in order to do this, the Iraqi leader would have needed access to fissionable material such as enriched uranium or plutonium, both of weapons grade. 'Also not impossible. From what we know from our own intelligence and from defectors, he had dozens of offers from Former Soviet Union states for the stuff.' Albright disclosed that at the same time Iraq (as well as Iran) had been the target of several well-planned nuclear-related stings in the past, all of which had the effect of making Baghdad unusually cautious.

A former IAEA inspector in Iraq himself, Albright detailed the Iraqi (and other) nuclear weapons programs in a book published by the Stockholm International Peace Research Institute and in various related reports. In an article in the May/June 1998 issue of America's *The Bulletin of the Atomic Scientists* he recalled that immediately after the Gulf War ended, Saddam gave orders to 'begin salvaging bomb-making equipment from damaged buildings and returning hidden items to where they had been before the war.'

He was soon hiding things again, Albright disclosed. 'Like materials that might have revealed the extent of his nuclear weapons program. These were boxed up and hidden in underground bunkers or even in private homes.'

Some key documents, he recalled, were placed in a freight car which was welded shut and then sent off, for years, to travel continuously up and down the national railway grid. Very few people knew about it, or even that the contents of the box car was top secret. It wasn't even guarded.

'They went to unusual lengths to conceal all activity related to nuclear issues,' Albright maintains. Even after September 1991, when there was a major IAEA breakthrough and fifty thousand pages of sensitive documentation was seized which detailed the activities of "Petrochemical 3" (the code name for Saddam's nuclear program) the Iraqis continued to play tag with us.'

The documents proved conclusively that Iraq had been in the middle of a full-blown program to produce highly enriched uranium and turn it into a deliverable, implosion-type nuclear weapon: The same kind of bomb that was dropped on Nagasaki by the Americans in 1945. 'However, not many items related to the weaponization of the device were ever retrieved,' Albright told me.

'That sort of thing went on for another five years with the result that there were numerous critical aspects that remained obscure,' he observed. For these and other reasons, he stated, Iraq's nuclear potential needed to be very carefully scrutinized for a long time to come.

He recalled that the West was fortunate that Saddam's son-in-law, General Hussein Kamel, defected when he did (to Jordan, in August 1995). As a result of that action (which cost him his life), the IAEA found evidence that Iraq aimed to put a nuclear warhead onto an intermediate-range ballistic weapon following a crash program to build a bomb that was launched only after Iraq invaded Kuwait. Saddam intended using IAEA 'safeguarded' highly enriched uranium for that purpose which was contrary to nonproliferation treaties that Baghdad had signed.

It is interesting, he reckoned, that Iran right now is in exactly the same position as Iraq might have been prior to the recent invasion. Like Baghdad, Tehran signed all the relevant treaties, yet it was now working simultaneously on a public as well as a covert nuclear program, the latter involved with weapons.

To achieve its aims, Baghdad went to extraordinary lengths to deceive International Atomic Energy Agency as well United Nations inspectors.

At Al Atheer for instance - which became the hub of Iraq's atom bomb program - Saddam's scientists built not one but two false floors in some buildings. They figured, correctly, says Albright, that those who were doing the looking would remove only one of them.

Elsewhere, they would declare only parts of a program, as they did with their centrifuge R&D program at Rashdiya. Brick walls were built that excluded vital aspects from prying eyes. They would then move superfluous equipment elsewhere, as they did at Al Furat maintaining that it was all innocuous. Only after Kamel's defection did the truth emerge. 'They would smile when they were cornered and forced to admit it,' Albright recalls.

The Iraqis also delayed (until Kamel defected) before revealing the seminal roles played by two Germans, Bruno Stemmler and Karl Heinz Schaab, in developing a centrifuge separation process for enriching uranium. Schaab ended up pleading guilty for treason in Germany after being extradited from Brazil. Stemmer has since died. Their exploits on behalf of Saddam Hussein are described fully in the next chapter.

Curiously, in the light of more recent statements, the IAEA remained skeptical of Iraqi claims that it had destroyed all key centrifuge documents. 'But without them,' says Albright, 'they are unable to fully assess the program's progress or its procurement efforts. It will also be recalled that UNSCOM did actually discover large magnets for use in calutrons to separate ^{235}U, a technique that the Manhattan Project used with some minor success, but that was outweighed eventually by gas diffusion.'

The question most often asked in the West these days is whether it was possible, had the two Gulf Wars not happened, that Iraq might eventually have obtained enough nuclear fuel illegally to complete the construction of atom bombs. Certainly with the breakup of the Soviet Union there were - as the record shows - multiple opportunities.

A few recent examples will suffice. Important here, is that while none of these incidents were geared to any Iraqi WMD initiative, they could have been. As Director of Intelligence George Tenet disclosed to Congress, Iraq (like Iran today) was always remarkably fluent in plausibly denying everything that related to weapons of mass destruction. He added: 'That has been so since day one of the weapons inspection program.'

Random examples of some of the attempts to acquire fissile material by nations unknown are as follows:

- It came to light in Moscow in the late Nineties that the chief of the Federal Security Service (FSB) in the Chelyabinsk region told *Itar-Tass* that their agents prevented the theft of forty lbs of fissile material.

Kevin O'Neill of ISIS reckoned that while he hadn't seen the specifics, he was told on good authority that the stuff was 'radioactive materials used for nuclear weapons production'. Another source mentioned weapons grade HEU.

- According to a submission made to a Senate Select Committee on Intelligence in Washington DC in January 1998, seven lbs of HEU was seized by Russian police in St. Petersburg.

- Mayak (where over thirty tons of weapons grade uranium was stored) was in the news when former President Boris Yeltsin ordered an overhaul of security measures at the plant that reprocesses nuclear materials for weapons. Mayak handles spent nuclear submarine fuel as part of the Chelyabinsk-6 nuclear complex, one of Russia's main weapons development facilities. According to Bill Gertz of the *Washington Times,* the CIA told a Senate Intelligence Committee that while nuclear warheads in Russia were relatively secure, 'declining morale and discipline in the military as well as economic conditions, raise our concerns about the potential for warhead theft'. The report added that 'Russian nuclear weapons-useable fissile material - plutonium as well as HEU - are more vulnerable to theft than nuclear weapons or warheads'.

- In several instances, in non-Russian republics (after being asked by plant officials to help measure the fissile stocks at their sites) the IAEA found fissile stocks to be in excess of what was on record. In one area, dozens of pounds of fissile materials unexpectedly turned up. Until then, nobody was quite sure exactly what the tally was. Even today, says O'Neill, US Energy Department officials and some Russian scientists are concerned that many of the facilities in the FSU lack complete and accurate stock records.

- An American team visiting the Kurchatov Institute in Moscow was shown a building that contained more than two hundred lbs of HEU which had been totally unguarded 'for some years'.

- A report in the American publication *Nuclear Fuel* stated that the six lb cache of HEU grabbed in a car in Prague late 1994, matched the specifics of similar material seized in Germany four months earlier. Following a tip-off, a number of people (including a Russian atomic scientist from the Nuclear Research Center at Rez) were arrested. The report states that the material found in containers identifying them as from the ex-Soviet Black Sea fleet had been stolen from a stockpile at Mayak, Siberia.

California's Center for Nonproliferation Studies at the Monterey Institute of International Studies produced a paper that has a substantial bearing on some of the questions surrounding the illegal movement of nuclear material. The Institute observed that all of these illegal substances originated in FSU states.

In that report, the Monterey report focused specifically on Turkey in the years 1993 to 1999. Of interest is the fact that there was not a single FSU state (or any country bordering on what was once the Soviet Union) that during the past decade had *not* reported instances of such illegal activity. Turkey is highlighted if only because it borders on several countries known to be or to have been interested in weapons of mass destruction, specifically Iraq, Syria and Iran. There are several more states that have borders with Turkey – notably the FSU countries of Armenia, Georgia and Azerbaijan.

The Institute makes a specific point about this issue: 'The concentration and types of incidents reported in Istanbul, and the lack of reported incidents on Turkey's borders with the three FSU states mentioned are somewhat surprising.'

Also, instances cited are only those that the West knows about: they involve groups or individuals that were actually caught trying to smuggle fissile material. Other, more sophisticated attempts, says Monterey, could very well have escaped attention.

Obviously, considering that penalties under the Turkish penal system are notoriously harsh, those involved wouldn't be doing it if the returns were not remarkable and concludes that the possibility of proliferation-relevant nuclear materials reaching Iraq (and elsewhere) through Turkey, must merit concerted attention.

The 17 incidents are listed in reverse chronological order

(For sources and further details, see Center for Nonproliferation Studies, Monterey <http://cns.miis.edu/research.wmdme/flow/turkey/index.htm>

Material(s) Seized	Origin of Materials	Reported Destination	Location of Seizure	Suspects
A certificate for the purchase of ^{235}U container with ^{235}U (Exact quantity not reported)	Moldova	not reported	Dounav Most, (Bulgarian/ Turkish border)	One Turkish national
100g of enriched uranium	Azerbaijan	Greece	Bursa, Turkey	4 Turkish nationals

Material(s) Seized	Origin of Materials	Reported Destination	Location of Seizure	Suspects
4.5kg 'non-active' solid uranium and 6g 'active' plutonium	Russia or Ulba Plant in Kazakhstan	not reported	Istanbul, Turkey	4 Turkish nationals, 3 Kazakhis (incl a Kazakh army colonel) + 1 Azerbaijani
13 cylinders of uranium marked	Iran	Istanbul	Van, Turkey	5 Turkish nationals and 1 Iranian
850g uranium dioxide	not reported	not reported	Bursa, Turkey	4 individuals (nationality unknown)
Osmium (quantity not reported)	Romania	not reported	Turkey	3 individuals (nationality unknown)
509g 'raw' uranium	Georgia	not reported	Ipsala, Erdine, Turkey	3 Turkish nationals
17g low-enriched uranium	Golcuk, Kocaeli, Turkey	not reported	Antalya Turkey	11 individuals (unknown nationality)
20kg uranium	Russia	not reported	Antalya, Turkey	5 Turkish nationals
1.2kg uranium	Georgia	Libya	Yalova, Turkey	2 Turkish nationals
12g highly-enriched uranium	Georgia	Libya	Zurich, Switzerland	1 Turkish national
750g weapons grade or enriched ^{238}U	Azerbaijan	Baku, Turkey	Istanbul	1 Azerbaijan national
12kg uranium	Unspecified FSU state	not reported	Istanbul	7 Turkish nationals
Uranium (quantity not reported)	not reported	Russia	Istanbul	1 Turkish national, 1 Azerbaijani + 1 Russian
4.5kg uranium	not reported	not reported	Bursa, Turkey	3 Georgian nationals
2.5kg uranium enriched to 2.5/3.5 percent ^{235}U	Russia	Iran	Gayrettepe, Istanbul, Turkey	4 Turkish nationals + 4 Iranians (suspected secret service agents)
6kg enriched uranium	Tashkent, Uzbekistan	Istanbul	not reported	not reported

1   *World Tribune.com:* Middle East Newsline 'Libya May Be First Arab State with Nukes, Sharon Warns.' September 6, 2002
2   Telephone interviews during the period September 2001 to the summer of 2002
3   Fissile material is composed of atoms that fission when irradiated by slow or 'thermal' neutrons. The most common are uranium 235 and plutonium 239. The term is often used to describe plutonium and highly enriched uranium
4   Center for Nonproliferation Studies. Monterey Institute of International Studies, Monterey, California: http://www.cns.miis.edu
5   FAS Weapons of Mass Destruction 'Iraqi Nuclear Weapons' under Iraq Special Weapons: Website: http://www.fas.org/nuke/guide/nuke/program.htm
6   According to the ISIS Report *The Challenges of Fissile Material Control* edited by David Albright and Kevin O'Neill, (Washington DC, 1999*)*, Uranium 235 is the only naturally occurring fissile isotope: in its natural form, it contains only 0.71 percent uranium 235. To make it into weapons grade uranium it needs to be enriched to more than 90 per cent uranium 235
7   Plutonium 239 is a fissile, artificial isotope created when uranium 238 captures a neutron through irradiation. Plutonium 239 is one of the principal materials used for nuclear weapons, the other being uranium 235
8   Among the most vocal critics of Hamza is another Iraqi physicist Dr Imad Khadduri who states in his CV that he has a MSc in Physics from the University of Michigan (United States) and a PhD in Nuclear Reactor Technology from the University of Birmingham (United Kingdom). Khadduri says he worked with the Iraqi Atomic Energy Commission from 1968 until 1998 and was allowed to leave Iraq late in 1998 with his family. It is on record that Saddam threatened all Iraqi scientists (and their families) with retribution if they so much as spoke to UN weapons inspectors shortly before 'Operation Iraqi Freedom'. The last part of Khadduri's statement consequently makes no sense. Jon Lee Anderson allows us a peek under Iraq's security barriers under the old regime in his 'Letter from Baghdad' (*The New Yorker,* May, 2003). He was able to spend time with one of Saddam's closest aides who was quite clear about travel restrictions: even he was prohibited from going abroad without his leaving family behind as hostages. It was a blanket restriction for anyone doing anything sensitive. But top Iraqi nuclear scientist Khadduri was allowed to emigrate to Canada...
9   Thermal

8

WAS HE BUILDING THE BOMB... AGAIN?

India and Pakistan were, by some estimates, the forerunners of a new kind of nuclear power, ahead of the field but hardly alone. Iraq may be solved, but North Korea is regarded as already nuclear. Iran is believed to be moving rapidly toward acquiring nukes. Libya and Syria are watched with suspicion. Experts talk speculatively of the ripple effects - of a nuclear Iran inspiring nuclear lust in Egypt, Turkey, even Saudi Arabia, of a nuclear North Korea prompting a breakout in Japan, South Korea, even Taiwan.

Bill Keller, *The New York Times,* May 4, 2003

It is no longer a secret that Western intelligence sources were aware until the end that Saddam had in his possession the components for at least three complete atom bombs in the twenty kiloton range (or roughly what was dropped on Japanese cities by the Americans in World War 2). All he lacked, it was averred, was enough weapons grade uranium or plutonium with which to arm them.

Since there are scores of documented instances of attempts being made to smuggle fissile material out of the Former Soviet Union (FSU) – both by Iraq and Iran (and, we now know, North Korea) - it is not impossible that some of these illicit shipments might have got through. There is much relating to the production of weapons of mass destruction (WMD) in Iraq that conclusively points to it.

Following Dr Hamza's arrival in America, he has made some astonishing disclosures. David Albright and Kevin O'Neill of Washington's Institute for Science and International Security (ISIS) extensively debriefed him. Once they were done, I was allowed access to bundles of pages consisting of questions and answers assembled during this period. What remarkable insight that exercise provided.

Among issues raised were the nature and extent of Iraq's nuclear weapons program. These included:

- indigenous production as well as overt and covert procurement of natural uranium compounds for use in an atomic bomb.

- Industrial-scale facilities for the production of pure uranium compounds for fuel enrichment and/or isotope enrichment.
- Research and development (R&D) of the full range of enrichment technologies, culminating in industrial-scale exploitation of electromagnetic isotope separation (EMIS) i.e. calutrons. There was also progress made towards similar exploitation of gas centrifuge enrichment technology in Iraq.
- Design and feasibility studies for an indigenous plutonium production reactor.
- R&D of irradiated fuel-reprocessing technology.
- R&D of weaponization capabilities for implosion-based nuclear weapons at the Al Atheer nuclear weapons development and production plant near Baghdad.
- A 'crash program' (after the first Gulf War) aimed at diverting safeguarded research reactor fuel and recovering weapons grade uranium for use in an atom bomb.

Which leads us to some of the news reports following the Allied invasion of Afghanistan and the neutralization of the Taliban and an Al Qaeda power base in that country. Many journalists followed in the wake of American, British, Australian, German and other troops and there was much speculation about Osama bin Laden's possible flirtation with mass killing weapons, nuclear included.

The nonsense written by some of these correspondents about a purported Al Qaeda nuclear program was mindblowing, some of it emanating from a few scribes very well known to their readers.

While there were those pundits who had made an effort to familiarize themselves with the ramifications of the disciplines involved in nuclear physics, most had not. In the first flush of the Afghan invasion, there were consequently quite a few who got it wrong.

The truth about developing nuclear weapons is that any fool with a fundamental understanding of science is aware that building such a device not only involves complex scientific proficiency right across the industrial spectrum, it is also an extremely difficult undertaking. Were it not, there would be many more members of the 'nuclear club'. It is also cripplingly expensive, which is why no nation undertakes such a venture lightly.

Some, like Argentina, Brazil, the old Yugoslavia, Taiwan, Algeria, Egypt and others, have on occasion expressed nuclear aspirations. Even Nigeria has thought about getting into the act. But when faced with the prospect of having to invest a sizable chunk of the country's GNP for what after all, is an exercise in national prestige, the majority have opted out. India and

Pakistan are the exceptions: those two belligerents have already fought three wars since Britain abdicated power in the sub-continent and developing nuclear weapons is purely strategic.

For those states that have taken the giant step, it has been a thing of concerted national effort. Such a program requires a large industrial base from which to operate and draw resources. South Africa is the most industrialized nation on its continent, which is why Pretoria was able to produce six atom bombs. In the end, the level of investment needed to achieve nuclear parity hurt the South African economy even though, at the time, South Africa was the world's largest single producer of gold.

So what is building the atom bomb all about? For a start, power in abundance is essential for any nuclear weapons program. Had Afghanistan dallied with that kind of infrastructure it would immediately have shown: the truth is that Kabul's government can hardly light its existing conurbations never mind still have electricity to spare.

It is consequently axiomatic that power grids are among the first things that Langley and Cheltenham look for in their spooks' perennial search for clandestine weapons operations.

To get a more complete picture, you only have to look at the extent of the Iraqi nuclear program, which is not difficult because it's all there in the open literature and on the web. Many specifics are provided by such entities as Britain's Jane's Information Group, Barry Rubin's always-informative *Middle East Review of International Affairs*, ISIS in Washington, the Federation of American Scientists (FAS), Stratfor, The Monterey Institute of International Studies, the Washington Institute for Near East Policy, the Carnegie Endowment and a host of others, the majority of them reputable.

With that kind of information in hand, one can understand why Saddam's nuclear efforts eventually cost him at least $20 billion. At one stage his program - which included the PC-3 Fourth Group (or weaponization stage) - employed twenty thousand people, many of them scientists. So much then for a bunch of raggedy Afghan tribesmen hiding in caves in the Tora Bora Mountains developing atom bombs, or for that matter, any other kind of sophisticated weaponry.

Interestingly, I wasn't the only one appalled at the amount of misinformation regarding matters nuclear that has been doing the rounds since the September 11 attacks. Dr S. Fred Singer, a physicist and emeritus professor of environmental sciences at the University of Virginia and a visiting Wesson Fellow at the Hoover Institution at Stanford University also chided some of the 'experts'.

As he said, 'for some reason the public seems to be more afraid of radioactivity than poison gas or even biological agents…this, even though radioactivity is easy to detect, is rarely lethal and cannot cause epidemics as can viruses or bacteria.

'This fear is being exploited by opponents of nuclear power who keep coming up with a multitude of scary scenarios,' he stated.

Because the threat remains persistent and is seldom out of the news, it is worth quoting the professor in more detail.

There are three general types of nuclear terrorism reported in the press, he pointed out. 'One is the so-called "dirty bomb" which does not create radioactivity but simply disperses radioactive material packed around conventional explosives. Another concerns the release of radioactivity from an aircraft impact or the internal sabotage of an operating nuclear reactor or of storage of highly radioactive spent nuclear fuel. Green activists who would love to shut down reactors assiduously promote this particular fear, he states. Finally, we have the possible explosion of a nuclear bomb.

'Of the three, the dirty bomb makes no sense at all: impact or sabotage is extremely unlikely to succeed. Only a real nuclear bomb using fissionable uranium or plutonium (like Saddam's) poses a serious threat, but even there countermeasures can be taken,' he suggests.

According to Dr Singer, the 'dirty bomb' is mostly hype. He refers to a three-year study by the National Council on Radiation Protection and Measurements that claimed that contamination from such an attack would likely extend to several city blocks and that radiation would be 'catastrophic but manageable'.

Singer: 'However, quite simple considerations show that such a bomb is merely a terror weapon without teeth. It would cause panic but it does not kill. Media stories actively promote such panic since the public fears anything that's even remotely connected with radioactivity.

'So too, with a "dirty bomb", which makes no practical sense. To produce significant radioactivity over an area of, say one square mile, the initial concentration within a small bomb would have to be roughly ten million times greater and would quickly kill the terrorists trying to assemble the material. The radioactivity also creates large amounts of heat energy, sufficient to melt most containers. What's more, such a bomb would be easy to detect at long distance if it emits gamma rays.

'Similarly, damaging a nuclear reactor by impact or sabotage is unrealistic. As compared to the World Trade Center towers, a reactor presents a very small target that would be a lot more difficult to hit. Furthermore it is protected by at least three feet of reinforced concrete, which even a large plane is unlikely to penetrate.'

He also makes one of the most balanced assessments of the consequences of a total reactor accident, which he regards as 'an extremely unlikely event'. It is his view that the consequences are less severe than generally pictured.

'We have already seen the worst scenario that one can imagine: even so, Chernobyl killed only some thirty people - those who were directly involved in putting out the fire.'

Vienna's IAEA reported some years afterwards that the subsequent health effects as a consequence of the Chernobyl catastrophe had been minor, with no increases in leukemia or birth defects; only in cases of thyroid cancer was there some increase that could have been avoided by taking protective potassium-iodide tablets.

So there we have it. It is all worth remembering when the West eventually does go after the handful of other illegal nuclear aspirants, North Korea and Iran among them.

While Saddam's efforts to build a nuclear weapon is a thing of the past, nobody will ever be sure how close he came to pulling it off. Twice, according to *The Washington Post,* UN arms inspectors in 1996 and 1997 reported that they had credible intelligence that indicated that Iraq had built and maintained all the working components for three 'implosion devices'. All that Iraq lacked were cores of enriched uranium to make the purported twenty-kiloton atom bombs.

The research to put all this together came from all over the world. According to Dr Hamza, a valuable source of nuclear-related programs was, interestingly enough, in Northern Ireland's Belfast.

'There is a library there, which has an international repository of (computer) programs. You can join in and gain access for a few thousand dollars a year. So we joined and I was the corresponding member,' he explained. Iraq also purchased a professional package from some companies that designed equipment for CERN (the European nuclear authority).

Dr Hamza identified several reasons for Iraq's (or any other proliferant's) search for sensitive nuclear weapons-related information. Obviously, the focus was centered on the need to build an indigenous capability to design and manufacture nuclear weapons, he said. There was also, for security reasons, a requirement to avoid reliance on outside experts as well as the need to gain a basic, rudimentary knowledge of how to handle and process nuclear materials and high explosives.

Seminal to all this, he explained, was the ability to devise credible 'cover stories' for the program and the desire to obtain leads on potential suppliers of information and items needed for nuclear weapons.

Although the Iraqi physicist provided no concrete case where he was involved in obtaining classified US documents, he did point out that 'rubbing shoulders' with those who might have had access to sensitive information often led to potentially important rewards.

As we have seen, much of the equipment needed for Iraq's atomic bomb program was classified as dual-use: material that might also have a civil application, like advanced explosives for mining purposes or the most sophisticated metals technology which could be diverted to Saddam's missiles program and so on. Thousands of items were searched for and the innocuous use that the Iraqis said they would be used for was rarely if ever questioned, at least in the early days. That situation prevailed for some years, until the West became aware that it was being duped. All that took time, which was of inestimable help to Baghdad.

In his debriefing prior to 'Operation Iraqi Freedom', Dr Hamza noted that other government activities - including agriculture, oil and other trade activities were, as he put it, 'used when needed to smuggle equipment and obtain information not otherwise available.

'The (Iraqi Atomic Energy) Chairman would send me a list and ask what I needed. I would tell him that I would perhaps like more on EMIS technology or that I needed something advanced on diffusion. He would split the list up and send it back to various ministries so that it wouldn't be traceable directly to Atomic Energy. Then he would split the supply companies and perhaps order two or three related items from one firm, more from another and the rest from several more. This was an ideal system that we used for covering our tracks.'

One particular Iraqi government organization - the El Hazen Institute - played a significant role in acquiring information. Dr Hamza said that El Hazen 'started all WMD programs and had excellent contacts with the University of Arizona because of its affiliation with Los Alamos. Lots of Iraqi students were sent to Arizona to study laser technology, which was fundamental to Saddam's weapons programs.

At his press conference, Joseph Cirincione of the Carnegie Endowment questioned Dr Hamza as to how all this activity was kept secret from Vienna's International Atomic Energy Agency.

'Of course,' he replied, 'Israel made a lot of fuss about it so it was difficult to stay off the topic. When we went into the initial stages, the French reactor at Osiraq (subsequently destroyed by the Israeli Air Force) was not working so there were no problems. Later we went into the enrichment program and that was in clear violation of the Nuclear Nonproliferation Treaty. Then the inspectors arrived and we would just lock the doors to the areas where we were working. We would take them on a path that was constructed so that we could bypass the locked doors behind which we were feverishly busy trying to enrich uranium and design the bomb.'

After the attack on Osiraq, said the Iraqi physicist, the nuclear weapons team went from about five hundred to seven thousand people over about five years (Western intelligence sources have indicated that by the time UNSCOM left, the staff was about twenty thousand).

Asked how long he would expect it would take Iraq now to produce a 'workable nuclear device', Dr Hamza replied:

'We had a clear nuclear program that you could look at as having two parts to it. The fissile part (material that is especially amenable to fission and readily usable for the core of the atom bomb) was always a bit of a problem. It took us ten years to solve it.

'Don't forget that with such a bomb, there are a number of basic components. The trigger system, which was working, was not the greatest but it was good enough. Also, the explosives (to detonate the bomb) were not as good as we would have liked.'

Question: If (Saddam) were to try to use a bomb on Israel, for instance, would it be air dropped?

Answer: 'Yes, I think that is why work was still being done. When you have a nuclear weapon, you need to harden it so that it can take the stresses of the journey, staying together and working. Hardening it effectively (so that its components wouldn't come apart in transit) was not possible in 1990. We barely managed to make a mock-up of an actual bomb without a core. Working on the actual hardening started after the war: (by the late Nineties) they had most of the components hardened so that a bomb could stay together during a trip. I also think explosive groups are more effective now since they have a smaller design.'

Asked about the consequences of sanctions against Iraq, the potential of an inflow of scientists to Iraq, and how that affected his timeline for the reconstitution of a viable Iraqi nuclear threat, Hamza replied (before Gulf War 2):

'Right now, I don't know if the uranium is there, but the design is there. The construction is difficult and would probably take a few months. It all depends on how they get the fissile material. Saddam can either start a fissile material program in Iraq – the enrichment program – in which case it may take him two or three years to have it. Or he can get it (smuggled) from abroad, like from Russia. Then he will have it immediately.'

Another issue raised was how Saddam would physically deploy an atom bomb if he were to acquire nuclear capability. Queries were raised as to whether the atom bomb project would be a secret weapon to be used in an emergency or would there be a declaratory policy. How did he envision that Saddam would actually deploy nuclear capability?

Dr Hamza's reply was that he did not believe Saddam would keep it a secret. He went on: 'If he has one (atom bomb), he will keep it a secret. If he has more than one, there is no advantage for him to keep it a secret any longer. I think he will test one because that is what the project was for. Then he will declare himself a nuclear power and he will use it to his maximum advantage.'

To this Hamza added a rider that Saddam would definitely *need* to test one to assure himself that he actually possesses the atom bomb.

Another issue was whether Iraq's bomb(s) would it fit into (Scud) missiles?

'Originally, no,' he declared, 'because the explosives were too large. They were something like four feet wide and weighed a ton-and-half. That was just too big.' Since then, he intimated, the bomb had been considerably reduced in size.

Following numerous debriefing sessions, David Albright made the point that Dr Hamza's story was not the last word on Iraq's efforts to acquire nuclear weapons-related information from the US or other Western countries. According to a technical specialist who subsequently reviewed many of his transcripts, he did not disclose many other avenues of acquiring information that were available to Iraq in the 1980s (or Iran in the 1990s).

Hamza himself concludes that once information had been declassified (or is otherwise in the public domain) it can spread rapidly. Advances in information technology and communication systems now enable an individual to access data electronically from just about any place in the world. It was his view that a more effective approach would be 'to understand the bottlenecks' of the would-be proliferator and act accordingly. That way, he suggested, suppliers could alert authorities that such information or equipment was being sought.

By way of example, Hamza and his team late in 1987 discussed with several German companies the procurement of a $200 million foundry that would be able to melt, purify, cast and machine refractory metals. Iraq specifically mentioned tungsten, but the real plan was that the foundry be used to process uranium into components for nuclear weapons.

He elaborated: 'During the negotiations we suddenly realized that the firms involved were actually willing to sell all these technologies to us. At the same time we were warned that they were complicated. For all that, some astonishment was expressed that we were entering such a field and that the costs would be high. It seemed that the companies were prepared even to disregard the requirements for export licenses by making special arrangements and packing equipment under covers which made the export seem natural.'

Dr Hamza disclosed that they 'even indicated that they knew the equipment was not for peaceful purposes'. It could only have been intended for the most sophisticated type of weapons manufacture, he reckoned.

In the end, Iraq did not accept the foundry offer. Saddam's scientists feared that the 'turn-key' job would have provided the Germans with the ability to learn the location of the Al Atheer facility and possibly discover that it was involved in nuclear weapons production.

What this episode did provide was the guidelines needed for Saddam to subsequently procure, piecemeal, all the foundry equipment needed for its nuclear weapons plant which was eventually bought from several countries. It also used the design of the foundry offered by the Germans to manufacture its own uranium processing plant at Al Atheer.

To come back to the two Germans involved in Iraq's nuclear weapons program, Bruno Stemmler and Karl Heinz Schaab, it was two years before the Iraqi role in developing a centrifuge separation process for enriching uranium at the walled-off Building 22 at Rashdiya was revealed.

Schaab worked for many years as a specialist at MAN New Technology in Munich, a contract company that developed many components for the gas-ultracentrifuge, a sophisticated technique for the enrichment of uranium: It is also the source of energy in modern light-water reactors. But the same separation technology can be applied to the enrichment of weapons grade uranium, which was why European governments had so strictly categorized it.

Schaab's aptitude was ultra-specific, focused as it was on the core of the centrifuge, the so-called rotor. Some rotors run at 60,000 rpm, i.e. over 1,000 Hz, which places extremely high demands on the structure of the materials employed in the manufacturing process. The rotor-blades, consequently, are made either of flow-forming managing (alloy) steel or carbon fiber or composite materials since steel rotors have a physical limit.

This man had little compunction in handing over years of complex and secret European research to his newfound friends in Iraq. Up to that point, it had already cost the Munich company millions of dollars. At his trial, after returning voluntarily to Germany from Brazil, where he had fled, Schaab admitted that he sold classified MAN blueprints of a subcritical centrifuge to the Iraqis for $40,000. Thirty-six carbon fiber rotors, equipment and technical assistance for about a million dollars followed soon afterwards.

Another German involved in clandestine nuclear activities was Alfred Hempel, who supplied nuclear items to many countries, including Pakistan, India and South Africa.

He sold hundreds of tons of heavy water, an item used in natural uranium-driven reactors as a moderator for triggering neutron-flow, thus gaining plutonium directly from the natural uranium without the difficult process of enrichment. In correspondence found in subsequent investigations it was shown that Hempel declared his heavy water shipments as 'Coca Cola'.

The true extent of foreign, and in particular, German involvement in the development of the Iraqi missile and nuclear program will probably never be known. As an UNSCOM spokesman put it to me, 'While we know most of what went on, there are some serious gaps. Our job was terminated prematurely and I fear that the West might ultimately pay a serious price for this lapse[1].'

Many more people were involved in Iraq's subterfuge to develop its weapons of mass destruction than those actually uncovered by UN arms inspection officials. What we do know is that a lot of what was delivered was useful technical information, without which nothing would have been achieved. Much else was secret and almost everything in documents (since released) was then highly classified.

What become clear long after the first invasion of Iraq by the Allies was the way that Iraq - in collusion with dozens of European firms (including some in Britain) - violated Western 'dual-use' laws relating to the export of equipment that might have been useful in developing WMD. Some of these details, arcane perhaps, to those not of a scientific bent, were unveiled in Washington DC later by Michael Rietz, defense attorney for some of the German nationals most closely associated with Iraq's clandestine weapons programs[2].

His client list included Dietrich Hinze and Karl Heinz Schaab as well as the owners of the firm that sold flow-forming machines to Iraq, Leifeld & Co. This material was used in the development of Saddam's missile program.

It was Rietz's contention that, in its own long-term interests, the West needed to be aware of what was taking place and how it all originally came together. As he stated, their intelligence agencies had to clearly understand the processes involved so that history did not repeat itself and that this was an ongoing process[3].

About the same time the head of Britain's Special Intelligence Service (SIS) warned that there were more than a dozen countries involved in developing their own WMD arsenals. Others, including the Americans, believed even then that there could be more. In this regard, Iranian aspirations to acquire WMD (including the bomb) have been highlighted several times in recent years.

What is important about the people that Rietz represented, is that almost without exception, money was the prime motive and the majority of those who opted to go underground for 'rogue states' often had decades of experience in some of Germany's defense-related industries. For instance, Schaab took with him to Baghdad everything he knew - including documents and blueprints - about centrifuge technology, which is at the heart of one of the systems involved in enriching weapons grade uranium.

In his talk, sponsored by Washington's Institute for Science and International Technology, Rietz made clear that he offered nothing remarkable. What he did provide was a behind-the-scenes glimpse at how some of these crimes were committed, how people and governments were manipulated as well as details about Iraq's massive undercover role in Europe. These agents operated almost entirely out of its embassies.

To achieve its objectives, Baghdad eventually bought into and, at one stage, actually owned some of the firms involved. Rietz detailed the manner and amounts of cash that changed hands and, more pertinently, how far advanced Saddam was in achieving his aim of building his bomb.

Dietrich Hinze's story is of particular interest. According to Rietz, he was an engineer with an impressive technical background in weapons-related matters. His contacts were worldwide and, as was shown at his trial, he was a key figure in helping Iraq contact other suppliers of high-tech items in Germany.

One of the main activities of his firm H+H (*Herstellung und Handel*) was the production and sale of vertical-flow-forming machines (most of them developed by Hinze). This process allows flow-forming (i.e. non-cutting machining) of thick-walled, high-tensile steel tubes to make them thinner and lighter in order to be viable for high-precision military purposes. The product that eventually emerges is especially useful in the field of rocketry. It can also be used as the steel-rotor in a centrifuge for uranium enrichment.

However, the flow-forming components produced by H+H also had civilian applications: they might be used in pressure tanks, gas cylinders and even pressure cookers. This gap was vigorously exploited by Iraq.

Rietz's explanation how Hinze first made contact with Saddam's people is important. It emphasizes the exploitative nature of Saddam's intelligence service and, to some extent, how the Iranians might possibly still be managing their acquisitions right now.

In April 1987, H+H was contacted by Meed International, a British firm owned by an Iraqi network responsible for the purchase of military equipment. The parent company, located in Taji, near the capital, was Nassr Establishment for Mechanical Industry Ltd. Since the Iran-Iraq war was still very much on the go and the West was much more predisposed towards Baghdad than towards Tehran's Mullahs, no objections were raised at the time by Western governments. In any event, it all appeared to be legitimate to Meed.

During contact negotiations between Hinze and Nassr's directors, it soon became clear that Iraq wanted to produce artillery in the 122mm-262mm range and for this they needed flow-forming equipment. At his trial, Hinze admitted that the objective became clear at an early stage, but he did or said nothing to halt the process.

The German's job, apart from the supply of equipment and know-how, was to visit Iraq several times for the purpose of installing it all. It was then that he became aware that some of the items were also related to Iraq's Scud missile program. Altogether nine flow-forming machines were sold by H+H, each worth between $1m and $2m.

Initially, the process was complicated by a lack of funds. When H+H first approached their German bankers for additional capital to expand production, they refused financial help since H+H couldn't provide the necessary securities. When the Iraqis offered to buy a fifty per cent stake in the venture, H+H had no option but to accept, which was how a Nassr subsidiary, Al-Arabien, came to have a shareholding in the German firm. Curiously, almost overnight, or as soon as the money appeared, offers from German financial organizations flowed in.

In the next three years, until about the time of the invasion of Kuwait, H+H supplied machines, tools and equipment for the production of rockets and ballistic missiles worth roughly $25m.

The technical side was also covered by the Iraqis. In the Scud program, for example, Baghdad had difficulties with combustion chambers that needed a double-walled design. The cavity between the two walls was only 2mm and, on their own, the Iraqi's couldn't get it right. Hinze consequently invented several new design aspects that were later experimentally verified and applied in modified versions of the missile called Al Hussein (four hundred mile range) and Al Abbas (range about five-hundred-and-eighty miles). Iraq was later alleged to have had a program for a larger intercontinental missile named Al Abid. This was a three-stage rocket with the booster made up of three linked Scuds.

Subsequently, in 1992, Hinze and a colleague, Hutten, were arrested for the violation of Germany's AWG/AWV Dual-Use Laws. It is notable that at

Hinze's trial, his lawyer (Rietz) pointed out that the German government as well as the international community were also to blame for what had taken place in Iraq.

For years, he told the assembly, the guiding rule of export controls in Germany (and some other European states) had been largely *laissez-faire*. This created an environment where an individual exporter could feel endorsed and comfortable about lacking political sensitivity with regard to illegal exports. This was especially so in Germany, he added, where there was an export policy that was driven by the aim of increasing export figures 'at any price'.

Significantly, the trial judges expressed the opinion that the German export control department BAW (today BaFa) had done a poor job. Their checks were cursory, superficial and clearly inadequate, they declared. This was perhaps understandable since many on their staff were poorly trained and there were about seventy people checking eighty thousand applications a year. That made it easy to skirt controls, they stated in their findings.

Rietz again: 'Even the BND, the German Secret Police, sold millions of dollars' worth of high-tech arms to Iraq in the Eighties through a cover company called Telemit. The BND also trained members of the Iraqi secret service in Augsburg and Munich in some of the latest espionage and other secret service techniques…and in Europe and America, too, Iraqi scientists were educated in advanced high-tech techniques, for example, in the nuclear field.'

Of related interest, according to Rietz, is the manner by which the Pakistanis originally got hold of Alfred Hempel, the man who was to eventually sell them heavy water for the Pakistani nuclear program:

According to the German lawyer, Pakistan first learned about Hempel through the German embassy in Islamabad. The ambassador was contacted by the Pakistani government, who requested the names of suppliers of heavy water. This request was passed through to the Foreign Ministry in Bonn who handed it on to the nuclear research plant in Karslruhe. They, in turn, gave them Hempel's details, from whom they had been buying heavy water for years.

Hempel, playing a discreet role, hired scientists from a variety of German institutions and reputable companies, none of whom guessed where their products were headed. Meanwhile, he founded a sister company in America called Scientific International.

'He participated through this cover company in US tenders and gained important information, and even blueprints that he later sold to Pakistan, India and South Africa,' Rietz disclosed.

How the international community should tackle what had clearly become a global problem involving countries that export products which might have a dual-use application, was also covered in Rietz's talk.

He referred to the publication of an article by John Friedman and Eric Nadler in *The Nation*[4]. Titled 'Nuclear Black Market', it was conceded by the authors that the issues involved were extremely difficult to control. It was they said, a multi-billion-dollar market. There are others who have suggested that the atomic powers should set up totally new international monitoring systems for the export of sensitive nuclear technology and enforce effective controls on multinational corporations.

At very least, suggested Rietz, 'politicians should publicly shame those who are involved in this kind of black market nuclear weapons commerce[5].'

Individuals acting on their own are also sometimes involved and here we have numerous examples over the years among some of the Former Soviet Union countries. Others are also affected.

During this writer's visit to Johannesburg in February 2000, he was approached by a couple of South African trading acquaintances who had been offered 'two bricks' of ^{235}U and ^{238}U by a Rwandan businessman in Kigali. Although the offer might have been bogus, it could not simply be ignored, especially since Rwanda, hamstrung by its own militaristic hubris, has been shown several times in recent years to have played some role as a conduit for uranium by-products from the neighboring Democratic Republic of the Congo.

1   Author's interview with Ewen Buchanan, former spokesman for UNSCOM at UN Headquarters, New York as well as erstwhile UNSCOM weapons inspector in Iraq, Scott Ritter

2   Talk prepared by Michael Rietz: delivered in Washington DC, December 10, 1999

3   Which is one of the reasons why some banned equipment used for making weapons is sometimes allowed to slip through from the West to countries that might be suspected of making WMD. What these people still need to complete the task is often a good barometer of progress that might have been achieved in any new weapons manufacturing venture

4   October, 1999

5   David Albright, President of ISIS, Institute for Science and International Security in Washington DC echoed these sentiments. He said that one way for the West to react would be to require those people and companies who work in sensitive nuclear areas to contact their governments whenever they are irregularly approached by other nations

9

QUESTIONS PERSIST ABOUT THE ROLE OF THE INTERNATIONAL ATOMIC ENERGY AGENCY IN IRAQ

Question: You indicated that Dr Mauricio Zifferero (chosen to run nuclear inspections in Iraq at the end of the Gulf War) while part of the International Atomic Energy Agency process, was knowledgeable about (Saddam's) centrifuge program. The centrifuge was part of Iraq's unsafeguarded (nuclear) program. What did the IAEA do with this knowledge?

Answer: Nothing.

The original question was put to Dr Khidir Hamza at a press conference hosted by Washington DC's Carnegie Endowment for International Peace. It followed the launch of his book *Saddam's Bombmaker* in November 2000.

Other disclosures emerged during the session. About two years before, Saddam had once again called together his nuclear weapons design team: All were mustered at a site about fifty miles from Baghdad.

According to Hamza (and subsequently confirmed by Ambassador Richard Butler, former head of UNSCOM, the UN weapons inspection team in Iraq), 'nuclear weapons work in Iraq never stopped...in fact, after the war we were able to perfect the barriers that made diffusing and enriching uranium possible'. He intimated that this was done, literally, in the face of International Atomic Energy Agency inspections.

What made the issue more immediate, he felt, was the possibility that Iraq by then might have acquired illegal (smuggled) fissile material. Saddam, he intimated, already had just about all the bomb components he needed, strategic assets that were supposed to have been handed over to the UN while UNSCOM was still alive. They never were.

Required to complete the job, Hamza believed, was weapons grade uranium. In this regard and confirmed by several independent sources, Iraqi agents had been vigorously trying to acquire fissile material in Eastern Europe and according to reliable sources quoted by British Prime Minister Tony Blair, in South Africa, itself once a nuclear state. Pretoria produced six atom bombs during the pre-Mandela Apartheid era[1].

In an interview with the author, the President of America's Nuclear Control Institute, Paul Leventhal, maintained that the history of IAEA inspections in Iraq were flawed from the start. 'In 1990, immediately after Iraq invaded Kuwait, the IAEA safeguards chief, Mr Jon Jennekins declared Iraq to be a "solid citizen" under the Treaty on the Nonproliferation of Nuclear Weapons (NPT).' Its cooperation in nuclear matters, Jennekins declared to the delight of the Iraqis, had been 'exemplary'.

According to Hamza, Iraq just then was secretly operating its own large scale Manhattan Project and often doing so 'sometimes within yards of IAEA inspectors'. Concurrently, Leventhal stated, it had launched a massive clandestine crash nuclear weapons program.

Codenamed 'Petrochemical-3' (PC-3) Baghdad was geared to build an atom bomb by diverting highly enriched uranium (HEU) fuel from its IAEA safeguarded research reactors.

Yet, less than three years later, the IAEA director-general Dr Hans Blix, contrary to the evidence available, declared that Iraq had 'never touched' this HEU fuel, despite his inspectors having discovered that Iraqi bomb scientists had cut open some of the fuel.

Interestingly, the person chosen by Blix to lead Vienna's on-site nuclear inspection team in Iraq after the Gulf War was Dr Mauricio Zifferero, the man quoted at the head of this chapter who, coincidentally, also uncovered Saddam's centrifuge (uranium enrichment) program. Of interest here is that prior to joining the IAEA, Zifferero (who died in the late Nineties and was never made accountable for these anomalies) had supervised Italy's supply of plutonium extraction equipment to Iraq.

Hamza: 'Top Iraqi scientists lavished the Italian scientist with gifts. They consistently referred to him as "our man at the IAEA". More salient, Professor Zifferero reported in 1992 that the Iraqi nuclear program "is at zero now". He also "verified" an Iraqi decision to halt the program.'

To cap it, said Hamza, 'three years later - following revelations of Iraq having initiated a program to build the bomb and enough evidence to conclude that Baghdad's nuclear weapons work had never ceased, Hans Blix reported to the IAEA Board that "nothing suggests that a change is warranted".'

Blix went on record as saying that it was the agency's conclusion that 'the essential components of Iraq's clandestine nuclear weapons program had been identified and destroyed, removed or rendered harmless'.

Zifferero's lengthy association with the Iraqi regime - first as a member of an Italian nuclear-related delegation and later as head of the IAEA inspection team - warrants close examination, if only because it gives the international community something of an insight to what the Iraqi dictator might possibly have been doing, declared Leventhal. According to a report by Jonathan Broder in the *New York Times*, the IAEA today refuses to comment on the specifics of Hamza's criticism[2].

'It denies that its inspectors were soft on Iraq before the war, saying that under the Nuclear Nonproliferation Treaty they were allowed to inspect only those installations that Iraq had declared,' Broder reports. David Albright, President of the Institute for Science and International Security, a Washington arms control organization, echoes this view.

'The IAEA system was never geared to detect nuclear weaponization,' Albright told me.

At the same time, Hamza concurred, there was a most elaborate system of obfuscation in place. He explained that 'we understood what the (IAEA) inspector's limits were. He was not allowed to ask questions outside these limits, so once he arrived at a nuclear plant, he would be taken along a set path and answered only within the scope of what he was permitted to inquire about. Then he would leave.

'All the while, right next door, we would be working on whatever we were doing at the time to enrich uranium or design an atom bomb.'

It was notable, said this former Iraqi physicist, that when news first emerged that Iraq was working on fissile material, 'we were terrified that we would receive questions from the inspectors. But even that didn't happen when international news reports claimed that we were doing something illegal. They didn't ask us any questions. They simply gave us the benefit of the doubt and never even asked us what we were doing or why we were doing it.'

Until the 1995 defection of General Kamel, 'the IAEA unreservedly, during years of ongoing inspections, accepted Iraq's story about its nuclear program being nothing more than a small research lab,' he added.

With the departure of Blix as head of the IAEA (coupled to disclosures about Saddam's large-scale nuclear weapons program), the Vienna-based organization acknowledged that the problems faced by the nuclear monitoring body were not unique to nuclear non proliferation. In a book on the history of the International Atomic Energy Agency, David Fischer declared in mitigation that 'any other arms control or disarmament treaty, for instance the Chemical Weapons Convention or Biological Weapons Convention, could run into similar problems'.

The Iraqi case, he said, showed that a determined and authoritarian state with very large financial resources and a skilled and dedicated nuclear establishment, could indeed defy its obligations under the NPT and evade detection 'for many years'. This evasion, he suggested, 'may have been helped by the fact that during the Iran-Iraq War, Western governments tended to tilt towards Iraq which, as all are aware, also received help from the Soviet Union'.

Fischer goes on: 'Whether the clandestine program would have remained undetected once the large electromagnetic isotope separation (EMIS) plants went into full production is still an open question.' So, too, is the uniqueness of Iraq's circumstances - its internal political structure, its technical and financial resources and its regional and international political environment.

One needs to carefully examine the official function of IAEA to understand what went wrong in Iraq and exactly why this happened. We also have to look at what has been done since to correct matters.

The IAEA was originally established as an autonomous organization under the United Nations Charter in 1957. It offers a broad range of services and programs based on the needs of its one-hundred-and-thirty member states (which includes Israel).

The first function of the IAEA Safeguards Division is essentially to ensure that inventories of known fissile materials such as HEU or plutonium are accounted for within annual error margins (about 17.5 lbs of 239Pu and 55 lbs of HEU). Broadly speaking, the purpose of the monitoring process is to detect possible diversions of what may be very small quantities of material from civil to military use (such as the weapons grade uranium that the international community knew Iraq had before 'Operation Desert Storm') and which was monitored by the IAEA on a bi-annual basis.

In Iraq, the duties of the IAEA and UNSCOM were strictly delineated, the latter being thoroughly intrusive - a vigorous international police action if you like - in trying to uncover Saddam's weapons of mass destruction. For his part, Saddam did everything he could to stop the inspectors from doing what they were tasked. Curiously (with subtle support from the French, Beijing and Moscow) Baghdad was quite successful in this kind of obscurantism.

One also needs to bear in mind that Iraq still had the fuel it intended to use in the original partly-completed Osiraq nuclear reactor destroyed in an Israeli air strike in the Seventies and which the IAEA inspected regularly. It is (or was) roughly ninety lbs of HEU - with an average enrichment of 84 per cent - contained in a hundred-and-seventy-five fuel elements.

By the time this stuff was removed, Iraq's processing line to make weapons grade HEU was all but 'ready to go and it would have taken Saddam only months to complete the task', said Hamza. But that is a story in itself. When it was eventually shipped out of the country, the IAEA had a devil of a job trying to find a country to accept it for safekeeping, since some of it had already been irradiated.

Another Hamza confirmation was that Saddam originally intended using this safeguarded fuel in his weapons program. The Iraqis felt that they could possibly accomplish this between inspection routines. We know this, too, from documents uncovered by UNSCOM inspectors. There is evidence that he had already tampered with the fuel rods by shearing off their caps in preparation to moving them for further enrichment to weapons grade level.

Also interesting is that in recent years, the IAEA has upgraded its nuclear inspection routines. These now cover some of the gaps that were vulnerable before information regarding the Iraqi nuclear program was exposed. Vienna also admits that several of the atom bomb drawings that should originally have been handed over to its action team by Iraqi scientists never were, a critical lapse in judgment. The West almost paid dearly for that oversight. Of note, they are still missing in spite of Iraq having been overrun by Coalition Forces in 2003.

The bulk of Iraq's nuclear effort only came to light initially in 1995 following the defection of Saddam Hussein's son-in-law to Jordan. General Hussein Kamel was able to reveal what had been going for the simple reason that he had been at the head of its Ministry of Industry and Military Industrialization (MIMI). This was the same body that ran Saddam's nuclear (and other WMD) weapons programs.

In exile, Kamel told the West about the mysterious 'chicken farm' where millions of documents that had a direct bearing on many illegal weapons programs could be found. Though these had been pretty well 'sanitized' by the time the inspectors got there, his revelations laid the basis for uncovering the rest of what Saddam was trying to achieve nuclearwise. Ultimately it also resulted in the destruction of many more Iraqi WMD-related facilities. Further details about the Iraqi atom bomb project were provided by the Federation of American Scientists in a paper[3] titled 'Iraqi Nuclear Weapons'.

The FAS makes the point that while Iraq's nuclear weapons program plan (started in 1988) had the objective of producing a small arsenal of weapons, with the first to be completed in 1999, there were three main components. These were design and weaponization, production of weapons grade uranium and the production of a missile delivery system. As might have been expected, they had not progressed at an equal pace, the Federation disclosed.

Working from captured resources or from information provided by defectors, FAS reached the following conclusions:

- The weapons design component was the most successful of the three interrelated disciplines. With the solution of the few problems that remained in January 1991, the PC-3 Fourth (weaponization) Group was confident that a viable design could be produced fairly close to schedule.

- Production of HEU by enrichment of domestic uranium pursued through the two parallel lines of EMIS and gas centrifuges lagged. Other sources have indicated that by then Saddam had already put into motion the clandestine means of acquiring plutonium or HEU illegally from Former Soviet Union states.

- Design and development of the Al Hussein missile (with modifications) had progressed to a point where development was anticipated for completion within about six months. But 'Operation Desert Storm' intervened. The design incorporated a missile with a separate warhead capable of delivering a one-ton payload over a distance of four hundred miles.

Notably, the crash program that was initiated in 1990 was planned to include the chemical processing of both unirradiated and irradiated research reactor fuel placed under IAEA safeguards. This was initiated in a bid to recover enough HEU to use in the first atom bomb that Saddam's scientists hoped to build.

The re-enrichment of part of it was to have been through the use of a fifty-machine centrifuge cascade that was to have been specially constructed for the purpose. Had HEU recovery and the enrichment process been successful, it would have resulted in the availability, late in 1991, of enough HEU to arm a single atom bomb in the twenty-kiloton range.

By then Iraq was in the process of constructing a facility deemed to be capable of producing a few thousand centrifuge machines a year, a hundred of which would have produced enough HEU for two small nuclear devices. Also planned were additional measures such as the fabrication of the implosion package.

Subsequently, according to Barton Gellman[4] of *The New York Times*, the IAEA started to acknowledge gaps in its information about the Iraqi nuclear program. However, Vienna was unable to verify exactly how much the Baghdad government had accomplished in its efforts to devise a working nuclear weapons design because several of the drawings that should have been handed over to the IAEA Action Team went missing. Shortly afterwards there were reports from several sources - including UNSCOM weapons inspector Scott Ritter (told to this writer, in case his memory again fails him), that Saddam had the components, though not the HEU for three completed atom bombs.

In another development, according to the IAEA, Iraq at first denied that it had built molds for the manufacture of explosive lenses. Then it admitted that it had, but said that it couldn't 'find' them. Similarly, Baghdad at first denied casting an explosive lens. It subsequently admitted casting one cylindrical charge of about five inches (120mm) that was tested for velocity and pressure.

As we now know, the man appointed by UN secretary general Kofi Annan to head UNMOVIC, UNSCOM's successor shortly before the second Gulf War was, to the astonishment of all, Hans Blix. This was the same individual who cocked things up so badly the first time round. There were quite a few UNSCOM old timers in the UN office when I called after hearing about the appointment and to a man, they were aghast.

That he blundered badly in the past is a view not only shared by certain members of his staff, but also by people like Charles Duelfer, former chief weapons inspector. He told David Wastell of London's *Telegraph* that he 'feared that Hans Blix would concede too much during discussions with Baghdad officials on arrangements for inspections[5].'

While the Coalition invasion put paid to that, the question still begs why anybody in his right mind – never mind the UN secretary general - would choose somebody to do a job when that individual had shown the international community *repeatedly* that he had neither the courage nor the strength of will to manage it properly in the past. To this cynical hack, it sounds a lot like jobs for pals.

We already know what Per Ahlmark, a former deputy prime minister of Sweden originally said about Blix's appointment: comments along the lines of the world having been amply warned about Blix's weaknesses. 'He has a track record of compounded failure,' was apparently his off-the-cuff statement to a reporter who asked him about it.

Writing for Project Syndicate, Ahlmark said that he had known Blix for more than forty years. The man was his deputy in 1960 when he was leader of the Swedish Liberal Youth organization. Since then he had closely followed his career when he became Sweden's foreign minister for a year and was later a director of the International Atomic Energy Agency in Vienna.

'Personally,' he wrote, 'Blix is amiable and has a sense of humor: Politically he is weak and easily fooled. I can think of few European officials who would have been less suitable for a showdown with Saddam. Indeed, it was with utter disbelief that I watched the television news about Blix's negotiations with the Iraqi dictator's henchmen.' Ahlmark was of the view that Blix was 'a total misfit in his appointment to head UN weapons inspectors in a new round of confrontations with the Iraqi government.'

He added: 'He is naive and relatively ignorant about technical details, his field is international law and he is easily misled.'

At the same time, Blix's appointment could very well be construed as an indictment of the way the United Nations is being run in the New Millennium. Having a useful fool in such a top position was necessary to please at least three important UN Security Council, members, namely: China, Russia, and France discreetly referred by their colleagues in the chamber, I'm told, as 'The Tempestuous Troika'. Ahlmark also maintained that regardless of how the Iraqi situation developed, 'the United Nations neglected its duties by asking a wimp to lead the inspectors who are supposed to stand up to the Brute of Baghdad'.

Nor was Vienna left out of the equation: the IAEA had blundered in Iraq. Many specialists were concerned that that the agency had originally permitted Saddam to retain sufficient low-enriched uranium (LEU) to make at least two atom bombs if his scientists had been able to run it through a small clandestine enrichment plant to make weapons grade HEU. Indeed, Washington's Nuclear Control Institute[6] warned as much late in 1999.

Moreover, Paul Leventhal subsequently told this writer that IAEA inspectors had by then not examined this uranium for several years. Also disturbing was the fact that Vienna had allowed Iraq to retain 1.7 metric tons of LEU enriched to 2.6 per cent, as well as about thirteen tons of natural uranium stocks[6].

Which brings us to the most recent developments. Prior to the invasion we were given the dossier published by Tony Blair in September 2002. The British Prime minister made a number of allegations that are worth investigating.

'Following the departure of weapons inspectors in 1998,' he stated, 'there had been an accumulation of intelligence indicating that Iraq was making concerted covert efforts to acquire dual-use technology and materials with nuclear applications. Iraq's known holdings of processed uranium were then supposed to be under IAEA supervision, but there was intelligence that Iraq had sought the supply of significant quantities of uranium from Africa. Iraq had no active civil nuclear power program or nuclear power plants. Therefore it had no legitimate reason to acquire uranium.'

Mr Blair indicated that intelligence sources had shown more procurement activity since 1998, including attempts to purchase:

- Vacuum pumps that could be used to create and maintain pressures in a gas centrifuge cascade needed to enrich uranium.
- An entire magnet production line of the correct specification for use in the motors and top bearings of gas centrifuges. It appears that Iraq was attempting to acquire a capability to produce them on its own rather than rely on foreign procurement.
- Anhydrous Hydrogen Fluoride (AHF) and fluorine gas. AHF is commonly used in the petrochemical industry and the Saddam regime imported significant amounts. Fluorine is also used in the semiconductor fabrication industry and again, Iraq did not have much of an industrial base for that either. But it can be diverted to converting uranium into uranium hexafluoride for use in gas centrifuge cascades. AHF would also be useful in at least some synthetic processes for nerve agents, mainly sarin (in the case of Iraq), but also for producing difluor - the latter readily forms sarin when added to the proper amount of isopropyl alcohol, and GF (cyclosarin) with cyclohexanol.
- One large filament winding machine which could be diverted to manufacture carbon fiber gas centrifuge rotors.
- A large balancing machine that could be used in initial centrifuge balancing work.
- Iraq also made repeated covert attempts to acquire a large quantity (sixty thousand or more) of specialized aluminum tubes. Since this item is subject to international export controls, because of its potential application in the construction of gas centrifuges used to enrich uranium, there was no definitive intelligence that it was destined for a nuclear program.

During the period that UNSCOM was active in Iraq, Mr Blair noted that the body surveyed more than a thousand sites. It also carried out two-hundred-and-seventy-two separate inspections. In this time, despite Iraqi obstruction, obscurantism and intimidation, UN inspectors uncovered details of chemical, biological, nuclear and ballistic missile programs.

Major UNSCOM/IAEA achievements included the destruction of forty thousand munitions for chemical weapons, more than two thousand tons of chemical precursors and roughly four hundred tons of chemical warfare agent. Also completed was the dismantling of Iraq's prime chemical weapons development and production complex at Al Muthanna together with a range of key production equipment; the destruction of forty-eight Scud-type missiles, eleven mobile launchers and fifty-six sites, thirty warheads filled with chemical agents as well as twenty conventional warheads.

There was also the destruction of the Al Hakam biological weapons facility and a range of production equipment, seed stocks and growth media for biological weapons and the discovery in 1991, of samples of indigenously produced highly enriched uranium. All this, together, ultimately forced Iraq's acknowledgment of uranium enrichment programs as well as attempts to preserve key components of its prohibited nuclear weapons program. Finally said the Prime Minister, there was the removal and destruction of the infrastructure for the nuclear weapons program, including the Al Atheer weaponization/testing facility.

Dealing with the situation since 1998, Mr Blair disclosed that there had been no UN-mandated weapons inspections in Iraq since that year. In an effort to enforce Iraqi compliance with its disarmament and monitoring obligations, the UN Security Council had passed Resolution 1284 in December 1999. This established UNMOVIC as a successor organization to UNSCOM and called on Iraq to give its inspectors 'immediate, unconditional and unrestricted access to any and all areas, facilities, equipment, records and means of transport'.

Full compliance with these conditions would be a prerequisite for the eventual suspension and lifting of sanctions, said Mr Blair.

His dossier also noted that Iraq had allowed the IAEA to carry out an annual inspection of a stockpile of nuclear material (depleted natural and low-enriched uranium) for the previous three years. This, he said, had led some countries and western commentators to conclude that Iraq was meeting its nuclear disarmament and monitoring obligations, erroneously as it turned out.

But, says Blair, as the IAEA had already pointed out, this annual inspection did 'not serve as a substitute for the verification activities required by the relevant resolutions of the UN Security Council'. He also recorded that Dr Hans Blix, in his capacity as Executive Chairman of UNMOVIC, and Dr Mohammed el-Baradei, Director General of the IAEA, had declared that in the absence of inspections, it was impossible to verify Iraqi compliance with its UN disarmament and monitoring obligations.

Significantly, Blair added: 'In April 1999, an independent UN panel of experts noted that "the longer inspection and monitoring activities remain suspended, the more difficult the comprehensive implementation of Security Council resolutions becomes, increasing the risk that Iraq might reconstitute its proscribed weapons programs".'

In fact, said Blair, 'the departure of the inspectors greatly diminished the ability of the international community to monitor and assess Iraq's continuing attempts to reconstitute its chemical, biological, nuclear and ballistic missile programs.'

And Now Iran...

Meanwhile, several international authorities have equated the Iraqi scenario in the past with what the West believes is happening in Iran today.

In a submission before Congress in March 2000, CIA Director George Tenet told the Senate Foreign Relations Committee[7] that Iran also aspired to acquiring an arsenal of nuclear weapons. Only months before, General Anthony C. Zinni[8], formerly responsible for US military forces throughout the Middle East, believed that Tehran 'would acquire nuclear weapons within a few years'.

The CIA challenged Zinni's time frame, stating in Congress that Iran could only be a serious nuclear factor within anything between seven and fifteen years. Critics of this reckoning point to Langley's botched estimates of Pakistan's thermonuclear efforts: Estimates have since been upgraded to anything between three and eight years for Tehran to conduct its first atom bomb test.

1   South Africa acquired some strange bedfellows following the accession to power of President Nelson Mandela. He had not been in office long before the head of Tehran's Atomic Energy Organization of Iran and deputy president for Iran's Atomic Affairs, Reza Amrollahi arrived at the Pelindaba offices of Dr Waldo Stumpf, chief executive of the South African Atomic Energy Corporation (AEC). Amrollahi told Stumpf that he had a 'shopping list' of items required for the manufacture of atomic bombs. Despite vocal South African and Iranian protestations to the contrary (the issue was even raised in Parliament in Cape Town), Pik Botha, then a minister in the new black government subsequently confirmed the incident. He told Mungo Soggit, a senior writer on Johannesburg's *Mail & Guardian*, that the event not only took place, but that he was there at Stumpf's insistence. For a more complete report on that event see Jane's *International Defense Review*, September, 1997

2   'Saddam's Bomb' by Jonathan Broder, *The New York Times*, October 1, 2000: 'Arms Control and Verification - Safeguards in a Changing World': International Atomic Energy Agency, Vienna, 1997

3   'Iraqi Nuclear Weapons': Federation of American Scientists (FAS), Updated by John Pike; November 3, 1998

4   'Iraq Work Toward A-Bomb Reported - US Was Told of Implosion Devices' by Barton Gellman: *New York Times*, September 30, 1988

5   *The Weekly Telegraph:* Issue # 584 October 2, 2002

6   'New Inspection Plan for Iraq Leaves Loopholes Big Enough to Drive an Atom Bomb Through': Nuclear Control Institute, Washington DC

7   'Weapons of Mass Destruction: A New Dimension in US Middle East Policy' by George Tenet, Director, Central Intelligence in testimony before Senate Foreign Relations Committee, Washington, March 21, 2000

8   *Aviation Week & Space Technology*, December 13, 1999, p33

10

NEW ERA THREAT;
IRAQ'S BIOLOGICAL WEAPONS

'Chemical (and biological) weapons work. They are undergoing revolutionary developments which make them practical and very lethal participants in those human affairs which are ultimately resolved with blood and iron. Be ignorant and be damned, and condemn your children as well.'

Dr James A.F. Compton: September 1987

About the time Dr Compton wrote that well considered introduction to his primer, *Military Chemical and Biological Agents*, another American, Dr Jane Orient published an article on the subject in *The Journal of the American Medical Association*. It was titled 'Chemical and Biological Warfare: Should Defenses be Researched and Deployed?'

Dr Orient made observations that were strident at a time when such matters were regarded by the medical world as arcane; especially where they concerned Third World nations and their relationships to the West[1].

She pointed out that, against civilian populations, chemical and biological weapons were extremely attractive because of simple economics. Casualties, she wrote, might cost $2,000 per square mile with conventional weapons, $800 with nerve gas and a single dollar with biological weapons. This was a groundbreaking prognosis and her peers acknowledged it accordingly.

It is possible that the now departed Saddam asked himself long ago why he needed to go nuclear since other options were so much cheaper?

Richard Butler, the Australian executive chairman of the UN Special Commission (on Iraq) reinforced this view. Deadly germs, he said in one of his interviews, were still the most mysterious and dangerous weapons in Iraq's hands. 'They are easier and cheaper to make than any other arms and they can be deployed with less difficulty.'

Looked at from another perspective, he stated that they must be of immense value to the country 'if it is important enough (for Iraq) to forgo the billions of dollars in revenues that it could have obtained if its (weapons) programs were fully disclosed to the UN'.

It is estimated that Baghdad has lost as much as $200 billion in oil receipts since sanctions were put in place by the world body. This figure is roughly half the value of the international aid package given to Korea in 1997 to put its economic house in order, or about as much as was given to Brazil in 2002. It is vital to ask, then, why does Iraq choose to deprive itself of so much of its wealth?

Ewen Buchanan, a spokesman for the now defunct UN Special Commission (UNSCOM) might have provided us with part of the answer. He told Washington's *Middle East Policy* at a time when his organization was still active, that Iraq's refusal to allow the United Nations weapons inspectors to do their work, 'represents a black hole of uncertainty that faces the international community'. It was a serious matter with enormous long-term consequences, he reckoned.

Particularly relevant was Baghdad's refusal to cooperate on biological warfare issues. 'That side of UNSCOM's work had not only been the most difficult, but of the four options - nuclear, chemical, biological and long-range missiles - Iraq had been singularly intransigent about what it has done with all its biological weapon assets,' he said adding that Baghdad had gone to absurd lengths in order to prevent biowarfare inspections, 'and it is this aspect that really worries us.'

Still unaccounted for, Mr Buchanan explained, were thirty tons of Iraq's biological warfare agents. The tally included four-hundred-and-twenty gallons of botulinum toxin, more than four hundred gallons of anthrax as well as two tons of aflatoxins that, in its various mycotoxinic states (and if dispersed in aerosol and droplet clouds) could, in theory, poison the entire world. An unlikely event, but that was the way that an authority described the situation.

Trichothecene mycotoxins (the by-products of fungal metabolism) were probably used by the old Soviet Union as a toxic weapon that could cause death and misery by inhalation and contact on the skin in a variety of wars that included Afghanistan, Laos and Kampuchea.

Significantly, the thirty tons is only Iraq's declaration, and one which UNSCOM was never able to verify. Also, the commission for which Mr Buchanan worked told the Security Council that the quantity of yeast extract (one of the growth agents for making biological agents) and known to UNSCOM to have been imported for Saddam Hussein's biowarfare program by the Technical and Scientific Materials Import Division, would be sufficient for three to four times more anthrax production than was declared by the Saddam regime.

Which is why Al Hakam, one of those obscure, sand-brown, quasi-military establishments stuck away in the desert a short distance from the

Tigris River, south-west of Baghdad was found to be so interesting shortly after the UN organization started its work.

Initially, it had nothing more to recommend it than its size; a succession of oddly-dispersed large buildings, warehouses, living quarters, workshops as well as recreational areas spread out over an area of about a dozen square miles. Apart from the standard security fence and nominal defenses (which included guardposts such as one finds everywhere in the Middle East, together with some well-camouflaged bunkers), there appeared to be almost no defenses. Consequently, the place seemed innocuous and was ignored by Allied Forces during 'Operation Desert Storm'.

How different the Iraqi chemical warfare plant at the Al Muthanna State Establishment. This place was the original location for Iraq's biological weapons program. In contrast to Al Hakam, it was totally flattened by Allied bombers in 1991.

Al Muthanna had air defenses, gun towers together with three separate and well-defended perimeter fences. Researchers there carried out lethality evaluations of several biological weapons (BW) agents in animals and examined their growth characteristics and survivability. Agents investigated were anthrax, botulinum toxin (among the deadliest biological agents known to man) and, to a lesser extent, aflatoxin and ricin, work on which was concentrated elsewhere.

That was before the Iraqis moved everything to Salman Pak, a thirty-minute drive south-east of the capital and for a while the national BW headquarters.

Directly after the war, Al Hakam (with its fermentation tanks and ancillary equipment) was one of the places declared by the Baghdad regime as having a legitimate biological capability. The Iraqis stressed that everything that went on there had, what they euphemistically termed, a 'strictly peacetime application'.

Al Hakam, they told UN inspectors, was involved in the production of single-cell protein in yeast as a supplement for chicken feed and in the cultivation of BT (*Bacillus thuringiensis*), a bacterium that acts as an insecticide when applied to crops. On the face of it, there was no reason to believe otherwise. In any event, those products presented to the UN as proof were found to be professionally made and not unlike similar products marketed in the West.

It took UN inspections four more years to discover that the Iraqis were lying. By the time it all came out, it was discovered that of all the sites, Al Hakam was the key to Iraq's BW program. It was then that the world learnt that the Al Hakam Single Cell Protein Production Plant began mass production of anthrax in 1989. Eventually, approximately eight thousand liters of solution with an anthrax spore and cell count of 109/mL was produced. Of this, six thousand liters was used to fill weapons; the remainder was stored on site

Iraq later admitted to Rolf Ekeus, former head of UNSCOM, that it had produced about half a million liters of botulinum and anthrax (again, enough to kill an awful lot of people) and that research work on mycotoxins had begun[2].

In contrast, it is the view of chemical and biological specialist Eric Croddy, that half a million liters seems more than a bit high. And in any event, he declares, it is certainly nothing that Iraq would have freely admitted to[3]. 'Using a *Clostridium botulinum* strain imported from the United States, the Iraqis produced twenty thousand liters of solution containing botulinum toxin of unknown strength and type at Al Hakam and Al Manal during 1989 and 1990. Of this, about half was used in field testing or to fill warheads; all unused toxin was stored at Al Hakam.'

UN officials in New York say they were always suspicious about what was going on at Al Hakam. According to a USAMRIID source, there had been much prodding, probing and false leads before the Iraqis finally admitted that Al Hakam was the site of a plant that produced agents for biological warfare[4]. That happened shortly before the defection of Hussein Kamel, after which Iraqi officials were forced to concede that they had begun an offensive BW program by July 1975.

The first breakthrough came late in 1994 when UNSCOM discovered that the Technical and Scientific Materials Import Division (TSMID) of the Ministry of Industry and Military Industrialization had imported quantities of culture media on behalf of the Ministry of Health. Although Baghdad claimed that the material was intended for disease diagnosis in hospital labs, the TSMID shipment totaled thirty-nine tons packed in 25-100kg drums (which in itself, created suspicion). Usually the stuff comes in packages weighing between 100gm and 500gm.

Also, the quantity was wildly inconsistent with medical needs as, in normal circumstances, hospitals use only small amounts. Moreover, the types of media imported were not suited for diagnostic purposes; rather, they were ideal for the cultivation of BW agents such as anthrax. By early 1999, almost twenty tons of this imported culture media remain unaccounted for.

That was followed by disclosures made by Iraqi General Waffiq al-Sammara'i, former head of Saddam's Military Intelligence who fled the country in 1995 fearing for his life. Speaking from London where he was subsequently granted asylum[5], he said that apart from nuclear, chemical and missile assets, Iraq had 'retained two-hundred-and-fifty containers of BW materials. About half was in dry form (which had no expiry date), he explained, and twenty-five were in liquid suspension', which, he said, would deteriorate with time. The powder is surmised to have been anthrax and the liquid botulinum toxin.

The ultimate break came with the defection to Amman, Jordan in August 1995 of Lt Gen Hussein Kamel Hassan. His revelations forced the Iraqis to admit that they had produced and weaponized one lethal bacterial agent and two toxins[6].

There was more. General Kamel provided information about twenty-five warheads, sixteen of which were filled with botulinum toxin, five with anthrax and four with aflatoxin. By his own account, there were enough of the first two agents, under optimum conditions, to kill a million people. The original target, he admitted, had been Israel as well as Allied Forces together with some of the Arab states that had sided with the West in Gulf War 1.

Subsequent disclosures in Iraq revealed that the missiles had survived the war as well as searches by UNSCOM. They were hidden in railway and irrigation tunnels or buried on the banks of the Tigris River to protect them from bombing raids. Months later, the Iraqis said, everything was transported to a desert site called Nebai and destroyed, though the UN had expressed doubts that this was ever done. The consensus is that they are still hidden away somewhere in the wastes of Iraq. Also, none of the warhead production records have been surrendered, raising questions as to exactly how many were made[7].

That the Iraqi dictator had every intention of using these weapons in combat is evidenced by two American intelligence reports, one sourced to the DIA, the other to the CIA[8].

The Defense Intelligence Agency report (October 11, 1991) describes a modified Su-22 Sukhoi *Fitter* of which a photo had been taken during 'Operation Desert Storm'. The plane, with Iraqi markings, was at the Tallil air base outside An Nasiriyah, roughly halfway between Baghdad and Kuwait.

It revealed 'what resembled a chemical/biological spray tank on the port-side pylon. Enlargements of the original photo showed an air scoop on the top front of the tank, giving rise to the hypothesis about a possible biochemical spray tank'. Hoses and tubing attached to a partly destroyed vehicle parked alongside might have indicated a non-standard decontamination vehicle for biological and chemical munitions. A later (sanitized) CIA report, titled *Iraqi BW Mission Planning* reads:

'In the fall of 1990 (the Iraqi President) ordered plans to be drawn up for the airborne delivery of a BW agent... It called for a test mission of three MiG-21s to conduct an air raid (deleted) using conventional high explosive ordnance. If these aircraft were able to penetrate (deleted) then a second mission was to take off within a few days of the first, using the same flight path and approaches. The second mission, also comprising three MiG-21s and carrying conventional ordnance, was to serve as a decoy for a single Su-22. They would follow the same route but fly (at an altitude) of between 50m and 100m. Optimum delivery altitude for the BW agent was judged at 50m at 400 knots...'

On the first day of the war the three-MiG-mission took off from Tallil but were almost immediately shot down. The launch of the Su-22 (the same aircraft mentioned in the DIA report with the modified tanks) was canceled. There were also reports of a Mirage F1 at Kut Air Force Base with belly drop tanks, which could take three-hundred-and-fifty gallons of biological media.

If there had been any doubts about Saddam's intentions in the Gulf War, these two reports are explicit enough to set them to rest. And since Tallil is much closer to the Gulf than to Israel, Allied ground forces were almost certainly to have been the target. Some doubt has been expressed about the potential efficacy of the operation because the warheads on the BW bombs had no altitude fusing: for all that, there would certainly have been casualties.

Some idea of the damage that might be caused by one aircraft spraying a single biological agent - in a one mile line with downwind travel of twelve miles-an-hour - was given by the World Health Organization in a publication *Health Aspects of Chemical and Biological Weapons* (Geneva) in 1970. An urban attack where about one-hundred-and-twenty lbs of dried anthrax in a suitable aerosolized form is disseminated, would affect an area well in excess of twenty square miles, it states. Such an act could result in thousands of deaths, 'in addition to causing primary casualties, the spores of the bacteria that cause anthrax are hardy and could survive for decades, possibly making the region hazardous for years'.

It is instructive that British germ warfare experiments in 1942 with *B. anthracis* (which took place on Gruinard Island off the coast of Scotland) caused the place to remain off-limits for more than forty years. Tests conducted in 1981 showed that anthrax spores were still detected in twenty out of a hundred-and-fifty-three soil samples, most of them embedded in the ground three inches down in the area where they had been strewn on impact.

Once the real purpose of Al Hakam had become evident, UNSCOM went to work 'removing, destroying and rendering harmless' everything that might be construed to be associated with a BW program at the base.

It took six weeks; May through June 1996. Machinery and equipment was stripped, crushed, mashed, cut apart with oxyacetylene torches or buried in cement; a very thorough procedure. Meanwhile, following other leads, UN inspectors discovered similar facilities at Salman Pak, Fudaliyah, Taji and the Daura Foot and Mouth Disease Vaccine complex on the outskirts of Baghdad.

Some facilities were left intact; Daura's vaccine production was regarded as essential for livestock survival in the region, though evidence that there was also research on viral warfare agents (including hemorrhagic conjunctivitis, [enterovirus-70] human rotavirus and camelpox) came later. Here, too, offending items were taken away for destruction. To prevent further BW work, Daura's air handling facilities were filled with concrete.

During the November 1997 confrontation between Saddam and the UN, there were several reports that UNSCOM had managed to uncover further evidence that Saddam Hussein was engaged in a clandestine chemical and biological warfare program. London's *Observer* trumpeted a headline story to that affect, but, as we found out later, it was not the case.

What gradually became clear is that there were many more BW assets than previously believed, as there were probably more nuclear facilities, evidenced by the incompatibility of declared nuclear related items compared to those recovered, as well as the attempt by Iraq to acquire hydrofluoric acid, a chemical used in the production of uranium hexafluoride [UF] feedstock not long afterwards.

The truth, according to Ewen Buchanan, UNSCOM's External Relations Advisor in New York, is that while the inspectors might have come close to doing so, they found nothing new. 'What is relevant,' Buchanan added, 'is that by the time we pulled out, the Iraqis were at the very end of the road with their arsenal of lies and duplicity. We followed every lead that they ever gave us. Consequently, by the time the crunch came, they had no room left in which to maneuver.' Buchanan maintains that in the end UNSCOM would accept no more stories or excuses, almost all of which led to red herrings in the past and which was one of the reasons for the impasse[9].

It is instructive that by mid-1998, UNSCOM was monitoring almost ninety biological facilities throughout Iraq, including a variety of institutions such as universities, breweries, food processing plants as well as production facilities for vaccines, antibiotics, biopesticides and single cell proteins [SCP] (Baghdad claimed earlier these were produced at Al Hakam).

It is important to look closely at what was being done at other Iraqi BW establishments:

Laboratory-scale research on anthrax (caused by *B. anthracis)*, botulinum toxin *(Clostridium botulinum)*, gas gangrene *(C. perfrigens)*, fungal toxins (including aflatoxin and trichothecene mycotoxins) as well as ricin (extracted from the seeds of the castor bean plant, *Ricinis communis)* were among tasks performed at Salman Pak, an average-sized place about twenty-five miles out of Baghdad. Dr Richard Spertzel, Chief of the Biology Section at UNSCOM, confirmed much of this.

Spertzel, a 28-year veteran of biological warfare and biomedical defense in the US Army, had visited Iraq as a senior member of UNSCOM many times. He was there, in January 1998, when another group of UN weapons inspectors demanded that they be given access to the prison at Abu Ghraib where, they told the Iraqis, they believed that BW and CW experiments had been conducted on dogs. This group headed by German microbiologist Gabriela Kraatz-Wadsack had evidence that humans, not dogs, were being experimented on. More damning, there were photographs to back up their claims, he told me (See Chapter 11).

There were other reports that spoke of BW experiments on people, though obviously, on this aspect, Iraq was expected to have been strenuous in its denials. Revelations that occurred after 'Operation Iraqi Freedom' in 2003 tell another story.

What was found in June 1994, was a mass grave near Salman Pak, though obviously nothing like what was uncovered in May 2003 at Al Mahawil, south of Baghdad. Earlier, a source told UN personnel that the victims were human guinea pigs 'that had been exposed to bacteriological agents'. The Iraqis swore that this was not so. The dead were 'political agents' who been executed, an Iraqi representative explained. Sadly, the UN did not follow up the investigation at the time and all efforts to return to that site again were blocked by Iraqi security personnel; another of the places to which UNSCOM has been denied access.

Had they done so, we are now aware, both President Bush and Prime Minister Tony Blair might have had easier passage with their arguments for bringing down the fratricidal regime of Saddam Hussein at a time when almost the entire international body was marshaled against them. There is blood on the hands of somebody at the UN originally responsible for this obfuscation.

While Baghdad continued to cautiously cover its tracks with regard to any evidence of human testing of BWs, there are a good number of circumstantial clues that such research did take place. A German microbiologist member of Spertzel's team led inspectors to Baghdad's notorious Abu Ghraib Prison in January 2001 in a search for evidence. They discovered that all records from the two-year period 1994/5 had been expunged. No explanation for doing this was either offered or given by the Iraqis. It is worth placing on record that this was the period, according to information received by the UN, when such activity, involving humans took place.

UNSCOM inspectors also uncovered sealed chambers large enough to house people where, it has subsequently been confirmed by dissidents, experiments were conducted on humans. By the time Coalition Forces arrived the second time around, it had all had been thoroughly sanitized with chemicals by Saddam's people. Earlier, the UN was assured by Saddam's people that they had been used to conduct bacteriological experiments on animals such as goats, monkeys and donkeys. Somebody will eventually have a lot to answer for at The Hague.

It was the view of Rolf Ekeus, former UNSCOM chief inspector, that the UN had been suspicious 'for a long time' that the Iraqis had been conducting experiments on humans. He referred to photos uncovered following the defection of Kamel. These showed gruesome remains of animals and, in one instance, human limbs with lesions that appeared to be consistent with such research. Ekeus said that the Iraqis gave him no credible explanation.

In truth, what was happening at Salman Pak was that staff were carrying out toxicity evaluations of all the agents mentioned above, as well as a host of others. Iraqi scientists also examined their growth characteristics and survivability. Eventually they conducted initial scale-up production research with a view to ultimately incorporating BW (and CW) in the warheads of Scud missiles being adapted for the purpose. Some of these were ready for firing at the start of 'Desert Storm'.

At Fudaliyah (the innocuously-named the Agricultural and Water Resources Research Center) in the north-east suburbs of Baghdad, the Iraqis say about four hundred gallons of concentrated aflatoxin came off a production line, a figure disputed by UNSCOM as being far too high for the size of the place. The Taji Single Cell Protein Plant (also north of the city) was being used for the production of botulinum toxin during the latter part of the Eighties.

The inclusion of aflatoxin in Saddam Hussein's BW program is puzzling. Aflatoxin is a carcinogen derived from wheat or ground-nut mold. It causes cancer, but this debilitating process might take years and needs repeated exposure. It's immediate toxicity is respectable, perhaps 100mg when injected in humans, but hardly more potent than nerve agents like sarin. Consequently aflatoxin has no application to modern-day warfare.

The rationale for proceeding with this project seems to be based on the premise that 'while we in Iraq will suffer your bombs, a certain percentage of your attackers will develop liver cancer by the time they are fifty'. Its 'use' underscores a distinctly lopsided approach to a few of the weapons programs on which some of Saddam's staff were embarked over the years and on which an awful lot of money was spent.

It is worth noting that Iraq initially experimented with aflatoxin mixed with chemical riot-control agents. UN officials told me that the intent was to spray the chemical on Kurdish and other ethnic minorities and also Shi'ite 'revolutionaries' (all of whom were opposed to rule from Baghdad) in the hope that it would eventually produce an untraceable spike of cancer in the years ahead. This is one of the worst examples of ethnic cleansing to emerge since Hitler's war. Curiously, the silence from the rest of the Arab world following the exposure of this barbarism was, like a lot of other Iraqi injustices, anything short of deafening.

In its reports, UNSCOM listed five more Iraqi sites involved in research in CW agents. These were in addition to the ten nuclear and nine ballistic missile sites, the latter including weaponization, production and test facilities.

Iraq's biological warfare program was started in 1974, five years before Saddam Hussein took power.

Although Iraq joined what were then a hundred-and-forty other nations and signed the BWC to forgo the production or acquisition of all BWs or toxins in 1972, Baghdad's Al Hazan Ibn Al Hathem Institute was founded secretly two years later. It was placed under the command of a chemical corps officer who reported directly to the president.

Much of the early work was targeted at opponents of the regime. An effort was also made to destabilize Iran economically by poisoning crops; and that happened a good fifteen years before open war broke out between the two countries. It is axiomatic, too, that Sunni-Shi'a enmity is fierce and deep-rooted throughout the region and goes back almost fourteen hundred years.

For its seed stock, Iraq turned to American and European suppliers of biological materials to supplement indigenous strains. Much was bought in gram-sized vials 'over the counter', as it were, from The American Type Culture Collection (ATCC) in Rockville, Maryland.

From 1985 onwards the company supplied anthrax, *C. botulinum* and *C. perfringens* at a cost which averaged $78 per order, all of it sent by post.

Negotiations for the purchase of growth media were begun in 1987. A year later the first order of almost forty tons was delivered, enough to produce four or five tons of bacteria, of which the equivalent of a tiny fraction of a drop can be lethal. Some came from a company in Bedford, England; more from the Swiss firm Fluka Chemie. It says much for the political climate of the period that no one questioned what the stuff was to be used for. By now, just about every intelligence service in the West must have been aware what was going on in Iraq, yet nothing was done about it until after the Gulf War.

Nor did the Iraqis themselves experience any problems acquiring industrial-scale fermentors. All are dual-use and the same as those found in any brewery or for making yeast-based products. Western companies were queuing up to oblige; Baghdad paid, as usual, in bundles of large-denomination dollar bills. Spray dryers (which turn germ-laden slurries into dry powder) were bought from the Niro Atomiser Company of Denmark.

As with all such facilities, decontamination was always a problem. At Al Hakam and elsewhere, most equipment was fitted with plug-in segments that could be rapidly connected and disconnected for better flexibility. For this purpose, the Iraqis used a mixture of potassium permanganate and formaldehyde which did a thorough 'cover up' job, though everything first had to be dismantled. It took a day or two get through the process. And since the UN, for reasons best known to those in charge, only conducted three dedicated biological inspections in the first four years after the Gulf War, it seems that Saddam was confident that he could do pretty well as he pleased without the UN being aware of it.

This omission is unconscionable. The West, by its own admission, was aware of Iraq's BW potential. Much had appeared in print on the subject over the years, underscored by the effort that went into inoculating the soldiers who took part in 'Desert Storm' against an acknowledged chembiowarfare threat. One might well ask why was such a serious lapse of security was allowed to occur?

This issue has been raised often enough in the past. Each time the reply from the UN officer responsible has been along the lines that there was 'no smoking gun'. This is a curious admission and for several reasons: The West knew from the start what it was up against. It had reams of evidence of previous BW programs. It was fully in the picture as to what Iraq had been shopping for.

Yet almost all effort expended in the first forty months of UNSCOM activity in Iraq was devoted to uncovering nuclear, chemical and missile assets. The BW side seems to have been placed on the back-burner. In terms of immediate military or possibly a clandestine retaliatory potential - as far as a crippled Iraq was concerned - the BW program, arguably, was the most potent.

Where, one might ask, was Osama bin Laden when Saddam needed him most? Put another way, the West can be truly thankful that Al Qaeda only became a reality when many of these shenanigans were over. The developed world has indeed been extraordinarily lucky.

Colonel David Franz, former commander of the US Army Medical Research Institute of Infectious Diseases (USAMRIID) and himself a member of various UNSCOM contingents, counters that while some might be critical of UN efforts in Iraq, it was never easy. The UNSCOM/Iraq example, he said, 'is the best case we will ever have, and even after Dick Spertzel got the job and really pushed hard, we were never able to adequately verify the stuff. It is just more difficult than the chemical or nuclear side under such circumstances[10].'

Dr Spertzel was still trying to uncover Saddam's BW programs right up to the last day that UNSCOM inspections were permitted in 1998 and he has his own views on the subject. He takes a strong view that the evidence was there for exploiting all along, saying that 'the problem was that there was no driving force, no impetus to exploit the BW issue within UNSCOM'. He concurs that much more could have (*and should have*) been done.[11]

Furthermore, it is one of the modern-day conundrums that so much of it escaped the notice of countries always considered most adept at monitoring such things in remote corners of the globe, the Middle East especially. These powers included Israel, Britain and the US. They badly underestimated the amount of botulinum that Iraq made (by a thousandfold) and anthrax, by a factor of eight[12], although Spertzel reckons that it could be very much higher.

Also, with a vanquished Iraq, the Allies had the clout to do something constructive (or rather, destructive) about Iraqi intransigence. But in the end they didn't use that option either until 'Operation Iraqi Freedom' in 2003. And by then it was almost too late.

With time, persistence and prevarication, the UN's potential influence was unrestrictedly allowed to dissipate to the point where an unresolved confrontation eventually allowed Saddam Hussein to do exactly as he pleased. Eventually, wearing down the patience of the Allies, he reached the point in the late Nineties when there was no longer anybody looking over his shoulder.

Dr Jonathan Tucker of the Monterey Institute of International Studies has since pointed out that there are many factors that made this imbroglio extremely difficult to resolve: 'Overhead reconnaissance proved of limited value for estimating production capacity in the BW area. Then - and now - international intelligence services had to rely almost exclusively on humint (human intelligence sources, such as agents and defectors) which, by definition, is fortuitous and unsystematic.'

Much of the early BW research in Iraq was conducted (on small mammals) at Salman Pak and Al Muthanna, which, until then, had been devoted to CW research under the supervision of two British-trained Iraqis. The BW Team leader was Rihab Taha, who obtained her doctorate in microbiology at East Anglia University and following the fall of Saddam, was listed among Iraq's 'Most Wanted' war criminals and was taken into custody by the Americans weeks after the war ended.

Married to a general in the Iraqi Armed Forces and asked to characterize her, one observer said she was petite, and rather dour with a dry, precise manner. For years she was assisted by her husband, Amer Saadi (another war criminal) who was later promoted to the rank of major general.

Most observers in Iraq regard 'the Taha woman' as the *eminence grise* behind Iraq's BW program. Dr Rihab Rashid Taha was listed as an 'Al Hakam Factory Director'. Forty-something and hardly conspicuous in a crowd, she was described by one UN inspector as 'manipulative'. Nor is she averse to an occasional tantrum that can include throwing chairs about the room. Faced with something intractable, especially after she has painted herself into a corner with unsubstantiated half-truths, Madam Taha can resort to tears[13].

For many years, her mentor - until he was arrested by the Iraqis on charges of espionage - was Abdul Nassir Hindawi, who had made a name for himself in microbiology after graduating from Mississippi State University (he also specialized in single cell protein [SCP] manufacture). It was he too, who originally inspired Saddam with theories of cheap military victories using gas and germs.

UN officials say that Hindawi's papers were never surrendered. Iraq told UNSCOM in September 1997 that the scientist's perceived objectives 'were to produce a viable deterrent in answer to a possible Israeli nuclear attack.'

It was Dr Richard Spertzel, among the most prescient of Saddam's critics, who ventured the opinion that because the UN devoted so little effort to Saddam's BW program, the Iraqis eventually became over-confident. 'Perhaps they eventually came to believe that sampling would never take place,' he told a symposium on bioweapons proliferation in Washington DC in October 1996[14].

It has always been his view that Iraq was remarkably skillful at using disinformation techniques to twist seemingly trivial events to its political advantage. In 1994, for example, UNSCOM conducted a biological audit at the Al Hakam facility in which samples were collected from fermentors and other equipment within the site. Sewers and septic systems were also tapped.

The sampling, he says 'took place at a time when we were trying to persuade the Iraqis to acknowledge their past BW production activities, including the biowarfare role of the Al Hakam plant. Yet Iraq tried to convince some members of the UN Security Council that there was nothing in UNSCOM's allegation by claiming that we had "sampled all over Al Hakam including the toilets" and found no evidence of misdeeds.'

Considerable effort was needed to counter this perception, he told the gathering. Later the same month an inspection at the plant obtained samples that provided the first positive indication that Iraq was producing a small particle-size *Bacillus thuringiensis* (BT) product that lacked pesticidal activity. While not the stuff of biological warfare as far as Iraq's efforts at obfuscation were concerned, it was a turning point - 'a smoking gun', as the Americans like to call it - even though BT is not a BW agent. Under normal circumstances, it is a quite legitimate product.

What should be explained is that since the BT found being made at Al Hakam did not have insecticidal potential (and had a dry particle size far too small to be of use for application to crops) UNSCOM could only conclude that it was being produced and dried as a training exercise for the production of anthrax. This pathogen is cultured under similar conditions.

Asked whether UNSCOM took samples to confirm that the microbial agents declared by Iraq were present (or rather, that they tended to identify undeclared BW agents that might be present in the samples) Dr Spertzel said that both approaches were used.

He explained: 'Although UNSCOM was obligated to verify Iraq's declarations, samples were analyzed for a variety of BW agents, both declared and undeclared.' The UN had not tested samples 'for every possible microbial pathogen,' he said. Instead, he added that the organization tended to look for the standard list of BW agents and for very good reasons.

There was clearly a limit to how much testing could be done without producing some sort of a result, Dr Spertzel disclosed. 'The commission could not afford to make repeated allegations about illicit BW agent production that was not corroborated by sampling and analysis. After several negative results, we were aware that the commission might lose all credibility with the UN Security Council if we went on producing negative results.' In fact, we now know that Baghdad was banking on this.

Dr Spertzel went on: 'The situation is such, that if there are grounds to suspect that Iraq is producing agents (other than those which it had declared), it would be worthwhile to sample for the undeclared agent and risk a negative finding.' Indeed, he stated, 'rumors and unverified intelligence suggested at least one site where Iraq had produced a BW agent that it had not yet acknowledged.' This aspect was among his objectives when he returned to Iraq in 1998, immediately prior to the final withdrawal of UN personnel.

Looking back, it seems clear that if Iraq were going to make some kind of mischief with its biological warfare assets, and remember, Saddam has a unique history of recidivism, it would have been carefully co-ordinated. It would almost certainly have had to be clandestine, though by their very nature, biological agents lend themselves to subversion.

Consider the implications[15] if the *Aum Shinrikyo* cult had made 'proper' use of botulinum toxin that was toxic to humans, or a much more virulent strain of *B. anthracis* instead of the sarin chemical agent in their attack in the Tokyo subway system.

The sarin count that they used was only about 30 per cent pure and was disseminated in a highly inefficient manner (by evaporation from plastic bags punctured with sharpened umbrellas). The death count and the scale of terror, had they used these BW media and disseminated them as a particulate aerosol (a complicated and difficult task), casualties might have been higher by orders of magnitude.

There could have been a fatality rate well in excess of 50 per cent instead of the 0.2 per cent actually experienced. That would have meant thousands of dead civilians. And considering that the volume of sarin needed to saturate any given area is roughly equivalent to ten thousand times the amount of botulinum toxin needed to cause the same effect, the consequences might have been devastating[16].

Also, not much publicity has been given to a binary cyanide device that was to have been triggered at the same time by an explosive charge, but that was spotted by an alert janitor in a subway restroom. It was subsequently deactivated[17].

This was not the first time that the *Aum Shinrikyo* had been criminally active. It had been instrumental in releasing botulinum and anthrax three times before with no discernible effects, largely, it is thought, because of an unexplained failure in production or weaponization. In April 1990, the cult rigged a vehicle to disseminate botulinum toxin through the engine's exhaust around Japan's Parliament. Three years later, in June 1993 the leaders decided to disrupt the planned wedding of the Crown Prince Naruhito in downtown Tokyo, again from an adapted vehicle. Later the same month they attempted to spread anthrax around the capital using a sprayer system on the roof of an *Aum*-owned building in Eastern Tokyo. It was the failure of these three biological attacks that led the cult to try sarin.

What is of concern is that it is not impossible that Iraq could have employed a free agent to do its dirty work; Baghdad in its prime, hardly had the monopoly on ideological nuts. Or Saddam could have paid someone to take a package across to the West. Others have tried. Again, we can be thankful that bin Laden was not active five years earlier.

Before that, though, there had been other incidents involving deadly agents. In October 1980, it is said (but never substantiated) that the French authorities made a startling discovery that demonstrates how vulnerable the world is to biological terrorism. The French Police are said to have raided a Paris residence suspected of being a safe house for the German Red Army Faction. As they conducted their search, they found documents that revealed a strong working knowledge of lethal biological agents. They also came across a bathtub containing many flasks filled with a substance that turned out to be clostridium botulinum. By all accounts, these were to have been dispersed around the French capital and in the Paris Metro[18]. It should be mentioned that some authorities in the US are skeptical about this story and whether it ever actually happened.

For all that, there have been quite a few such people active in the United States. In 1995 for instance, some members of a lunatic fringe militia group in Minnesota were convicted for the possession of ricin, which they had produced themselves for use in retaliation against local government officials[19]. A year later, an Ohio man, Larry Wayne Harris (with connections to another extremist group) was able to obtain bubonic plague cultures through the post. In both cases, it mattered little to these anarchists that innocent family members might die.

During my own visit to Beirut, mid-1997, I was told by contacts who had close links with Pasdaran (Iranian Revolutionary Guards) in the Beka'a Valley that the Sudan government had recently taken an unusual interest in BW. Curiously, here too there appeared to be an Iraqi connection.

A report in November 1997 in the Paris-based *Al-Watan Al-'Arabi* newspaper[20] claimed that with the blessing of the-then Sudanese strongman Hassan al-Turabi, The Sudan 'had started a chemical and bacterial factory in the Khartoum-Bahri suburb of Kubar'. The report even gave details about the location of the meeting, which was held at Turabi's home in the Khartoum suburb of al Manshiya.

What it came down to is that Iraq had apparently moved some of its BW agents first to Libya, and then overland into The Sudan. This was done, it said, with the support of Osama bin Laden, the by-then Afghan-based Saudi Islamicist who for a long time had maintained close ties to Tehran's

Supreme Guide Ayatollah Ali Khameini. Bin Laden's operations then were apparently coordinated by Iran's Revolutionary Guards (Pasdaran), but that was before he moved to Afghanistan from where he (and his Taliban hosts) were eventually ousted by a powerful Allied military force.

Apart from the destruction of the Twin Towers in New York, bin Laden has since been circumstantially linked to many other adventures that involved terror. These include the bombing of the Khobar Towers in Saudi Arabia in June 1996, where nineteen American military personnel were killed and hundreds injured[21]. Since then, bin Laden has also been tied to the two US embassy bombings in East Africa (more than three hundred killed) and, more recently, bomb blasts in Bali and Mombassa in Kenya in which hundreds of people who had absolutely nothing to do with either America or the Islamic World were slaughtered.

While the United Nations is no longer directly involved in Iraq (though this could change) such issues continue to fester, especially where there is loss of life.

Until it was replaced by UNMOVIC, the UN Special Commission remained as active as it was allowed to be by Saddam's goons. In January 1999, it forwarded two reports to the President of the Security Council, one on the current state of affairs in Iraq with respect to the disarmament of that country's proscribed weapons and the other on ongoing monitoring and verification in Iraq.

There were other developments. Questions were raised by the UN a year before about the possible sale by Russia of equipment to Iraq that might have been useful to produce biological weapons. This was a serious matter. According to an UNSCOM spokesman, the answers given by Moscow were 'unsatisfactory, and also incomplete'.

US and British officials maintained that the plant said to be under discussion was to have included several fermentation vessels with a total capacity of about fifty thousand liters. They pointed out to Moscow that such things could be used to grow anthrax spores or cultivate botulinum toxin. An American intelligence source reckoned that talks between Iraq and Russian companies about supplying dual-purpose equipment included 'at least one official from the Russian government'. For its part, the UN wanted to know why this had been allowed to happen in the first place considering existing strictures in place.

In a letter to Sergey Lavrov, Russian Permanent Representative to the UN, UNSCOM Chairman Richard Butler said during the course of routine inspections, his teams had discovered documents relating specifically 'to a project for a program of cooperation between Iraq and Russian companies in the field of single cell protein production'.

Mr Butler reminded the Russian Ambassador that Iraq in the past had used dual-purpose SCP production 'as a very effective cover for pursuing a most sophisticated bioweapons program'. He was in possession of evidence, he wrote, that Iraq was 'still interested in this sort of work'.

Observers noted that the issue raised questions about exactly how much Moscow knew about these dealings. Also, if there were Russian companies 'freelancing' in Iraq, why didn't Mr Yeltsin's government put to a stop to it? Mr Butler stated that at very least such action would have been in line with agreed UNSCOM principles to which the Russians were signatories.

He also disclosed that there were documents in hand, which showed that Russia had presented an offer to the Iraqi delegation, and that Saddam Hussein's Military Industrialization Corporation later decided to accept it. 'The UN had no information regarding the present disposition of the venture,' Mr Butler wrote to Mr Lavrov on January 5, 1998. He waited months for a reply.

A UN source told this writer that the issue was not solely about 'technologies'. The Iraqis had proved conclusively, and repeatedly, that they had all the expertise needed to cultivate the most advanced bacteriological pathogens.

'What they don't have,' he said, 'is hardware.' Much of their old equipment, he explained, was destroyed at the behest of UNSCOM following various inspection tours within Iraq. 'Clearly, the Russian stainless vessels would have been ideal for launching another germ warfare program,' Mr Butler declared.

It is necessary to look closely at the most sobering prospect of all: A biological weapons attack on a Western city, and not necessarily American.

We've seen the effects on society following the mailing of anthrax spores after the destruction of the Twin Towers in September 2001. The brouhaha that resulted was out of all proportion to the number of people affected and the handful who died. This obviously worried both the American capital and London.

Prior to those incidents, the US Office of Technology Assessment did studies of damage likely to be caused if even non-contagious agents were used in Washington DC. The pundits afterwards put their findings before Congress.

Imagine the scenario: A hundred pounds of anthrax is disseminated over the main business and residential areas of any big city. It could be quietly and quickly done with the help of a small private plane adapted with appropriate aerosol sprays. The report stated that the number of deaths occurring in the first few days was estimated to be almost a half-million.

Thousands of others would be at risk of dying if a program to deliver antibiotics to all those potentially exposed was not immediately begun. There would be a stampede of millions, all of them fearful that they or their families might be exposed[22].

Beyond the immediate health implications, the potential panic and civil unrest created by such action would require an equally dramatic response from the government. It wouldn't take long for local law enforcement agencies to be overwhelmed and not able to operate effectively without the assistance of federal agencies[23].

The vulnerability of the United States, if exposed to this type of terrorism, might provoke other similarly-minded people to attempt the same kind of onslaught for extortion or, possibly, some sort of impact related to terrorism. It is also essential to consider the probability of what would happen if three or four such attacks were launched simultaneously. And then, one needs to question, how does one retaliate? Would (could?) Washington act in a way that would almost certainly involve the use of nuclear weapons?

The reality of such a disaster is that while terrorists can often be implicated by association or implication with state sponsors (Iraq, Iran, Syria, North Korea, Libya and others), the quantum of proof that the West would require *before* responding to such a perceived linkage would have to be high. Consider, for example, the forensic difficulty in assigning responsibility for the attack on PanAm Flight 103 that exploded over Lockerbie in 1988. Only in May 2003 did Libya finally acknowledge that its agents has orchestrated the attack over Scotland, *and then under tremendous international duress.*

In the event of a BW attack, it would be comparatively easy to mask the source. The perpetrator could arrive at any airport in the world with a deadly BW agent like smallpox sealed in one or more plastic bags. The entire package could easily fit in the pocket of a raincoat.

And then, how does any nation retaliate? Washington cannot simply 'eradicate' the capital cities of those countries that are at the top of a suspect list on the basis of unsubstantiated intelligence. Even more clear is that ultimately, someone will have to provide a solution, for no other reason than if nothing is done, one such attack could lead to others.

It was former USAMRIID commander Colonel Franz who made the point that the UNSCOM experience in Iraq (and the current perceived threat of biological terror to the cities of the West) underscored many issues. Among them was 'the unique difficulty that the Free World faced in dealing directly with regimes who would use legitimate dual-use facilities and equipment to develop mass-casualty weapons cheaply for covert use[24].'

'The threat demands an integrated approach. That includes effective intelligence programs, the availability of physical and medical countermeasures, education of health-care providers and other responders,' he told me.

Most important of all, he added, 'conventional military strength and a clear national policy regarding response to a biological warfare attack on Americans or American cities is a vital requisite.'

1   Dr Jane Orient in *The Journal of the American Medical Association*: August, 1987, pp644/648
2   Mylroie, Laurie & James Ring Adams: 'Saddam's Germs; *The American Spectator:* Vol 28, No 11, November, 1995 pp60-62
3   Eric Croddy: *Chemical and Biological Warfare: A Comprehensive Survey for the Concerned Citizen* (with Clarisa Perez-Armendariz and John Hart): Copernicus Books, New York, 2002, together with a succession of personal interviews from December 1997 onwards
4   Colonel David Franz, former commander, US Army Medical Research Institute of Infectious Diseases: Fort Detrick MD; January 12, 1988. Personal interview
5   'Iraq Unlikely to Give up Nuclear Option'; *Jane's Intelligence Review - Pointer;* Vol 003/009: Sept 1, 1996
6   Dr Jonathan Tucker: *Biological Weapons Proliferation Concerns:* p25: Center for Nonproliferation Studies, Monterey Institute of International Studies, Monterey, California: (Prepared for NATO Advanced Study Institute in Budapest, Hungary, July, 1997)
7   R. Jeffrey Smith: 'Iraq's Drive for a Biological Arsenal': *The Washington Post,* November 21, 1997
8   Defense Intelligence Agency: US DOD GulfLINK file # 22010067.92.a; CIA GulfLINK file # 062596_cia_74624_01.txt
9   Ewen Buchanan, UNSCOM'S External Relations Advisor; UN HQ: Succession of interviews, December 1997
10 Franz: Personal communications including letter dd January 12, 1988
11 Dr Richard Spertzel: Personal Interview: UN New York HQ; January 6, 1998
12 R Jeffrey Smith: *Ibid* pp3/4
13 UNSCOM, UN HQ New York; personal interview: Ewen Buchanan, December 1997
14 Dr Richard Spertzel: 'Lessons from the UNSCOM Experience With Sampling and Analysis' in Jonathan B Tucker (ed): *The Utility of Sampling and Analysis for Compliance Monitoring of the Biological Weapons Convention:* (Livermore California: Lawrence Livermore National Laboratory, Report #CGSR-97-001), pp17-25
15 It was only in the Spring of 2003 that details were released of some of the biological warfare experiments that South Africa was working on both during the Apartheid era and afterwards. They had actually developed a kind of 'stealth' anthrax that could fool tests designed to detect the disease (See *Jane's Terrorism Monitor*, London, May, 2003 as well as 'Biotoxins Fall into Private Hands' by Joby Warrick: *Washington Post,* April 21, 2003)
16 Kathleen C Bailey ed., *Director's Series on Proliferation:* Lawrence Livermore National Laboratory, Livermore, California: May 23, 1994
17 Croddy: Personal interview, January 1998
18 Joseph D Douglas: *America the Vulnerable: The Threat of Chemical and Biological Warfare:* Lexington Books, Lexington, Mass. 1987
19 Commentary: Why Should We Be Concerned About Biological Warfare? *The Journal of the American Medical Association* August, 1997, pp431-432
20 *Al-Watan Al-'Arabi,* by Jihad Salim (in Arabic) Paris, 31 October, 1997: 'Secrets of al-Manshiyah: Meeting between Hasan al-Turabi and Ayman al-Zawahiri'
21 *Jane's Intelligence Review,* 'The Bombing of the Khobar Towers: Who Did it and Who Funded it': Chris Kozlow, p555
22 Congress, Office of Technology Assessment: *Proliferation of Weapons of Mass Destruction: Assessing the Risks* (Washington DC: GPO, 1993)
23 'Biological Warfare: The Poor Man's Atomic Bomb'; *Jane's Intelligence Review,* London, 1999
24 Franz: Personal communication; USAMRIID, Fort Detrick, Maryland

11

SOME FEARSOME POSSIBLE NEWCOMERS TO THE MIDDLE EAST EQUATION: SMALLPOX, ANTHRAX AND NOVICHOK

'It is an agonizing way to die. First there is fever and dreadful aching pains. Then come the pus-filled boils which appear all over the body and develop scabs. Slowly the immune system surrenders...'

'Smallpox: The New Bioweapon' *The Times,* London, January 8, 2001

German microbiologist Ms Gabriele Kraatz-Wadsack, former chief inspector of the UN biological weapons commission in Iraq was interviewed by Sophie Muehlman of *Die Welt* not long before 'Operation Iraqi Freedom'[1]. Her observations are instructive because she traveled to Baghdad on twenty-six inspection missions for UNSCOM. A veterinarian specializing in microbiology, she worked in Iraq from 1995 until the UN body was forced out of Iraq.

Asked whether Saddam Hussein actually had biological weapons, Ms Kraatz-Wadsack was unequivocal: Iraq had something to hide, she declared, 'otherwise there would be no reason *not* to allow weapons inspectors into the country'. Under the headline 'Iraq Has Produced Huge Amounts of Biological Weapons', this discussion was a key factor in the debate about the feasibility of a military strike by the West against Iraq.

One of the points made to the German newspaper by Ms Kraatz-Wadsack – she is also an advisor on biological terrorism at the Robert Koch Institute - was that Iraq first revealed its biological weapons program to the UN in 1995, a good four years after it had been required to do so by the world body following the first Gulf War in 1991. 'And even then Iraq didn't come clean as to the full extent of the program.' More important, she stated, while an international commission of experts found some discrepancies, 'they came to the conclusion that it could not be determined whether the Iraqi bioweapons program had ever really been terminated'.

Referring to American vice-president Dick Cheney's comments about 'a deadly threat from Baghdad', her immediate reaction was that 'the Iraqi government disclosed to us that it had produced anthrax and nerve toxins in very large quantities. It also admitted that it had produced aflatoxin, a fungicide that causes liver cancer (and that these pathogens) had been loaded into weapons, in missile warheads and bombs. It had gas gangrene and the plant-derived lectin/toxin ricin (together with) the pathogens that cause economic damage, for instance wheat blight. There was also research and development work on various viruses.

'So, if you look at this large spectrum of pathogens that kill people and make them sick, then you are able to recognize the kind of know-how behind it. Also, the program was industrialized and open-air tests and animal tests were carried out. Iraq produced huge quantities within a very short time,' she added.

Does this threat still exist?

'Certainly...the expertise still exists. Further, the scientists are there, the documents were not turned over, and weapon systems and production data were never completely clarified.'

Were there exclusively Iraqi scientists involved or did Baghdad have help from other countries for its bioweapons program?

'We dealt only with Iraqi scientists. With respect to their biological weapons, the Iraqis never claimed that they received help from abroad. Of course during the (first) Gulf War there were imports from abroad that could not obviously be attributed to a bioweapons program. Indeed, much is hidden in the industrial infrastructure, for example, in installations for the production of vaccines, which they then modified. In the area of bioweapons, everything can be used both in the civilian and in the military area and that cannot be classified so easily.'

The German scientist was explicit about the detection process: 'As an inspector, one follows up on the information provided by Iraq. One speaks with scientists and looks for trails. The official information must then be verified. One must visit the installation, analyze equipment, take samples from equipment and raw materials, and install cameras and sensors to determine how often the device is used. We also had helicopter inspections and satellites, that is, a very intensive inspection regime. What it did depend on, however, was Baghdad granting us access to all facilities and information anytime, anywhere and without hindrance. And that was the handicap: Iraq did not agree with that UN mandate.'

Ms Kraatz-Wadsack was also critical of Iraqi obfuscation, a topic about which most former UNSCOM members, because of the nature of their job, tend not to be overly explicit.

'Simple hindrance looks like this: (the inspectors) come to an installation and the Iraq representative says that there is no key. A more extreme situation is when Baghdad says that it will not admit you to (a particular) facility. Then a government representative must come in before they can proceed further. These are delaying tactics. Then you are dealing in part with falsified documents or with false representatives. You simply have no access to correct information.'

Did the Iraqis actually lie to her? 'Yes,' she replied bluntly.

Meanwhile, in the United States, smallpox has been in the news again. According to Dr Richard Spertzel, in a submission before the House Armed Services Committee[2], the Middle East was possibly the nexus here too. Others named by him before Congress as possibly having access to the deadly *Variola major* (smallpox) virus for military use are Iran, North Korea and of course, the Russians.

Almost as if preordained, Dr Jonathan Tucker published his book on smallpox almost exactly a year before. Some of his observations are compelling[3] and it was Iraq once more that interested him.

He disclosed that following the first Gulf War, United Nations officials determined that Saddam's scientists had manufactured smallpox vaccine and immunized the Iraqi armed forces with it. However warned Tucker, 'the Iraqi action was not necessarily incriminating, because the US military had also continued doing so until 1990 for strictly defense purposes.'

United Nations weapons inspectors - while still in Iraq - discovered that Baghdad manufactured smallpox vaccine as late as 1989 - *or more than a decade after the disease was supposed to have been eradicated throughout the world.*

Suspicions were further aroused when an Iraqi scientist, Hazem Ali, admitted that Saddam instructed his germ warfare specialists to study camelpox virus, which causes fever and skin rash in camels. Because camelpox rarely infects humans, some analysts believe that Baghdad may have used it as a surrogate for smallpox in order to refine their production techniques. They will have looked at the possible dissemination of the virus as a warfare agent.

'Further evidence for Iraqi military interest in smallpox came to light in the mid-1990s when UNSCOM inspectors visited the maintenance shop of the State Establishment for Medical Appliances Marketing, a branch of the Iraqi Ministry of Health that had been involved in the biological warfare program,' wrote Tucker. He added that it was during this inspection that the weapons inspectors found an old freeze-drier labeled 'smallpox' in Arabic.

'Though the Iraqis claimed that this piece of equipment had been employed for the production of freeze-dried smallpox vaccine, it could just as easily have been used to convert a liquid suspension of Variola virus into powder form for dissemination as a fine-particle aerosol,' Tucker maintained. Once aerosolized, this powder - whether anthrax or smallpox - becomes the ultimate biological weapon. In that form it can, in theory, be easily sprayed over any sleeping city from Stuttgart to Sydney and everywhere else inbetween.

Suddenly, after decades of smallpox being a non-issue, Western intelligence services are once more focusing on its use as a weapon of mass destruction. The US government is taking the threat seriously enough to prepare the nation for a possible germ attack in which smallpox might be involved. As Tucker points out, 'while the disease itself may have been eradicated, laboratory stocks of the virus continue to exist and may have fallen into the hands of pariah countries'.

Tucker quotes a Defense Intelligence Agency (DIA) report from May 1994 (of unknown reliability) stating that virologists from one of the Soviet Ministry of Defense's military microbiology institutes transferred smallpox virus cultures to Iraq in the late 1980s or early 1990s. There was also (unsubstantiated) evidence he stated, that the Russians 'assisted the Iraqis with their biological warfare program'.

Significantly, Dr Kathleen Vogel, a scientist at Cornell University who toured biological warfare facilities in the Former Soviet Union, told a meeting of the American Association for the Advancement for Science not long before that, that she suspected secret stocks of smallpox virus were still being held at Russian military microbiology facilities. These were outside the WHO-approved repository in Novosibirsk, she warned.

Dr Vogel reported that scientists formerly employed by the Soviet biowarfare program had been offered lucrative jobs in countries categorized by the US State Department as 'supporting international terrorism'. She also expressed concern that samples of smallpox virus might have been sold to some of these rogue states which might include Iran, Syria, Libya and others.

There are several reasons why international terrorists might be tempted to use smallpox as a weapon some time in the future (and one of the reasons why Western nations are quickly pushing through with as many immunizations against the disease as possible). By the time this book is out, all health workers in Britain would have got their shots and, as in the US, it will probably be available to others who want it.

The first reason for this uncharacteristic haste is that the United States stopped vaccinating its civilian population against the disease in 1972. All other nations had taken the same approach by the early 1980s. Also, since smallpox vaccination provides full immunity for only about ten years, nearly the entire US population would now be susceptible to infection. At greatest risk would be the hundred million or so more Americans – or roughly 45 per cent of the population – born since routine vaccination ceased.

Given this vulnerability, Atlanta's Centers for Disease Control (CDC) warned not long after the implications of the threat had been released that even 'a limited terrorist release' of the smallpox virus would constitute a major emergency. In the absence of sufficient stocks of the vaccine worldwide, smallpox could potentially result in the return of a global health threat, the Atlanta spokesperson declared.

Tucker highlights an accident in 1978 - a year after smallpox was eradicated worldwide - when smallpox virus escaped from a research laboratory at the University of Birmingham Medical School in Britain. A medical photographer working on the floor above the laboratory became infected (through the air vents, it was thought at the time) and later died. The disease also spread to her mother, who survived. It was only a matter of luck that a major smallpox outbreak did not result.

Could terrorist groups use smallpox as a weapon? Dr Tucker has his own views of the subject.

Since the virus no longer exists in nature, the only way that terrorists could have acquired seed cultures would have been on the international black market, he said. For this reason, he believes that smallpox would be an unlikely weapon for ordinary terrorist groups, but more likely, state-sponsored operatives might obtain it.

But should a terrorist group (perhaps state-sponsored by a rogue government) manage to acquire and produce the virus in liquid form, it would be a relatively easy matter to disseminate it. Of use here would be a small aerosol device, for instance in an enclosed space such as the London Underground or the New York City subway.

The pattern of infection is chilling. Within two weeks the first victims would come down with fever, aches and other nonspecific symptoms before developing the distinctive pustular rash. By the time the first patients were diagnosed, they would have infected the next wave of cases.

Professor Vincent Fiscetti, head of the Department of Bacterial Pathogenesis and Immunology at The Rockefeller University, observed that in a mass transport environment there are people from all over the world traveling together. 'It takes several days for the symptoms to show, by which time they will have carried it back to their own countries.'

An interesting aside here, is that exactly this pattern of infection (out of Hong Kong) was instrumental in transmitting China's much less potent SARS virus early in 2003: It didn't take long to spread the virus all over the globe though comparisons end there. Smallpox deaths, among those who have been vaccinated, could, by comparison, be measured in terms of hundreds of millions.

Professor Fiscetti is of the view that an even more effective delivery method might be to use a low-flying aircraft to disperse an aerosol of the virus over an international event like the Olympics or a World Cup football game or, unthinkably, those making the *Haj* (pilgrimage) to the Saudi Moslem holy cities of Mecca and Medina. Geographically small countries such as Sri Lanka, Israel, Singapore and Jordan would be especially vulnerable.

Because of fears that smallpox could be used as a terrorist weapon Washington announced not long ago that it was pouring money into developing new drug treatments for the virus and was also expanding its supply of smallpox vaccine. Some American Special Forces were inoculated against the disease prior to going into Iraq in 2003.

The most feared of all infectious diseases, smallpox was first identified in ancient Egypt and gradually spread throughout the world. Over the centuries it caused hundreds of millions of deaths; it killed rich and poor, royalty and commoners and repeatedly changed the course of history.

Highly contagious, the smallpox virus spreads through the air and it takes only a few particles to infect. The more potent form of the disease, *Variola major*, kills about 30 per cent of its victims. Survivors in the past were almost always disfigured with ugly scars.

About a quarter century ago a worldwide vaccination campaign organized by the World Health Organization (WHO) successfully eradicated the disease. The last natural outbreak occurred in Somalia in 1977. Three years later, the WHO declared the disease extinct and urged all member-countries to halt routine vaccination because it entailed a significant risk of complications. Even after smallpox was eliminated from nature, some countries retained laboratory stocks of the virus for research purposes. Although Soviet leaders had been the driving force behind the WHO smallpox eradication campaign, they cynically exploited the world's new vulnerability to the disease by turning it into a strategic weapon.

During the 1980s, the Soviet army mass-produced the smallpox virus as a biological weapon. Tons of the virus in liquid suspension were stored in refrigerated tanks; in wartime, the agent would have been loaded into aerial bombs and ICBM warheads targeted on US and Chinese cities.

Dr Ken Alibek, who served as First Deputy Director of Biopreparat, a major component of the Soviet biological weapons program, revealed Moscow's mass-production of smallpox to Western intelligence agencies after his defection to the United States in 1992. He also claimed that stocks of smallpox virus were distributed 'to places in Russia beyond the known laboratories - possibly where there were less effective security controls'.

Alibek added that while smallpox was an effective weapon, Soviet scientists had attempted to make it even more deadly by adding foreign genes from other viruses such as Ebola, although this work was apparently halted after the breakup of the Soviet Union.

Specialists at a Johns Hopkins University conference on bioterrorism at the turn of the Millennium said that much of Dr Alibek's information had been confirmed by other sources. It must be said though, that there are specialists who remain skeptical of the genetically engineered 'double kill' concept (reinforcing the acknowledged lethality of one virus by adding another).

Dr Joshua Lederberg, a Nobel laureate in biology who advises Washington on germ warfare, commented: 'We have no idea what may have been retained, maliciously or inadvertently, in the laboratories of a hundred countries from the time that smallpox was a common disease.' These would be the most likely sources of supply for potential biowarfare terrorists, he warned.

It is also noteworthy that in 1996, the WHO agreed to destroy all stocks of smallpox virus stored in two official repositories at the US Centers for Disease Control (CDC) in Atlanta and the Vector Laboratory near Novosibirsk, Russia. But because nobody was certain that there weren't other countries that might have retained undeclared samples of the virus, the US persuaded the world health body in 1999 to delay destruction of the official stocks for another three years. It needed to conduct more research on the virus and to develop anti-smallpox drugs, Washington argued.

Anthrax, in marked contrast to *Variola major*, is a very different proposition when viewed as a potential terrorist weapon. Here, too, Iraq had been unusually active.

In one sense, the trouble with anthrax is that contracting the disease is much like a shark attack:

While it can be lethal, many times it isn't. The inhalation form of the disease is highly lethal (more than 85 per cent) unless treated promptly with antibiotics, but the skin form is less threatening. This doesn't prevent the media from having a field day speculating on the consequences each time there is an outbreak, no matter how minor.

The reality is vastly different. For a start, it's not all that easy to become infected by anthrax simply by handling the spore in powder form such as that disseminated by envelope, unless you inhale it or have a cut or sore and it enters your body subcutaneously. The ideal, in the kind of biological warfare (BW) perfected by the Russians (with emulation attempted by, among others, Iraq, Syria, Libya and Iran) is to infect the target through the lungs - inhalationally. But that, too, is easier said than done.

The process of using anthrax as a weapon involves a sophisticated system of disseminating huge volumes of spores that have been 'weaponized', in itself a sophisticated process necessitating some form of government involvement rather than private individuals or terror groups. Again, as with smallpox, quantities of the pathogen might be sprayed over a specific area by aircraft or possibly delivered in the warhead of a missile, very much as the Soviets planned to do in their darkest days.

What is important is that in order to become contaminated with the disease (which, untreated, is fatal about 80 per cent of the time) each subject needs to inhale between eight thousand and fifty thousand anthrax spores[4]. According to Eric Croddy, these numbers probably need to be revised: a range of four thousand to eight thousand is more likely, and is also conservative. In fact, he feels, it may take considerably less.

While such an attack might result in terrible loss of life, that will only occur if a variety of other factors such as spore size, wind, temperature and climate are ideal, the conclusion here is that anthrax is an inordinately difficult medium to deploy as a weapon.

In the incidents involving sections of the postal system in Florida, New Jersey and New York being contaminated with anthrax after the World Trade Center attack, the consensus of most authorities was that the perpetrators, while deadly in their intent, were amateurs.

The attack on Congress, however, placed them in a different league. One should mention that in his submission before Congress, former UNSCOM chief inspector (biological weapons) Richard Spertzel felt confident that while it might take time, the responsibility for those attacks might eventually also be laid at Saddam Hussein's door.

Let us look then at the implications of a full-scale anthrax attack. The potential threat from aerosol clouds is evident from a WHO estimate that about eighty pounds of dry anthrax used against a city would kill as many as thirty-six-thousand people and possibly incapacitate another fifty thousand or so. Other estimates indicate a higher fatality rate.

But why go aloft when a simple subterranean option would provide the terrorist with a much better prospect?

Dr Seth Carus, erstwhile Visiting Fellow at the National Defense University's Center for Counterproliferation Research in Washington DC, told me that in order to disperse anthrax in a New York subway or through the London Underground, you would need to produce a dried, milled, powdered agent. Also, size is of critical importance: the spores need to be from one to ten microns in diameter.

'Anything smaller and they don't deposit in the lungs. Bigger and the body starts its natural filtering process,' he declared. Also, the *bacilli* would tend to settle more quickly instead of remaining suspended in the atmosphere. Carus stressed that it is extremely dangerous to handle agents of this kind: Those involved need to have an extraordinarily efficient containment program.

'If you don't, you could end up killing everybody involved.' As he points out, producing a dry agent is a much more difficult task than actually growing the organism. In theory, a schoolboy with the right paraphernalia might be able to do that. However, he would first need to find a source of anthrax seed stock.

'But once you get to a more advanced level, it becomes relatively easy in military terms to disseminate the agent and infect a large number of people.'

What is clear is that with *Bacillus anthracis* spore in powder form, the perpetrators encounter none of the problems usually found with a liquid agent where nozzles and pressure have to be just right. But the slurry also has to be of the right consistency or wrong-sized particles might result, he pointed out.

Preparing anthrax as a large-scale biological weapon requires a sophisticated level of technological skill. The essentials include industrial centrifuges, repeated washings and intensive drying of the spores, all of which take place inside a specially built sealed environment. That's hardly the stuff of some primitive lab in Afghanistan.

And let us not forget that even the Russians had difficulty with some of the more arcane aspects of these disciplines. In one instance in 1979, as a result of an accident at a biological weapons factory in the industrial city of Sverdlovsk (now Ekaterinaburg) east of the Urals, some of their own people died when the disease was unintentionally released into the atmosphere and disseminated by wind. The figure officially quoted, is almost seventy dead, though skeptics of this unsolicited Russian candor tend to put the fatality figure much higher (if only because only civilian deaths were tallied in an accident that took place in a military establishment).

What we do know is that anthrax is an insidious disease that has long been associated with human history.

The fifth and sixth plagues described in *Exodus* may have been anthrax in domestic animals followed by cutaneous anthrax in people - the same form of the disease that appeared to have affected most of those involved in the sporadic attacks in America in 2001/2002. The disease that Virgil described in his *Georgics* is clearly anthrax among animals. We also know that anthrax was intimately associated with the origins of microbiology and immunology; a disease for which the French scientist Louis Pasteur developed a live bacterial vaccine in 1881. For centuries, anthrax in humans was associated with exposure to infected or contaminated animal products.

In 1958 it was estimated that, worldwide, between twenty thousand and about a hundred thousand humans were infected by the disease. In recent years anthrax in animals was reported from more than eighty countries, the largest epidemic in modern times occurring in Zimbabwe from 1978 through 1980 with an estimated ten thousand cases. It was about then that I landed at a small airstrip near Fort Victoria on the way back from a diving trip in Northern Mozambique: there were animal carcasses strewn everywhere alongside the length of the runway. More lay where they had fallen in the adjacent bush.

Military interest in anthrax in the West in the past quarter-century or so, such as research being conducted today at the US Army USAMRIID germ warfare facility at Fort Detrick, Maryland, has been linked strictly to defense against its use as a biological weapon. That is not the case in some other countries. By the start of Gulf War 1, Iraq had already weaponized tons of it.

Saddam's intent (recently confirmed by declassified CIA and DIA reports) was to spray it over Allied forces moving up from the south. He even modified several MiG-21 aircraft, complete with special tanks adapted for the purpose, though all were destroyed in the first day's air strikes. Were his scientists able to master the intricacies needed to fit Scud missiles with warheads containing anthrax and botulinum toxin, these almost certainly would have been showered over Israeli cities had the circumstances been 'right'.

For years, UNSCOM searched Iraq for these weapons, very much as US inspectors did after the second Gulf invasion. Though they found some of Saddam's WMD assets, almost everything associated with his biological warfare program remained hidden another five years, or as Ms Kraatz-Wadsack elucidated to *Die Welt*, until he was forced by the world body to admit that he had been involved with these deadly weapons all along[5]. Several Iraqi defectors subsequently maintained that about two dozen projectiles primed with anthrax still lie buried somewhere in the desert between Baghdad and the Gulf.

What is clear is that anthrax remains potent for a very long time, largely because it is a remarkably hardy pathogen. This was illustrated by the British, who used Gruinard Island off the coast of Scotland as a bombing site for the testing of dropping anthrax during World War 2. As stated in the previous chapter, more than four decades later the area was still contaminated and the place stayed off-limits.

An interesting hypothesis regarding anthrax was submitted as a paper in the *Journal of Emerging Infectious Diseases* in July/August 1990. It dealt with an aerial anthrax attack on an outdoor stadium where a football game was being played before tens of thousands of spectators. This is interesting because it fairly accurately tracks what could still happen in actuality if terrorists were able to dispense anthrax at a large gathering.

The scenario envisaged was a truck passing along an elevated highway at a stadium. For thirty seconds it released an invisible, odorless anthrax cloud about a third of a mile long into the atmosphere. About sixteen thousand fans - or about a fifth of those present were infected and so were another four or five thousand people living in adjoining areas.

Two days after the game, hundreds of people become ill with fever, coughing fits and, in some cases, shortness of breath and chest pain. Some of the sick self-administered. Others went to their doctors. Because it was that time of the year, influenza was commonplace, nobody made too much of the outbreak to begin with. A day later however, a large number of serious upper respiratory illnesses were reported. By nightfall some victims were dead.

Though the study was fictitious, it does make the point that when anthrax is properly disseminated among the unsuspecting and left untreated, the disease becomes a potent killer.

And then there are some deadly chemical weapons that the Iraqi dictator may or may not have acquired from Former Soviet Union dissidents and others. We will find all this out in the end, but meanwhile, much of it is conjecture. Dr Richard Spertzel, testifying before Congress, believes that there is a good chance that they might very well have[6].

Novichok, is one of them and in a class of its own as an extremely potent binary nerve agent about which most chemical warfare specialists were only able to speculate until recently. There seems always to have been very little information in the public domain about it.

Eric Croddy, author of *Chemical and Biological Warfare: An Annotated Bibliography*[7] told me that 'for a while I thought novichok might never have existed.' What he did eventually discover was that the Russians had developed a unique toxic compound that was seven to ten times as potent as other CW agents such as VX, sarin and soman. He is candid that its purported potency is awesome.

Early reports spoke of novichok being able to defy medical treatment, that it could filter through all known Western gas masks and that CW field detectors were not able to spot it.

Strategically, said one of those who had worked with novichok, it has a singular advantage over other nerve agents: It can be used in ultra-cold temperatures and won't freeze on the battlefield.

'Worse,' says Croddy, 'novichok binary components were specifically designed to be indistinguishable from civilian pesticide manufacture. It can (or so it is claimed) be made in any fertilizer factory.' He points out that though it violates the Chemical Weapons Convention, novichok is apparently not listed among the treaty-controlled schedules of chemicals subject to routine verification.

A binary weapon is made of two ingredients that become lethal only after they are combined, usually in those few seconds when the chemical munition is on its way towards the target: That makes novichok easily and safely transportable. In contrast, with unitary chemical weapons such as VX and sarin (which Syria, Iraq, Iran and some other Middle States have in quantity) in which the ingredients are already combined in the manufacturing process.

Unitary weapons, consequently, are lethal from the start and thus dangerous when there are shells being hurled about on the battlefield. Your own people could be killed if your ammunition takes a hit.

When it was first disclosed that Moscow had been working on a succession of top-secret binary weapons programs, the news could not have come at a worse time for the Russians. It immediately followed the signing of a bilateral agreement between the US and the USSR in 1990 for both countries to reduce their respective CW stockpiles. The end of the Cold War had arrived and the event was a milestone in the thaw. In any event, the 1972 trilateral agreement between the US, Britain and Russia precluded such activity: Revelations that Russia had not played by the rules were a public relations disaster.

Thus, in 1992, the intelligence community was rocked when they read a report titled 'A Poisoned Police' in the weekly *Moscow News*. Written by Russian scientist Dr Vil S. Mirzayanov, he disclosed that all along Russia had been clandestinely building a new class of secret, highly effective binary weapons. This program was so successful, he declared in his article, that those involved were actually honored with the Lenin Prize at a Kremlin function.

Dr Mirzayanov, a 26-year veteran of the Soviet CW program and his associate, Lev Fedorov[8], went public about novichok in what they termed were 'the interests of humanity'. For his efforts, Mirzayanov was arrested and jailed for 'revealing state secrets'.

Also associated with the exposé was another Soviet scientist Valdimir Uglev. He stated in an interview that he not only knew about novichok but had helped invent the nerve agent. Though he was locked out of his laboratories by the authorities, Uglev warned that unless charges against Mirzayanov and others were dropped, he would disclose publicly the chemical formula of the controversial binary agent

The ploy took a big pair of balls to implement. It had been a bluff, but the threat worked. After Yuri Baturin, security advisor to Boris Yeltsin convinced him to keep the details secret, Uglev admitted that he really didn't have the information after all. Mirzayanov meanwhile, once released from prison, emigrated to the US where he met Americans more than eager to talk to him about what he had done in Russia's secret BW laboratories. For his part, Fedorov has since written two historical accounts of the Soviet Union's development of chemical weapons[9] .

Another scandal followed not long afterwards. Russian Lt Gen Anatoly Kuntsevich, a graduate of the (Soviet) Military Academy of Chemical Defense in 1958, and himself an author of over two hundred works, was dismissed from his position as head of Center of Ecotoximetry at the Academy of Sciences Institute of Chemical Physics. After a furious exchange with his fellow generals, he was charged with helping smuggle a quantity of CW nerve agent precursors to Syria.

Unlike most of his colleagues, many of whom made no secret of the fact that they despised Arabs, this officer - a maverick and totally outspoken - had apparently always maintained close ties with the Syrian president's advisors.

Kuntsevich's political sentiments can perhaps be gauged from the fact that while this drama was unraveling, he tried to win a parliamentary seat in the Russian Duma with the late Zhirinovsky's reactionary party which was characterized by anti-Semitic utterances during the election process.

It is noteworthy that Kuntsevich (who shared the Lenin Prize for his work in binary chemical weapons with three other former Soviet scientists[10]) never specifically denied his actions[11]. He simply justified his contacts with Syria on the basis that it was part of a deal that had been authorized under a 'long-standing contract obligation' with the Assad regime .

Now novichok (in Russian the word means 'newcomer') is once more in the news. Following an assignment to several Former Soviet Union states,

Judith Miller of *The New York Times* visited the so-called Chemical Research Institute in Nukus, Uzbekistan, which, Soviet defectors and American officials maintain was the site of a major research and testing site for novichok. By then the US and Uzbekistan had quietly negotiated a bilateral agreement to provide $6m in American aid to decontaminate and dismantle one of the FSU's largest chemical weapons facilities. In an interview in Tashkent, Isan M. Mustafoev, the Uzbeki deputy foreign minister, told Miller that 'we were shocked when we first learnt the real picture'.

> '...in one room stood a large test chamber into which smaller animals were placed for testing...another room contained treadmills for dogs and dozens of testing harnesses, to cram dogs' muzzles into gas masks, leaving their bodies exposed,' she reported[12].

According to Uzbeki and American experts, the device enabled scientists to expose either the dogs' skin or lungs to lethal chemical agents.

Miller reported that only in recent years has information started to emerge about hundreds of open-air chemical tests at the Nukus plant and on the neighboring Ustyurt Plateau in the Turgey steppe. She described the region as an inhospitable desert several hundred miles to the west of the Aral Sea with which Uzbekistan and Kazakhstan share common waters.

As she recorded, by the time it was all over in 1992, and the Soviet Union started to unravel, more than three hundred scientists at the plant packed up everything and went home.

The question most often asked by Western defense and intelligence analysts is what exactly is novichok? Croddy has consistently maintained that 'the answers are hidden in classified reports somewhere'. He explained to me what it is *not*:

- It does not owe its toxicity to being an acetylcholinesterase (AChE) inhibitor, at least according to Vil Mirzayanov: it might inhibit AChE, but that may be only a minor or secondary effect.
- If it is not covered by the technical parameters of the substance and precursor lists of the CWC, it does not have a direct P-C bond (if it contains phosphorous at all).

Croddy goes on: 'If the reports that we already have are to be interpreted literally that novichok can be produced (at least one of the binary components, anyway) at a fertilizer plant, then we need to think very carefully about what is produced at a real fertilizer plant. The chemical fertilizer that I buy at my local store is your basic ammonia, potash and phosphate.

'Now potassium is a dead end for finding a compound that might be used as a weapon, at least for these purposes. Nitrogen and phosphorus, of course, are readily found in all kinds of chemical weapons They serve different purposes and depending on how they are attached to other organic and inorganic structures. There are some organophosphoric compounds called "caged" which are reasonably toxic, but the analogs that I am aware of, are nowhere near as toxic as soman or VX.'

There is another reality, Croddy declares: 'The general-purpose criterion of the CWC notwithstanding, such compounds are technically not listed under CWC control lists. But again, any nation that has signed on to the treaty, cannot (and should not) make chemical weapons regardless of whether or not they are explicitly listed in the schedules,' he declared.

Inconclusive disclosures in a Decision Brief by the Center for Security Policy[13] claimed that '…soldiers can mix the innocuous starting materials (of novichok) to create the lethal product in the field: One, by means of a simple addition of alcohol (presumably ethanol) and another by mixing it with acetonitrile.'

Novichok's pedigree goes back a long time. Lev Fedorov wrote[14] that the USSR Council of Ministers in 1973 initiated a 'Flora' program in order to develop herbicides to be used in wartime. As he explained, various programs fed off a bureaucratic windfall to fund both chemical and biological weapons projects entitled 'Flute', 'Fouette', 'Fagot', 'Flask', 'Ferment' and 'Factor'. That was followed a decade later with a special decree tasking 'Foliant' program scientists to work on a new and very advanced generation of binary weapons.

According to Fedorov, there were five 'promising' nerve agent prototypes that were later developed. Novichok-5 included A-232 and its 'ethyl analogue' A-234.

Dr Jonathan Tucker provided this writer with a footnote of his own[15] to the quandary facing the West.

Quoting[16] an interview in the Russian publication *Novoye Vrema*, Mirzayanov claimed that under the 'Foliant' program the Soviet Union secretly developed and tested three new unitary CW agents. The first was Substance-33, a compound similar to the persistent nerve gas VX, of which fifteen tons were produced in the early 1980s (in a full-scale production facility near the city of Novochebokarsk in the upper Volta Region). Mirzayanov stated at the time that while the West was under the impression that the Novochebokarsk facility was involved in VX production, it was actually working on the much more potent Substance-33.

More than one authority, including Howard T. Uhal, formerly of Clemson University, South Carolina[17] has since asked whether it was not Substance-33 that was used by Iraqi Forces during the Gulf War.

Two other unitary agent substances were also developed: A-230, which was officially approved by the Soviet Army in 1988 and A-232 (an agent similar to A-230) but that was never actually formally approved by Moscow. Tucker disclosed that all three unitary agents became the basis for later research into the development of the novichok series of binary weapons started at the State Union Scientific Research Institute of Organic Chemistry and Technology (GosNIIOKht) in Moscow and its affiliate in Volsk-17 (near Shikhany).

The first Soviet binary agent, novichok-5 was derived from the unitary nerve agent A-232. A test batch of five to ten metric tons of it was produced at a pilot-scale plant in Volvograd and field-tested at the CW testing ground at Nukus, the very same one that Judith Miller visited.

GosNIIOKht also developed a binary form of Substance-33 that has no established name, but which Mirzayanov calls novichok-#. It, too, was tested at Nukus and was adopted as a CW in 1990.

Mirzayanov stated that the organization developed a third binary agent called novichok-7, which has a similar volatility to soman but is about ten times as effective. It was produced in experimental quantities (tens of tons) in Shikhany, as well as Volvograd. Two other binary nerve agents, novichok-8 and novichok-9, were under development but never went into production.

Mirzayanov: 'Although the chemical structures of the novel new CW agents are unknown, they are reportedly organophosphate compounds that were derived from accessible raw materials.' He quoted Valdimir Uglev, the inventor of A-232 as saying that 'the weapon's originality lies in the simplicity of its components, which are used in civilian industry, and which cannot therefore be regulated by international experts'.

Moreover, he stated[18], since binary components are much less toxic than unitary nerve agents, the novichok series might well be produced at commercial chemical plants that manufacture fertilizers and pesticides. In its final form, he warned, it is deadly. 'Even accidental exposure to it is invariably fatal.' Those who came into contact with it remained disabled for the rest of their lives. Also, its effects are incurable[19]. Croddy says that the disabling effects of novichok as described by Russian scientists, remind him of tri-ortho cresol phosphate poisoning which has a low anti-AChE activity but permanent neuropathy can follow.

Questioned by Uhal as to whether Russia sent CW to any Middle Eastern states, Dr Mirzayanov was certain that they had not. But, he added, Baghdad might have received Substance-33, an analog of VX gas. All Soviet/Russian CW agents have their own 'substance' code numbers. Sarin, for instance is referred to in Soviet argot as Substance-35 while soman is Substance-55. Similarly, Substance-33, the Russian expatriate explained, was known as Soviet V-gas and produced in the USSR instead of VX gas.

When discussing these nerve agents with their American counterparts, the Russians always referred to their V-gas as VX-gas, which was incorrect, since V-gas has its own unique chemical structure and properties. Mirzayanov felt that this subtle but vital piece of Soviet deception might ultimately have had some tragic consequences, especially with regard to Allied forces in Iraq during Gulf War 1.

For while US troops were prepared for the full range of known CW agents (including mustard), they couldn't have known about Substance-33. Certainly, they might not have been able to recognize it if it had been deployed, accidentally or otherwise, Mirzayanov told Uhal. He qualified his statement by admitting that he wasn't at all sure whether Iraq had actually used the Russian V-gas.

Conversely there is some evidence that Washington was not quite as unprepared as Dr Mirzayanov suggests. A recently declassified document[20] titled 'Defense Intelligence Assessment - Iraqi Military Developments Through 1992' stated that as early as 1989, 'Iraq is expected to begin producing the persistent nerve agent VX or an analog of VX this year.'

There is also the matter of nerve gasses possibly being linked to the gradually developing Islamic missile threat. Several countries including Syria, Egypt possibly and certainly Iran are at issue here. Tehran has the most advanced missile development program in the region.

Under a previous administration, the-then Israeli Air Force chief of staff Major-General Ben-Eliahu went on record as saying that Israel was concerned about the growing number of ballistic missiles that posed a threat to the Middle East and, in particular, to his country.

'Our strategy, as well as our politics and tactics, have to be adaptive (to these threats). The number is growing and the range of these missiles is getting longer,' he said.

'It is also worth remembering that as long ago as 1997 there were reports that Syria's Scud-C missiles were being armed for long-range chemical weapons delivery. Syria at that stage was reported by US intelligence sources as having developed its own version of cluster bomblets for loading nerve agents into its 884mm Scud-C warheads.

The Israeli newspaper *Yedi'ot Aharanot,* quoting Harold Hough, an independent US analyst, reached the following conclusions after studying satellite imagery of suspected Syrian missile deployment sites. The Scud-C missile has an estimated circular error probable (CEP) of about a mile. That made it improbable that it could hit specific military targets. More likely, said Hough, the Scud-C would deliver a chemical warhead to create mass casualties and havoc.

While most systems behind contemporary Scud missiles of the kind deployed in the Middle East date from the Second World War, it remains a reasonably potent close-range weapon, especially if tipped with WMD. Advances made by both Iran (with South African rocket scientists' help) as well as North Korea, have added markedly to this clumsy weapon's efficacy.

Syrian Scud-C deployments include a relatively high ratio of launchers to missiles, thus enabling the young President Assad to launch most of his ballistic missiles in a limited number of salvos. Most Scuds, worldwide, are matched to about one launcher for every ten missiles. In contrast, he stated, 'Syria appears to have a 1:2 ratio. East Germany in its heyday had about one launcher for every five of its nuclear and chemically armed Scuds,' said Hough.

It is clear that Israeli military planners are acutely aware of any potential Arab missile threat. Damascus, they say, has the largest and most advanced chemical weapon (CW) capability in the Arab world, with Egypt and, until recently, Iraq as near contenders. Moreover, apart from having tipped its Scud missiles with nerve gas, Damascus has developed chemical gravity bombs for delivery by aircraft.

Historically, Syrian CW development was spurred by a succession of disastrous conventional military defeats at the hands of Israel in 1967, 1973 and again in 1982 when it lost a huge proportion of its air force without a single Israeli fighter having been brought down.

There are indications that as early as 1972, Syrian CW scientists began serious work on the program as a possible answer to the reality of overwhelming Israeli military supremacy.

By 1986, President Assad's father possessed a large arsenal of both blister and nerve agents. There is also evidence - including intelligence testimony from Russian specialists now living in the United States - that he received considerable aid from the Soviets. Trouble is, while there was still some Russian involvement in these departments until recently, this has been a painfully difficult issue to pin down. At present just about everybody in the FSU is in denial.

At the same time the Syrian stockpile of nerve gas and other CW agents is reckoned by Eric Croddy to be measured in terms of 'hundreds of tons'.

Agents include sarin, VX and mustard gas. Less than a single drop of VX on a man's skin will kill him, says Croddy.

While Assad's CW program remains dependent on foreign chemicals and equipment, much of the work is now being conducted at a facility north of Damascus known as CERS: *Centre d'Etudes et de Recherche Scientifique.* Other production facilities for WMD are near Damascus, Aleppo and Homs.

One Jane's source maintains that hundreds of tons of nerve agents are being produced in Syria annually. Damascus denies it, even though satellite photos of all of Syria's WMD are available on the web[21].

In an exchange of correspondence with this writer, Brigadier-General (Res) Aryeh Shalev of Tel Aviv's Jaffee Center for Strategic Studies said that in the long term, it was not impossible that Syria could go to war in a bid to recapture the Golan Heights even though the statement was made prior to 'Operation Iraqi Freedom'. There were a number of imponderables to such a scenario, he warned.

'If the young Assad decides to take that course, then he will start as his father did in 1973, with a surprise attack. He is likely to take advantage of the positive ratio, for Syria, of the numbers of active armed forces (compared to Israel).' General Shalev explained that this was because Syria's armed forces 'are always on an active footing whereas Israel needs at least forty-eight hours for mobilization and deployment'. Under special circumstances, he added, Assad might just be tempted to capitalize on this advantage. Like his departed father, the Syrian President would like to see his country's flag over the Heights.

The main hurdle then, as now, has been the IDF's determination - for clearly delineated strategic reasons, to hold on to its three early warning electronic outposts. There is one on Mount Hermon and others have been built on the eastern crest of the Heights, including Lucifer, the most extensive of them all.

I was able to view these sites from the UN Area of Separation, about an hour's drive south of Damascus. All three installations with their powerful arrays of aerials, radar masts and defenses might easily have been mistaken for a *Star Wars* film set. Though I visited the place under the auspices of the UN mission in Damascus while on a visit to Syria a few years ago, I was warned not to be seen there with a camera.

The Israeli government has always maintained that the status of the Golan facilities were not negotiable, even though that of Jewish settlers on the Heights, as with their counterparts in the Sinai a generation ago, might ultimately be.

There is some concern, too, in the way that Syria, in spite of its impoverished economy, has been beefing up its armed forces. The latest development in this regard is that President Assad, with Saudi and some Iranian financial help, launched an ambitious program to strengthen his armored corps and acquire a more modern and effective missile arsenal in the New Millennium. Almost all the hardware ordered was Russian, as had been the tradition for decades. As I was to see during my own visit, Moscow continues to maintain a large cadre of military advisors and technicians (said to be about a thousand) in Syria.

According to Shalev, one of that country's objectives for embarking on a program would be to bolster the country's weakened image in the Arab world. Now, with Saddam gone, the issue might not warrant the same priority.

1   *Die Welt*: Berlin: Internet text in German; 30 August 2002: FBIS translated text
2   House Armed Services Committee, Congress, Washington DC, September 10, 2002
3   *Scourge: The Once and Future Threat of Smallpox:* Dr Jonathan Tucker, Atlantic Monthly Press, New York, 2001
4   There is a significant difference of opinion within the scientific community on actual quantities needed for an infection to take place: some authorities opt for the higher figure, others for much less
5   *Die Welt: Ibid*
6   House Armed Services Committee: *Ibid*
7   Eric Croddy: Scarecrow Press, London & Lanham Maryland, 1997. Also *Chemical and Biological Warfare: A Comprehensive Survey for the Concerned Citizen* (with Clarisa Perez-Armendariz and John Hart): Copernicus Books, New York, 2002
8   Lev Fedorov: 'We Were Preparing For an All-Out Chemical War,' *Obsgchaya Gazeta*, in Russian: #4 January 26, 1995. p9 translated by FBIS
9   Lev Aleksandrovich Fedorov has followed up on his *Chemical Weapons in Russia: History, Ecology, Politics (Khimicheskoye Oruzhiye V Rossii: Istoriya, Ekologiya, Politika*, 1994, pp1-95, (translated in FBIS) with another monograph not yet available in English
10 A Gayev, A Kisletsov and V. Petrunin
11 J. Michael Waller, 'The Chemical Weapons Cover-up', *The Wall Street Journal,* February 13, 1997; p18
12 Judith Miller, *New York Times:* May 25, 1999: p3, personal communication: August 1, 1999
13 Decision Brief, The Center for Security Policy, No 97-D-19, February 4, 1997 using a *Washington Times* report as a source
14 Fedorov: *Ibid*
15 Dr Jonathan B. Tucker, Monterey Institute of International Studies; personal communication, February 4, 1998
16 With Lev Fedorov: No 44 (October, 1992). pp 4-9 in JPRS-TAC-92-033 (November 14, 1992)
17 Howard T. Uhal; The UKOPRP: 'Soviet Chemical Warfare Agents Novichok and Substance-33
18 Mirzayanov: *Ibid*
19 Uhal: *Ibid*
20 Department of Defense GulfLINK file 02200639.89
21 www.globalsecurity.org

12

IRAQ'S MISSING WEAPONS OF MASS DESTRUCTION

John Gannon, Chairman of America's National Intelligence Council and the CIA's top official in charge of analysis, recently told a Stanford University conference on the threat of biological and chemical weapons that 'the battlefield of the future could be Main Street, USA'. He disclosed there were now at least twelve countries that possessed or were actively pursuing offensive capability with such arms. 'As the Iraqi case so dramatically illustrated, even a residual biological or chemical capability can be highly dangerous,' he said, noting that 'years of international pressure has been unable to stop Baghdad's weapons programs entirely...I don't think even friendly governments recognize how ominous the trends are.'

In his series of unprecedented disclosures on September 24, 2002 British Prime Minister Tony Blair shared with his public the reasons why he believed the Iraqi issue had become 'a current and serious threat' to the UK national interest.

The document, subsequently subject to much controversy and titled 'Iraq's Weapons of Mass Destruction', made a few astonishing pronouncements. Among them was that British Intelligence had uncovered the fact that Saddam's military planning allowed for some of his weapons, and in particular his missile batteries, to be ready within forty-five minutes of an order to use them[1]. Mr Blair said that there was little doubt that 'Saddam will now do his utmost to try to conceal his weapons from UN inspectors'. He added that 'the picture presented to me by the JIC (Joint Intelligence Committee)[2] in recent months has become more, not less, worrying.'

He went on: 'Under Saddam Hussein Iraq developed chemical and biological weapons, acquired missiles allowing it to attack neighboring countries with these weapons and persistently tried to develop a nuclear bomb. Saddam has used chemical weapons, both against Iran and against his own people. Following the Gulf War, Iraq had to admit to all this. And in the ceasefire of 1991, Saddam agreed unconditionally to give up his weapons of mass destruction.'

The Prime Minister said that much information about Iraq's weapons of mass destruction was already in the public domain from UN reports and from Iraqi defectors and 'this points clearly to Iraq's continuing possession, after 1991, of chemical and biological agents and weapons produced before the Gulf War. It shows that Iraq has refurbished sites formerly associated with the production of chemical and biological agents. And it indicates that Iraq remains able to manufacture these agents, and to use bombs, shells, artillery rockets and ballistic missiles to deliver them.'

Blair maintained that an independent and well-researched overview of this public evidence was provided by the International Institute for Strategic Studies (IISS): This was *Iraq's Weapons of Mass Destruction: a Net Assessment*, published in London on September 9, 2002. The IISS report, he stated, suggested that Iraq could assemble nuclear weapons within months of obtaining fissile material from foreign sources.

'As well as the public evidence, however, significant additional information is available to the Government from secret intelligence sources, described in more detail in this paper. This intelligence cannot tell us about everything. It did however provide a fuller picture of Iraqi plans and capabilities.

'It shows that Saddam Hussein attaches great importance to possessing weapons of mass destruction which he regards as the basis for Iraq's regional power. It shows that he does not regard them only as weapons of last resort. He is ready to use them, including against his own population, and is determined to retain them, in breach of United Nations Security Council Resolutions (UNSCR).

'Intelligence also demonstrates that Iraq is preparing plans to conceal evidence of these weapons, including incriminating documents, from renewed inspections. And it confirms that despite sanctions and the policy of containment, Saddam has continued to make progress with his illicit weapons programs.

'As a result of this intelligence, we judge that Iraq has continued to produce chemical and biological agents and has military plans for the use of chemical and biological weapons, including against its own Shi'a population. Some of these weapons are deployable within forty-five minutes of an order to use them; command and control arrangements are in place to use chemical and biological weapons.' The (period) used here is the approximate time required to fuel up and fire Iraqi Scuds.

According to Blair, while authority in Iraq ultimately resided with Saddam Hussein, some intelligence suggested that he may have delegated this authority to his second son Qusy. Prime Minister Blair went on:

'He also developed mobile laboratories for military use, corroborating earlier reports about the mobile production of biological warfare agents;

pursued illegal programs to procure controlled materials of potential use in the production of chemical and biological weapons programs; tried covertly to acquire technology and materials which could be used in the production of nuclear weapons; sought significant quantities of uranium from Africa, despite having no active civil nuclear power program that could require it; recalled specialists to work on its nuclear program; illegally retained up to 20 Al Hussein missiles, with a range of 400 miles, capable of carrying chemical or biological warheads; started deploying its al-Samoud (SA-2 derivative) liquid propellant missile, and has used the absence of weapons inspectors to work on extending its range to at least 120 miles, which is beyond the limit of 95 miles imposed by the United Nations; started producing the solid-propellant Ababil-100, and is making efforts to extend its range to at least 120 miles; constructed a new engine test stand for the development of missiles capable of reaching the UK Sovereign Base Areas in Cyprus and NATO members (Greece and Turkey), as well as all Iraq's Gulf neighbors and Israel; pursued illegal programs to procure materials for use in its illegal development of long range missiles; learnt lessons from previous UN weapons inspections and has already begun to conceal sensitive equipment and documentation in advance of the return of inspectors.'

Divided into time periods that correspond to the years during and after United Nations weapons inspections, the section provided by Britain's Joint Intelligence Committee for the period 1999-2002 is informative

The report tabulated various intelligence findings including the fact that since the withdrawal of the inspectors, the JIC had monitored evidence, including some from secret intelligence, of continuing work on Iraqi offensive chemical and biological warfare capabilities.

In the first half of the year 2000, it said, the JIC noted intelligence on Iraqi attempts to procure dual-use chemicals and on the reconstruction of civil chemical production at sites formerly associated with the chemical warfare program. Iraq had also been trying to procure dual-use materials and equipment that could have been used for a biological warfare program.

Personnel known to have been connected to the biological warfare program up to the Gulf War had been conducting research into pathogens.

There was intelligence that Iraq was starting to produce biological warfare agents in mobile production facilities. Planning for the project, begun in 1995 under Dr Rihab Taha, was known to have been a central player in the pre-Gulf War program[3].

The JIC concluded that Iraq had sufficient expertise, equipment and material to produce biological warfare agents within weeks using its legitimate biotechnology facilities. In mid-2001 the JIC assessed that Iraq retained some chemical warfare agents, precursors, production equipment and weapons from before the Gulf War. These stocks were to have enabled Iraq to produce significant quantities of mustard gas within weeks and of nerve agent within months.

The JIC concluded that intelligence on Iraqi former chemical and biological warfare facilities, their limited reconstruction and civil production, pointed to a continuing research and development program. These chemical and biological capabilities represented the most immediate threat from Iraqi weapons of mass destruction, it declared.

Another consideration was the fact that since the withdrawal of the UN arms inspection team in 1998, Iraqi development of mass destruction weaponry had been helped by the absence of inspectors and the increase in illegal border trade, which provided hard currency.

Significantly, the JIC believed that in the six months prior to issuing its report, its earlier judgments on Iraqi chemical and biological warfare capabilities had been confirmed. So too, had an assessment that Iraq had the means to deliver chemical and biological weapons.

On a different tack, shortly before Ambassador Richard Butler's UN Special Commission (UNSCOM) was forced out of Iraq in the late Nineties, that organization revealed to the Security Council a range of devices that Iraq intended to use in its biological weapons (BW) program during 'Operation Desert Storm' in 1991.

At least three of these involved either aircraft or drones. Of course Baghdad denied most of it, even though these claims were backed by aerial and satellite photography and, shortly afterwards, the discovery of a squadron of Delphin L-29 jets converted to unmanned aerial vehicles (UAVs). They had been reconfigured by Iraqi technicians to carry chemical and/or biological weapons[4].

Iraq did admit that a succession of Mirage F1 drop tanks were modified for the dissemination of BW agents, one of them by mid-January 1991, and in time for deployment in the first Gulf War. Video footage obtained by UNSCOM showed Iraqi jet aircraft laying down a line source of anthrax simulant (*Bacillus subtilis*, or *Bacillus globigii*). The photographs were incriminating. Subsequent interviews with UN weapons inspectors indicated that a total of a dozen such aircraft drop tanks had been produced. All disappeared after the invasion.

Baghdad also produced a pilotless MiG-21, though it is unclear whether it was to have carried CW or BW. UN inspectors suggested that both were envisioned and there was nothing to show that this project had been dropped before completion. More evidence was provided by UNSCOM of the development by Iraq's Technical Research Center (TRC) of aerial drones to deliver WMD onto Allied troop deployments north and north-west of Kuwait at the same time.

Constructed by the TRC at Salman Pak in addition (and believed at UN Headquarters to have had considerable significance in future operations), there were about a dozen modified aerosol generators for the dispersal of BW agents or toxins from helicopters or slow-moving aircraft.

While it was obvious that these devices were intended to be used against the Allies, they never were because all Iraqi aircraft were destroyed either on the ground prior to take-off, or moments afterwards, so effective was Allied and Coalition air cover during both invasions. Another issue continues to fester: whether they were intended for use in another country, perhaps Israel.

Referred to as the Zubaidy Device, these systems were successfully field-tested in August 1988, to spray *Bacillus anthracis* spores. UN experts assessed these devices as an effective BW munition[5]. All have since disappeared and remain to be accounted for. After hostilities ended, Baghdad was vociferous in its claims that either this equipment did not exist or that it had 'no idea where they are'.

It is notable that these catalogues of dishonesty and duplicity were symptomatic of Saddam's official line throughout his rule, particularly during the course of the last two decades. In some respects, particularly where members of the old order continue to be involved or have been taken into custody, the deceit continues.

Other weapons systems that Iraq was working on were:

Cluster Bombs Although Baghdad always denied that any were produced, an Iraqi official mentioned to UNSCOM that they were part of the biological warfare program, though he formally retracted his remark after he had been visited by Iraqi security police, the *Mukhabarat*. Afterwards, Baghdad stated that cluster munitions played no part in its BW program.

122mm Rocket Warheads The majority of the declared BW field trials carried out by Iraq involved testing 122mm rocket warheads, some of which were later uncovered by the UN and destroyed (see the photos on the back cover of this book). By all accounts, this part of the program proceeded in an ordered and logical fashion and commenced with static tests of single warheads, culminating with salvoes of rockets charged with BW agents or simulants. There are sufficient documents, videotapes and interview information detailing this work to make it irrefutable. Despite progress made over a period of years, the rationale for their use and the seemingly abrupt end of the project was never satisfactorily explained.

Land Mines When Iraq was considering which weapons to use for the dissemination of BW agents, landmines became an option. One of the scientists involved was sent to Al-Qa'a Qa'a, an Iraqi explosives factory, to look for types of anti-personnel mines that might be filled with nerve agents. Baghdad claimed that he found nothing suitable but, says the report, some doubt lingered as to whether this was true.

Artillery Shells A single 155mm shell was found at Iraq's main BW production facility at Al Hakam. It had been recovered from the River Euphrates and was of the same type used for CW agents. Another, smaller shell was also uncovered and detonated by UNSCOM. Four similar shells were used in a trial for the dissemination of the BW agent ricin, a stash of which was later discovered in the possession of a terrorist group in Britain in early 2003.

LD-250 Aerial Bombs Static trials of LD-250 aerial bombs to disperse BW agents were conducted in 1988. It was likely that further trials were conducted, though Iraq says they were not, even though earlier tests were considered successful. Despite these efforts (and the adaptation of the weapon for BW agent delivery) Baghdad claimed that no further development occurred.

Fragmentation Weapons Experimentation on the subdermal introduction of *Clostridium perfringens* spores, applicable to fragmentation weapons was acknowledged by a senior Iraqi worker in the field. He admitted that the work was relevant to fragmentation weapons that were designed to cause gas gangrene. Questioned about this revelation, officials in Baghdad denied carrying out any developmental work on weapons exploiting this research. However, they conceded that some research involving aerosolizing gas gangrene spores went ahead. This suggested that Iraq was looking to see if it could be used as an aerosolized threat.

350mm and 1,000mm Caliber SuperGun The Iraqi SuperGun program with the aid of Canadian national Gerald [Gerry] Bull, who was later assassinated by Israel's Mossad in Belgium[6] was developing long-range projectiles for both caliber weapons. Drawings of various designs for the 350mm device depict a projectile with a guidance and control section, control surfaces on the fins and a payload of around thirty-five lbs. Plans existed for a 1,000mm caliber weapon that would have had a longer range with a payload in excess of about two-hundred-and-twenty lbs.

Iraq maintains that there was never any connection between the BW program and that of the 'SuperGuns', though it was managed by the same authority responsible for such work, the Military Industrial Commission (MIC). Like the BW project, no objective or planning was acknowledged, even though this weapons system was well advanced with several sites used and plans prepared for a succession of new and more versatile weapons. Nor was its intended purpose ever revealed, though a succession of weapons and Middle East specialists maintain that considering the range, the ultimate target of any such weapon was Israel.

A long-range delivery system, with its guided projectile capable of delivering relatively modest payloads, UNSCOM specialists agree, suggests very potent warheads such as CW or BW agents or even radioactive material. Chairman Butler concluded that without a more comprehensive disclosure by Iraq, the possibility that this weapon was being developed for the delivery of BW payload could not be ruled out.

Until 'Operation Iraqi Freedom' took place, it was clear to most strategists in the West that the Iraqi weapons of mass destruction issue would continue to loom large within the framework of the Middle East equation until something positive was done about it. That too, was the consensus among former members of UNSCOM, some of whom were later incorporated into its successor, UNMOVIC.

In particular, Ewen Buchanan told me, not only had the Iraqi government gone to extraordinary lengths to hide its biological weapons' assets, it had done everything it could to prevent weapons inspectors from finding them – or, for that matter, any paperwork relating to them. This was detailed in two reports compiled by UNSCOM's head, Ambassador Richard Butler. The two-hundred-and-seventy-two-page document (which covered a variety of priority issues in the chemical and biological areas as well as missile production) underscored discrepancies between what Iraq declared and what UNSCOM believed was the true picture in relation to these assets.

Ambassador Butler made three basic points about the disarmament record in an annex to the report:

> During the first four years following 'Operation Desert Storm', UNSCOM was 'very substantially misled by the Baghdad government both in terms of its understanding of Iraq's proscribed weapons programs and the continuation of prohibited activities'.

Second, the Commission was obliged to undertake a degree of forensic work that was never intended to be the case.

Last, in spite of a vigorous effort by the UN (countered by a vigorous level of obfuscation on the part of the Iraqis) it was never possible to fully verify Iraq's statements with respect to the nature and magnitude of its proscribed weapons programs.

This, said Butler, caused Saddam Hussein to claim that 'Iraq had fulfilled all its disarmament obligations, had ceased concealment policies and actions and possessed neither WMD nor the ability to make them'. Which, he declared, was clearly not the case.

For instance he stated, in response to the Commission's requests for relevant documents, that 'Iraq had repeatedly claimed that they no longer existed or could not be located, which was shown to be false.' That was followed, in August 1998, by a statement from Iraq, 'that unless the Commission can demonstrate that Iraq has retained prohibited items, then it must declare that Iraq had fully implemented its obligations under Section C or Resolution 687'. In his preamble, Mr Butler listed a number of priority issues under the different weapons' headings:

Chemical Munitions Priority Issues In July 1998 UNSCOM inspectors found a document during a routine search that indicated serious discrepancies with Baghdad's declarations in respect of the expenditure of CW in the 1980s. According to this find, Iraq consumed about six thousand chemical aerial bombs *fewer* than it stated in its declarations to the UN. It claimed, too, that five-hundred-and-fifty shells filled with mustard gas had been 'lost' shortly after the Gulf War and maintained that, in any event, the agents would have degraded long before. In truth, though, there is no reason for properly distilled mustard, or even some of relative impurity, to go 'bad' even decades after manufacture. However, a dozen mustard-filled shells were recovered from a former CW storage facility in the period 1997/98; a chemical sampling revealed that the mustard was still of the highest quality.

Of one-thousand-five-hundred R-400 bombs produced by Iraq, more than a two-thirds were declared as having been unilaterally destroyed by Iraq (including a hundred-and-fifty-odd stated as having been filled with BW agents). There has never been any accounting for the five hundred outstanding bombs even if Iraq were to be taken at face value in its initial declaration.

Also, the degree of verification achieved with regard to the accounting for the production of Agent VX, the Commission said, was not satisfactory.

Iraq maintained that it had produced almost four tons of VX nerve agents. While it provided documents for the 1988 output, nothing was forthcoming for its activities for 1990 and after. Iraq also strenuously insisted that it had never weaponized VX gas whereas sampling of special warheads resulted in significant doubts upon this claim, said Butler. That is to say, there is *no doubt* that Iraq weaponized VX, including filling Scud warheads with it, along with dicyclohexyl carbodiimide, a well-known stabilizing agent for VX.

Then there is the disappearance of a hundred-and-ninety-seven pieces of CW production equipment that was secreted prior to UNSCOM's arrival in 1991. Only a small proportion was ever found and destroyed.

Biological Weapons Priority Issues Until August 1995 (and the defection of Lt General Hussein Kamel Hassan) Iraq consistently denied that it had been involved in any proscribed BW activities. Moreover, in spite of evidence to the contrary (which resulted in the destruction of some BW assets) it neither provided UNSCOM with an account of that program nor detailed materials or items which may have been used or acquired for that purpose. This was in spite of the Commission having provided Baghdad with specific evidence that the program did in fact exist.

Since August 1995 (until the forced withdrawal of UNSCOM from Iraq) Saddam provided the UN with a succession of 'Full, Final and Complete Disclosures (FFCD)', not one of which was found to have been *fully* accurate. In particular, the Commission asked for details about BW agent weaponization, bulk BW agent production and acquisitions for BW program. None were given.

Mr Butler stressed that 'it needs to be recognized that Iraq possesses an industrial capacity and knowledge base, through which BW agents could be produced quickly and in volume'.

Of the more than three hundred sites that were eventually included in UNSCOM's monitoring database, a fair proportion involved the potential production of BWs. But this department also provided some of the biggest headaches and for several reasons: Firstly, BW agents can be produced in small facilities using relatively simple equipment. Second, there are limited signatures to look for, especially if small quantities were being produced and were not being weaponized. Hence the net cast for monitoring must be extensive. Following standard procedures, a great number of facilities incorporating dual-use capabilities were routinely inspected and were under varying degrees of monitoring. These included such facilities as production sites, R&D facilities, laboratories and other apparently innocuous sites such as breweries and drug production plants.

Priority Issues in the Missile Area There was evidence from three independent laboratories that in pursuing a WMD program, Iraq tipped some of its missile heads with VX gas. There were also numerous instances of Iraq having declared that it had destroyed missile warheads when there was proof to the contrary.

'The discrepancies between Iraq's declarations and the physical evidence collected need to be resolved,' said Butler.

Also, the remnants of some fifty warheads (twenty-five imported and a similar number Iraqi-manufactured) declared as unilaterally destroyed, were never recovered. There were also seven missiles in the possession of the Iraqi Army that nobody knew anything about, as well as a variety of major missile components. These included combustion chamber and nozzle assemblies as well as other priority items associated with WMD.

Also missing was the full accounting for imported proscribed missile propellants, totaling roughly five hundred tons.

Butler devoted an entire section (Annex D) to the history of the work done by the Special Commission which, he said, 'has been plagued by coordinated efforts to thwart the full discovery of Iraq's proscribed programs'.

Immediately following the Gulf War, he says, the Iraqi Presidency collected reports on weapons remaining with its Armed Forces. A decision was then apparently taken to provide UNSCOM with only a portion of its proscribed weapons. This policy was based on the following Iraqi actions:

- Providing a portion of their extant weapons stocks with an emphasis on those which were least modern.

- Concealing the full extent of chemical weapons programs, including its VX project and retain production equipment and raw materials.

- Concealing the number and type of BW and CW warheads.

- Concealing indigenous long-range missile production specifically with respect to guidance systems and missile engines.

- Concealing the existence of its offensive BW program and retain all production capabilities.

Of interest here was the discovery in January 1996 by a Commission inspection team of computer files with a missile simulation program at a missile facility. These contained evidence that in July 1992, more than a year after the Gulf War, a flight simulation of a three-stage missile had been executed. It was based on the Scud-B missile. Iraq described the product as a 'Space Launch Vehicle' produced by an unidentified engineer working on his own, which of course was nonsense.

Forensic examination later also revealed that the computer discs were part of a larger collection that was never found. Notably, the report said that due to the manner in which Iraq interfered with the team's analysis, a proper chain of evidence was not maintained.

Shortly before that, late in 1995, Iraq declared that it had imported a large vacuum furnace without notifying the Commission. It was intended for use in the Al Hussein missiles and it was subsequently placed under UNSCOM monitoring procedures. In mid-1998 Iraq undertook to assemble the furnace and began its installation at one of its declared facilities for production of missile engines.

The ninety-one-page section headed 'Status of Verification of Iraq's Biological Warfare Program' provides some of the most intrusive data to be found in UNSCOM's report.

Butler stressed that his inspectors only started looking for biological weapons after Kamel's defection and that was four years after the start of the war. It was only then that the UN was able to show that Iraq had been producing biological weapons, virtually under the noses of the UN weapons inspectors. Why else, the question was posed, would Saddam Hussein have been so secretive about everything to do with his BW program?

Significantly, after July 1995, Iraq produced three FFCDs of its proscribed biological weapons' programs. The last, in September 1997, was a review by a panel of international experts. The declarations made by Baghdad were considered to be deficient in all areas. Claiming that it had not been given an adequate opportunity to present its case, it was allowed to do so again at a Technical Evaluation Meetings (TEM) in Vienna in March 1998. Again, nothing new was submitted.

Then, in July 1998, another review of the FFCD was conducted by a team of international experts in Baghdad. It focused on those elements directly related to the material balance; weapons, bulk agents and materials such as bacterial growth media. Conclusions were as follows:

- On weapons, the team concluded that the materials and their sub-components (production, filling and destruction) declared in the FFCD for biological bombs (R-400) and Al Hussein warheads could not be verified. Further, the account on biological spray devices, modified aircraft drop tanks and the aerosol generator (Zubaidy device) could not be verified.

196

- The material balances for bulk BW agents and their sub-components (production, filling, losses and destruction) for all declared agents (*Clostridium botulinum* toxin, *Bacillus anthracis* spores, aflatoxin, *Clostridium perfringens* spores and wheat smut) could not be verified.

- Nor could the media material balance and its sub-components (acquisition, consumption, losses and destruction) be verified.

- Iraq's FFCD in its totality could not be verified. The team concluded that while the Commission had an incomplete understanding of the philosophy of the program, including the military and other (such as security service) requirements for BW, verification simply could not be achieved.

One of the points repeatedly made by Butler was that from day one Baghdad insisted it never had a BW program. Certainly, it took active steps to conceal the activities at such places as Al Hakam and Kimadia from UNSCOM inspectors.

Only when the Iraqis were presented with evidence of imports of bacterial growth media in quantities that no civilian utility within Iraq's limited biotechnology industry could possibly have used, did it acknowledge that it had produced anthrax and botulinum toxin in bulk. Iraq also admitted to having undertaken weapons tests that involved the use of BW from about 1987 onwards.

Iraq's BW research program goes back a quarter-century. Initial research efforts were begun in 1974 at Al Hazen Ibn Al Haithem Institute. For the next four years, Baghdad admitted that the biological part at Al Hazen was 'research on micro-organisms for military purposes and included antibiotic and environmental resistance, means of production and agent preservation'.

UNSCOM reckoned that apart from anthrax and botox, there was also work on *Vibrio cholerae* and *Shigella* spp, among a host of other organisms studied there. Research was begun in 1985 and, by all accounts, never stopped until Saddam was ousted.

Curiously, once General Kamel defected and Iraq was forced to release a hoard of documents related to its WMD programs, papers relating to biology represented just two hundred pages out of more than a million. The Emergency Session of the Commission held in November 1997 concluded that the biological weapons file was the most serious area in which Iraq had consistently disregarded its obligations under the Security Council Resolution 687.

There is a lot of detail regarding Iraq's material balance declarations for growth media acquisition, usage, consumption and disposal by four key media types: casein, thioglycollate broth, yeast extract and peptone. If there was work done in developing BWs, it would have been linked to one of these. UNSCOM made some interesting comments in this regard (*figures in metric*):

Casein: Iraq claimed that 17,544 kgs of casein was acquired of which 7,074 kgs was used for botulinum toxin (botox) production, 145 kgs were lost or wasted and the balance, 10,335 kgs, was destroyed under UNSCOM supervision. The UN said that apart from initial orders that were derived from three large batches (which arrived in 1988) there was no supporting evidence for any of the figures presented by Iraq.

Thioglycollate Broth: Iraq claimed that 6,036 kgs of broth was acquired and about two-thirds of this was used for botox production. Again, there were no supporting documents. The original order stated the UN failed to account for additional smaller, but still significant, orders for the BW program. Only 1,848 kgs were destroyed under UN supervision and Iraqi and UNSCOM inventories differed markedly in this regard.

Yeast Extract: Yeast extract acquired, said Iraq in a FFCD, was 7,070 kgs. Of this, 1,768 kgs was used for botox, 185 kgs for anthrax spores and 11 kgs for perfringens, but these were only 'estimates'. Once more, UNSCOM declared, there were no supporting documents. The 5,090 kgs yeast extract that Iraq said remained in 1991 appeared to be based on a 1985 inventory and may have had little relation to the actual amount in 1991. Also, Iraq claimed that it had sent 1,807 kgs to Kimadia which offered still more inconsistencies. Ultimately 4,942 kgs of yeast extract was destroyed under supervision.

Peptone: The 1,500 kgs that Iraq said it acquired did not include several other smaller but significant orders. By the time UNSCOM started asking questions, Baghdad said they had 750 kgs in stock and 705 kgs had been 'stolen'. To sum up, Mr Butler's report stated that, as with the other media agents, Iraq and UNSCOM figures differed greatly.

Thus, said Butler at the time, 'there were still 460 kgs of casein unaccounted for and enough to produce 1,200 liters of concentrated botox. Also missing was 80 kgs of thioglycollate broth. The 520 kgs of yeast extract unaccounted for was sufficient to produce 26,000 liters of *Bacillus anthracis* spores, or over three times the amount declared by the regime, another serious inconsistency. Then there was the 1,100 kgs of peptone outstanding, enough to produce 5,500 liters of concentrated perfringens (or about sixteen times the amount declared). In a comment on the subject, the document declared that UNSCOM could not believe the claim that 700 kgs of peptone was stolen. It should be noted that it appeared that the peptone was nearly all devoted to production of *C. perfringens*, and to this bug alone and that this was a significant part of Iraqi BW activity.'

The UN report also stated that although the expiry date for the media would have passed, advice from manufacturers was that, given appropriate storage conditions, particularly away from moisture, it would still have been useable several years later. Croddy maintains that Iraq quickly became self-sufficient in producing its own growth media.

1   See http://www.bbcnews.co.uk under the subheading 'Iraq's Weapons of Mass Destruction'
2   Blair stated: The JIC is at the heart of the British Intelligence machinery. It is a body chaired by the Cabinet Office and made up of the heads of the UK's three Intelligence and Security Agencies, the Chief of Defence Intelligence and senior officials from key government agencies
3   Among some UNSCOM scientists, Dr Taha - because of her obsession with lethal agents - was surreptitiously referred to as 'Dr Death'
4   This emerged after an RAF *Tornado* on a bombing raid in Iraq destroyed the roof of a hangar in which these trainers were hidden. By all accounts they were ready to be deployed
5   Joby Warrick in an article in *The Washington Post* on September 5, 2002 wasn't so sure. He said that that the so-called Zubaidy device was 'an adaptation of an industrial aerosol sprayer for crop-dusting. The nozzles were modified for spraying bacteria and the device was prepared for mounting on helicopters.' The other device that UNSCOM regarded as the most troubling of all was a simple aircraft 'drop tank' mounted on the wings of fighter jets as a reserve fuel tank. 'The Iraqis added a British-made electric valve and aerosol sprayer adapted for biological and chemical warfare, UN documents show,' writes Warrick
6   Dr Gerald Bull's clandestine role included developing the 155mm G-5 artillery system for South Africa during the Apartheid era. It remains a remarkable weapon with a range potential in excess of most artillery systems. A number were sold to Iraq with ammunition, some of it base bleed, prior to 'Operation Desert Storm'. In the summer of 2002, the US Department of Defense was examining the potential of the G-5 with a view to acquiring the weapon for the US Army

13

THE GAS MASK IMBROGLIO

'That Iraqi armed forces have had chemical and biological weapons is beyond doubt. The seven years of UN inspections after the 1991 Gulf War clearly established the existence of weapons programs in all three areas. The world knew as far back as the Iraq-Iran war that Iraq had successfully developed and used chemical weapons...and despite declaring in 1991 that it did not possess any biological weapons and related items, the UN Special Commission (UNSCOM) uncovered a well-developed BW program in 1995.'

BASIC Special Briefing, April 30, 2003
by David Isenberg, Ian Davis and Paul Ingram

'Buying a gas mask is simply a waste of time.' That was one of the points made by biowarfare specialist Eric Croddy when speaking on the need for the average American to face the realities of a chemical or biological warfare attack after the events of September 11, 2001.

He declared that for most of us, were there perhaps an ongoing, clearly identified biological warfare (BW) threat, such as the anthrax threat that faced postal workers for some months following the Al Qaeda attack, then all that was needed was a surgeon's (or procedure) mask. 'That should be adequate to filter out the particles that matter,' he declared.

The same applied to a chemical threat: 'The likelihood of having the right mask on hand at the right time makes this kind of preparation, in my view, impractical.' He points out that there are some nerve agents like the Russian-developed novichok that can permeate through all known gas masks in use in the West (See Chapter 11).

More unsettling is news of uncorroborated reports indicating that one or more Russian scientists might have handed their Syrian counterparts specifics about the novichok formula. Indeed, it was one of the points made in Congress before the House Armed Forces Committee by Dr Richard Spertzel in September 2002. Rumor or not, the implications are disturbing, if only because Damascus has a history of association with Arab terrorists, including the Tehran-backed Hizbollah movement in Lebanon.

Eric Croddy's recent book *Chemical and Biological Warfare: A Comprehensive Survey for the Concerned Citizen*[1] couldn't have come at a better time. He has this to say about recent events along the East Coast: 'While it is true that we now have to think about clouds of anthrax or possibly mists of sarin, it's just as important that we pay attention to that large truck parked in a suspicious spot.'

To that he adds a critical rider: 'Right now I'm actually more concerned with attacks involving conventional weapons than an enemy using chemical or biological weapons. Bullets, explosives and incendiary agents are still the most widely used tools for causing death and injury.' In this regard he points to the genocidal wars in Rwanda where, in the slaughter of a million or more souls, the weapon of choice among the majority was still the machete. 'More salient, the instruments of mass murder in two successive attacks on New York's World Trade Center were not chemical or biological agents,' says this author.

A former long-time Senior Research Associate at the Monterey Institute of International Studies, Croddy's area of focus has always been chemical and biological warfare. It says much that he is one of a handful of international sought-after experts on the subject, having discussed armaments issues on CBS, the Fox News Network, NHK Tokyo Television and NPR. He has also written extensively for Britain's Jane's Information Group.

One of the issues that come through forcibly in Croddy's book – and something that he deals with at considerable length because he believes it is seminal to the issues discussed here – is that right now, in some parts of the world, there are actually groups of people fabricating, stockpiling and, in a few cases, actually using chemical and biological armaments.

He observes: 'Words that in the not-too-distant-past were obscure and seldom heard – anthrax, sarin, smallpox – have become impossible to avoid, especially if you read your newspapers.' Also disturbing is his disclosure that prior to toppling Saddam, Iraq had been playing about with anthrax for years. In 1986 and 1988, for example, Iraqi scientists purchased pathogen seed stocks from reputable American dealers for a variety of biological weapons. These included, among others, anthrax, botulism and gangrene.

Despite their having signed the Biological and Toxin Weapons Convention of 1972, disclosures following the first Gulf War indicated that Iraq was involved in a massive biowarfare program: By 1990 it had cultured almost ten tons of anthrax and six tons of botulinum toxin. At the same time Iraq's Daura Foot-and-Mouth Disease Institute produced another six tons of botox and another four hundred gallons of the pathogen at the Taji facility outside Baghdad. There was evidence that work was going on at Salman Pak with the large-scale fermentation of *Clostridium perfringens* (gas gangrene).

As he explains, all this labor was military-orientated. There were even some French-built Mirage jet fighters, complete with modified tanks and spray nozzles that were about to be used against our own forces had the Iraqi Air Force planes involved not been destroyed on the ground during initial aerial assaults.

Croddy makes another interesting observation: Contrary to the accepted wisdom, he declares, the United States is not without its own resources to retaliate against people who might be considering using some of these weapons against the West.

While President Richard Nixon, in the interests of rapprochement with the Soviet Union scrapped US biological warfare research programs in 1969, America is still well equipped to retaliate with chemical weapons should it wish to do so more than three decades later. Indeed, some evidence recently made public reveals that US Army scientists haven't been quite as inactive as some government departments would have us believe. Since the late Sixties, American scientists have actually produced a lethal, powdered form of anthrax that could be used as a weapon. Officials at the Army's Dugway Proving Ground in Utah were not prepared to comment on exactly how long this work had been going on or whether anybody else in government was involved in pathogen research.

The legalities of all such actions remain moot. The US not only has huge stocks of nerve agents (such as sarin, VX and one or two others that are not public), it also possesses quite a lot of weapons in storage with which to dispense them.

Whether Washington would actually use the stuff in conflict, is another matter. What is clear is that it would have to be pressed pretty hard to do so, and then only if the other side had used them first.

Right now, these same chemical weapons await destruction, though it's not inconceivable that Washington – with the recent Iraqi scenario in mind, and others developing in places like Syria, Libya and North Korea - might have second thoughts about relinquishing a valuable military asset. Especially when there are so many other nations that right now, are adding to their own chembio arsenals.

There are some interesting observations in Croddy's book. As he says, the term 'weapons of mass destruction', like any defining or categorizing word, has its shortcomings. It explains some things, but goes only so far.

Says Croddy: 'Distinctions like this are grim. But they are also useful. They help us to define and sharpen our sense of things and to face up and describe in words what would otherwise be overwhelming, confusing, frightening.'

Fear is another motive for the study of disciplines that are both terrible and arcane. One can hardly read a newspaper or listen to the news today and not hear reports about other wars, repressive regimes and terror groups that have access to, or are working on the development of some of these weapons. The mere existence of chembio weapons, the West is continually being told, poses a very significant threat to the stability of international order.

Thus he states, even if we believe that the nuclear stand-off between superpowers – the so-called 'balance of terror' that characterized so much of the Cold War – is a thing of the past, we now have a whole new set of characters to worry about. Then, surprise, surprise, he adds the punch-line: If he were a betting man, opines Eric Croddy, 'I would put my money on the likelihood that we *will* see chemical or biological weapons attacks in the not-too-distant future.'

Possibly the most disturbing aspect of Croddy's book deals with the fact that those interested in developing chemical weapons in the present climate of uncertainty can, in theory, do so in a farmyard factory by using common precursors that are available locally. They can be bought either from outside suppliers or synthesized from raw materials to which the potential proliferator has access.

Saddam Hussein succeeded in clandestinely structuring an entire WMD industry on this basis, and, to the surprise of even the most advanced intelligence groups (which included the British, the Israelis and Washington), all that only came to light after the first Gulf War. Worse, there is a considerable body of evidence that he continued in these pursuits in the twelve years that preceded 'Operation Iraqi Freedom'. So too, incidentally, have Iran's mullahs.

Many of the chemicals in the hands of people like the Iranians, the Syrians and others involved in such activities are referred to in the argot as 'dual-use' compounds. What this means is that they have legitimate commercial uses as well as applications in the production of armaments. Take these examples:

In the case of biological weapons, one of the problems with dual-use technologies (other than dual-use precursors) is what challenges those investigating its proliferation.

In Iraq's case, UN weapons inspectors often found factories with large fermentors which might otherwise have been used in yeast cultures (or breweries, for that matter). The Iraqis were so well-informed about the movements of these officials that they knew long beforehand when a specific facility was to be visited and then they would go to great lengths to sanitize this equipment of any traces of, say, anthrax spores.

Similarly, on encountering a plant used in aerosolizing, Saddam's scientists would maintain that they were perfecting equipment to be used in agricultural spraying. Thus it is quite possible, and indeed feasible, that much of the equipment, knowledge, technology and infrastructure required in medicine and agricultural disciplines can be put to peaceful use or for making WMD.

Moreover, as Croddy points out, 'newly advanced techniques for sterilizing contaminated equipment now help BW proliferators to do a better job converting equipment back to its legitimate purpose. The new generation of weapons investigators now have a much tougher time definitively proving that a particular facility was used to test or develop these armaments.'

Then there is Russia. In spite of Presidents Bush and Putin having become kissing cousins, Washington intelligence sources maintain that work on both chemical and biological weapons goes on in Russia, though at a much-reduced scale than previously.

We know for instance, that in 1992, former President Yeltsin finally admitted that the source of the Sverdlovsk (today Yekaterinaburg) anthrax outbreak had been an accidental release of spores into the atmosphere from a military BW facility. Even then, the writing was on the wall; strong steps were already being taken to convert some of these institutions to produce legitimate products for the civilian economy.

Still, the notion persists that things aren't quite as they appear to be in the Former Soviet Union countries.

There are known BW and CW weapons plants that remain off-limits to joint investigations and the situation remains unclear. More disturbing, according to Croddy, is the existence of earlier plans by Soviet BW scientists to genetically alter smallpox, as well as evidence from Russian scientific literature that suggests some state bodies might have continued with this kind of work.

'This includes the introduction of Ebola and Venezuelan Equine Encephalitis (VEE) genes into smallpox to create a whole new kind of BW agent, a so-called chimera virus.' As he states, this would not only resist treatment, but also have synergistic effect. It's worth noting that according to Ken Alibek (who was interviewed by this writer several times) a strain of a combined *ectromelia* (mousepox, a close relative of smallpox) and VEE genes created symptoms of both diseases in laboratory animals in the late 1980s. In fact, he is convinced that this BW-related research work still continues in Russia despite presidential decrees banning all such activity.

In the chapter headed 'Threats and Responses', Croddy takes a look at the reality of many of these threats and how they are likely to affect our lives. He also offers useful hints, stressing that anybody actually using this stuff offensively is faced with some powerful obstacles.

With anthrax, for example, it's not enough to have weaponized this pathogen. 'Even if the terrorist has a large quantity (tons?) of this material and were they are able to store it in such a way that it stays dry and suitable for dispersal over a wide area, they still have the intractable problem of delivery.' Therein lies the rub, because to achieve the required objective of, say, wiping out half of Los Angeles or Chicago, it has to be dispersed in a 'perfect cloud' over the target population.

'Thus, if it were to rain while it was being dispersed, it would present a serious problem for the attackers. A thunderstorm, or even a light shower is a very good dilutant and would lessen the effect of most CBW agents, even those CW agents that don't hydrolyze very quickly. The wind more so, he reckons. Even intense sunlight would dilute the lethality of agents. All these factors would have to be just right for the attack to succeed on any scale,' Croddy tells us.

On any kind of mass attack he is even more forthright, stating that it would be absurd to say that such things will never happen. 'But if I accomplish nothing else with the book, I hope to make people a little less terrified and perhaps more realistic in their assessment of the actual risks.'

For a start, he maintains, a mass attack is *highly* unlikely. But he does suggest that as a society, Western nations need to be vigilant and to start preparing for such an eventuality. Being in a constant state of terror is not one of his prescriptions. 'A lot of people have said that if we live in unending terror, then the terrorists will have achieved some kind of victory. They are right. What is needed is for people to become a lot better informed. In so doing, they will negate fears that are unrealistic or possibly a handful that might have been overblown by the media or hype.'

So, do you buy a gas mask? Here, the situation depends solely on the threat, and changes from one agent to another. A mask to combat mustard gas won't have any effect on, for example, sarin nerve gas. Consequently, the likelihood of having precisely the right mask on hand at the right moment, as he points out, makes this kind of preparation totally impractical.

What should be known is that different agents act in very different ways. Apart from VX and mustard gas (which also act through the eyes), most chemical agents take the more typical pulmonary route. Only one biological toxin (T2) is active through topical skin contact.

Some agents such as *Francisella tularensis* (tularemia) can also infect through broken skin, as does the cutaneous form of anthrax. Often, we may have abrasions or cuts that are hardly perceptible to the naked eye, but which may be big enough to allow ingress of some pathogens. Then infections could very well result.

An issue often debated in the media is whether our water supplies could easily be contaminated. Croddy tends to dismiss the threat.

As he states, 'water supplies (in the US, at least) are remote, meaning that it would take a long time for an agent introduced into the system to reach its end users, by which time it would be so diluted that it could cause little or no harm. Moreover, most US water systems not only chlorinate and aerate their water supplies, but these resources are constantly monitored and checked for foreign substances that might be introduced into the system.'

Croddy's final words deal with an aspect that has been given little publicity: That people involved with chemical or biological weapons are possibly the most susceptible to themselves being infected. Even the Russians with their space age technology and laboratories made serious blunders. It is his view that this is likely to be even more the case in some of the developing countries: countries like Syria, Libya, Iran, Iraq and others, hardly any of them renowned for either technological ability or progress. There is also the hygiene issue in cities like Damascus, Tripoli or Tehran...

As he points out, many Iraqi soldiers became casualties during the Iran-Iraq War because of the unsafe handling of their own chemical weapons.

The CW agent VX, for instance, is so toxic that the utmost care and refined technique would be required to use it in any form. So are potential BW agents like tularemia and Lassa Fever, caused by a bacterium and a virus respectively. These pathogens are notorious for causing laboratory-based infections and are extremely difficult to handle safely. In America nobody goes near the stuff with donning late-generation laboratory 'space suits'.

'So the inherent danger of these agents in itself, is an obstacle to their deployment,' Croddy comments.

'And that, as far the West is concerned, is a powerful plus.'

1   *Chemical and Biological Warfare: A Comprehensive Survey for the Concerned Citizen*, by Eric Croddy, with Clarisa Perez-Armendariz and John Hart: Copernicus Books: New York, 2002

14

DID IRAQ ACQUIRE FISSILE MATERIAL?

Washington was abuzz following the fury expressed by the US Energy Department at the inability of the Russians to 'adequately safeguard nuclear bomb making materials'. America has poured millions of dollars into Russian complexes that, in spite of good relations between Putin and Bush, remain off-limits to US teams. This has effectively prevented them from determining whether the money is being spent appropriately. 'Taxpayers' money is being misspent by the Russians,' said Gregory H. Friedman, the inspector general.

The Washington Post: November 6, 1999

Looking at the bigger picture with regard to safeguarding (or trying to protect) Russian fissile material, a lot of American money has been wasted on these efforts since the fall of the Soviet Union. Much was misappropriated, some of it ending up in Swiss banks.

In recent years, the so-called Nuclear Material Production, Control and Accounting Program provided more than $150m for about a hundred projects. What becomes apparent after a good deal of scratching about, is that some of that money has not been used for the purposes for which it was intended. Rose Gottemoller, who headed the DOE (Department of Energy) Office of Nonproliferation attributed some problems to the 'difficulty of opening doors to Russia's weapons-making facilities'.

The interception of a cache of stolen uranium at Batumi, a few miles from the Georgian/Turkish border, prompted the initial verbal reaction. The State Department disclosed shortly afterwards that this was the second such incident in two weeks. There have since been quite a few others

According to an American intelligence source, these - and many other such events - suggested a possible security breakdown either at a Former Soviet Union nuclear fuel fabrication factory or an atomic energy plant. And that, despite Russia and America having signed an agreement on cooperation in the monitoring and safeguarding of nuclear material.

Then followed a Tbilisi report that mentioned a quantity of uranium pellets found in the possession of Valiko Chkmivadze, a sixty-year-old

Georgian with a history of illegally trading in fissile materials. He had previously been arrested by Turkish authorities on suspicion of dealing in smuggled uranium but was never brought to trial. Nobody is prepared to say why.

Turkish nationals (with their country bordering on several countries with dubious political agendas) seem to have taken the lead in smuggling prohibited material in recent years. There are known to be scores of attempts at trying to move such contraband to countries in the Near East using Turkey as a conduit.

In early 2000 for instance, a man was apprehended with a 'certificate for the purchase of uranium-235' (^{235}U) together with a quantity of uranium in a five lb lead container. Its origin was given as Moldova and the illegal substance was recovered at Dounav Most on the Bulgarian/Turkish border.

About the same time roughly ten lbs of 'non-active' solid uranium together with thirteen lbs of 'active' plutonium from the 'secure' Ulba Metallurgy Plant in Ust-Kamenogorsk, Kazakhstan, was taken from a man arrested in Istanbul. Linked to him, established later, were four Turkish nationals as well as three Kazakhis.

One member of the gang was a Kazakh army colonel. That was followed by thirteen cylinders of uranium marked 'UPAT UKA3 M8' destined for Iran and seized at the town of Van in Turkey. In a separate incident at Bursa, also in the Turkish state, about a quarter-pound of enriched uranium from Azerbaijan was recovered.

Interestingly, there were also two shipments of almost three lbs of HEU out of Georgia recovered. One lot was impounded in Switzerland and the other in Yalova, Turkey. Both were destined for Libya: That was followed by more than five lbs of enriched ^{235}U intercepted in Istanbul. Once it was established that it was intended for Iran, several Turkish nationals and suspect Iranian secret service agents were arrested.

Following these disclosures, a State Department official told me that there were other nuclear-related issues that remained unresolved. For instance, US nonproliferation and disarmament experts were having a great deal of difficulty in trying to get the Russians to disclose specific details of their fissile material stocks. These referred specifically to plutonium, though highly enriched uranium (HEU) was also part of it.

The imbroglio, he stated, stemmed from the fact that US nuclear facilities, curiously, had the same problem with their own statistics.

'Each time we ask them to give us an *exact* rundown, they counter by asking us whether we can do the same. Of course we cannot, because this is an incredibly complex issue,' the specialist disclosed.

Speaking on a condition of anonymity, he said that the last time a survey of stocks of US plutonium was done, 'there was an uncertainty of about 2.8 metric tons (MT) of plutonium at American nuclear plants. In addition, losses to waste were put at about 3.4 MT.'

Part of the reason for this, he explained, was that while the plutonium manufacturing process is very well understood in general, there were some specifics about which the scientists were still a little uncertain. This was more marked in the early days. For instance, numerous computational irregularities at the beginning were really only resolved in the Seventies: these might have included things like how much plutonium a specific reactor might produce or how long the facility had been operational.

'One needs to keep in mind that apart from some pretty obvious uncertainties, a lot of this stuff is still classified. Restrictions apply as much to Russia as to America,' he stated, stressing that the so-called 'missing' plutonium at US nuclear establishments hadn't actually been stolen. Instead, there were several other factors involved.

'These range from trying to estimate the amount of plutonium still trapped in trans-uranic waste (TRU), to possibly something as mundane as inadequately kept books.' Since the first plutonium was produced in 1944, the industry had to 'feel its way' through a successive series of phases and establish its own parameters.

In order to comprehend how and why fissile or nuclear material goes missing in Russia, one needs to look carefully at how DOE stocks are stored and managed in America. Some striking differences come to light.

For example, the Department of Energy disclosed that in the United States before 1978, inventory differences were identified as 'materials unaccounted for' or MUF. At various times, MUF included the fractional amounts of nuclear materials lost in regular day-to-day operations. These were listed as normal operating losses. There were also accidental losses as well as materials possibly removed from a facility for quality control and safeguards analysis. He also made the point that since it was not prudent to discount the fact that a small inventory difference in US stocks might be due to theft, all losses were invariably investigated, analyzed and resolved to ascertain whether an actual theft or diversion had taken place. If necessary, a spokesman stated, an entire operation might be shut down until these differences were resolved.

It was his view that matters for the Americans had improved markedly since the Seventies. It was worth noting, he added, that almost seventy per cent of inventory differences had occurred during a period when the learning curve was being established, largely through a complex process of trial and error.

In answer to a query, the DOE released details relating to American plutonium removals from the period 1944 to September 1994 (there had been very little change in the previous six or eight years).

Of a total of 111.4 MT of plutonium produced or acquired in the half century (of which eighty-five per cent was weapons grade), only 12 MT was removed from the DOE/Department of Defense inventory. Of this, 3.4 MT was expended in wartime and nuclear tests; 2.8 MT was due to inventory differences; 3.4 MT was waste (normal operating losses); 1.2 MT was consumed by fission and transmutation while 0.4 MT was lost to decay and other removals.

A total of 0.1 MT was transferred to US civilian industry and 0.7 MT went to foreign countries, details of which remain secret.

A source at the Hanford nuclear facility disclosed that the core of the problem with shortages lay with the production process. The system had always been fraught with uncertainties. For instance, nuclear physicists were aware from the start that plutonium was subject to a variety of natural losses.

'Some of it was trapped in process lines and waste streams (and it is still there) some tons of it,' he disclosed. There is even more in liquid waste dump grounds. Another eight-hundred-and-eighty lbs decayed.

Until fairly recently it was believed that radioactive waste products that had been left standing for many years (and sometimes for decades) might be close to criticality. Consequently, for a long time the authorities were simply unwilling to tamper with it. Some was certainly unstable, but at facilities like Hanford, Savannah River and Los Alamos, clean-up programs resulted in much of it being stabilized and stored in preparation for the move to the Waste Isolation Pilot Plant at Carlsbad, New Mexico.

Thus, claimed the man from the State Department, exactly the same situation prevailed for Russian or FSU nuclear processing plants when faced with similar problems.

'The only difference between the two countries is that while it is all but impossible to get into Hanford or Colorado's Rocky Flats undetected, never mind try to take something out illegally, that has not always been the case in Russia since the collapse of the Soviet Union,' he stated.

'Not only are these installations badly guarded, but we have discovered that some of the sophisticated monitoring equipment supplied free by Washington was sometimes not put into service, unworkable, perhaps not properly understood, faulty or subjected to power cuts.' In one or two instances, he confided, the equipment was never installed.

More important, he said, 'Russian security personnel were often not paid for months at a stretch in the past,' though things have improved a lot since then. It was so bad, he suggested, that staff sometimes lacked the motivation to do a proper job, especially during the winter months when some were more interested in keeping themselves warm than watching dials. 'You can accept that it is probably a lot worse on an empty stomach.'

One result of Russian nuclear disparities was that such issues were somewhere near the top of most agendas each time there was a meeting between Russian and American heads of state. As one official at State phrased it, 'Bush and Putin have taken on very much where Clinton and Yeltsin left off'.

Early in 2000 for example, Reuters reported that a woman had been arrested in Vladivostok for trying to sell radioactive metal. Although she was employed at a base at Bolshoi Kamen (near the home of the Russian Pacific Fleet), the alloy wasn't from there, a director of the Zvezda maintenance plant, Grigory Pavlenko, stated. What he did confirm though, was that his company serviced nuclear submarines and worked with nuclear fuels.

In a statement, the Vladivostok police said that their investigation showed that the stolen ^{238}U and other rare metals probably came from one of the many atomic plants in the region. Police and factory investigators carefully checked stocks but could find no missing atomic materials.

The woman was arrested after she tried to sell a six-pound piece of metal for $65,000. It had been kept in a local lock-up garage near her home and at the time of the arrest, had been wrapped in newspaper and was being carried about in a shopping bag. What astonished the investigators was that the radioactive substance exceeded safe radiation levels by more than two-and-a-half thousand times, a Russian source disclosed[1].

In another incident shortly afterwards, Kyrgyz security service agents arrested an Uzbeki national trying to smuggle thirteen lbs of plutonium aboard a flight to the United Arab Emirates. The man said that he had been offered $16,000 to smuggle the shipment out of the country. The plutonium, used in the detonation devices of nuclear bombs, had been carefully packed in a rubber container. Unconfirmed reports indicated that it was intended for Iran.

As with the Vladivostok incident, *Itar-Tass* said afterwards that the origins of the radioactive metal could not be established.

Richard Meserve, chairman of the US National Research Council (part of the US National Academy of Science) issued a statement shortly afterwards. He said that although joint efforts by Russia and America had strengthened security at many sites, 'we believe that terrorist groups or rogue nations have more opportunity to gain access to Russian plutonium and highly enriched uranium than we had previously estimated'. A Moscow spokesman Yuri Bespalko immediately countered this: he declared that 'the safety and protection of Russian nuclear materials met and, in some ways, even exceeded international standards'.

Shortly afterwards, the Norwegian nuclear watchdog organization Bellona reported that the Russian security police had arrested five people in St Petersburg for trying to sell a radioactive Californium-252 as well as thirty-seven lbs of mercury from the nuclear icebreaker base Atomflot, in Murmansk. Police said that the radiation source 'could be used for the perfect murder'.

Californium-252 is a strong emitter of neutron radiation and is used to start up nuclear reactors. It was customarily stored in containers of about four-hundred-and-fifty lbs onboard the *Imandra*, a Russian fleet supply ship. To transfer it to an icebreaker, a bucket-sized container, carried by one man, was used. After it was depleted, the vessel would be transferred to the Atomflot storage facility.

Bellona - the Norwegian nuclear watchdog organization - has made the point many times over that there are certain aspects of the case that simply don't make sense. In recent years, it says, the DOE (through a program called Material Protection and Accountability) supplied both the *Imandra* and the Atomflot base with physical protection equipment. Also, radiation detectors had been installed at the entrance to the Atomflot base. Because the stolen material emitted radiation three-hundred-and-fifty times higher than background levels, it should have automatically triggered electronic alarms already in place (courtesy of the Americans). They did concede, however, that the stuff could have been taken through a hole in the fence. Or the equipment wasn't working or the guards might have been bribed to look the other way.

Questions have also been raised about the ease with which the Russian FSB security police made the arrests and whether the operation wasn't a set-up to convince Washington that they were doing a good job protecting Russian nuclear assets[2].

In a related comment, the US Department of Energy's Pacific Northwest National Laboratory (PNNL) in Washington State suggested during this writer's visit to this facility, that what was often overlooked in trying to assess the Russian problem, was 'weapons-radioactive materials that could be used in terrorist acts as pollutants rather than as fissionables'. Part of the reason why this issue was not being confronted, it was indicated, was that 'it would need to expand coverage to everything including radon waste-storage sites, medical waste and the rest'. It was also the view of PNNL's Dr Michael Foley that in the long term, radioactive contamination by hostile elements could very well become a serious security threat, a sentiment incidentally, echoed by other specialists dealing with such issues.

Other incidents involving the illegal movement of radioactive materials or equipment include the following:

A theft at the Kola Nuclear Power Plant in 1999, when thieves removed two items that were part of the automatic radiation monitoring system at the facility's fourth reactor unit. For a full day the plant lost control over radiation levels but managed to regain it[3]. The thieves were never identified and there were indications that the goods might have been targeted for outside or foreign interests.

Only a month before, a theft in the Kola plant's turbine machinery led to an automatic shutdown of its No.1 reactor unit. Kola Nuclear Power Plant operates four VVVR-440 reactors commissioned between 1973 and 1984.

A conscript onboard one of Russia's Northern Fleet's nuclear submarines at the Vidyaevo base pillaged more than twenty lengths of palladium-vanadium wire from the reactor room at about the same time. The significance here is that it could have been highly radioactive. The Murmansk newspaper *Polyarnaya Pravda* reported that the wire was used in communications systems of vital control devices onboard nuclear submarines. When removed, they prevented the installation from being operated. The next day the sailor sold the wire to a Naval petty officer for $45. Vidyaevo is a base for Russian Akula class submarines, the most advanced attack-class submarines in Moscow's Navy. In September 1998 another conscript shot eight of his mates and hijacked an Akula Class submarine at Skalisty on the Kola Peninsula. He was killed by Speznatz troops after a twenty-three-hour standoff.

Six containers with radioactive cesium-137 were stolen from a refinery in Volvograd in May 1998. Each of the three hundred-lb containers held a single capsule with about one cm³ cesium-137. If taken out of its container, the capsule could radiate up to 400 roentgens/hr. Volvograd police spokesman Pyotr Lazarev disclosed that the cesium was used in electronic equipment that monitors chemical processes in the oil refinery and that the thieves would probably try to sell the isotopes abroad. He added that there was a certain demand on the black market for cesium, which could be used by terrorists in 'dirty bombs' and other terrorist acts. The Volvograd theft was the second that month: Two containers of cesium were stolen from a cobalt smelter in the southern Siberian Republic of Tuva but later recovered.

The previous March, a number of radioactive pipes were stolen from the premises of the Chernobyl Nuclear Power Plant. In a theft characterized by *Deutche Presse Agentur* as 'not the first of its kind', thieves removed irradiated pipes.

Smugglers attempted to move a quantity of weapons grade uranium that had been stolen in Novosibirsk in March 1997 into Kazakhstan, according to a local paper *Novoya Sibir*. A year later, the gang was smashed by a police follow-up team shortly before they were due to hand over the uranium pellets. Again, the origins of the uranium were not identified. Questioned about the incident, Vladimir Orlov, Director of the Center for Political Studies in Moscow, said that by then, more than twenty criminal cases had been launched in Russia: all were related to the theft of radioactive materials. In an article in *Nuclear Control,* Bellona quotes Orlov as saying that 'the possibilities to smuggle nuclear materials for organized professionals remains quite high'.

Also in 1997, a cache of almost nine lbs of uranium was seized by police at the home of a man in the north Caucasus town of Ivanov. Police traced the ^{238}U to the nuclear research center at Sarov (formerly Arzamas-16) from where it had been stolen three years before. Meanwhile, the report said, it had been kept at the man's home in a metal cylinder inside a lead isolator[4].

'Russia today cannot guarantee that nuclear explosive materials have not found their way to proliferating countries such as Iran or Iraq or to terrorists seeking nuclear weapons.' Harsh words, perhaps. Kevin O'Neill, deputy director of ISIS uttered them during this writer's last visit to Washington.

He went on: 'The lack of security and accounting of these materials is one of the most troubling and immediate proliferation threats in the post-Cold War world.'

O'Neill said that the Russian economic free-fall that had started four or five years before had had a dramatic impact on Moscow's ability to implement upgrades at its nuclear sites. For example, 'US Department of Energy officials relate stories of MVD guards leaving their posts to look for food. Also, there were numerous cases of inadequate clothing and heating units for guards, coupled with unreliable communications, as well as cuts to electricity supplies at the various sites housing nuclear materials,' he said. In a last-ditch effort to help the Russians cope, the US provided emergency rations, portable generators, warm clothes and other items at sites participating in the upgrade programs.

Elsewhere – around the northern ports of Murmansk and Archangel in the Kola Peninsula in the Russian Arctic, about a thousand miles north of Moscow, hundreds of redundant nuclear submarines were then being dismantled (as they still are today). To assist the Russians in their efforts to upgrade nuclear safety, the West has pumped tens of millions of dollars into the region. But because this naval work is handled in what are termed 'closed cities', there was simply no way of telling whether the money was being devoted to the purposes intended. The Kremlin assured the West that it was. Others were more skeptical[5].

As he explained, the problem, briefly, was that by the time it collapsed in 1991, the Soviet Union had produced the world's largest stockpile of plutonium and highly enriched uranium. These materials come in many forms – in nuclear weapons and components, metal and oxide reactor fuel elements (including both fresh and spent fuels), bulk oxides for processing, metal 'buttons' as well as in a huge amount of radioactive waste.

Moreover, O'Neill elaborated, fissile materials were located in hundreds of buildings and in dozens of sites spread across the entire Former Soviet Union, but principally in Russia. Most of it (and all the nuclear weapons) were under the control of either the Russian Ministry of Atomic Energy (Minatom) or the Ministry of Defence[6].

While nuclear weapons in the FSU were generally better accounted for and protected than non-military fissile materials, a number of Western authorities regarded weapons to be vulnerable at some storage sites and, possibly, during transport. Worse, many of Russia's fissile material production facilities and other related locations lacked fundamental material protection, control and accountancy systems (MPC&A) which were needed to detect or prevent theft.

Look at the record:

Also newsworthy out of Moscow at about the same time was the fact that the chief of the Federal Security Service (FSB) in the Chelyabinsk region told *Itar-Tass* that in December 2000, their agents had prevented the theft of forty lbs of fissile material[7]. O'Neill maintained that while he hadn't seen the specifics, he was told on good authority on his last visit to Moscow that the stuff was 'radioactive materials used for nuclear weapons production'. Another source mentioned weapons grade uranium.

According to a submission made to a Senate Select Committee on Intelligence in January 1998, seven lbs of HEU was seized by the Russian police in St Petersburg.

Mayak (where over thirty tons of weapons grade uranium is stored at any one time) was also in the news when Russia's previous administration ordered an overhaul of security measures at the plant that reprocesses nuclear materials for weapons. It also handles spent nuclear fuel as part of the Chelyabinsk-65 nuclear complex, one of Moscow's main weapons development facilities. According to Bill Gertz of *The Washington Times,* the CIA told a Senate Intelligence Committee that while nuclear warheads in Russia were relatively secure, 'declining morale and discipline in the military as well as economic conditions, raise our concerns about the potential for warhead theft'. The report added[8] that Russian nuclear weapons -useable fissile material, plutonium as well as HEU, 'are more vulnerable to theft than nuclear weapons or warheads'.

Significantly, the plant in the South Urals (and its associated residential community) has had several names over the years. It was originally Chelyabinsk-40, then Chelyabinsk-65, all with anonymous Chelyabinsk post office box numbers. Recently, the residential side (a closed Russian city) was allowed to rename itself Ozersk (pronounced Ozyorsk) – City of the Lakes – because it nestles up against Lake Kyzyltash and has a beachfront park. The reactor/reprocessing/industrial complex is called the Mayak Production Association and is now distinguished apart from Ozersk.

In a presentation to the Defense and Security Committee of the North Atlantic Assembly in 1998, William Potter, director of the Center for Nonproliferation Studies, Monterey Institute, disclosed that at some Russian facilities recently-installed security equipment was not being used because there wasn't enough money to maintain it. Similarly, at some installations entire security systems – alarms, surveillance cameras, portal monitors and more – have been shut down because electricity was cut off for non-payment of bills[9].

Thereafter, Barbara Slavin reported in *USA Today*[10] that at other facilities 'guards had intentionally turned off alarm systems or even cut their cables because they were annoyed by frequent false alarms'.

In several instances, in non-Russian republics, after being asked by plant officials to help measure the fissile stocks at their sites, Vienna's International Atomic Energy Agency found fissile stocks to be in excess of what was on record. In one area, dozens of pounds of fissile materials were discovered. Until recently, nobody was certain what the tally was. Even today, says O'Neill[11], US Energy Department officials and some Russian scientists are concerned that many of the facilities in the FSU lack accurate records of their stocks.

V.N. Obarevich, Head of the Inspectorate for State Oversight of Nuclear Weapons Security, told the Russian Duma (Parliament) in October 1996: 'I really cannot imagine how people who work with nuclear weapons are managing to live, especially at the Ministry of Defense. People have no money. They do not have the means to live. A major who is going to be doing technical maintenance on nuclear munitions tomorrow is fainting from hunger today. How can these nuclear weapons be serviced? And these are nuclear weapons that require materials as well. There's no more money with which to buy these materials…as I understand it, things are getting worse[12].'

'At our (nuclear warfare) facilities, 70 per cent of the technical security devices have become worn out and 20 per cent have been in operation for two or three service life periods. Attempts are being made to repair them but this is no longer possible. Most control and checkpoints do not have resources for detecting the unauthorized transport of nuclear materials, metal or explosives.' This is the gist of a statement to the Russian Parliament by Lev Ryabev, Deputy Russian Federation Ministry of Atomic Energy.

In 1998 a US team visiting the Kurchatov Institute in Moscow was shown a building containing 220 lbs of HEU that was totally unguarded[13]. The Institute apparently could not afford the $200 a month salary for one guard, never mind the full quota for round-the-clock surveillance that would have been regarded as essential anywhere else.

A report in *Nuclear Fuel*[14] states that the six-lb cache of HEU grabbed in a car in Prague late in 1994 matched the specifics of similar material seized in Germany four months earlier. Following a tip-off, a number of people (including a Russian atomic scientist from the Nuclear Research Center at Rez) were arrested. The report states that the material found in containers identifying them as from the ex-Soviet Black Sea fleet had been stolen from a stockpile at Chelyabinsk-65. A correction later said that all of it had originally come from Mayak and was only part of what had been seized in Prague and Germany. A year later, 0.4gms of the same material was being offered as a sample for sale in Prague.

Similarly, there are other issues in the Former Soviet Union that need attention, some of them urgently, if only because they, too, are nuclear linked.

For instance, nuclear safety in the Russian Arctic where redundant former USSR strategic missile submarines are being dismantled, is a cause for grave concern in Western Europe especially. Conditions there are bad enough to have prompted Nikolay Yegorov, Russia's deputy atomic energy minister to comment that with nothing being done, 'matters worsen every year…and could turn into a catastrophe worse than Chernobyl'.

The Oslo watchdog organization, Bellona, with its own website, specifically targets work (or more appropriately, the lack of it) being done in several 'closed cities' in the remote Kola Peninsula. Some nuclear storage sites are only a twenty-minute drive from the Norwegian border.

Bellona issued a report[15] that stated that more that forty-five thousand spent nuclear fuel elements were being stored in the region. Some of these assets were in temporary on-shore storage tanks. Others had been placed aboard a variety of run-down service vessels. In the old days, excess or spent nuclear fuel would have been transported by rail to the Mayak reprocessing plant in Siberia. Now all that has changed.

To start with, shipments went intermittent about four years ago, though with American pressure and financial incentives, regularity has to some extent been re-established. In the past, issues were hampered by a lack of funds and specific orders from the Mayak county administration that declared that no more nuclear waste was welcome in this already-contaminated South-Ural region.

Other complications abound. Not only is there no more space available at Mayak (because storage facilities are filled to capacity) but the reprocessing plant is often inoperative because of technical problems. Here, too, more cash is needed for spares. In fact, the facility is so dated that an entirely new system needs to be installed but Moscow hasn't the cash to do that.

In some of the Arctic naval ports, says Bellona, many of the discarded reactors of 'Yankee' and 'Delta'-class dismantled submarines still contain their nuclear fuel elements and a number have been left unattended for years, often lying where they were abandoned along the shore. More ominous, the report states, concrete tanks (in which spent nuclear fuel elements were being stored) were so run down that the stability of their radioactive contents was threatened.

The report also explained that the distance between each element was only about an inch and that the concrete separating them had developed cracks, some serious, because of extreme temperatures.

'There is consequently a substantial risk for criticality (initiating a chain reaction such as occurred at Chernobyl). Because of the sheer volume of nuclear fuels stored there, a meltdown in the Russian Arctic would in all likelihood be on a much bigger scale than anything yet experienced this century. It could, conceivably, affect the entire Northern Hemisphere.'

Dr Michael Foley, a geologist specializing in nuclear-related issues at PNNL who was responsible for producing, in English, a Russian book on the subject *Deep Injection Disposal of Liquid Radioactive Waste in Russia*[16] disputed this in an exchange of letters[17].

He maintained that 'we have never taken the criticality threat very seriously. Perhaps we are being naïve, but that is one of the first and last things nuclear workers worry about and, let's face it, the Russians have had enough criticality accidents to be serious about preventative measures'.

Also, he told me, 'criticality developing from infrastructure degradation would start locally rather than involving the whole mass of a storage area. That would limit the consequences and allow remediation before things got too far out of hand'. As he explained, the submarine reactor accident at Chazhma Bay was an example of how things could go bad once a criticality gets going 'and it's interesting that we recently discovered that it was a fresh fuel accident and that the released radioactivity was less than 500 Ci[18] after the first few weeks'.

He added that since the accident occurred in a reactor, the geometry of the event was designed to promote criticality. 'Accidental fuel proximity criticality would probably not be so efficient; however this is a judgment-call area and we are still thinking about it.'

Dr Don Bradley, a nuclear engineer and group leader at PNNL for the past twenty years, backed Dr Foley's comments. An acknowledged expert on the Former Soviet Union's nuclear waste management programs, he suggested that any meltdown of spent fuel cells could never be anything as bad as the Chernobyl disaster[19].

Fortunately, a good deal of all this is now history because, with US assistance, conditions in the FSU have markedly improved. At the same time, nobody would put good money on whether some shipments of fissile material *have not been* filtered out of the country. On the face of it there seems to have been thefts galore, but only those instances where the perpetrators have been apprehended, have become public knowledge. The bulk of it we'll never ever know about.

There is good reason for Moscow to put its house in order in this department and it is called Chechnya. The Russians face a powerful Islamic-led insurgency in the enclave that has already claimed many thousands of lives. Worse, these Muslims are known to have links to Moslem dissidents elsewhere, including Osama bin Laden's Al Qaeda. It is also known that Chechnyan fighters have found themselves in a dozen anti-Western/anti-American conflicts in recent years in places as far afield as Afghanistan, the Philippines, Indonesia and Somalia.

Putin knows all this. He is also aware that Chechnyan dissidents have shown a good deal of interest in former Soviet nuclear installations and perhaps, the rumor mill has it, stolen nuclear warheads. He does not need Washington to tell him that if any of this material is acquired by Chechnyan separatists (or any other FSU rebels), it could end up in some sort of device that may have Moscow's name written on the shell casing.

There are several programmed moves afoot to stop the trafficking of nuclear materials.

One of these involves intrusive new advances in the United States that allows fiber-optic technology to be embedded in roads of several East European and East Asian nations. These are being laid specifically to detect smuggled nuclear weapons. A research program launched at PNNL has developed what the laboratory calls 'a one-of-a-kind scintillating optical fiber for sensing both neutrons and gamma rays'.

Named PUMA – for Plutonium Measurement and Analysis – the sensor is designed to be embedded in a variety of materials or literally, 'wrapped like fingers around objects of different sizes for content analysis'. Also, it is adaptable to a wide range of applications including environmental restoration, cancer treatment and nonproliferation of weapons of mass destruction.

Most important, it can be embedded into asphalt roads to detect the transportation of unauthorized or diverted nuclear weapons material. Alternatively, it can be wrapped around drums and other containers to inventory contents. Nuesafe LLC is licensed to commercially manufacture the technology under the PUMA name.

Head of program research is Dr Mary Bliss. She advised that developments at the laboratory were quite revolutionary and that the sensors could be used for body-worn detectors for nuclear materials and airborne weapons detection. Portable monitors, she reckoned, were the single biggest commercial application.

Unlike the gas tube, she explained, 'PNNL sensors are less sensitive to vibration, they are rugged and flexible and versatile in both length and numbers, ranging from about a quarter-inch to two yards long. Also, they may consist of a single fiber or clusters of tens of thousands of fibers'. There was an important advantage: High-speed electronics could be utilized to give detectors 'an improved, dynamic range, which is simply not feasible with gas tubes', she said.

PUMA is based on the rationale that ionizing radiation interacts with the scintillating fibers and produces light. It works like this: Light is trapped within the fiber and goes to its end where conversion to an electrical signal takes place. This can be interpreted as either a neutron or a gamma-ray interaction, depending on size.

A spokesperson for PNNL stated that teams of materials, nuclear, optical and electrical scientists began testing applications of fiber-optic radiation sensors at the lab about twenty years ago and the work has been going on ever since.

Until now, the single biggest problem facing the West has been detecting secret nuclear blasts. There is real fear in Washington, London and elsewhere that more countries might follow India and Pakistan in testing nuclear weapons. Here North Korea springs to mind. So, judging from the amount of illegal fissile that appears to have been headed there, does Iran. Tehran has recently been shown to be eager to join the 'Nuclear Club' as soon as possible. The refusal of the US Senate to ratify the global (CTBT) test ban treaty complicates matters still further.

Several new monitoring developments are already impacting on the industry: A succession of revolutionary American monitoring procedures is likely, if not to permanently eliminate secret nuclear tests, then at least detect them. Systems developed involve technology a hundred times more sensitive than the best previously available for detecting atomic testing. Monitoring stations on all five continents will cover applicable seismic, hydro-acoustic, infrasound and radionuclide data.

With the CTBT stymied, new monitoring systems are urgently needed to provide for total global verification. The monitoring of nuclear testing will be more intensive than ever and, as we go to press, several new systems are being put in place. These include a network of more than three hundred stations worldwide incorporating new instruments such as those developed by PNNL and operated for the DOE. During treaty negotiations, the US Department of Defense was tasked to spearhead an international effort to develop a prototype International Data Center (IDC) at the Center for Monitoring Research in Arlington, Virginia.

There are several reasons. The first is to support future test ban treaty negotiations. Another is to test new concepts necessary for effective global monitoring. Yet another to establish an infrastructure for cooperative, international verification. Finally, the objective is to provide the foundation for a future international data test ban center to be located in Vienna, Austria. Such a center is envisaged to include a communications system, the prototype IDC as well as an international on-site inspection component to monitor compliance.

PNNL has produced two systems to monitor nuclear debris: A Radionuclide Aerosol Sampler/Analyzer (RASA) that measures radioactive debris from aboveground nuclear weapons testing (regardless of where or when the bombs were detonated) and ARSA, an Automated Radioxenon Sampler/Analyzer. This device fills the CTBT requirement for near-real-time, ultra-sensitive field measurement of short-lived noble gases. Like RASA, ARSA operates automatically.

All programs are remotely programmable. Both projects are funded by the DOE's Office of Nonproliferation and Security from Washington.

Dr Harry Miley of PNNL is responsible for the development of RASA (in conjunction with researchers at DME Corporation, Orlando, Florida) which was given The Most Outstanding Technology Development With Commercial Potential Award by *R&D Magazine.*

Essentially, Miley explained, the analyzer passes air through a large area, low-pressure drop filter at a high rate of flow for selectable time periods. This action captures verifiable airborne trace particles on six strips of filter paper that are packaged in a single bundle to be analyzed by a gamma-ray detector.

'In so doing,' he said, 'the system actually captures a part of the nuclear weapon: Minute, yes, but still a verifiable part.'

The resultant spectra are then transmitted to central data locations thousands of miles away. It simultaneously achieves a very high sensitivity coupled with a low-power/small footprint.

He explained that since short-lived fission products have no natural background, weapon blasts could also be easily discriminated from reactor accidents. Thus, he said 'a simple one kiloton atmospheric blast will be detected by multiple isotopes at multiple stations'.

He explained that special features within the system archived each sample. They then identified them with their own unique barcodes. Containing a ninety per cent relative-efficiency germanium detector, he reckoned that the new technology, which identifies debris in an environment of ubiquitous radon background, was a hundred times more sensitive than its nearest commercial rival.

The US Air Force and the DOE have authorized DME Corporation to sell RASA units to all potential CTBT participants and other interested parties.

The philosophy behind detecting xenon in the ARSA process, in contrast, stems from the fact that it homes in on all the byproducts of a nuclear blast. Radioxenon is a particularly useful signature of an underground nuclear explosion for no other reason than it is the most likely radioactive debris to escape. In layman's terms, explained Miley, 'we actually end up with a physical piece of that explosion, microscopic, but something tangible, nevertheless'.

What happens is that the high-volume analyzer passes filtered air through an aluminum oxide bed for the removal of moisture and carbon dioxide, then through a charcoal sorption-held-bed near 100°C for xenon collection. The gas is then thermally desorbed, purified and measured by beta-coincidence x-/gamma-ray spectrometry.

That done, gamma-ray spectra are automatically transmitted to appropriate organizations. The gas samples, meanwhile, are tagged and retained for a later central laboratory confirmatory process.

Notable is the fact that ARSA continuously separates xenon from the atmosphere at a flow rate of 48m³ per eight-hour collection period. The system has a sensitivity of about 0.1mBq per cubic meter of air in the subsequent twenty-four-hour period, during which four of the samples can be measured simultaneously.

ARSA was field tested in April 1997 in New York City. The first units were delivered to the USAF not long afterwards, and work has progressed on commercial units.

1   Internal State Department memo; dd September 6, 1999

2   Bellona: 'Nuclear Icebreakers Base Robbed': by Igor Kudrik: July 14, 1999

3   *Polyarnaya Pravda*, a Murmansk daily, May 28, 1999

4   Interfax, Moscow

5   Bellona: 'Five Subcritical Nuclear Tests': Oslo, Norway, December 29, 1998

6   David Albright and Kevin O'Neill (Editors), *The Challenges of Fissile Material Control:* The Institute for Science and International Security, Washington DC, 1999

7   Jump-Start: Retaking the Initiative to Reduce Post-Cold War Nuclear Dangers: *Arms Control Today*, Washington DC, January/February 1999

8   *The Washington Times:* October 21, 1998

9   Todd E. Perry, *Preventing the Proliferation of Russian Nuclear Materials: Limit to the Current Approach:* paper prepared for the annual meetings of the International Security Studies Section (ISSS), International Studies Association, Monterey, California, November 8, 1998

10 November 24, 1998

11 Albright and O'Neill : *Ibid*

12 *Yaderny Kontrol Digest #5:* Stenographic Record of the Parliamentary Hearings on Issues Concerning the Security of Hazardous Nuclear Facilities, October 1997

13 Elisabeth Rindskopf : *Where Nuclear Peril Lies Waiting,* Chicago Tribune, October 12, 1998

14 Mark Hibbs: *Smuggled HEU seized in Germany, Prague came from Mayak Stockpile, Police Say,* 'Nuclear Fuel' September 21, 1998

15 *Naval Nuclear Waste Management in Northwest Russia*: Bellona, Norway: bellona@bellona.no

16 Edited by Michael J. Foley and Lisa M.G.Ballou: Battelle Press, Columbus: Richland, WA, 1998

17 A series of personal communications with the author from 1998 onwards

18 Curies - the accepted international measurement of radiation

19 *Behind the Nuclear Curtain: Radioactive Waste Management in the Former Soviet Union* by Don Bradley, edited by David R Payson: Battelle Press, 1997

15

SPIES:
WHY AMERICAN INTELLIGENCE
WAS CAUGHT SHORT

**'Four things come back not: The spoken word; the sped
arrow; time past and the neglected opportunity.'**

Omar I Ibn al-Khattab, Caliph (AD 581-644)

Michael Ledeen, resident scholar in the Freedom Chair at the American
Enterprise Institute, has expressed dissatisfaction with the state of the
country's intelligence services often enough in the past, but rarely as
critically as he did in an article for *National Review*[1] in early 2002.

Much of the invective was prompted by the experiences of former CIA
spy Robert Baer, whom he quoted at length. Baer, he said, is 'plenty
disgusted' with Langley and, indeed, this ex-CIA man pulls no punches in
his best-selling exposé, *See No Evil*[2]. The Baer book, incidentally, provides
Ledeen with even more anti-CIA ammo.

'The CIA had the book (on Iran and the Middle East) at least five years
ago,' he points outs, 'but either Bill Clinton never noticed or John Deutsch
or George Tenet, the Director of Intelligence (DI) never let him into the
secret.'

Ledeen also takes the media to task for ignoring or, at best, downplaying
Baer's amazing kiss-and-tell revelations involving the Near East and
Langley. 'He tied it all together,' says Ledeen, 'like a suspense novel.' And
Ledeen himself has some telling observations to make on Yasser Arafat's
links to what President George Bush has referred to on occasion as 'The
Axis of Evil'.

One of the more remarkable revelations to emerge from Baer's book was
the seeming ease with which he was able to cultivate some powerful assets
in Northern Iraq. Amazingly, he even set the ball rolling for a possible coup
d'etat against Saddam Hussein himself. And then, inexplicably, he was sent
a terse message from one of Clinton's national security advisors ordering
him to call the whole thing off. At the same time, he was warned that if he
did go ahead, 'you're on your own'.

As if that weren't enough, on his return home Baer was hit with the
news that he was to be investigated on charges of attempted murder. And

the man he was supposedly guilty of plotting to kill? None other than the Iraqi dictator himself. Charges were eventually dropped; how could they not be on something as absurd as this? But it was obvious that someone deep within government, possibly in the White House itself, must have tipped off the Feds about Baer's activities or they would never have embarked on such idiocy.

Clinton's cronies still have a lot to answer for on this issue, and, if things go badly wrong because of previous botched or compromised intelligence activities that were negated through their efforts, some of these individuals could end up having to answer for their actions. As it is, unnecessary lives were lost in 'Operation Iraqi Freedom'.

While working for the CIA, Robert Baer covered most of the Middle East and in his day, he has made some startling pronouncements. This is what he has to say about Iran's efforts at creating mayhem in the United States:

'It was clear from all the documents that I dredged up that, by at least 1997, the CIA knew the Pasdaran's command structure[3] inside and out, just as it knew that Ayatollah Ali Khamenei and President Rafsanjani approved every terrorist operation to come out of Iran. As I looked at the evidence in front of me, the conclusion was unavoidable: The Islamic Republic of Iran had declared a secret war against the United States and the United States had chosen to ignore it.'

In conversation, this former CIA spook who orchestrated several major clandestine operations during the course of a professional career that was both enterprising and illustrious, comes across as quiet, affable and, by all accounts, totally unflappable.

First impressions can be deceptive. Get him talking on his favorite topic and he becomes as forthright as a laser beam. For instance, observe his opinion today on the Directorate of Operations (DO), where he spent most of his adult life: 'A professional criminal organization.'

Coming from Baer, thoroughly 'old school' where espionage is concerned, the maxim is fairly complimentary of the nuts and bolts of America's national intelligence gathering apparatus. His disdain for the contemporary organization - compared to the one where he started his very successful career as a spy - is palpable.

He is also forceful is his view that the entire US intelligence subculture is a shambles. For instance, he has few words of praise for the majority of people who work there today. He recalls that while he and his agent friends risked their lives gathering intelligence, all these folks back home could do was watch helplessly as the CIA consistently downgraded the single asset at which it had always excelled in the past: Operations Abroad. The United

States is paying a bitter price for that lapse right now in Afghanistan, Iraq, Iran, Syria, Indonesia, Somalia, Libya and elsewhere, he points out.

'They failed to put in place people who were familiar with the regions to which they were posted. And when they really got going and were producing results, they transferred them out of there because they said they were "getting involved". In spy trade parlance it's called "falling in love".'

Instead, he revealed during the course of a number of interviews, that 'Langley rewarded workers who knew how to play the political games of the agency's suburban Washington headquarters. They did so at the expense of recruiting people on the ground who, as in this present phase when the security of the nation is at risk, could be of inestimable value in the quality and depth of the intelligence that they might deliver'.

What makes Baer's argument compelling is that he uses a multitude of his own experiences to make his case. What's more, these are the exploits of a secret agent that reveled in the unconventional. It's quite a ride.

Clearly, espionage is a filthy and often disgusting business. For those involved in America's clandestine services, the words should be cast in concrete and hoisted aloft over the main entrance to CIA Headquarters at Langley, Virginia. It is also the first message imparted by Baer, who had twenty-one years of service in the CIA. His revelations were equated by one observer with whom he was acquainted 'as akin to a doomsday augury'.

What does come across in his book is that the CIA has massive problems. One of the most intractable is the suburban mentality towards intelligence that Washington seems to inculcate among people working there. 'The comfortable home in Virginia syndrome,' he calls it. 'Many realize that they could get promoted faster and with less risk by staying in Washington. They tend to ignore the reality of the business that collecting information, especially sensitive stuff on which history sometimes turns, quite often needs dirty hands. It's one of the fundamentals of the job. The British have been showing us that for more than a century and they're good at it.

'If you're into intelligence gathering you must get out there and mix and talk with ordinary people of the society in which you've been placed: It's the only way to build up trust and confidence. To get to the point where people are willing to confide in you or react favorably when you finally confront them, takes time.' Essentially, he explains, it is a sharing of experiences.

'It's not going to work by commuting between a flashy hotel and the meeting place. Choose that route and you're always a stranger among those whose friendship you're trying to cultivate. Get on to common ground and that's half the battle won.'

Robert Baer is a powerful proponent for the need for case officers to be able to speak the language. Instead, he says, Langley takes the indirect, Harvard Business School approach to management and expertise. He makes the point that since the Middle East provides a huge proportion of America's oil needs, the Arab world, like it or not, is integral to the nation's long-term strategic wellbeing. For this reason he is critical of Langley's failure to get closer to, and, as a consequence, have a better understanding of the people in the street in the Arab world.

Just one example of how this could have been achieved was for America to have taken a leaf from Britain's book and set up its own national Arab language school in some Arab country.

'But nobody in Washington took any notice, early last century, when Whitehall established its own Arab language school in Lebanon,' he says, though he concedes that with recent developments in the Near East and Central Asia, there might be something in the pipeline.

Beirut's Shamlan School was one of the best in its day, he says. That institution churned out generations of British and Commonwealth Arabists, many of whom - in commerce, industry, diplomacy or good old-fashioned spy craft - played sterling roles in maintaining steady interest in a part of the globe that seems always to have been volatile. He suggests that it is perhaps no accident that for all its problems, the British connection with the Islamic world has remained steadfast for many generations. He suggests, too, that as a consequence, it is no accident that London remains the financial hub of most Arab money movements. 'Why not New York?'

As Baer succinctly puts it, 'Langley has screwed up mightily'. The way it's going, he reckons, it'll take a generation or more to put things right. Others disagree.

What he does stress is that 'they're starting to repair some of the damage, but not much has changed'. Indeed, in some respects things have got worse, he says. The company seems gripped by a multitude of incompetent legacies, many of them inherited from previous administrations.

His accounting of how the CIA's Directorate of Operations has declined under the last three leaders (he describes them as a recalled retiree, an analyst and a 'political pal') makes for chilling conclusions and here he's not talking policy or methodology, but the long-term security of the American nation.

It's interesting that Seymour Hersh, in his introduction to Baer's book, felt that 'we've hit intelligence rock bottom in America'.

Baer explains, by way of illustration following the events of September 11, that the CIA, desperate for more solid intelligence input, rehired squads of retirees to help address the situation. This was fine in theory, he stated, but they're a mixed bunch. 'Some of these veterans are solid old timers. Others are the original bunglers that caused years of abuse and neglect, the very same people that contributed to breaking the system in the first place. Included in this group was the knucklehead who mistakenly targeted the Chinese Embassy in a Belgrade attack during the Kosovo War.

'Right now there's a housewife in charge as deputy head of a division directing CIA's overseas operations. Originally she was a reports officer, a clerk who did minor editing of field reports!'

Could that ever happen at the Pentagon? He speculates 'Can't see it. Can you imagine the military bringing in a nonentity – and a housewife to boot – to help run operations in Afghanistan? The US military runs its shows professionally, the way we once did in the CIA.'

He's not altogether uncritical of certain military developments. 'Operation Desert Storm' he says, gave the Americans a remarkable opportunity to recruit agents from among the tens of thousands of Iraqi prisoners of war that were captured: 'Some of these people were very senior in the Iraqi military and, considering the circumstances, it should have been easy to turn a select few. Had we done just that, we'd have had people in sensitive positions right under the nose of Saddam Hussein when Gulf War 2 came along.' As things developed, says Baer, the CIA was prohibited from doing any intelligence recruiting after the 1991 invasion and the man responsible for this decision was none other than the much-revered General 'Stormin' Norman Swartzkopf.

'In fact he was totally opposed to it and it makes no sense whatever,' he adds. Baer states that throughout his career, whether in Vietnam or in the sands of Arabia, Swartzkopf seemed to have been opposed to CIA activities on his stretch of turf. 'In much the same way he was against deploying Special Forces.'

In the light of the consequentially serious long-term implications, that kind of myopia was unconscionable, he says, adding that 'today we're paying for it'.

As for CIA Director George Tenet, he does not spare the man. Even allowing for obvious lapses of concentration in critical issues, or the fact that the worst terror attacks in the history of the nation occurred on his watch, nothing justified the CIA being caught with its pants around its ankles as has been the case in several campaigns in which America found itself in the past few years. Baer can hardly contain his surprise that he's still at McLean: 'Anywhere else, when your boat kisses the bottom, you lose your command...'

However, he says that he now understands a little better the political realities and constraints of Washington. As he says: 'Tenet has the ear of the president and maybe he should stay...the last thing the CIA needs right now is another director who can't get into the Oval Office.'

This sad chapter can perhaps be encapsulated by an exchange that took place at an open Congressional hearing in February 2002 between Tenet and Senator Pat Roberts. The Kansas Republican asked the head of the CIA how it was that an obscure American member of the Taliban by the name of John Walker Lindh could not only meet with (Osama) bin Laden and be totally accepted, while his organization couldn't get an agent anywhere near him? Tenet appears not to have been able to answer.

Robert Baer is not shy to detail events that must be embarrassing to his former spymasters. It is also a timely exposé.

Briefly, Baer's brisk explication is a terse dynamic between the realities of everyday espionage and the environment in which so many of these people operate. Put another way, what he has to tell deals with what British master spy and KGB secret agent Kim Philby, paraphrasing that arch imperialist Kipling, once called 'the great game'.

Plurilingual, this former California ski bum with a degree from Georgetown University slotted easily into any environment in which he was placed once he had joined the 'company'. Too easily, say some of his detractors. They claim that in the field, Robert Baer was a risk taker, which the Arab specialist accepts more as a compliment than a slight 'since that's exactly what gathering intelligence is all about', he retorts. His candor can be disarming.

As a case officer in the DO for the Central Intelligence Agency, Baer saw service in many of the world's trouble spots: Iraq, Khartoum, New Delhi, Rabat, Dushanbe and elsewhere. During the course of his duties, he became fluent enough in Arabic to be able to operate clandestinely in Lebanon as a native Arab.

At the end of it, tired of bureaucratic bickering (at one stage Langley's mandarins tried to implicate him in the Iran-Contra shambles and failed) and with the CIA pulling back from aggressive covert actions to appease their political masters, he resigned from the service in December 1997.

As he told me, 'I left in utter disgust.'

Some of the more interesting observations in his book deal with CIA shortcomings, which, if they didn't matter so much would be hilarious. In fact, some are so improbable that they hardly seem plausible.

For instance, following the end of the Cold War, Langley went to absurd lengths to exonerate Russia from charges that it might still be spying on the US. Baer recalls how 'Uncle Milty', his old Khartoum boss (and by then chief of the Central-Eurasian Division) informed the CIA office in Rabat, Morocco, that 'henceforth Russia would be treated like Germany, France, Italy or any other friendly country'. The Cold War was over! Period.

Of course, that was before the traitor Dick Ames was taken into custody and exposed as having caused the deaths of dozens of people abroad who were working for US intelligence, almost all of them murdered by Moscow's agents. Issues were further compounded after Robert Hannsen of the FBI was uncovered after spying for the Russians for twenty-one years.

'It was so obvious,' recalls Baer. 'The man was driving a brand new Jaguar XJ-6 and it must have been the only one in the parking lot. My gut reaction was that nobody in the CIA owns a car like that.'

What Langley's revised approach towards America's new-found friends, the Russians, meant was 'that if the KGB *resident* were to walk in and volunteer to tell us everything he knew, we weren't authorized so much as to give him a nickel to catch a bus back to his embassy. Actually, once the CIA had to turn away Vasili Mitrokhin a KGB archivist, who then went to tell all to British intelligence. He provided them with the kind of information that ultimately led to the identification of dozens of spies, including a US colonel. You figure that one out', declared Baer.

Also interesting was his own FBI investigation for murder (he was cleared, it was a set-up), and, at one point by the US Secret Service in an attempt to shed new light on the complete breakdown of internal security processes within the CIA. Finally, he was pressured by his Director of Operations with the threat of a psychological evaluation to determine his 'fitness for duty', which another former clandestine case officer Robert D. Steele equated to a variation of one of the original Stalinist ploys. Baer, savvy to Langley's machinations, would have none of it.

Steele added that it was an underhanded technique for declaring officers unfit for duty, based solely on psychological hatchet jobs and was a common practice in the two decades when Britt Snider was appointed Inspector General at the CIA.

CIA agent Robert Baer could see the changes coming long before they began to manifest as negatively as they eventually did.

He takes bitter pleasure these days in recalling the antics of a female case officer working in France. He'd arranged to meet her, together with a European informant who, for years, had been a solid source of information about all sorts of dirty deeds. These ranged from illegal weapons shipments to snippets of information out of the darkest corners of the Elysée Palace. For the purpose of elucidation, he called him Jacques and the woman Becky.

The first time Baer met with Becky and Jacques was after the American woman had decided that the spying business wasn't for her. So she handed Jacques over to Baer.

'From the start,' says Baer, 'it was obvious that the informant wasn't at all happy. In fact, relations between Becky and Jacques were like ice. So I set out to do what I could to get things back to an even keel and decided it would be a good start to take the man to a first-rate restaurant.' There, in true James Bond style the American spy displayed a respectable knowledge of a good claret. Warmed up by a second bottle of 'white burgundy from a terroir I knew', Jacques startled him by asking if he believed in God.

'Er...no, not exactly,' Baer replied. The Frenchman beamed with relief.

The contact went on to explain that Becky (his prior handler) was interested only in saving him from a life of sin by attempting 'to lead me back to Christianity'. When Baer complained to his Paris COS Chuck Cogan, he got the brush-off. The station chief, though sympathetic, was fearful that any interference with Becky's First Amendment rights might get the agency into an unwelcome lawsuit.

In the end, Jacques came up big with the goods. One of his coups included giving the CIA information about a Swiss-British merchant of death living in Zug who was selling boatloads of *Iglas* (advanced Soviet surface-to-air missiles) to Iran. 'Jacques got the prices, letters of credit, end-users certificates, everything.'

Baer provided other graphic examples of how America's prime intelligence gathering agency gradually deteriorated to an organization where most of the operatives, rather than face risks in the field, preferred to wear smart suits, work in embassies and live in comfortable homes. The level of obfuscation got worse with each new Director of Information.

Another example: 'We'd ask the Paris office to put together a surveillance team to watch the apartments of a suspected terrorist. Paris came back and told us that it couldn't be done because the local spooks would find out.

'Another time we asked Bonn to recruit a few Arabs and Iranians to track the Middle East émigré community in West Germany. It responded that it didn't have enough officers.

'Then we asked Beirut to meet a certain agent traveling to Lebanon: It refused because of some obscure security problem.'

As Baer explained, 'Security was never *not* a problem in Beirut, for God's sake. Instead of fighting terrorists we were fighting bureaucratic inertia, an implacable enemy...analysts were in charge, which was insane because these were people who'd never met an agent in their lives, didn't know what a dead drop was and rarely traveled out of the Washington metropolitan area. Yet they were directing field offices abroad on how to run their cases. It was like assigning a hospital administrator to head the surgical team,' Baer argued.

Some of the best work of this CIA professional's career had an Islamic backdrop. As he told me, 'Maybe it sounds wacky, but I loved working in Beirut. Instead of dealing with the distractions of headquarters, the meetings and paperwork that ate up time, I'd move around on the streets where I was always more comfortable.'

At one stage he was able to get to the core of Iranian subterfuge in the Be'qaa Valley. He employed a local contact that he had spent a lot of time cultivating in order to get him into the ancient city of Baalbek, then a serpents' nest of Ayatollah Khomeini's interests in Lebanon. It was during this visit that he came within yards of the compound then holding kidnapped CIA chief in Beirut, Bill Buckley, who was later executed.

From the start, Baer was deeply affected by the bombing of the US Embassy in that city more than twenty years before. It was a debacle that cost the lives of several of his CIA buddies. Having experienced the consequences of what was then still a relatively new phenomenon, a totalitarian brand of terrorism, he spent years piecing together the leads. In the end it became almost an obsession to get at the truth of who was really behind the bombings. It took a lot of time, together with a good deal of human, documentary and circumstantial evidence, but he finally reached something of a conclusion in his last months at Langley: He actually uncovered who was masterminding it all.

The American explained that picking up the trail of the embassy bombing was like putting together a Roman mosaic scattered in an earthquake and scorched by fire. 'You had no idea what was a lead, something to go on, and what wasn't.'

In the end, he declared, 'I unraveled the...bombing, at least to my satisfaction: Iran had ordered it and Yasser Arafat's Fatah network carried it out.'

The story does not end there. Washington built a new embassy in Beirut, a two-story villa about a hundred yards from the skeleton of the old one that had been bombed by terrorists. This new structure became one of the most heavily protected properties in the world.

'The ten acres of land surrounding it were covered with a sea of coiled razor wire, fortified bunkers, watchtowers, machine-gun positions and sandbagged trenches. Foot-thick steel walls cushioned the villa from artillery and rockets. Anti-rocket screens covered the roof. With more than six hundred local guards, the US Embassy had the fourth largest standing militia in the country: Even an armored division would have had to fight like hell to capture it.'

However, the ring of protection extended only so far, he says. During the previous three years - Baer was working there for part of the time - the CIA lost two of its chiefs, another five of its officers and plenty of agents. In the same period, thirty-seven foreigners were taken hostage, half-a-dozen of them executed.

Interestingly, Robert Baer provided a grim indication of the true intentions of the PLO leader. Graphically he is able to depict the movement's historic ties and support, not only for the Ayatollah, but also for the fundamentalist Muslim Brotherhood as well as a dozen other shady terrorist groups. In 1972, he says, Arafat and the Ayatollah Khomeini signed an accord in Najaf (during his period of exile in Iraq) to train Islamic fighters at Fatah camps in South Lebanon. Some of these were in Tyre, always a hotbed of Hizbollah activity, even today[4].

'Almost every leader of the Iranian revolution passed through these camps, from Khomeini's son Ahmad Khomeini to Mustafa Chamran, the first commander of the Iranian Revolutionary Guards or Pasdaran. When the Shah fled Iran in January 1979 and Khomeini returned to Tehran two weeks later, it wasn't surprising that the first telephone call that the Ayatollah received was from Arafat.'

Nine months later, on October 19, 1979 - two weeks before the Iranians seized the US Embassy in Tehran - Arafat flew there to congratulate Khomeini in person.

'I think of all that when I see Arafat standing in the Rose Garden at the White House, or when I hear that a CIA director has met privately with him at some desert tent.

'I wonder sometimes if Arafat's example didn't make Osama bin Laden consider that he, too, might have become a statesman in time.'

1   'Unnoticed Bombshell' - *National Review Online*, Print Edition, February 11, 2002. See also Ledeen's *The War Against the Terror Masters:* St Martin's Press, New York, 2002

2   Robert Baer: *See No Evil: The True Story of a Ground Soldier in the CIA's War on Terrorism*: Crown Publishers, New York, 2002

3   Pasdaran (officially, the Islamic Revolutionary Guards Corps or IRGC) is the most secret of Iran's clandestine bodies. Many thousands strong, it is linked to terror movements and subversive operations in numerous countries, the West especially, and more recently, Iraq. Lebanon's powerfully anti-Israeli Hizbollah movement is directed, funded and motivated by Iran's Pasdaran. Following 'Operation Iraqi Freedom' in 2003, the first Iranian elements to infiltrate westwards from Iran were Pasdaran. This body also handles the security for Tehran's clandestine nuclear program

4   For a backgrounder on Hizbollah, see the author's report on the revolutionary movement in *Jane's Islamic Review,* May, 2003

16

SCOTT RITTER'S CURIOUS ABOUT-FACE

'Mr Ritter has been rewarded for his truth telling with a stern warning from the United Nations, a Federal investigation into his association with Israel and the ludicrous assertion of American officials that he does not know what he is talking about. This treatment is an embarrassment to the country.'

Editorial, *The New York Times,* October 5, 1998

It has been suggested that the maverick UN weapons inspector Scott Ritter is either a double agent working for the American government or the Iraqis have corrupted him. Personally, knowing the man as I do, I wouldn't wager money on either option.

Rather, I'm of the opinion that Ritter having worked at the sharp end in this Arab State for several years, got to know Iraqi people rather well. He understands their plight. He also showed himself able to empathize with the enormity of the problem that faced a people saddled with a demon for a leader.

Having said that, Mr Ritter did a rather curious tactical about-turn in the face of a colossal amount of incriminating evidence that he, no less, played a vigorous role in accumulating. He was so successful in his search for banned weapons with the UN Special Commission (UNSCOM) that at one stage he was complimented by his superiors for a level of dedication and insight as being 'beyond the normal demands of duty'.

Indeed, it's fair to say that few UN arms inspectors spent as much time digging for evidence as did this reserve US Marine Major, now into his early forties. Nor was any member of UNSCOM quite as critical or as vocal of dilatory UN and American efforts to find them.

Having achieved that much, his activities on his return were curtailed by the US State Department. For a while, he was under investigation by the FBI. At the top of this page there is an observation made during those difficult times by one of the world's leading newspapers which reflected kindly on Scott Ritter's travails.

It is worth mentioning that following his abrupt (and to some, astonishing) mind change, I spent a while on the road in Europe and Africa in the Fall of 2002 and found Ritter's comments being quoted everywhere. Though amusing at first, it eventually became a bind to discover that no single person linked to the Iraqi imbroglio was more consistently hailed by Continental and Third World youth as proof that America was lying about Iraq. He created a consensus among millions of impressionable young (and not so young) people that Washington had a catalogue of intentions that had something to do with expropriating Iraq's oil assets. He even came out in print on the subject.[1]

Overnight, Ritter became a hero to tens of millions of people of every possible political persuasion. To the majority, he was a modern-day messiah called down from the heart of the American Establishment to damn Washington's imperialist aspirations, in the Arab world especially. His newfound disclosures about Iraq were even used by governments to prove that Saddam had no weapons of mass destruction and that 'neoconservatives' working out of the West Wing fabricated the entire story.

For all that, and the controversy that he whipped up - worldwide, mark you - there is a sentiment in the United States that might suggest that this illustrious New York resident could end up with criminal charges. These might include those of treason and, arguably, consorting with the enemy: Iraq, after all has been a military adversary for many years. Personally, I doubt if any of this will happen, even though there is an argument that runs something along the lines of him having been a pliant instrument in propagating Baghdad's lies.

Listen to this one, Ritter quoted by London's *Daily Telegraph* on May 7, 2003: 'I see no difference between the invasion of Iraq and the invasion of Poland in 1939.' His detractors point too, to documents recovered after the fall of Saddam that show that very expensive gifts of jewelry were bought by Baghdad for Ritter's wife. As this ex-US Marine warns, it was not his idea and he wanted none of it.

So why the change of story? The reality, it seems, is that Scott Ritter has always been a bit of an upstart. He was certainly one of the most controversial figures to emerge from among a fairly large body of UNSCOM weapons inspectors in Iraq.

What Ritter feared most - the emasculation of UNSCOM - became a reality not very long after he got back onto American soil. The UN body conducted its last search for hidden Iraqi WMD assets in August 1998. As a result, Ritter told me then, Saddam Hussein retained a substantial armory of illicit weapons 'and there is nothing that anybody, or any nation, can do about it'. Even the UN secretary general Kofi Annan conceded at the time that without massive use of force, the issues involved were insurmountable.

Immediately afterwards, the head of UNSCOM, Ambassador Richard Butler, resigned.

Ritter first started his search for Iraqi nuclear, chemical and biological weapons as a low-level staffer with the UNSCOM-24 inspection team of December 1991. His last tour of duty was the controversial and aborted UNSCOM-255 inspection effort seven years later. In between, there was much controversy. Ritter was accused by the Iraqis of being a CIA spy. By his own admission, he worked closely with Israeli intelligence, though this was to the benefit of UNSCOM, he declared when the brouhaha became public. He was remarkably forthright about the inability of the secretary general of the UN and the US government to support either him or UNSCOM when push became shove.

By the time Ritter resigned from UNSCOM, he had become the central figure in a risky 'spy versus spy' enterprise launched by the UN under the code name of 'Shake the Tree'. UNSCOM, in the words of *Washington Post* staffer Barton Gellman, 'took on a role in consuming and acquiring intelligence that was unprecedented for an international organization'. Ritter, it was averred, had become a repository of the most sensitive secrets of a job that no person had ever held before; a UN intelligence operative, said Gellman.

Already, only months after he left Iraq, it was Ritter's view that because no UN spot checks were happening, Saddam might very well have again resuscitated his biological warfare program. And because biowarfare time frames are calculated in months rather than years, he reckoned that it was not impossible that Baghdad could already have produced tons of anthrax and botulinum toxin.

'There is simply no organized, unscheduled UN activity to prevent the man from doing so,' he exclaimed with some resignation.

It is Ritter's contention originally, and he is on record as saying this, that most governments would be stunned if they knew the full breadth of Iraq's hidden weapons' inventory. In June 1997, in a frank, verbal confrontation with Lt General Rasheed, Iraq's oil minister, Ritter was asked what he believed was being hidden from his search teams.

His answer: 'As many as half-a-dozen fully operational ballistic missiles and twenty-five more in disassembled form. There were also one or more complete nuclear weapons minus their fissile cores, VX nerve toxins in salt form for extended storage, a mobile biological weapons production facility (including fermentors and freeze-drying apparatus), freeze-dried anthrax as well as other items which remain classified.' With that, General Rasheed excused himself and left the room.

Similarly, said Ritter about then, Baghdad might very well have got its nuclear program on track again, especially since several hundred nuclear physicists and technicians were still on Saddam's payroll. While a lot of assets were destroyed after 'Operation Desert Storm', still more were secreted before UNSCOM could get to them.

Still more of his comments:

- There is evidence that Iraq may have been conducting chemical weapons activity outside Iraqi territory, notably in The Sudan. This tied in with reports from Western journalists who had returned from South Sudan a short while before. There they uncovered numerous reports of The Sudan Peoples Liberation Army (SPLA) suffering casualties consistent with the use of chemical weapons such as sarin or VX. Ritter stated that he had been unable to investigate these reports because UNSCOM's mandate did not extend beyond Iraq.

- An UNSCOM inspection of the Iraqi air force HQ at the time uncovered a document which showed that in a Baghdad presentation of the material balance for chemical weapons, it had *overdeclared* the number of bombs dropped and the tonnage of chemical agents used during the first Iran-Iraq War. As a result, Ritter declared, several thousand bombs and seven hundred tons of chemical agents (all previously listed as expended) were still hidden by the time UNSCOM was forced out.

- There was substantive evidence that pointed to Saddam having possibly tested biological weapons on live humans in 1995. The mastermind behind Iraq's bioweapons program was, again, the notorious Dr Rihab Taha. It was of some embarrassment to the British government that she took her PhD in plant toxins at the University of East Anglia between 1981-84.

- Ritter confirmed that it was Israel that passed on the intelligence that Oxoid, a Basingstoke company, had sold Iraq forty tons of biological growth medium, none of which Baghdad was able to account for. This raised the question whether Britain's SIS at the time was myopic or just absurdly inept?

- At one point, UNSCOM received detailed information from a north European country, as well as from three Iraqi defectors, that Saddam was hiding almost all the necessary components for 'at least' three atomic bombs. According to Ritter, these were implosion-type nuclear bombs in the 20kT range; similar to, but larger than the A-bomb which obliterated Nagasaki. It is still not clear whether the size of the bombs met Iraq's design goal for fitting inside the 88cm warhead of a Scud, though it seems unlikely. While it is surmised that Iraq did not at the time have highly enriched uranium (HEU), Baghdad, on Saddam's orders, did hide away a lot of uranium hexafluoride feedstock (UF6) prior to UNSCOM activity. UF6 is a precursor used to deliver HEU, and is the gaseous form of metallic uranium that is used during the enrichment process to get weapons grade isotopic mixture of over ninety per cent.

- A confusing aspect about all this information is that while American intelligence assessments officially concurred on the credibility of the nuclear report in 1998 (and went on record to that effect), US policy makers on Capitol Hill said in October of that year that the government never received such information from UNSCOM 'and, in any event, did not regard (Ritter's) claim as credible'.

- Ritter's intelligence contained detailed information on how the weapons were concealed (including the names of Special Republican Guard [SRG] and Special Security Organization [SSO] officers involved). It included the types of vehicles (ice cream trucks with white cabs and red stripe markings used to move embargoed assets about during the day and green Mercedes tractor-trailers from the Segada Transportation Company's fleet for night work) as well as the location of seven transport depots where these vehicles were housed. A subsequent review of US surveillance imagery found five of them. Ritter's requests for permission to pursue these objectives were rejected on instructions from the US State Department. It is notable that Segada, or phonetically, Sajida, is the name of the wife of the Iraqi dictator.

On ballistic missiles, Ritter maintained that Iraq consistently refused to talk about those that had been produced indigenously. Baghdad repeatedly told UNSCOM that it had never produced an operational ballistic missile. Yet

Iraqi documents held by the UN provided evidence that after the first Gulf War, seven locally produced Al Hussein missiles were destroyed. Ritter reckoned then that there were still up to about a dozen that had been dismantled and dispersed in hidden sites throughout the country. Experts agree that if Saddam wanted it, his scientists could have reassembled them all at short notice.

- Defector reports, said Ritter, indicated that Iraq's leadership had devised a plan to produce operational Al Hussein ballistic missiles within six months of a decision being made to do so. This tied in with other reports (some of Israeli origin) that Saddam was importing machines and tools (ostensibly for other purposes) to enable him to achieve this objective. Among items which Ritter - in conjunction with US intelligence agents seized in August 1995, while being shipped through Jordan - were Russian-made precision gyroscopes and accelerometers that had been salvaged from decommissioned former Soviet submarine ICBMs. These were intended for Iraq's missile program.

- Ritter maintained that Iraq went to extraordinary lengths to conceal its WMD assets. '(They) originally changed their concealment mechanisms every ninety days or so,' he said. What's more, as Ritter's efforts fructified, this regimen was altered every month. 'Consequently, to avoid such intelligence becoming dated, we needed to act quickly on any information that came in,' he told.

More evidence of clandestine WMD work emerged afterwards. French tests inside Iraq appeared to have found traces of chemicals linked to the production of VX nerve gas on Iraqi missile warheads. Asked about it, Ritter confirmed to me at the time that he had been aware of the findings 'for a while now', but his question was: Why had France delayed releasing the final results in the first place? In the end there was more vacillating on the part of the Elysees Palace.

Another source maintained that the delay was intentional and that Paris did not wish to undermine Iraq's push at the UN to get sanctions lifted. It is no secret that, of all countries, France stood to gain an immense economic advantage in any eventual restructuring of the pariah state, though no French diplomat that you talk to at the UN (or anywhere else) would have been crass enough just then to admit it.

Following 'Operation Iraqi Freedom' a lot more has emerged as to why France took the staunchly anti-American line that it did. Some reports talk of substantial economic rewards from Saddam personally if Paris was to stay out of it (See Chapter 17).

The discovery of clandestine WMD work had other implications. The system of VX production in Iraq was then quite unique. It contained not only a phosphorous-carbon bond, but sulfur as well.

For instance, the sample taken from the grounds of the Al Shifa Pharmaceutical factory in Khartoum (prior to the US cruise missile attack on The Sudan) had this exact same consistency. There was a strong suspicion that one of the processes Iraq used to manufacture VX, combining EMPTA with another chloride compound, was similarly employed by technicians in The Sudan at Al Shifa.

The West had been aware for some time after 'Desert Storm' that Iraq had moved some of its WMD assets abroad, first to Libya and then, overland, into The Sudan: This was actually one of the reasons why the attack was predicated.

The significance of Ritter's disclosures about Iraq's nuclear aspirations, according to an earlier *Washington Post* article (September 30, 1998) was that they 'would revise the conclusions of recent reports by the IAEA, which, it seems, was always a bit of an uneasy collaborator with UNSCOM'.

There was good reason: A year before, Vienna's International Atomic Energy Agency reported that active inspections were nearing the point of 'diminishing returns', a finding that led Russia, France and China to suggest that the Security Council's 'nuclear file' on Iraq be closed.

'In effect, this would have been tantamount to a certification that Baghdad had no capacity whatever to build an atomic bomb,' said the *Post*, which, it implied, was ridiculous. The newspaper took the matter a step further; it contacted Gary Dillon, chief of the IAEA Action Team on Iraq who, while rejecting Ritter's claims as 'unsubstantiated', did not respond to several messages requesting an interview.

Significantly, the IAEA had previously acknowledged gaps in its information about Iraq.

In a confidential report on August 19, 1997 its Action Team wrote that it could not verify how much the Baghdad government had accomplished in its efforts to devise a working nuclear weapons design. After the 1995 defection of Lt General Hussein Kamel, Baghdad was forced to turn over technical drawings on the use of precision-shaped charges known as 'explosive lenses'. These are interlocking hexagonal blocks of explosives designed to implode a nuclear device. Also surrendered were details of how to crush HEU to a critically dense mass for inclusion in the warhead.

What transpired later was that Iraq first denied that it had ever built the molds: Then it said that its personnel couldn't find either the molds or the lenses. Ritter's comment was along the lines of it being typical of the sort of obfuscation he had encountered throughout.

Meanwhile, the West gained an immense windfall with the 1995 defection of Iraqi scientist, Dr Khidhir Hamza. As we have noted, for several months Hamza worked closely with David Albright, President of Washington's Institute for Science and International Security (ISIS). Albright for a while was of the opinion that Hamza – at the time - was probably the most important source to reach the West with information about Saddam's nuclear weapons program. All of Iraq's nuclear projects were still very much alive, he was assured by Hamza.

Albright reckoned that Hamza had come across with a lot of evidence, including details of his having trained a cadre of young scientists who, while working with more senior people, would be able to quickly resume Iraq's atomic bomb program once sanctions were lifted. The nuclear program had been personally directed by Saddam from its inception almost three decades before, he maintained, and was abetted by a host of Western countries that sold Iraq sophisticated equipment as 'they winked and laughed' at patently false cover stories (See Chapter 8).

A disturbing sidelight here, he also confided, was the number of Iraqi students at Western universities and lengthy periods spent by senior Iraqi scientists at American universities studying the latest scientific journals and technical accounts of America's nuclear efforts.

At issue, following the Hamza disclosures (which were passed on to the IAEA) was how that body, having been apprised from the start about what was going on in Iraq, could have possibly considered giving Saddam a clean nuclear Bill of Health once these details were made public. Hamza said from the start (and he had evidence to prove it) that Iraq would continue to build atomic bombs.

UNSCOM had a difficult time in Iraq and the stories are legion; of inspection teams arriving at a site and demanding access only to be told that their documents weren't in order.

While these were being 'fixed' they could often do no more than watch helplessly as Iraqi officials burnt drums of documents in full view of where they were stopped. Or being held at the front gate while Iraqi army trucks full of equipment drove out the rear. Sometimes they would arrive at a factory or warehouse that was being targeted by an inspection with good intelligence that something was going on, and there would be a sudden, inexplicable power failure.

'There was the case towards the end when we actually deployed a team of forty-five inspectors into the country to carry out inspections,' said Ritter. The US, together with Britain, actually intervened and conferred with Richard Butler. They wanted the Australian head of UNSCOM to put pressure on him to cancel intrusive inspections, despite the fact that everybody was set and waiting to go. Then, a month later, Ritter had another team ready.

'We had *very* good intelligence about certain sites. This time Washington - through intervention from both Madeleine Albright and Sandy Berger - had the inspection first postponed for some days and then ordered that it be canceled outright.' The weapons inspectors were flabbergasted at the about-turn, but it was symptomatic of so much that went on during the Clinton Watch, or as somebody chided, the lack of it.

In Ritter's discussions with Washington journalist Martin Gellman, there were some unsettling indications of security leaks from within UNSCOM and, more ominous, that weapons inspectors' 'Shake the Tree' had become what was termed 'a competing operation' with the Central Intelligence Agency. For instance, Ritter was aware that an Iraqi defector told the Americans in 1995 of secret underground weapons storage facilities at Jabal Mokhul, one of Saddam's presidential complexes on the west bank of the Tigris, north of Tikrit. This information was never passed on to UNSCOM, with the result that a valuable search opportunity launched by him later was thwarted.

Following a tip, his people looked through all the main Jabal Mokhul structures, but the SSO had already shifted away a variety of WMD assets into those same underground storage passages that the CIA had earlier been told about.

'Had we known about the tunnels, who knows what would have been uncovered?' Ritter declared.

Also, just as the UN tried to penetrate Iraq, Saddam made every effort to penetrate UNSCOM. 'Ritter and his superiors learnt to their disquiet that the Baghdad government showed signs of having six to ten days' notice of most inspections,' Gellman disclosed.

One consequence of these breaches was that UNSCOM staff responded by compartmentalizing information and inventing classifications like 'Green Code' to limit access to information. For some time prior to the withdrawal, Ritter stated, UNSCOM operated on the 'need to know' principle. Meanwhile, the FBI was warned of Iraqi agents on the UN janitorial staff in New York and senior UNSCOM personnel routinely left the building for their most confidential discussions.

According to group leader Ritter, the number of UNSCOM personnel in the country at any time averaged about a hundred-and-twenty. This figure could be upped if unscheduled searches were envisaged. When that happened, teams of between thirty and seventy would make surprise visits to sites where it was believed items relating to WMD were hidden. Ritter stressed that they rarely acted before being in possession of reliable information. As the flow of intelligence increased, these 'raids' became more intrusive.

Obviously, the Iraqis would object vigorously, both in Baghdad and in New York. Several times - with UNSCOM on the brink of making new discoveries - Saddam would become confrontational. When that happened, negotiations would be initiated, usually culminating (after some pretty determined Iraqi intransigence) with American threats to retaliate. And, then, as we repeatedly saw, Saddam Hussein would back down, but always at the last moment.

This would rarely happen before entire Allied battle groups, including aircraft carriers and squadrons of military aircraft had been moved into the Gulf. The cost of this kind of brinkmanship was enormous. It's worth noting that with Saddam having set the example, the same game was afterwards played with a equal skill and sleight-of-hand by Yugoslavia's Slobadan Milosovic. That kind of opportunism was eventually halted by pre-emptive military action.

Ritter's contacts with Israel were pivotal to an FBI investigation launched after he resigned his Iraqi position and returned home. It focused almost solely on his links with the Jewish State while he was with UNSCOM.

By his own admission, while Washington tended to treat the Iraqi affair as an academic exercise, 'I thought that Israel regarded it as a matter of life and death. So we went to Israel'. Whatever was done, he stressed, was sanctioned by the Chairman of UNSCOM (first Rolf Ekeus, and then his successor, Richard Butler).

'At the same time,' said Ritter, 'every aspect was approved by Washington, all the way to the top,' adding later: 'I am not a spy for the United States, or for Israel or any other country. Let us be quite clear about that.' Ritter contended that he was in charge when he went to Israel and that Israel had responded. 'Nor did (Israel) control the special commission in any way, or did they try to,' he said.

Ritter always maintained - privately and in public - that Israel was very conscious of the hovering threat of UNSCOM possibly being accused of partisanship and the damage that such a charge might have had on the UN body. 'These are extremely responsible people. They knew what was at stake,' he declared.

Asked how often he went to Israel, he would only say that from 1994 until the time he left in 1998 that it was 'a lot'.

Towards the end of 1994, Ritter was leading regular delegations to Tel Aviv for meetings with Major General Uri Saguy (then chief of Israeli military intelligence) as well as with panels of analysts from other Israeli security agencies. There were also meetings with representatives of the Jerusalem government in New York, usually held in basements or obscure bars scattered throughout the city; as he recalls, it was very discreet. It had to be. Sometimes he met with Amidror, Saguy's deputy.

Part of the reason for this work, he disclosed, was that there came a time when operators within UNSCOM needed some new methodologies that they weren't getting from the US. 'So we took them from Israel instead.'

What did he think of the Israelis that he met? Ritter was blunt when he spoke to me about it: 'First, they are a remarkably professional bunch. They worked their asses off. In Washington, in contrast, you have to cope with the nine-to-five mentality.

'But the Israelis would have none of it. If we weren't finished at the end of the day, we'd go on, well into the night.' Ritter was scathing about what he termed Washington bureaucrats 'thinking out of the box'. This implied that everything was done according to the book. It possibly tells you something that former CIA staffer Robert Baer saw it in exactly the same light[2]. There was no latitude for flexibility, both Ritter and Baer suggested (See Chapter 15).

'The Israelis are different,' said Ritter. 'If they come up against something, they say, OK we can't do it this way, so how else?' To these people, he sensed, alternatives were simply a natural progression in solving issues: 'they looked for solutions. A problem was just another obstacle that needed to be overcome. They are not afraid of having ideas shot down within a think-tank milieu. In this they were remarkably courageous and innovative in terms of putting forward new ideas.' By the time it was over, in his opinion, they had become a pretty formidable team.

In a subsequent interview with Israel's *Ha'aretz* on September 29, 1998, Ritter conceded to having provided first-hand information about the Iraqi concealment program. It was run by Abed Hamid Mahmoud, at the time probably the most powerful man in the country after the president. Like his boss, Hamid was a Tikriti: they hailed from the same village[3].

The two main organizations involved in Mahmoud's operations, both presidential forces, were the SSO and the SRG.

Commented Ritter: 'The Special Security Organization is one of the most secretive organizations anywhere, with a strength of about five thousand, possibly more. The SRB, in contrast, is the military component. It has four brigades with about twenty thousand people in all.' It was Ritter's job while with UNSCOM to try to break through the inscrutable, almost impenetrable security shell that surrounded both bodies.

'And in the end we did it. We managed to establish what procedures they followed and gradually, because it was a slow process, we came to understand their methodology. I asked Israel to help us formulate analytical models and techniques and to advise on operational issues, which they did.

'Remember it is Israeli cities, not the people of Chicago or New York that are in the line of fire from any of the crazy weapons of mass destruction that Iraq might produce. The Jewish State has a vested interest in the outcome.'

Abed Mahmoud's influence within Saddam Hussein's 'inner sanctum' at that time was remarkable. Even his son couldn't get to his father in those days unless he went through Abed, which was why he was termed his 'gatekeeper'. Abed was not only responsible for coordinating the national security policy of Iraq but also responsible for the day-to-day operations of the SSO.

According to Ritter, the entire program operated like Mafiosi, with select cells being responsible for specific tasks. One cell never knew what another did.

'Here, I think we're talking about hundreds of people in several cells doing chemicals; others, biological work, missiles or imports and so on. You might be talking about as many as fifty or sixty sites at any one time. Then you have those whose job it is to do nothing but monitor the activities of UNSCOM personnel; trying to get information about our next move or, more likely, what we had been able to uncover of Iraqi clandestine activities.'

Ritter stressed that his people were always being challenged by security obstacles placed in their way by the authorities, and that the UN role needed to be viewed within the intractable framework of a regime of terror and control.

'Make no mistake, they can tap into any resource in the country and they don't need permission to do so.' Any Iraqi national even suspected of disloyalty was simply liquidated, he disclosed.

On relationships maintained by him with the chairmen of UNSCOM, first Rolf Ekeus and then the later incumbent Richard Butler, Ritter in the Clinton era had nothing but praise.

'I had a similar relationship with both men, and I can only say that theirs was one of the most difficult and challenging jobs in the world. It was made more onerous by a weak and fractured Security Council, coupled to a United States Administration which will not and cannot lead, as well as a meddling, pro-Iraqi secretary general, all of whom refuse to stand up to the real culprit, an obstructionist and defiant Saddam Hussein,' Scott Ritter stated.

In a later interview, shortly after his first book[4] was published in 1999, Ritter told me that UNSCOM and he were aware that Iraq had kept all of its infrastructure and personnel associated with their nuclear program intact. 'It was very cleverly hidden under dual-use covers.'

'Similarly, UNSCOM had plenty of information linking Saddam Hussein's Special Security Organization (SSO) with an ongoing biological warfare program. All that is happening right now. The US government is aware of it. All I can say at the moment is that this is a huge mistake on the part of Washington. For me to discuss it in detail would only embarrass persons and agencies who do not wish to be embarrassed.' It was significant, he added, that 'although I am critical of developments, it would be dangerous to ignore the role that America has played in successes achieved by UNSCOM so far'.

Ritter stated that his comment about Iraq having components for 'three or four nuclear devices, minus the fissile core' was taken out of context by the media. They stemmed from answers to questions asked of him on Capitol Hill by Senator McCain.

'I answered yes. UNSCOM did have this information which had been provided by a third government (but not Israel). It was deemed at the time (in 1996) to be credible enough to warrant investigation. It was also passed on to the US government and to the International Atomic Energy Authority in Vienna.

'What we did *not* do, was give the IAEA everything that we had, and this was simply to protect sources and methods. This information dealt primarily with how Iraq concealed components from us and from the Atomic Energy Agency. However, coordination between IAEA and myself indicated that gaps in Vienna's knowledge of Iraq's nuclear weapons' program existed in the areas of explosive lenses, neutron generators and electronic initiators, all components for an implosion device,' he explained.

Ritter added that, likewise, the IAEA was aware that Iraq had made lens molds. UNSCOM also had information that Iraq had lens drawings and had actually pressed lenses. But while he was with UNSCOM, nothing had been turned over by Iraq[5].

'The information was deemed credible and relevant and we pursued it, but I never said flat-out that Iraq had three or four nuclear devices.'

He explained that explosive lens work was done at Al Qa'a Qa'a, an explosives factory located next to Al Atheer. He thought it curious that at the time that the IAEA was destroying Al Atheer in 1992, the weaponization program had been transferred from there to Al Kawthar. 'What we do know is that from 1992 until 1996, Al Kawthar operated as a weaponization laboratory without Vienna's knowledge. As to exactly what was happening there, nobody knows for sure.'

He makes an interesting observation about Iraq's chemical warfare program: '...the method used by Iraq to manufacture stabilized VX (as found in missile fragments) can be done in stainless steel reactor vessels. But UNSCOM monitored only glass-lined reactor vessels largely because nobody thought stainless steel vessels were useful and because monitoring stainless steel vessels was too difficult.

'Given what we now know of Iraq's VX program, how can we safely say that the Iraqi government did not produce VX between 1991 and 1998?' For instance, he said, information suggested that the Baiji fertilizer complex could, during the period under review, have been used for such an effort, which would, of necessity be covert.

On missile development, Ritter believed that Al Karama and Ibn Al Haytham were two sites where 'permitted activity' was being employed as cover for long-range missile development. 'The Rashid factory, we know, illegally imported CNC machine tools for use in its missile programs.'

Asked why it was that Iraq claimed that UNSCOM had found almost no Iraqi biological warfare assets in almost sixty months of searching, his view was that Saddam had taken the initiative to keep this WMD firmly under wraps.

'Likewise, you must not think that we did not do anything. We did... the UN body continued to hold some of its information close to its chest and it's not my place to reveal it.' He added that Iraqis generally were not only very clever in the way that they went about this business, 'they are (also) sharp and could be extremely devious'.

Ritter was asked to clarify an earlier *Ha'aretz* report[6] that UNSCOM had eventually 'broken the Iraqi code that Saddam was using to issue instructions involving the movement of hidden WMD'.

'Nothing that I said about this matter should in any way infer such a capability. I was simply referring to a figurative code that we had solved the problem, broken the code, untied the Gordian knot, as it were.

'What had taken place, was that Iraq had indeed developed a concealment mechanism to hide its prohibited weapons. Through analytical techniques of examining available information, we "solved" that puzzle. It was a slang usage of the word "code" and that's all it really was.' He believed strongly that the *Ha'aretz* correspondent should have known better, but accepted that there might have been something of a nuance problem in its explication.

Answering questions about reports that the FBI was looking into the possibility of making a case against him because he had spoken out on sensitive issues and, possibly, worked in association with a foreign power (Israel), he declared: 'I cannot comment other than to say that everything - *everything* - that I did was known and approved by the executive chairman (Richard Butler). It was also reported in full to the US government. And Washington, while probably not pleased with everything that I did, never said "Stop!" I presume that this is because my work was "driving the madman into a corner".'

Earlier, he accepted that it was possibly 'a huge mistake on the part of the US government (and for me) to discuss all this in detail and that it would only embarrass persons and agencies who do not want to be embarrassed.' By same token, he insisted, the FBI was 'chasing a shadow...there was no wrongdoing on my part because everything was approved and in keeping with my instructions. The facts and the truth are on my side'.

Scott Ritter commented on reports that he had handed over aerial surveillance films taken by U2 aircraft seconded for UNSCOM surveillance purposes and that he had 'received help' from Israeli intelligence agents (a charge made in a letter to UN secretary general Kofi Annan by Tariq Aziz, the Iraqi deputy prime minister).

About this, the former UN arms inspector was forthright: 'That's all wrong! I never "handed over" anything. I took such reconnaissance imagery to Israel where it remained under my control while it was *jointly* exploited. It was strictly a working relationship of benefit to UNSCOM.

'If they want to drag this thing out in a manner in which I have to defend myself, then I will. But that will bring down the whole shop and that is not my purpose here.'

1   William Rivers Pitt, with Scott Ritter: *War on Iraq: What Team Bush Doesn't Want You to Know*. Context Books, 2002

2   Robert Baer, *See No Evil*, Crown Books, New York, 2002

3   The majority of the Iraqi dictator's bodyguards were also of Tikriti extraction and were thus regarded as part of an extended tribal 'family'

4   Scott Ritter: *Endgame: Solving the Iraqi Problem Once and For All*: Simon & Schuster, New York, 1999

5   Indeed, none were ever surrendered by the Iraqis, even though UN arms inspectors repeatedly asked for them

6   *Ha'aretz : Ibid*

17

THE IRAQI SAGA: WAGING THE PEACE

'Mass graves are weapons of mass destruction. End of argument.'

John E. Ayto's Letter to *The Times*, London, May 16, 2003

The sudden, but not altogether unexpected change in attitude in many Western countries formerly opposed to 'Operation Iraqi Freedom' has been cathartic. Opposition to the campaign became much less pronounced once reports started to filter through about the mindless excesses of Saddam. Images of row upon row of cadavers, together with untidy bags of bones lined up in their hundreds, infused horror into the minds of thinking persons.

Overnight, the international community was bludgeoned with headlines like 'Huge Mass Grave Found in Iraq' (BBC May 13, 2003). Another, on the front page of *The New York Times* on May 17 reported 'Mass Grave In Iraq May Hold Kuwaitis Missing since 1991'. Earlier, Britain's BBC News heralded an article by Stephen Sackur titled 'In Saddam's Killing Fields'. It was a savage indictment of a system that had escalated to a level of barbarity that most people found incomprehensible.

Clearly, as the scale of brutalities began to emerge, even the most vocal opponents of the Iraqi invasion were stunned. Almost by the day more mass graves were being found and more and more bodies disinterred. It seemed that many women and children had been targeted by Saddam's *mukhabarat*. As one British newspaper commented, it was murder on an unintelligible scale[1].

In one burial ground at Al Mahawil not far from Baghdad, relatives trying to identify the dead claimed that eighteen thousand corpses had been buried there. A farmer living nearby told how he'd watched the goings-on at Al Mahawil from a distance as victims were bussed in, executed and bulldozed into oblivion. And that, he said, had been going on for years. Asked why he did nothing, he shrugged, adding after a pause that if he had whispered a word he would have been rewarded with a bullet.

It was not only Baghdad's inhabitants who were at risk of being carted away in batches and liquidated by Saddam's executioners. In the aftermath of 'Operation Iraqi Freedom', reports were coming in of mass burial sites around Basra in the south, Nasiriya, Mosul and elsewhere.

Since then, more mass graves were uncovered including two thousand bodies in the oil city of Kirkuk in the north. There were also many childrens' bones found in another execution site outside Babylon and hundreds more at a military complex at Salman Pak. There, some of the dead had been bound and others blindfolded before they were executed with single shots behind the head. Most of these victims were youthful Shi'ites from Baghdad's Sadr City. There was no part of Iraq that was spared these executions.

Ian Fisher of *The New York Times* wrote from Abu Ghraib late April[2] about one of the biggest and most feared jails in Iraq, about nine miles west of Baghdad. As American armored columns approached the place, he said, prisoners were led out the back and executed.

Quoting Saleh Hassan, a forty seven-year-old merchant who had been arrested a month before, Fisher recounted that 'one night in the first week of April about thirty prisoners were taken away. Then he heard shots outside the cell block's walls...they were a combination of people - Kurds, Arabs, Islamists...all suspected of being spies'. The man explained that anybody caught with a *Thuraya*, small satellite telephones that were banned in Iraq for all but Saddam's elite, was arrested as a spy.

Not long afterwards, stories began to emerge about the six hundred or so Kuwaiti prisoners of war who had disappeared after Gulf War 1. Only in May 2003 did evidence emerge that they had all been shot and their bodies dumped near an Iraqi Army base that faced Lake Habbaniya near the capital.

The last time the civilized world saw anything as macabre as this it had had a Buchenwald or Auschwitz label. In Iraq, these atrocities were Saddam's personal testament to his disregard for life. Meanwhile, observers in Baghdad were talking about another two hundred thousand missing souls. Human Rights Watch upped that by about a third, citing events in 1991, after the Shi'ite uprising in the south had been suppressed.

The Republican Guard trawled through the Shi'a holy city of Najaf with loudspeakers, summoning men aged seventeen to seventy to gather at a crossroads on the outskirts to meet Saddam's son-in-law. When they arrived some were immediately shot. The rest were carted away in forty buses and trucks that had been flagged down for the purpose.

Only one man survived the slaughter that followed. He managed to jump off his truck when it stopped at a traffic light.

In truth, nobody will ever be able to measure the full extent of what is now regarded as the worst abomination of recent times. Through it all, there was a deafening quiet from some Arab capitals. It is interesting too, that the ether surrounding many of Hollywood's usually provocative anti-establishment figures went strangely silent. To some of them, Saddam's grim calculus of violence had become a non-issue.

There had been many early atrocities, some dating back a decade or more when Iraq fought its bitter eight-year war of attrition with Iran. American writer Jeffrey Goldberg gave us a fascinating insight to a notorious chemical warfare attack on the Northern Iraqi town of Halabja that took place while these hostilities were in progress.

Writing in *The New Yorker*, (March 25, 2002) the event that he described displayed a shocking indictment of the use of a deadly nerve gas. Worse, Saddam Hussein killed his own people.

Goldberg recounts: 'In the late morning of March 16, 1988, an Iraqi Air Force helicopter appeared over the city of Halabja, about fifteen miles from the border with Iran. The Iran-Iraq War was then in its eighth year, and Halabja was near the front lines. At the time, the city was home to roughly eighty thousand Kurds, all of them well accustomed to the proximity of violence and the effect it had on the vicissitudes of ordinary life. Like most of Iraqi Kurdistan, Goldberg recalls, Halabja was in a perpetual state of revolt against Baghdad. Its inhabitants were in strong support of the *Peshmerga*, a group of fighters whose name meant "Those Who Faced Death".'

He mentions a young woman named Nasreen Abdel Qadir Muhammad who was preparing food outside her family's house when she first saw the helicopter. The Iranians and *Peshmerga* had just attacked some Iraqi military outposts around Halabja, forcing Saddam's soldiers to retreat. Shortly afterwards, Iranian Revolutionary Guards infiltrated the city. Residents assumed that a counter attack was imminent.

'At about ten o'clock, maybe ten-thirty, I saw this helicopter getting closer,' Nasreen told Goldberg.

'It was not attacking. There were men inside it, taking pictures. One had a regular camera, and the other held what looked like a video camera. They were coming very close and then they went away.' Nasreen thought that the sight was unusual, but she was preoccupied with lunch. The bombardment began shortly before eleven.

As Goldberg explains, the Iraqi Army - positioned on the main road from the nearby town of Sayid Sadiq - fired artillery shells into Halabja. At the same time, the Iraqi Air Force began dropping what was thought to have been napalm on the town, especially the northern area. Nasreen and her sister Rangeen rushed to their cellar, Nasreen praying that her husband Bakhtiar would find shelter. The attack ebbed by about two o'clock and Nasreen made her way carefully upstairs to get the food for the family.

251

'At the end of the bombing, the sound changed,' she said. 'It wasn't so loud, rather like pieces of metal dropping without exploding. We didn't know why it was so quiet.'

A short distance away, in a neighborhood still called the Julakan, or the Jewish quarter (even though Halabja's Jews left for Israel in the nineteen-fifties) a middle-aged man named Muhammad came up from his own cellar and saw an unusual sight.

'A helicopter had come back to the town, and the soldiers were throwing white pieces of paper out the side,' he recalled. In retrospect, he understood that they were measuring wind speed and direction.

'Nearby, a man named Awat Omer - twenty at the time - was overwhelmed by a smell of garlic and apples.'

Nasreen gathered her food quickly, but she too noticed a series of odd smells carried into the house by the wind. 'At first, it smelled bad, like garbage,' she said.

'And then it was a good smell, like sweet apples. Then like eggs.' Before she went downstairs, she happened to check on a caged partridge that her father kept in the house. 'The bird was dying,' she said. 'It was on its side.'

Nasreen looked out the window and recalled that it was very quiet. 'But the animals were dying. The sheep and goats were dying.' She ran to the cellar and told everybody there was something wrong. 'There was something wrong with the air,' she ventured.

'We wanted to stay in hiding, even though we were getting sick,' Nasreen explained afterwards. She felt a sharp pain in her eyes, like stabbing needles. 'My sister came close to my face and said that my eyes were very red. Then the children started throwing up. They kept throwing up. They were in so much pain, and crying so much. They were crying all the time. My mother was crying. Then the old people started throwing up.'

What was clear was that chemical weapons had been dropped on Halabja by the Iraqi Air Force, which, in effect, meant that any underground shelter would become a gas chamber.

In an article[3] in *The New Yorker*, David Remnick reminded us that the Saddam Hussein who came to power in 1979 - declaring his intention to combine the glory of Nebuchadnezzar with the methods of Josef Stalin - no longer rules Iraq. As he says, 'not to feel relief at the prospect of a world without him is to be possessed of a grudging heart'.

Remnick went on: 'In a region well stocked with tyrants and autocrats, Saddam was singular in his ambitions, though not in the way proposed by his cult of personality. His record of murder, torture, aggression, intimidation, and subjugation is inscribed in the documentary reports of

Human Rights Watch and in the souls of the traumatized ex-subjects who have survived to hammer at his fallen monuments...'

The indictments are revolting. They are also contrary to the fundamentals of Saddam's Moslem faith. There wasn't a public or private gathering in Iraq at which he or his sons did not invoke the name of their beloved Allah. It was this hypocrisy, unabashedly histrionic, which caused Paul Wolfowitz - a key architect of President Bush's Iraq policy - to highlight the 'shaming effect' that Saddam's antics had had on Islamic peoples everywhere[4]. A historic precedent is the way that Hitler often called on the Christian God to eliminate Jews.

Looking at the broader picture, it soon becomes clear that Saddam was not, and is not the only political miscreant in the Moslem world. While members of the ruling Saudi oligarchy are hardly burying their opposition in mass graves, many of Riyadh's rulers are corrupted beyond the pale. The majority of the ruling House of Saud and their Wahhabist clerics are about as concerned with human rights abuses in their own country as they are in pork belly price hikes in Chicago. For a start, the brutal Saudi system of condign punishment predates the Middle Ages.

There are others of this dreadful ilk. Qadhaffi, we now know, blew up American and French passenger jets, killing all their occupants. Recent intelligence reports out of Washington maintain that he, too, is now involved in advanced weapons of mass destruction programs.

We also have Lebanon's Party of God, or more colloquially, Hizbollah, an offshoot of Iran's Shi'ite Pasdaran (See Chapter 15). Throughout 'Operation Iraqi Freedom' a lethal media offensive emanated from Hizbollah's Al Manar television, the most outspoken anti-Israel element in the region. Nor has it been lost on Washington that long before Saddam had been ousted, Al Manar followed the same paradigm and began a powerful campaign to incite opposition to the American-led force in Iraq. As the *Middle East Intelligence Bulletin* declared, there was an eerie similarity to its war on the airwaves against Israel[5].

Once war became imminent, records Avi Jorisch, 'Hizbollah began explicitly calling for acts of "resistance" against US forces in Iraq in a series of videos, powerfully produced and geared towards an already agitated audience that have since made up around twenty-five to thirty per cent of Al Manar's programming'. Some programs ended with footage of suicide bombers detonating their explosive belts, he stated. The Iranian connection to Al Manar is implicit.

There was a related development a month after the war ended when the Al Jazeera network, much acclaimed in the Arab world for objective reporting, was forced to parry questions regarding the impartiality of its news reports. That after its general director was sacked following allegations that 'he worked with Saddam Hussein's intelligence services', reported *Arab News*. The gist of it was that 'Mohammed Jassem Al-Ali visited Iraq before the US-led war, meeting Saddam during an hour-long interview. Both Al Jazeera and Ali were afterwards accused by the Western media of collaborating with the former regime in Baghdad'.

Nor should we absolve from responsibility the racist thugs who continue to mastermind an Arab-on-black civil war in The Sudan that has resulted in a million deaths among that country's black people. Slaughter in the sprawling, semi-arid south of Africa's largest state has been on the go for almost a half century, making it the world's longest war. A place in the Valhalla of Tyrants is secure for those responsible for these crimes against humanity, but imagine, if you will, the uproar had it been white people killing blacks.

Then there is Syria, Iraq's neighbor, stuck like pre-war Iraq, with an empty sloganeering shell of a Ba'ath Party that like its Baghdad counterpart brooks no opposition. Its functions over the years have been very much like its namesake prior to Gulf War 2. When the Syrian story eventually gets to be told, probably in a volume very like this one, there will be more examples of man's inhumanity to man.

At the end of the day, the Assad dynasty has a good deal to answer for. And when that happens, a litany of government excesses will be revealed by thousands of people incarcerated in Syrian prisons under conditions not dissimilar to those in Iraq while Saddam strode tall. Like Saddam, Hafez Assad, the current ruler's father, also murdered his enemies by the thousands.

In one insurrection in February 1982 Assad sent his army - backed by armor and the air force - into Hamah, a big city to the north of Damascus to quell an uprising by the opposition backed by the Moslem Brotherhood. The number of dead has never been confirmed, but we do know that huge tracts of the city were destroyed and that a figure in the region of twenty-five thousand killed was quoted afterwards in State Department reports.

It was a dreadful massacre. Underground reports coming out of Syria maintain that some people linked to that event remain in prison to this day. To paraphrase the old saw: uneasy lie the heads of those who cling to power in Damascus.

One of the enduring maxims that emerged centuries ago from somewhere east of Suez is that cities are where civilization ends.

Right now that condition pertains to Baghdad, especially with attempts at reconstruction going on. London's *Economist* called it 'waging the peace'.

It's a mammoth task, fraught with poverty, insecurity, distrust of others and of an uncertain emerging 'system', coupled to the kind of politico-religious factional disputes that can only happen in the Middle East. At its core, nobody can ignore the realities of a rekindled Shi'ite power based on age-old dogma. Like it or not, Tehran is integral to the equation.

What is seminal to understanding this mix, is that the followers of the historical Ali the Younger (the Prophet Mohammed's cousin and son-in-law of fourteen centuries ago) while making up only fifteen per cent of Moslems worldwide, are in the majority in Iraq, as they are in Mullah-led Iran. Consequently, should President Bush stand firm in his intention of instituting democratic rule in Iraq, there is no question that the country must eventually emerge with a Shi'ite head of state. In turn, he will be backed by a Shi'ite majority in parliament and, in all probability, a largely Shi'ite defense force.

Associated Press writer Steven Gutkin expressed it well in a report[6] published nationally in the United States on April 17, 2003. With the collapse of Saddam's Sunni-dominated regime, the Shi'ites of Iraq now aspire to claim dominance for the first time in modern Iraqi history.

True to form, within the first weeks of the invasion, Gutkin reports, the Shi'ite community had effectively taken over almost all functions of government within their own societies. They 'appointed governors, imposed curfews and offered jobs, health care and financial assistance to the poor', he reported, adding that Shi'ite clerics were 'leading self-declared governments in the holy cities of Karbala and Najaf'.

The Sunnis who formerly ruled Iraq - Saddam Hussein was a Sunni and Iraq's Ba'ath Party had a preponderant Sunni base - together with the country's very substantial Kurdish community, would obviously oppose this kind of transition. Indeed, their leaders are alarmed at this sudden Shi'ite resurgence. They point to the threat of an Iranian-style theocracy being installed in Baghdad.

While revolutions tend to take on the complexions of those that went before, one cannot discount the suspicion that here are all the ingredients of another civil war.

But there is hope. Roger Hardy of the BBC[7] declared in his analysis 'Shi'a Role in New Iraq' that while the country's Sunni and Christian minorities were uneasy about what he termed 'the new mood of Shi'ite resurgence' a common bond between the two does exist. Most Iraqis, Hardy suggests, 'are indeed united by allegiance to a common faith - and by a shared suffering under Saddam's rule'. He points out that intermarriage between Sunni and Shi'ite is commonplace and that both communities share an immense sense of national pride. At critical issue is whether the

Shi'ites (or a significant number of them, at any rate) will press for transformation into an Islamic state?

Meanwhile, the situation facing the 'Infidels from the West' who conquered this Arab state as vast as California, but potentially ten times as rich, has to be their 'finding some kind of order in the chaos'.

To some observers, the options being put on the table by some of the participants (there are radical Shi'ite factions that refuse to have anything to do with the Americans) are both intractable and insoluble. The issue is further compounded both by time and whether Washington has the political stamina to see the exercise through to finality. Many people doubt it.

To quote Roger Hardy again: 'If the Americans mishandle the post-war transition, this could radicalize the Shi'ite and foment unrest - with potentially damaging consequences for both Iraq and the entire region.'

Time's Joe Klein made some incisive observations of his own[8] early on in the campaign. The situation on the ground was confusing at best and quite possibly chaotic, he ventured. He then suggested the obvious: Invite the neighbors to help sort out the mess.

'President Bush should invite them all – Saudi Arabia, Jordan, Syria, Kuwait, Turkey and, yes, Iran...' as well as British Prime Minister Tony Blair to a conference on the future of Iraq.

'We did it in Afghanistan. The US, Russia and the five neighboring countries (including Iran) held a series of Five-Plus-Two talks devoted to preventing chaos, tribal warfare and a humanitarian disaster after the Taliban were routed.'

Adding his two bits' worth, James Dobbins, a former National Security Council staff member who was part of the US delegation to the Afghan talks, was of the opinion 'that you can't build a country if the neighbors are trying to pull it apart'.

Klein went on: 'The post-war situation in Iraq is far more volatile than it was in Afghanistan. The neighbors are more contentious, but they do have a common interest - preventing chaos in Iraq...(and) incredibly delicate negotiations lie ahead.' Ultimately, he declared, 'the proud, powerful and well-organized majority Shi'ites will have to cut a deal with the proud, well-organized and not-so-powerful Kurds'.

He added that even if there were to be an accord between the Shi'ites and the Kurds, it was axiomatic that they would then have to find a place in the sun for the Sunnis. Point taken.

Some interesting developments followed the collapse of Saddam's regime. One of these was the remarkable and unrestricted access that the international media gained when it was allowed into some of the inner sanctums of the old regime's power base, including its intelligence apparatus. It was almost like Moscow during *Perestroika's* brief summer of hope. As in the Russian capital, journalists in Baghdad were able to gain access to all manner of Iraqi government offices and some of them (including, no doubt, a fair body of spooks masquerading as scribes) carted away documents by the trailer-load.

Those without the luxury of such facilities could, with translators, comb at their leisure through piles of documents, some stacked in boxes to ceiling height. In the foreign ministry numerous examples of perfidy were uncovered, much of it anti-American.

David Harrison of *The Washington Times* gave us a classic example of German skullduggery when, following a session of digging through documents, he exposed Berlin's intelligence links with Saddam's secret service. He spoke about a file obtained in Baghdad that named Johannes William Hoffner as the 'new German representative in Iraq' attending a meeting with Lt General Taher Jalil Haboosh, the director of Iraq's intelligence service in 2002.

'Under diplomatic cover,' the Iraqis hoped to develop a relationship with the German intelligence agency, Harrison wrote. Haboosh is on record as having offered 'lucrative contracts to German companies if the Berlin government helped prevent an American invasion of the country'. Earlier, Hoffner had suggested that 'my organization wants to develop its relationship with your organization'.

Then it was France's turn. Paris apparently supplied Saddam Hussein's regime with details of its dealings with American officials, reported London's *Sunday Times*. This information, found in files and said to have come partly from 'friends of Iraq' at the French foreign ministry in Paris, no less, 'kept Saddam abreast of every development in American planning and may have helped him to prepare for war'.

One of the documents[9] included 'an account of a meeting between Hubert Vedrine, the former Socialist foreign minister of France, and [Colin Powell]'. Another revealed: 'According to French information, a discussion about Iraq is going on in Washington between Colin Powell and the Zionist Wolfowitz.' Powell, said the document, 'was against a military attack on Iraq whereas Wolfowitz was in favor of a strong military operation'.

Then there was a letter dated September 5, 2002 from Naji Sabri, the Iraqi foreign minister to Saddam's palace. Totally incriminating, it was based on a briefing from the French ambassador in Baghdad and covered talks between Presidents Jacques Chirac and George W. Bush. So much for North Atlantic Treaty allegiance. Well, might one ask, with friends like this, does America really need NATO?

The *Sunday Telegraph*, relying on papers found at the foreign ministry, reported that 'France colluded with the Iraqi secret service to undermine a Paris conference held by the prominent human rights group Indict'.

Another came from the Iraqi intelligence service which stated that 'one of our sources met the "deputy spokesman" of the French foreign ministry, "with whom he has good relations".' It claimed that the spokesman from the justice and interior ministries had sought to find a legal way of preventing the Indict meeting. The paper said it had been agreed that no Iraqi opposition leaders would be granted visas for France to attend the conference, but was not clear whether Iraqis living outside the country had actually been granted visas. Although the conference went ahead, the Iraqis regarded moves to undermine it as a striking success.

The *Telegraph* then found 'a six-page letter dated February 1998, from Saddam Hussein to Jacques Chirac, welcoming the French president's support in the campaign against sanctions and assuring him that Iraq did not have weapons of mass destruction'. In retrospect, this might put to rest the still current accusation in some quarters that the Bush Administration's 'botched diplomacy' was to blame for the UN Security Council's failure to approve an 18th Resolution authorizing the liberation of Iraq.

The British newspaper went on: 'If veto-wielding France was actively colluding with Saddam's regime to oppress the Iraqi people and to prepare for a prospective attack, then winning Paris's approval for a resolution explicitly authorizing regime change was never a possibility.' Looking at this kind of malevolence from a supposedly friendly power, those who urged Washington to subordinate American foreign policy to the French veto have a lot to answer for in the aftermath of the war.

Probably the most devious French action involved a number of reports which said that Paris had supplied fleeing Iraqi leaders with French passports in order to escape, possibly to Europe. The issue remains clouded and there are protestations galore, Syria's included, if only because Damascus Airport would have had to play a role in this mischief, and that certainly could not have been done without government collusion in that police state.

What is clear is that for all the smoke and grime that surrounds this most controversial issue, there must be some fairly substantial embers smoldering somewhere.

The dust had not yet settled when Bill Gertz, an investigative journalist with good links to the US intelligence community, disclosed that a US intelligence team inside Iraq had uncovered a dozen French passports[10]. He added that 'defense officials believe other French passports from the same batch were used by Iraqis to flee the country'.

Careful not to draw conclusions about an issue that by then had become somewhat intemperate (such things tend to seriously affect relations between nations) Gertz made the point that the French immediately denied culpability. But then, as another observer suggested, they would of course.

An immediate result of the passport fracas, perhaps innocuous in any other circumstance, is a European Union that is unable to delineate its long term relations with America. The two powers are supposed to be allies. They have fought together in several wars. Yet, the perception in the United States, right or wrong, is that France betrayed its valued ally who unstintingly gave of its sons during two great wars.

Things were then exacerbated by a group of French vandals who desecrated British and American war graves north of Paris. They painted demeaning slogans on many of them.

One of these read: 'Dig up your dead, the bodies are defiling our soil.' To the horror of the entire French diplomatic community in Washington, there wasn't an American daily that did not carry that story. That such things could have taken place almost within sound of where the buglers of Ypres sound the 'Last Post' each evening in honor of the fallen, makes it that much more banal.

You need to have lived in the United States to understand the depth of American reaction to that kind of insult. Even visitors to the diverse, pluralistic Land of the Free are allowed to say just about what they like, but some things are sacrosanct. They always will be. Visit the Vietnam War Memorial in Washington and you might begin to understand how the average American feels about those who laid down their lives, *and that was an extremely unpopular war that America lost!*

To the majority of these people - there are millions of them - it is not just 'the resting places of our brave boys' that were defiled. In thousands of ex-servicemens' organizations like Veterans of Foreign Wars, the grief and anger expressed afterwards cut deep into the nation's psyche. Most of those involved felt betrayed.

Chirac can apologize till kingdom come - as, indeed, he did afterwards with all the histrionics that he could muster - but the average American will not quickly forget that slight and certainly not this generation of Yanks. My bet is that the French will suffer the aftermath of that affront long after Chirac is gone and it will hit them where it hurts most: in their pockets.

An immediate consequence is that in places like Boise, Idaho or Bald Knob, Arkansas, if it's a car you're after, you simply don't look to be buying a Peugeot or a Renault. And while French claret will always have its aficionados, California's vintners can only score. So, too, with Americans visiting France. The list goes on.

Also jeopardized was an extremely successful Visa Waiver Program between America and many countries in Europe and elsewhere where visitors can travel to America without having first to acquire visas. It is a reciprocal gesture and an important measure of trust. Time will tell how it is affected by these shenanigans

Concerning the passport issue, one report out of Paris claimed that looters had possibly filched the passports. Then somebody at State pointed out that of all the foreign legations in Iraq, the French Embassy was among the best guarded while hostilities raged. Also, it was strange that Saddam's cronies were handing out only French passports: they had to come from somewhere. And what about the requisite stamps and seals for authentication? And why were there were no illegal Polish, Italian, Greek, Danish or other passports from countries whose legations had been looted?

Interestingly, intelligence on the disputed French passports followed reports that a French company had covertly sold military spare parts to Iraq in the weeks before the war, said Gertz. 'Other intelligence reports indicate that a French oil company was working with a Russian oil firm to conclude a deal with Saddam's government in the days before military action began on March 19,' he added.

Gertz also wrote that Paris denied US intelligence reports indicating that a Chinese chemical company used French and Syrian brokers to circumvent UN sanctions in providing Iraq with chemicals used in making solid missile fuel.

It took about a month for the first confirmed reports to surface concerning the roles played by Saddam's two vicious sons, Uday, not yet forty and his somewhat younger but no less wicked sibling, Qusy.

Time magazine devoted a good deal of space to the brothers in its issue of May 25, 2003 and it made for some unsettling reading[11]. By the time Gulf War 2 was launched, the twosome had dictatorial control over the country and its more than twenty-four million people. Kenneth Pollack, an ex-CIA and White House expert on Iraq who works for the Brookings Institution in Washington said that 'having those two boys to do (his dirty work) for him was a critical element in (Saddam's) reign of terror'.

It is well worth reading the article, if only because it underscores the age-old premise that absolute power really does corrupt absolutely.

BBC correspondent Harry Peart[12] also provided a sidelight to these goings on. When Uday became president of Iraq's National Olympic Committee, the International Olympic Committee accused him of torturing and jailing unsuccessful athletes at his headquarters in Baghdad. There were reports of athletes 'having been forced to crawl along roads covered in hot tar, being thrown into raw sewage and being beaten on the soles of their feet'. The national football team was similarly abused when they lost matches.

Uday apparently became unhinged after taking eight bullets in his side in an assassination attempt. His behavior became progressively more reckless, until the day, in a fit of rage, he clubbed his father's favorite food taster to death. For this misdemeanor he was jailed for forty days.

Uday was also a notorious paedophile and though Saddam must have been aware of his son's predilections, there was nobody in Baghdad who dared do anything about it.

At one stage, according to his personal aide Adib Shabaan, he kidnapped the fourteen-year-old daughter of a former provincial governor. The girl was attending a function at Baghdad's posh Jadriyah Equestrian Club with her parents and her younger brother and twelve-year-old sister. Not long afterwards Uday demanded that the ex-governor bring his daughter and her sister to his next party.

'Your daughters will be my girlfriends or I'll wipe you off the face of the earth.' The man complied, surrendering both girls.

In the aftermath of the war, one of the persistent questions being asked by military strategists of all shades is what on earth was it that possessed Saddam Hussein to go to war against such a powerful adversary. The man was not stupid. He must have realized that he could never win any kind of military struggle against the combined might of the Anglo-American Coalition.

The answer is provided, in part, by Ibrahim al-Marashi, a research associate at the Monterey Center for Nonproliferation Studies and a lecturer at the US Naval Postgraduate School. He offers us a penetrating study on the subject.

Published by the *Middle East Review of International Affairs*[13] in June 2003, al-Marashi had deduced that the Iraqi leader was 'highly influenced by his perception that America had been defeated in Vietnam by a lack of courage and willpower, a limit on its patience, and an inability to sustain casualties'. He went on to propose that this view was reinforced by his reading of American behavior after Vietnam, leaving Lebanon in 1983 and Somalia in 1993, among other events.

'Even in Afghanistan in 2001, where the United States had won a quick victory, Saddam noted that America preferred to use local forces rather than risking its own troops. Since US forces would have to do the fighting in Iraq, his best - and perhaps his only hope - was a protracted ground war in which America would tire of losing soldiers, which would occasion domestic demands to end the war.' He also hoped that international public opinion in other countries, as well as Arab protests, would demand that the war be ended.

In this context, using weapons of mass destruction would have been counterproductive since it would have destroyed the pretext that Iraq was a victim that needed to be saved by the world and by the American people.

Al-Marashi reckoned that Saddam knew that this strategy had worked in 1991 to save him. 'He thus, understandably, believed that this defensive strategy was his best bet for the regime's survival and was willing to pay the cost, Iraq's utter destruction, to serve that end.'

Christopher Andrew of Cambridge University pointed out in the same article that analysis of Saddam Hussein tended to vacillate between characterizing him as a rational, logical actor, and a fanatic, isolated from reality.

'The most dangerous fanatics, however, combine elements of both - they are shrewd operators with deranged views. Though Hitler was obsessed by the preposterous theory of a Jewish plot for world mastery, he was also remarkably astute - outwitting Western statesmen before the Second World War and driving his generals to achieve a spectacular sequence of rapid military victories,' said Andrew.

What is also true is that Saddam could be said to have combined serious misconceptions of the world, including a profound belief in conspiracies, with a shrewd sense of the political behavior and strategies required by his position as leader.

The most perspicacious comment made about Saddam Hussein by American journalist Michael Kelly before he was killed while embedded with the Third Infantry Division, was that one of the great constants in his rule, besides excessive cruelty, was excessive misjudgment.

Claims of conspiracies also justified many of the regime's policies and garnered loyalty to them by the security apparatus and sometimes by the population at large. As one example of the regime's use of this method, two statements are offered which justify Iraq's possession and possible use of chemical weapons. They appeared in an official Iraqi Army training manual:

These weapons were needed[14] 'as a result of the American-Zionist union against our country in order to steal the natural resources of the Arab world, under an international umbrella and the decision of the Security Council and the distortion of facts by some of the traitorous Arab leaders like the (King of Saudi Arabia) and (President) Hozni Mubarak (of Egypt). And as a result of the concentration of the hostile forces in preparation for unleashing hostilities on our dear country: (Intelligence) reports have indicated the possession of the American-Zionist union of chemical weapons, and their ill intention to use them against our country to increase our losses in persons, equipments, weapons and preparations'.

It is worth noting that while Gulf War 2 was officially named 'Operation Iraqi Freedom' (most Arab circles called it *al-Harb al-Khalijiyya al-Thalitha* - the Third Gulf War), Baghdad had a different appellation.

The Iran-Iraq War of 1980-1988, for instance, was referred to as *Qadisiyat Saddam,* coupling the leader's name with the first battle ever fought in history between the Persians and Arabs in which Arab Muslims emerged victorious. Similarly, while Gulf War 1 was termed 'Operation Desert Storm' by Coalition Forces, Saddam used *Umm Kul al-Ma'arik* or as it was popularly promulgated by the media, the 'Mother of all Battles'.

Al-Marashi states that the euphemism for the 1991 war revealed Saddam's emphasis on the scope and severity of the impending conflict with Washington. Nevertheless, he declared, the regime believed implicitly that it would emerge victorious. In a military memo circulated among military units it stated that 'we are guaranteed victory because we are standing up to thirty nations, and that is a point of pride for us'.

In the same way Saddam referred to 'Operation Iraqi Freedom' as *Ma'rakat al-Hawasim,* or 'The Defining Battle'. In a sense, it was his bid to mobilize the Iraqi masses against the impending American attack. And as he contemplated, though it might not have been intended, the rhetorical use of this title indicated that this was perhaps the final defining battle of the regime.

1   The international community was spared almost all the carnage that followed Pol Pot's assumption of power in Cambodia where, we now know, a lot more people died than in Iraq and then only because almost all the Western media had fled. If anything, the killings in Cambodia were more widespread and indiscriminate than in Iraq where, almost Nazi-style, it had with time, become a refined and ordered form of political terror

2   'As Hussein Faded, Prisoners were Executed' by Ian Fisher, *The New York Times,* April 28, 2003

3   David Remnick, 'War Without End; *The New Yorker,* issue of April 21/28, 2003

4   'Shaming Effect' on Arab World by Bill Gertz and Rowan Scarborough; *The Washington Times,* April 29, 2003

5   'Al Manar and the War in Iraq' by Avi J. Jorisch: *Middle East Intelligence Bulletin,* April 2003. See their website at <www.meib.org>

6   Steven Gutkin: 'Who are Iraqi Shi'ites and What Do They Want?' Associated Press, April 17, 2003

7   Published by BBC News, 22 April, 2003

8   Joe Klein 'To Remake Iraq, Invite the Neighbors Over', *Time* Magazine, May 5, 2003

9   'France Briefed Iraq on War': *Sunday Times,* London, April 27, 2003

10   'Intelligence Team Finds French Passports in Iraq' by Bill Gertz: *The Washington Times,* May 24, 2003. See also Gertz: 'France Helped Iraqis Escape': *The Washington Times,* May 6, 2003

11   'The Sum of Two Evils – Saddam's Nastiest Biological Weapons may have been His Two Sons...' by Brian Bennett and Michael Weisskopf: *Time,* New York, May 25, 2003

12   'Iraqi Athletes "Tortured and Jailed".' by Harry Peart; BBC News, London, May 18, 2003

13   The Struggle for Iraq: Understanding the Defense Strategy of Saddam Hussein by Ibrahim al-Marashi: MERIA; Volume 7, Number 2; June 2003

14   MERIA *Ibid*

18

AFTER SADDAM HUSSEIN

مَن قَتَلَ نَفْسًا بِغَيْرِ نَفْسٍ أَوْ فَسَادٍ فِي ٱلْأَرْضِ فَكَأَنَّمَا قَتَلَ ٱلنَّاسَ جَمِيعًا

'Whoever killed a human being, except as punishment for murder or other villainy in the land, shall be deemed as though he had killed all mankind.'

The Holy Qur'an V:32

In a remarkable document that appeared shortly after American forces entered Baghdad, Dr George Friedman declared that 'with the end of the Iraq campaign, things have become complicated for the United States'. This is not because (the war) was militarily trying, nor because the occupation is proving an insuperable problem. Rather, the US Administration has built the probability of post-war complexity into its original strategy. The Iraq campaign was designed to redefine the regional psychology and to create new strategic opportunities for the United States'. Dr Friedman's perspicacious analysis goes on to say that while this new psychology is certainly emerging, the redefining of regional sensibilities does not proceed with mathematical precision.

'As in all wars, the conclusion of a major campaign frequently creates a sense that leaders and commanders are not altogether certain about what comes next,' says Friedman. After the North African or Solomons Campaigns in World War 2, the United States had to define the follow-up operations. This required clarity as to the ultimate politico-military goal, an assessment of enemy capabilities and intentions, the generation of plans and the deployment of appropriate forces. It therefor appeared to the untrained eye to be a period of indecision, discord and uncertainty. That view wasn't unreasonable, but it was unjust...'

So too, with Iraq. But for all this, the question continues to beg: was Gulf War 2, the invasion of Iraq by the United States and Britain legal?

More salient, was it necessary? Is the world a better place without the Saddam family? There are a lot of people who, on all three counts, think not. Others ask whether the level of international terrorism has decreased. And, as a consequence of 'Operation Iraqi Freedom', is the world safer?

264

Dealing with the last question, the answer must be a resounding no. What else when groups of fundamentalist Islamics have managed to create a terrorist concept that in some countries has become almost a way of life? In this category is the Yemeni interior, or vast swathes of it, parts of Indonesia (with its Laskar Jihad movement), the southern islands of the Philippine archipelago, Pakistan's North West Frontier Province, some Afghan regions - particularly around the country's frontiers - as well as just about all of Chechnya and Somalia.

Some actually refer to this increased Islamisation as another form of what is called 'Talibanisation', in Pakistan especially.

Moreover, it has been a problem for a long time and there are Western Arabists who regard the ongoing trend as making the most dangerous inroads of all fundamentalist followings. Interesting too, is that many have Wahhabist undertones, complete with the covert backing of some sections of the Saudi establishment and, in places like Chechnya, Saudi war lords.

The same with hundreds of new mosques recently built or in the process of construction in Africa. Take one example: just about every large town in KwaZulu-Natal in South Africa boasts a splendid new mosque and these edifices don't come cheap. Nor is it coincidental that most of the funds for these ventures came from Saudi Arabia. A number of these institutions - as well as their adjacent religious schools, *Madrassahs* - also reflect Wahhabi patronage.

It is only now starting to emerge that these same groups of Islamic militants have achieved marvels of dislocation under the very noses of a score of unsuspecting and remarkably naïve Western nations. For that reason alone, one cannot underestimate Al Qaeda's role in the American and British decision to punish Iraq.

Terrorism, most of the experts agree, has a complex ecology that inhibits generalizations. But the fact is that neither the Afghan nor Iraqi invasions would have happened had it not been for September 11. The developed world can thank bin Laden for heightening its measure of threat perception, though obviously the Al Qaeda leader never intended things to work out the way they did.

As a consequence, what we do know is that radical Islam - bitterly opposed as it is to the Western way of life - has, in a bid to achieve its objectives, embraced those very same values that makes the developed world tick. Al Qaeda would have been stillborn had it not used Western systems of law, transport, communication and trade, as well as the most sophisticated financial and banking institutions that the world has seen.

How else could these people, some of them barely a generation out of their Bedouin tents and espousing Middle Age precepts, have communicated with each other as efficiently as they did. They moved millions of dollars about in a plethora of companies, subsidiaries and banks in a tangle of deals and money transfers that stultified London and New York when the full implications of their activities started to emerge.

Take another example: at his peak, Osama had a fleet of about twenty-five ships. These he used several times to move about people and equipment, including illegal weapons into the Eastern Mediterranean. We know that the Israelis intercepted at least two of these consignments and though both included top-drawer military hardware like SAM ground-to-air missiles, there was no paper trail. Consequently, the origins remain obscure, even though some of it was shipped out of Iranian ports.

With it all, the mindset of these recalcitrants remains focused on a single objective of harming 'the far enemy' as they like to call the US. Clearly, America's allies and perceived friends (Kenya, the Philippines, Bali, Morocco *et al*) are also in the line of fire because the world's biggest single industry, tourism, with its easy going bonhomie and scantily clad beach-goers and attractions are all manifest evils in the eyes of the Islamic devout. Thus, the Imams conclude, these nations must be harmed.

As with everything associated with international terrorism, the moment there is a hit - Khobar Towers, the USS *Cole*, two American embassies in East Africa in which hundreds of innocents were killed - just about everybody that is suspected of having been involved goes into denial mode. In a sense it is a bit like Germany after the Third Reich: you had to work hard to find anybody who admitted to Nazi connections.

With time (and ground roots support from the clerical order in Saudi Arabia, Pakistan and elsewhere) the long-robed, turbaned ones have been able to extend their grip on Moslem groups across the globe. Even 'moderate' South Africa has Moslem fundamentalist groups that almost routinely send 'volunteers' to Palestine. There are even South African Moslems in Chechnya. Before that, they had members 'embedded' with the Taliban. Previously, a hard core of several hundred Moslem enthusiasts from Cape Town and Port Elizabeth fought the Soviets alongside their Afghan *mujahadeen* brothers. By all accounts, they appeared to do pretty well.

The extent of this kind of Islamic proliferation might be gauged from what is going on in this, one of the least committed African countries: there were reliable underground reports in South African Special Forces circles that Islamic hotheads had even established five Al Qaeda training camps in KwaZulu-Natal. Both South African intelligence operatives and the FBI were said to be monitoring them with unmanned aerial vehicles (UAVs). I said as much in a report to Jane's *Islamic Affairs Analyst* and there was never a rebuttal.

More to the point, how would a group of Moslem fanatics have been able to coordinate extremely sophisticated bomb attacks in places as disparate as Casablanca and Bali (as well as Riyadh, Mombassa, Aden, Tunisia and Israel) had they not had powerful backing, often at government level, from those involved? Each time there was anything from eight or more dissidents taking part (a dozen in Morocco, twenty-nine in the Saudi bomb attacks on Western compounds in Riyadh and so on). That, alone, underscores the do-and-more-often-than-not die mentality of these fanatics.

It also points to the remarkable determination of these people to work towards a singular cause, never mind extraordinarily stringent levels of internal security in place. The cell system became pivotal very early with Al Qaeda's operations, which is why the Americans have had such a hard time trying to crack its infrastructure.

One can only speculate what might have been in store for us all had Washington not gone into Afghanistan when it did and eradicated the Taliban's leadership elements. That was only the start. Immediately apparent, is that if the United States had sat on its hands after the events that turned modern history on its head, these religious cadres (with strong Al Qaeda backing) would have subjected us to a more appalling regimen of terror than anything we've experienced since the World Trade Center was destroyed. To be sure, there is hardly a capital in the West - Russia's included - that would not have been targeted by suicide bombers. So too with some big cities out East that maintain ties to the West, among them Manila, Singapore and Tokyo. To this end, you only have to listen to some of the tapes circulated by Osama bin Laden before he was driven underground to make that much clear. Don't take my word for it: transcripts, together with translations are on the web.

In truth, the last battle in this ongoing ideological struggle that now has global proportions has really only started. To compound matters, there are diehards in both camps.

All this will ultimately concentrate the minds of future generations in much the same way that the Iraqi conflict, from its outset, dominated debate in America and Britain. The only difference is that with time, survival of the respective cultures is likely to become paramount in the minds of both sets of belligerents. For that reason alone, terror could become common cause in achieving specific objectives.

Nor is it lost on students of unconventional warfare, that Whitehall already began to point the way in its war against the IRA. Assassinations - on both sides - were commonplace in Northern Ireland throughout the Troubles. And though that war is over, there are still intermittent killings taking place in Northern Ireland.

Even with a succession of setbacks in Afghanistan, the Yemen, Lebanon, Saudi Arabia and elsewhere, these religious zealots have not been fazed. It will stay that way for as long as there are Moslems who believe that the West, and America in particular, is a degenerate entity with a culture that is both evil and has outlived its time.

In June 2003, Washington released a confidential report about new Al Qaeda training camps in the southern Philippines. Run by the organization's stalwart South East Asian affiliate Jemaah Islamiya, it was said to draw recruits from all the neighboring states. As in Indonesia and Afghanistan, their training systems reveal a distinct Chechnyan influence, as do many attacks on Russian and Western targets in recent years. They are similar to what their older colleagues in terrorism were taught in Afghanistan when that country served as Al Qaeda's base.

Another powerfully Moslem area to watch for future Al Qaeda activity is the East African coastline, stretching from Somalia all the way into Northern Mozambique two thousand miles away. Osama's people have already used Kenyan cadres to hit at Israeli-linked targets in their own country as well as in Tanzania. More recently, there have been unusual developments out of the Mozambique port of Pemba, with foreign Moslems buying up stretches of real estate and islands in one of the most remote regions on earth. Almost all of this wild, beautiful country is adjacent to the Tanzanian border.

Then questions need to be asked about Saddam's mysterious missing weapons of mass destruction, an issue inextricably bound to the legality of 'Operation Iraqi Freedom'.

For all that, months after Gulf War 2 was launched, little evidence emerged that there had ever been WMD programs in Iraq though it is worth recalling that on the eve of the invasion, Hans Blix's UNMOVIC reported 'a strong presumption' that more than two thousand gallons of anthrax might still exist.

But that was not unexpected. Following a spate of articles in the British and American media that early CIA and SIS reports about Saddam's illegal weapons' cache were flawed (Britain's *Guardian* even suggested that some UK and American leaders seriously doubted that they ever existed) US Secretary of State Colin Powell defended the intelligence used by both countries in justifying the war against Iraq, and he did so fiercely.

In an unscheduled riposte to a claim that he was against the invasion from the start, he stated that he had spent nights poring over CIA reports 'because I knew that the credibility of the country and the president were at stake'. Apart from what came out of Langley on Iraqi intelligence, he used these assessments 'along with satellite photographs and intercepted conversations between Iraqi military officers' to make the decision that he finally presented to the United Nations Security Council on February 5, 2003.

Asked whether these had been politicized to bolster the Administration's call to arms, Mr Powell proffered a resolute no. Instead, he called it 'solid information based on multiple sources presented to him by unbiased analysts'. It says something that the secretary of state is viewed by just about everybody in Washington as the most cautious member of Mr Bush's national security team on Iraq.

In a later report, quoted by the BBC on June 8, 2003, Mr Powell denied that the White House had exaggerated intelligence reports of Iraqi weapons of mass destruction to justify the war against Saddam Hussein.

'I can show you reports from United Nations inspectors all through the 1990s that demonstrated that the Iraqis had weapons of mass destruction,' he said on Fox News on the previous Sunday.

'I can also show you reports where the Iraqis were caught lying about their weapons of mass destruction.' By then, there had been mounting questions, both in the US and the UK, over the quality of the evidence given by the Coalition to back the case for war in Iraq.

In a damning indictment of the kind of sensationalist journalism penned by people who were barely qualified to assess sensitive and technical issues, Mr Powell declared that it was the media and not the people who were at the vanguard of criticizing pre-war Western intelligence on Iraq.

The bottom line in this issue is that weapons inspectors in Iraq attached to the UN body UNSCOM repeatedly and conclusively proved in the early and mid-Nineties that the Iraqi leadership had some very substantial nuclear, biological and chemical weapons programs, as the previous seventeen chapters show.

Saddam's missile program, for instance, was much in advance of anything that Iran might have had at the time. In fact, he was fiddling with what was referred to as 'Saddam's Super Gun', the brainchild of Canadian maverick arms developer Gerald (Gerry) Bull who was not altogether unexpectedly 'taken out' by the Mossad before the weapon could be used offensively. It was Israel that would have been in the sights of that device had it been completed (See Chapter 12).

But first the United Nations. Both America and Britain unsuccessfully attempted to hammer through several motions in the UN Security Council to bring the invasion to fruition. But having failed at Turtle Bay, they went ahead anyway. As their respective ambassadors made clear early on, these two countries were going to proceed with toppling Saddam whether the UN voted on the matter or not. Their argument was very much along the lines of something that acclaimed author William Shawcross had said earlier: 'I do think that if we in the West are confronted with horrible images...and say that something must be done, *then, indeed, something must be done!*'

Having spent a lot of time exploring the harsh realities of the new world order and presented his findings in a brilliant book titled *Deliver Us From Evil: Peacekeepers, Warlords and a World of Endless Conflict*, Shawcross is not flattering about UN efforts in Cambodia, Rwanda, Sierra Leone, the Balkans and elsewhere. It was then (and still is), as he records former UN secretary general Boutros Boutros-Ghali as saying, 'a world where everywhere we work, we are struggling against the culture of death'. And even that didn't prevent the United Nations from becoming one of the most mendacious, inefficient and bureaucratically hamstrung international organizations of the last century.

In many respects, the UN is far more ineffectual than its predecessor, the long-defunct League of Nations which, in its day, prior to World War 2, was also crippled by spates of hopeless inefficiency, excesses by the bucketful and an almost criminal measure of indecision at crucial moments that dictated whether communities lived or died. Italy's invasion of Abyssnia was a case in point. Like the UN, the League of Nations was long on debate and very short on demonstrable action. History, it seems, does repeat itself.

American commentator David Isenberg said in his review of Shawcross' book for the US Armed Forces' newspaper *Stars and Stripes*, 'after reading this book, nobody will ever again be able to contemplate a call to deploy United Nations Peacekeepers without gagging'. And though both Shawcross and Isenberg deal with ancillary issues involving conflicts in dozens of countries, Iraq included, recent events have demonstrated that as far as the UN is concerned, the rot starts at the top.

What happened recently in Sierra Leone and what is going on right now in the Democratic Republic of the Congo make the point.

In Sierra Leone, the UN had thirteen thousand troops from twenty-one different countries deployed in the year 2000 when eleven British soldiers were kidnapped by a bunch of drunken rebels. One stupid error of judgment set off a chain of events, putting the lives of British servicemen and their Sierra Leone guides seriously at risk. It was the job of Kofi Annan's UN Headquarters in New York to come to their rescue, but it was left to Whitehall to take unilateral action and launch an airborne effort from half a continent away. Part of it involved flying three RAF Chinook helicopters from Europe to West Africa non-stop but for refueling.

When the attack finally came - the entire operation was put together within a few days and is a classic example of a well-planned First World rescue effort - it took the tough, lightly equipped combined Special Forces and Parachute Regiment elements just forty-five minutes to free their countrymen. Though 'mopping up' went on all day and almost the entire rebel squad was either killed or captured, only one British SAS soldier died. He was killed very early on in crossfire.

This was something that could (and should) easily have been handled by the local UN commander. But the Indian general, a prevaricator of note, did nothing.

More recently, in April and May 2003, the moral authority of the United Nations was again questioned by a reporter from the London *Guardian*. Writing from Bunia, a city of almost a hundred thousand people in a far eastern Congolese province, he reported that 'UN peacekeepers aren't doing a very good job keeping the peace: Dead bodies litter Bunia's empty streets...from some the blood still drips from machete slashes, spear thrusts and bullet wounds. Others are two weeks old and stinking, half-eaten by packs of dogs flopping lazily about this once-prosperous north-eastern capital. There were also reports of cannibalism.

'There are women's bodies scattered in Bunia's main market place; a baby's body on its main road; two priests' bodies inside one church. Last week, a burning corpse was tossed on to the lawn of the main UN compound to show seven hundred Uruguayan peacekeepers what they were missing while they cowered under fire behind its razor-wire perimeter, unauthorized to intervene in the latest massacre of Congolese civilians...

Does the world care what happens to the Congo? No, said Lieutenant-Colonel Daniel Vollot, the French commander of UN forces in Ituri. 'We've been sending messages every day to (the UN headquarters in) New York (saying) this was going to happen, that we need more troops. Nothing was done.'

But would such troops have been a match for Saddam's Republican Guard? Or Uday Saddam's impressive Fedayeen Saddam, a tough, ragtag band of militants, mostly ex-felons? Hardly. There would almost certainly have been a repeat of what happened in Sierra Leone when UN forces faced large groups of armed rebels. When they didn't hand over all their weapons and armored personnel carriers on demand, they made a hasty dash for the capital.

On one notable occasion, a group of senior UN officers told the UN commander General Jetley that 'we're not in Sierra Leone to fight'. I detail the saga at length in my forthcoming book[2] *War Dog: Fighting Other Peoples' Wars.*

The United Nations has always had problems with Saddam Hussein's weapons programs. Indeed, almost from the start its efforts, sometimes confused, often indecisive and always ineffectual, were what one observer on the ground in Iraq termed 'an unmitigated disaster'. (UNSCOM's story is spelt out in Chapter 6.)

So what of Saddam's weapons? We do know that he had the ability to produce many different types of chemical, biological weapons and was on the verge of building the first Arab atom bomb by the time Gulf War 1 happened. And when UNSCOM weapons inspectors were kicked out in 1998, his government had four years in which to hide the stuff in a country which, in places, is as wild and remote as parts of Siberia. Personally, I'd reckon that if it were Arizona we were dealing with, I'd find enough spots in the back and arid beyond to hide an entire arsenal of equipment that nobody would ever find, especially if I had the army to help me.

An interesting comment was made in *The Washington Post* where MIT scholar Michael Schrage offered an acute analysis of why the finding of weapons of mass destruction was now not all that important: 'Even if Iraq proves utterly free of WMD - or if it merely possesses a paltry two or three bioweapon vans - the Coalition's military action was the most rational response to Saddam's long-term policy of strategic deception. Saddam Hussein bet that he could get away with playing a "does he or doesn't he?" shell game with a skeptical superpower.

'He bet wrong...Saddam Hussein's Iraq may or may not have had impressive caches of nuclear, biological and chemical weapons. But his regime surely behaved as if it might (have). Iraq's WMD threat remained credible for more than twenty years because that was precisely what Hussein wanted the world to believe. After all, he successfully deployed chemical weapons against both the Kurds and the Iranians. He'd earned his credibility.

'In fact, the UN's resolutions dealing with weapons of mass destruction took account of this. Saddam was obliged not just to destroy such weapons but to provide a full accounting of their destruction - something he unquestionably failed to do,' declared Schrage.

In scouring Baghdad sources, the UN emerges as a player of many shades, some dubious. That secretary general Kofi Annan and the UN Security Council powerfully opposed the Coalition invasion is history. What is not, is the unsavory behind-the-scenes role played by the world body before hostilities started.

An ABC News team out of New York further fueled American resentment towards the world body when the network reported that UN officials constantly looked the other way as Saddam Hussein's regime skimmed $2 billion to $3 billion in bribes and kickbacks from the UN Oil-For-Food program. And this had been going on for years. For their part, UN officials told ABC News that they were 'powerless' to stop this graft. Nor, apparently did they tell anybody about it until the scams were unmasked by an enterprising piece of investigative journalism.

The news agency went on to uncover widespread corruption in the UN 'aid' program, which it explained, had helped Saddam build his fortune in American currency.

'Everybody knew, and those who were in a position to do something about it, weren't doing anything,' said Benon Sevan, executive director of the Office of Iraq Program. When asked if that included him, he told ABC News: 'I have no power.'

So much for the international body that won a Nobel Peace Prize in 2001. But then Annan's people have a history of misadventure in a succession of recent wars that range from Sierra Leone, the Balkans (Bosnia in particular), Rwanda, Timor, the continuing debacle in the Democratic Republic the Congo and dozens of war zones elsewhere.

Since it was a United Nations team of weapons inspectors that originally unmasked Saddam Hussein as a proliferator of illegal arms, it is necessary to examine carefully what the Iraqi leader had been able to achieve before the truth came out and how this entire armory could have been made to disappear. It is no accident that Coalition Forces have not been able to come up with any substantial weapons finds in the aftermath of 'Operation Iraqi Freedom'.

Iraq, in its day, had the biggest WMD program of any country outside the Big Five. That much nobody can dispute. Saddam's prowess in developing nerve agents and a variety of pathogens as well as missiles - that he used destructively not only against his own Kurdish community but also against the Iranian Army (See Chapter 3) is well documented here and elsewhere. It is all on public record, though some opponents of US and British military action in March 2003 dispute even this self-evident fact.

An immediate consequence of Baghdad's illegal arms build-up caused Tehran to go down the same road in the aftermath of the Iran-Iraq War. Subsequently UNSCOM exposed a huge range of weapons that, had Saddam not been stopped, would probably have resulted in Iraq being the pre-eminent Arab power in a region that stretched from Suez to Afghanistan.

Left unchecked, Saddam would probably have used some of it on Israel. Aware of the perpetual threat of annihilation, the Jewish State has been consistent in stating that if such weapons were used against the Jews, it would retaliate with the best means at its disposal. By implication, these would be thermonuclear bombs, with yields a hundred times greater than anything dropped on Japan. Though it is incomprehensible that this could happen, had Saddam not been stopped short, some of the capitals of Israel's neighbors might by now have been vaporized, Egypt's included.

There are also those who argue that such thinking is nonsense and that there could never be another war between Egypt and Israel (there have already been three). They maintain that the Camp David Accords are watertight. So, supposedly, are nuclear as well as chemical and biological nonproliferation treaties signed by Iraq and Iran. Baghdad flouted these agreements in the face of UN inspections in the Nineties. Tehran is doing so by pursuing nuclear parity right now[3].

And what about the animosity between Israel and Egypt that has simmered since the Jewish State was founded more than a half century ago?

Some harsh words are being traded in the Middle East these days. A recent example: Ben Lynfield wrote in *The Jerusalem Post*[4] that 'exactly twenty years after the signing of the peace treaty, Egypt and Israel find themselves not so much in a cold peace, but, according to some, in a cold war...' Of twenty-two fields of cooperation envisaged in the peace treaty that originally brought them together, he declared, only agriculture had grown. Cairo even shunned cooperation on tourism, though it wasn't too long before the place swarmed with Hebrew-speaking visitors, not always on their best behavior. With disruption back home getting worse, Israelis have now become wary of visiting their neighbors.

More recently, another dimension crept into the dichotomy. In Israel it was underscored by Arieh O'Sullivan writing in *The Jerusalem Post* under the headline 'Egypt the New Enemy?' He offered the challenge: 'The army doesn't want to say it out loud, but behind closed doors the IDF (Israeli Defense Force) is changing its attitude about Egypt.'

At the time, O'Sullivan disclosed that the Egyptian armed forces had made a deal to buy more than ten thousand rounds of 120mm smoothbore KEW-A1 ammunition for its (American supplied) M1A1 battle tanks. This is no ordinary purchase, he wrote: 'It is the "silver bullet" of armor-piercing artillery, made of depleted uranium (DU) and is said to be able to defeat any armor system on earth.' Then he added something that chilled hearts in both countries:

'Twenty years of "cold peace" have never eliminated the deep-rooted insecurities and mutual distrust between the IDF and the Egyptian armed forces. While the peace treaty has given Israel's military leaders some breathing space in its planning, the command structure has never taken its eyes off our southern neighbor. War plans call for a hefty reserve force to be set aside for dealing with Egypt, no matter where confrontation breaks out.'

Were these comments the speculative ramblings of another Israeli hack, they might have been ignored. They were not. O'Sullivan networks very competently within his own system. Also - more than two decades of peace and growth aside - Jerusalem really is concerned about its long-term relations with its Arab neighbors, so much so, that several Israeli think-tanks recently offered prognostications about the possibility of a future war in the region. While nobody wants bloodshed, only a fool would ignore the portents, if not from across the border then from an extremely hostile and totally disaffected Palestinian minority in its own back yard.

Asked how he saw future Egyptian-Israeli relations, the noted Arabist Daniel Pipes - he lived in Cairo for three years, speaks Arabic and is Director of the Middle East Forum in the United States as well as an author of three books on Islam - was pessimistic.

'The problem is simple: Arabs in general, Egyptians in particular, have not had the requisite change of heart toward Israel. Yes, their governments sign treaties with Israel but no, the populations still are not reconciled to the permanent existence of a sovereign Jewish State in the Middle East. Until that happens, the Arab-Israeli conflict will go on,' Pipes declared. At the same time, he said, Egypt wasn't (as some observers had suggested) about to succumb to Islamic fundamentalism[5].

So where are Saddam's weapons of mass destruction? For now, the bulk is hidden, but like the three trailers that were deemed by the CIA to have been laboratories intended for the production of biological weapons, Saddam's cohorts had a lot of time to hide the stuff.

On their own, the three mobile labs are interesting, if only because it is clear that a huge amount of effort was made to sanitize them. 'The moving factories would have been capable of producing enough agents to kill thousands of people,' said Rowan Scarborough in a report[6] for *The Washington Times*.

The CIA report disclosed that the three mobile facilities were a production trailer found by Kurdish troops near Mosul in Northern Iraq, a second trailer discovered by American soldiers at Mosul's Kindi Research, Testing and Development and Engineering facility as well as a mobile truck lab found in Baghdad that the experts said was biological weapons-linked.

For once former weapons inspector Hans Blix had something sensible to say about Iraqi duplicity. He told Reuters that the mobile labs in the CIA report 'were not originally disclosed by the Iraqis as required by UN resolutions after Saddam's forces had been evicted from Kuwait in 1991'.

And the rest of it? We were given an inkling in an early report by Judith Miller who spoke to members of an American military team who had interviewed an Iraqi scientist who claimed to have worked on Saddam's chemical weapons program for more than a decade[7]. The unnamed scientist, from whom we are likely to hear more in the future when war crimes against the Iraqi hierarchy are pressed, said that his people 'destroyed chemical weapons and biological warfare equipment only days before the war began'.

More disconcertingly, he told the Americans that 'Iraq had secretly sent unconventional weapons and technology to Syria, starting in the mid-1990s and that more recently, Baghdad was cooperating with Al Qaeda.'

Nico Price, an Associated Press writer[8] reported from Baghdad at the same time that 'six Iraqi scientists working at different Baghdad research institutions were ordered to destroy some bacteria and equipment and hide more in their homes before visits from UN weapons inspectors' in the months leading up to Gulf War 2. Their accounts indicate that Saddam's people 'may have had advance knowledge of at least some of the inspectors' visits, as the United States had suspected, and that the former Iraqi regime was deeply concerned about any material that could raise the suspicion of UN experts', Price wrote. He explained that autoclaves (the use of superheated steam, most often to sterilize equipment) were employed to destroy any bacterium, any fungus and the contents of petri dishes.

A month later, even the US Defense Secretary Donald Rumsfeld admitted to the BBC[9] that while the search for hidden weapons was continuing, 'Iraq may have destroyed its weapons of mass destruction' and that 'it will take time to investigate hundreds of suspect sites'.

One reason for the reluctance of some of the weapons specialists to talk to the Americans is a very real fear that they might be charged with war crimes. This was expressed after Dr Rihab Taha (nicknamed 'Dr Germ' by UN weapons inspectors) had turned herself in after negotiating her surrender for some days. A microbiologist, Dr Taha holds a doctorate from Britain's University of East Anglia and is said to have carried out work on germs that cause botulism poisoning and anthrax on behalf of the Baghdad regime. A week before, Huda Salih Mahdi Ammash (called Mrs Anthrax by some wag in the media) was captured by Coalition Forces. She had played a key role in developing Saddam's anthrax program.

Shortly afterwards the BBC carried an interesting report about how easy it was for the average man-in-the-street to make the deadly nerve gas, sarin. Using a credit card and fake headed note paper for BBC's Radio 4's 'Today Program' a reporter was able to buy a cocktail of ingredients which could be used to make the stuff. This was the same sarin used by the Japanese religious cult Aum Shinrikyo to kill a dozen and injure more than five thousand people in the Tokyo subway in 1995.

The BBC investigation found that buying the chemicals was simple and that while there were stringent and rigorous import and export controls on them, there were no laws restricting their purchase in the United Kingdom. Further, a recipe describing the manufacture of the nerve agent was found on the Internet.

The program reporter, Angus Stickler was able to buy enough of the chemicals to make twice the amount of sarin used in the Tokyo attack. And that is a single individual. Saddam's scientists would have been able to make hundreds of tons of nerve agents[10].

So too with nuclear issues in Iraq which remain clouded in the aftermath of the war. What is known is that there was a lot of radioactive material being held by the Iraqi regime in seven nuclear facilities, some of it, in all probability, undeclared. One consequence is that as the Allies swept towards Baghdad, these facilities were abandoned by their Iraqi guards and looted.

Early reports mentioned bomb damage to the Baghdad Nuclear Research Center and the Tuwaitha Yellowcake Storage Facility. Afterwards it became apparent that the Tahadi Nuclear Establishment, the Baghdad New Nuclear Design Center and the Ash Shaykhili Nuclear Facility were also damaged and subsequently looted and/or destroyed by fire.

These reports also explain why hundreds of Iraqis today suffer from radiation poisoning. Radioactive materials, containers, documents, control systems and so on disappeared from all of them and hospitals in the area have had streams of patients arriving with symptoms which include bleeding, vomiting and rashes, all suggesting radiation sickness.

With the American Army in place, Iraqi officials with Geiger counters arrived and they reported later that in some areas radioactive readings had gone way over the limit. Shortly afterwards instructions were given to encase some of the worst affected areas in concrete.

As for Saddam's three 'almost-complete' atom bombs together with their mock-ups, diagrams, drawings and other paraphernalia that went missing but which were supposed to have been handed over to UN officials, there is not a word. Even Vienna's IAEA has gone unusually silent on the subject.

That much of it did exist is irrefutable and is backed by the testimony of a score of UNSCOM weapons inspectors including Dr David Kay who created an enviable reputation for himself in chasing down Saddam's bomb makers. A fear expressed in several quarters (and borne out to some extent by intelligence intercepts) is that some or all of this sensitive equipment might have been passed on to another country for safekeeping. And since the only 'friends' Saddam had were rogue, like himself, it is not only the British and Americans who are worried.

One source has suggested that Saddam's links with Al Qaeda might provide an answer, though this is unlikely. Following the discovery of a batch of documents in Baghdad, Inigo Gilmore of Britain's *Daily Telegraph* provided an insight to Iraqi ties with Al Qaeda, detailing a series of clandestine meetings having taken place in Baghdad and elsewhere from 1998 onwards[11].

In the game of illegal weapons acquisitions, every possibility is examined. And while Osama bin Laden's ragged bunch of Tora Bora cave dwellers were hardly likely to harbor such ambitions, there is evidence that this Saudi national himself would have liked to develop something more lethal. Like the rest, time will eventually reveal all.

At the end of the day, it is oil - the second largest deposits in the world after Saudi Arabia - that will grease the cogs of Iraq's recovery.

Following Gulf War 2, the industry is in disarray. In its heyday, Iraq produced more than three million barrels (bbl) a day, but this dropped to about five per cent of that figure after 'Operation Desert Storm'. Issues are further complicated by reports of Seventies-style equipment, old and broken pumps, fractured pipe-lines, rusting equipment and numerous instances of looters taking whatever hadn't been bolted down when the region was not under anybody's control. That didn't last long, but by the time Coalition Forces did arrive, immense damage had been done.

Nobody can deny that the Iraqi issue has a lot to do with oil. That much was underscored when US forces seized two offshore terminals capable of handling two million bbl a day to tankers. Also, whereas a fleeing Iraqi Army torched six-hundred-and-fifty Kuwaiti oil wells in 1991, they were able to set only nine of their own alight before they were driven off.

As *Time* points out in a well considered assessment[12] of the Iraqi oil industry by Donald Barlett and James B Steele published early May, Iraqi oil is a most valuable prize: 'Not only does (Iraq) have the potential to become the world's largest producer, but no other country can do it so cheaply. That's because, for geological reasons, Iraq boasts the world's most prolific wells,' write Barlett and Steele.

The figures are in the public domain. They record that in 1979, the year before Iraq's oil fields were devastated by the first of Saddam's three wars, its wells produced an average of 13,700 bbl a day. This compared favorably to the Saudi average of 10,200 bbl/day and a miserable 17 bbl in the United States where many of its wells have gone dry.

The equation extends to production costs. The average cost of bringing a barrel of oil out of the ground in America is about $10, says *Time*. In Saudi Arabia it is about $2.50. And according to Fadhil Chalabi, executive director of the Center for Global Energy Studies in London and former Under Secretary of Oil in Iraq, it is less than $1 there. What's more, reckon Barlett and Steele, 'most of Iraq's known oil deposits are waiting to be developed'.

The writers give good reasons why some countries have their own reasons for not wanting to open Iraq's oil spigots. They fear that unrestricted Iraqi oil flows could result in prices falling to the kind of lows last seen more than a quarter century ago. Russia, Saudi Arabia, Venezuela and Iran would be the hardest hit by declining prices.

Russia could never produce oil as cheaply as Iraq. Nor could Saudi Arabia's wells, which in 2000 pumped 8.1m bbls of crude oil a day. And even that, at a time when high quality Arabian light sold for an average of $26.81 per bbl, was not enough to balance Riyadh's budget. Push that figure below $10 per bbl and the Saudi government would be bankrupt. It is in the interests of both countries to keep oil prices as high as the market will allow.

France, like Germany, was strident in its rejection of the war and stands to lose massive post-war reconstruction contracts if America remains a player in Iraq. What has become clear since Gulf War 2 is that Paris was made promises by Saddam to allow French companies almost unrestricted access to Iraqi oil fields once sanctions had been lifted. That has since happened and France (as well as its confrontational allies) have been sidelined.

In China's case, feelings are mixed. For historical reasons Beijing does not need a US presence to the east of 'the ditch' as mariners like to call Suez. But it needs cheap oil and would probably welcome a lowering of prices because it will soon be importing about 2m bbls a day.

What is important about Iraqi oil is that both Washington and London have emphasized on numerous occasions that all Iraqi oil resources belong to the Iraqi people. Much has been made of the charge that America went to war to gain access to some of the world's richest oil fields. Had that been the case, the US would not have withdrawn its forces and gone home in 1991. It would have stayed put and exploited a situation that was temptingly exploitable.

In a bid to parry these accusations, both the British and the Americans quickly appointed an Iraqi to head the nation's oil industry and there is absolutely no chance that he will be supplanted by a foreigner. What that means is that Baghdad's oil resources and its exports will be closely monitored. Further, such controls will be efficient. They will also be free of the kinds of actions for which the Saddam family were notorious. Simply put, it is just not possible to sneak a two-hundred-thousand-ton super tanker into one of the southern ports and siphon off what some are now referring to as devil's excrement. Some system of accountability with regard to Iraq's oil industry will have to be installed. One solution might be to hive off the country's oil income into a stabilization fund controlled jointly by Baghdad and the major powers, Russia and China included. The 'dividends', for all to see, would then be used as and how it is needed so that the economy does not overheat. It will also prevent the newly elected from creating personal slush funds. Chile, one of the world's more successful developing nations has a similar fund for its copper revenues. So, in variations of their own, have Norway and Alaska.

The joker in the Iraqi pack for the foreseeable future has to be Iran. A quarter century of antipathy and suspicion characterizes relations between Washington and Tehran. While the two countries do talk, the Iranians regard an American presence within two or three days' tank drive from their capital as unacceptable. Also, they are prepared to do something about it, which is one reason why so many Iranian secret agents have infiltrated Iraqi cities. Robert Fisk went on record late May stating that Iraq was likely to become Washington's 'Second Beirut'.

Iran's mullahs regard an American military presence on their western frontier as a threat to Iran's regional hegemony and they are not afraid to say so. What is clear to all of us Middle East watchers, is that Iran will do its level best to undermine American influence in post-Saddam Iraq.

This leads to several imponderables. One Washington intelligence source with whom I have had much truck in recent years referred to Tehran's meddling as 'exposing the region to a potential for more religious-based conflict'. As with many Third World conflicts, he suggested that Qur'an or not, emotions among that country's mullahs tended to dictate their actions, many of them irrational.

'They simply didn't see beyond tomorrow and that can be dangerous. It could set the region alight,' he stated.

One consequence of such a confrontation, he declared, was that Washington, having taken the giant step with regard to Iraq, would fight to maintain its position if need be. Right or wrong, Iraq, together with Iran and North Korea were identified in turn by President Bush as nations that threatened the stability of their respective regions. Among others that have had fingers pointed at them for human rights or other transgressions are Syria and Libya: nobody will forget American lives taken when a Pan American Boeing 747 was brought down by a Libyan explosive over Lockerbie.

Sensing that a scrap might be in the offing, the Iranians have already warned the Americans several times that they won't find Iran the pushover it encountered in toppling Saddam. And they are right. But most strategists also agree that the United States would be crazy to get itself involved in a ground war in Iran.

However, ABC News in a report headed 'The Iran Debate: Pentagon Eyes Massive Covert Attack on Iran' declared that US military planners have already advocated a huge covert action to enforce a regime change in the neighboring state[13].

This could include surgical air strikes to destroy all known Iranian nuclear and other WMD sites, as well as backing armed Iranian dissidents inside the maverick state.

The danger is that having tasted blood, the Bush Administration will not easily be deterred from consolidating its position at the head of the Gulf. We could be a step away from another war.

Dr Friedman has the final word. In his piece in *The Stratfor Weekly* quoted at the head of this chapter, he goes on to say that the Iraqi campaign did two things. First, it reinforced the perception of the extraordinary political power of the United States, and it drove home the fact that (America) could not be restrained by diplomatic means. Second, the US military occupation of Iraq wasn't an abstract; it could be seen with binoculars from Syrian or Iranian border posts.

'In a region where the United States was known for its indecisive or inconclusive use of military power, (the Iraqi war was) a period in which the countries bordering on Iraq – and outside the region – including allies and enemies of the United States, have had to re-evaluate their understandings of how the world works.'

What the good doctor does not talk about is the long-term effect that the invasion is likely to have on such institutions as NATO and America.

As mentioned earlier, France's obstructionist role in the lead-up to and conclusion of the war in Iraq led many members of NATO to re-evaluate their links with the North Atlantic Treaty Organization. With the end of the Cold War, there were voices within some of the larger powers that echoed the refrain that NATO had outlived its usefulness. After all, it had originally been established to counter Moscow's military aspirations in the Northern Hemisphere and that epoch is behind us.

Arguably, France did more to bring the affairs of NATO to an almost permanent impasse than any of the other member nations. Writing in *The Calgary Sun*, Ezra Levant was spot on when he declared that all that was left for France after the Iraqi fracas, were dashed dreams of presiding over a European Union counterweight to the United States. Clearly Chirac views himself as following the Gaullist credo, which is absurd. Instead, most of his opponents view the man as an impostor, claiming that Chirac has neither the acuity nor the stature of De Gaulle. More significant, he is not blessed with the old man's guile.

'By fomenting a parliamentary rebellion against Britain's Tony Blair and publicly belittling Eastern European countries that backed (Coalition Forces), Jacques Chirac fractured the united Europe that he hoped to lead.'

Germany fared no better, Levant commented. 'Berlin suffered economic loss and strategic marginalization, since United States military bases there are gradually (to be) relocated to friendlier countries like Poland, Bulgaria or Romania.' Once again, it is a question of hitting those who oppose you in their wallets.

Brussels, too, according to *The Wall Street Journal* played a despicable role. As capital of the pint-size Western European nation of Belgium, this city is best known as the headquarters of the North Atlantic Treaty Organization.

Following 'Operation Iraqi Freedom' Brussels followed the French lead and also began to display unhealthy symptoms of an arrogant, unilateralist foreign policy that threatened to tear the half-century-old alliance asunder.

First Belgium (along with one or two other European countries) defied seventeen UN resolutions by taking the position that Saddam Hussein should remain in power. It followed that by seeking to try American General Tommy Franks who led the liberation of Iraq, for 'war crimes', all this under a bizarre law by which the Belgians claim jurisdiction over the entire world. Earlier they had threatened to throw Israeli Premier Ariel Sharon in jail if he attended an international conference. The charge: crimes against humanity.

It is worth noting that no such moral stand was ever taken on people like Yasser Arafat or members of Saddam Hussein's entourage attending meetings in this European capital.

With powerful opposition from Paris and a bunch of Islamic hotheads in a supposedly secular Turkey playing a spoiling game in the deployment of US forces into Northern Iraq (and putting American lives at risk), you won't find many people in authority in London or Washington who would advocate an enhancement of any of NATO's roles. In fact, it would be surprising if the body still exists in its present form five years from today. As for Turkey's hopes of joining the EU, that too is fatuous.

For all the bluster that came afterwards, Iraq proved convincingly that Ankara is no friend of Washington. The same with an ineffectual and intellectually atrophied United Nations. The consensus among people who count is that there is no need to prolong the agony as the organization heads for oblivion.

Obviously, there are some United Nations bodies such as the UN High Commission for Refugees, Vienna's IAEA, the World Health Organization and possibly UNESCO that still have a valuable role to play in their respective spheres. But certainly not the General Assembly or the Security Council. In the end, the UN suffered an extraordinary credibility gap, very much on par with the League of Nations, and, as Levant succinctly phrases it, 'for the same reason - caviling in the face of evil'.

As he says, 'this affects more than just the talk-shop called the Security Council. It also de-legitimizes the UN's pet projects, from the anti-industrial Kyoto Protocol, to the star chambers of the International Criminal Court, or the eugenics programs of the UN Population Fund. In short, the UN's reputation of high-minded morality has been shattered'.

Kofi Annan, he suggests, is no longer a politically correct symbol of a futuristic, international harmony. 'He is now seen for what he is: an unelected, unaccountable diplomat from Ghana who is paid a huge sum to act as a lawyer for the world's dictators and America-haters.' Coming from a Canadian, that's a hellova statement!

It will take a while for rigor mortis to set in, but the world body is finally being killed by a passivity that engendered indecision in times of crisis and a total lack of direction from the top. Saddam Hussein quickly learnt what he manipulatively needed to do to avoid concerted action from the big boys. And let's face it, he played his role like a master. So, too, in his day, did Yugoslavia's Slobodan Milosovic.

Consequently, when Washington needed muscle to back intent with force (as was essential with Iraq, a nation that, *avec un large sourire* mocked everything that Turtle Bay was supposed to stand for) the Security Council waffled at first, then played for more time and finally said no.

So Britain and the US went ahead anyway. They did their thing. And what monstrous human suffering was exposed once the tyrant had been toppled. If nothing more emerged as a dividend from the invasion of Iraq but the prevention of Saddam being able to take more lives innocent or otherwise, it will have been worth it. Next stop Syria or Iran.

Of the future, the portents are already there for all to see. The United Nations - or rather, some of its ancillary functions - are likely to be active into the foreseeable future. Ultimately, though, the UN will transmogrify into a world body that is both a lot more lean and mean than it is today. For two generations billions of dollars were thrown away on countless international projects, programs and 'peace missions' - many of which achieved nothing and served no real purpose. They were voted on by schools of bureaucrats with no experience of issues about which they were debating and who certainly had more regard for the good life in plush New York residences than the embattled millions they were supposed to be helping.

The United Nations lost its way in a labyrinth of hidden interests and obscure national agendas. France and Russia's concern for Iraq had absolutely nothing to do either with Saddam Hussein or with weapons of mass destruction. The interest of both nations in Iraq centered on putative contracts that were in the offing.

At the end of the day, this was avarice on an unimaginable scale for us mere mortals. Very few of those involved in these multifarious activities did more than line their pockets and the United Nations spawned some of the most avaricious of world citizenry: a fitting epitaph. It's always been a private joke within UN circles that a job at Turtle Bay always ensured comfortable retirement. More importantly, it involved little effort beyond trying to stay awake during endless speeches, a difficult task since so much of it was rubbish.

These would be unkind words if they were aimed at stalwarts like Ewen Buchanan and his colleagues, good people and enthusiasts for what was right that sparked the first Iraqi weapons inspection body, UNSCOM. These teams spent long, thankless hours trying to make sense of some of the most complex misinformation programs to emerge anywhere in the past half century. And at the end of it, the people in the offices above were simply not prepared to act on their findings. It is these iniquities that made another Gulf War necessary.

Will Iraq have the wherewithal to survive the next decade? All things being equal - and if the Shi'ites don't plunge the country into another round of hostilities and make the country unmanageable (which, with Tehran's help would not be impossible) Baghdad has the kind of resources that most nations only dream about.

At the end of Gulf War 2, London's *Economist*[14] told us, the tyrant left his nation in hock to the tune of about $350 billion. It acknowledged that this was a crippling burden given that a 'normal' country with the sort of GDP that seemed plausible for Iraq in the medium term, could probably service debts of only around $80 billion, this according to Edwin Truman of the Institute for International Economics.

'Of these potential obligations, over $200 billion is war reparations, mostly arising from the invasion of Kuwait in 1990,' says the paper.

But a draft resolution tabled by America and Britain early 2003 makes one intriguing comment. All revenues from sales of Iraqi oil, according to the proposal, 'shall be immune from judicial, administrative, arbitration or any other proceedings' relating to claims 'of whatever kind and whenever accrued' against Iraq or its agents.

According to Patrick Bolton, an economist at Princeton, 'laying legal claim to Iraqi oil revenues had seemed the likeliest way for creditors to get some money back'. At very least, he said, this wording would give Iraq a strong hand in any formal Paris and London Club debt renegotiations. It might even allow it to repudiate its old debt and still raise fresh capital, Mr Bolton suggested, adding that some American officials had made no secret of their preference for Iraq's debts to be written off and to let the new regime start with 'a clean slate'.

These sentiments are backed by Michael Kremer of Harvard University, who argued that after a change of regime, the country's new government should have no obligation to service the 'odious debt' of an illegitimate predecessor, an idea that dates back to the Spanish-American War of 1898.

Trouble is, he points out, Beijing might use the same polemic to try to shed an external debt of $170 billion 'of the odious, undemocratic regime' its present rulers replaced. For all the tales of woe that the international media has been pumping out of Baghdad, there is money in abundance Iraq. But most of it is in the wrong hands. No doubt as much attention will be given to finding it as uncovering weapons of mass destruction.

That became evident when American troops scouring one of Saddam's palaces found almost $1 billion in crisp new bank notes neatly packed in steel trunks. Though some of the cash temporarily disappeared into soldiers' pockets (it was quickly recovered), much of it went as security towards paying some, but not all, Iraqi civil servants later in the month. With Washington dipping into Iraq's seized assets abroad, there is no shortage of capital to keep the country's administrative machine ticking over, at least until an interim Iraqi government moves in.

Word has it that there are quite a few more such resources secreted by Saddam and his sons. The incredible pace of the Coalition *blitzkrieg* stopped the tyrants from doing what they intended, including hauling as much of the country's national assets across the border as they could.

Then there was a truck stopped at a US Army checkpoint near the Syrian border late May with about $500 million in gold bars onboard. Soldiers discovered two thousand, forty-pound ingots which, the drivers claimed, that they had been paid $350 to deliver to somebody in Al Qaim. They had been told that the bars were bronze.

In truth there is not a lot happening in the world right now that is not related to September 11. As Penny Noonan said in one of her columns for *The Wall Street Journal,* President Bush's meetings with the new head of the Palestinian Authority and Prime Minister Ariel Sharon of Israel, in Aqaba, Jordan in June was about 9/11.

'Mr Bush had no intention of going into the long chain yank that is the Mideast…until 9/11, which forced the toppling of the Afghan regime, the US counterassault on the Taliban and terrorism, the invasion of Iraq and the toppling of Saddam.' All of that came out of 9/11, she declared.

Ms Noonan went on: 'Mr Bush pushed a Mideast road map because he knew what all but children knew: 9/11 grew from (and) was gestated in the intense hatred of the Arab-Israeli conflict.'

Strong words, but indisputable.

The final word comes from Jim Morris, iconoclast, thinking man's soldier, very much wounded Vietnam vet and a respected author in his own right. Always skeptical of those who display undue sentiment, he had a few words of his own in a column that he wrote for the duration of the war and its immediate aftermath. I quote:

'A couple of weeks ago Jay Leno did a gag about how the Japanese had offered to send troops to help out in Iraq. "Great timing," he said, the message being that the Japanese had come on board when the war was over. Chris Matthews, on MSNBC's "Hardball" expressed great surprise that people are still killing each other in Iraq. One got the impression he thought that the administration had misled him, that once Saddam's statue was down, it should be clear sailing from then on.

'What universe do these people live in?

'To me the surprise is that we've faced so little opposition, not so much. In the world in which I live, when you put in an invasion you get a resistance movement. WW II saw them arise in France, Russia, Yugoslavia, China, the Philippines, everywhere the Axis Powers invaded. Ho Chi Minh began as an anti-Japanese guerrilla, and switched to being an anti-French guerrilla as soon as Paris sent its forces back, then an anti-American guerrilla when we replaced the French.

'I shouldn't be dismayed that reasonably intelligent people expected the war in Iraq would be over when the invasion was over. We were surprised when Ho took on the French, too. Remember when the Clinton administration announced that we would bring the troops home from Bosnia after one year? I laughed out loud. It was like telling a group of high school graduates they would start college in September and pick up their degrees just before Christmas break.

'Some things take time. Re-creating a society takes at least a generation, usually closer to two. In 1963 I was getting ready to go to Vietnam for the first time. I met a Special Forces sergeant who said flatly that it would take thirty-five years to accomplish what we had set out to do in Vietnam. He didn't say why, and I didn't learn why until I went there.

'I saw, we all saw, and nobody in Washington saw, that it takes at least a generation to re-create a society. Nobody ever really changes their

mind about anything. Once their basic attitudes about life, and how it is lived are formed, they are pretty much set. To make competent generals you have to train them as lieutenants, and keep at it through all their promotions until you have good senior leaders.

'We did exactly half of that job in Vietnam, threw up our hands, and sold out the competent lieutenant colonels we had made. Iraq has been under a fascist dictatorship for three decades. Self-reliance, initiative, personal responsibility; these things have all been beaten out of them. They won't come back by issuing a proclamation, or waving a magic wand. They will come back through patience, kindness, and setting a decent example.

'Americans tend to think in the near term. Government doesn't think past next year's budget. Big Business is even worse. It doesn't think past the next quarterly profit and loss statement.

'We insist on the quick fix, instant gratification, shake'n bake. We don't want to build it to last; we just don't want it to fall apart on our watch. We get played for suckers by cultures that plan a couple of centuries down the road.

'If we're out of Iraq in two years, it will be either another fascist dictatorship or an Islamic "Republic" in ten. Hell, Saddam Hussein could still come back. How humiliating would that be? We would be the world's sole remaining superdickhead. One of the greatest mistakes we could make would be to blow into Iraq and think we, the great Americans, are going to show the simple natives how it's really done.

'The resolution of every war is a process of cross-culturization. We're going to learn at least as much from the Iraqis as we teach them, like it or not. We didn't drive Toyotas, eat pizza, learn karate, or have army uniforms that resemble those of Nazi postal clerks before WWII. We didn't practice Tai Kwon Do before Korea. We didn't have a burgeoning culture of Asian scholars and entrepreneurs before Vietnam.

'There will be Iraqi war brides. Much that is worthwhile about Iraqi culture and Arab culture will become part of American culture. I don't pretend to be an expert on that culture, but my favorite poet is Jalaluddin Rumi, a 12th Century Sufi poet, born in Afghanistan, raised in Persia.

'I'm writing this from my sister's farm in Cabool MO, so I don't have the poems here to quote from directly, but I remember some of those great lines:

'I am the sweet water, and the jar that pours.
Come to the garden in spring.

287

There will be light and lovers, grapes and pomegranates.
If you come, these do not matter.
If you do not come, these do not matter.

'*Probably doesn't sound much like what you expect from Iran. Sufism predated Islam. When Islam came to conquer, the Sufis simply absorbed it, and went on. The fundamentalists hate them for their mysticism and their sensuality, and more than anything for their tolerance. But it was not the fundamentalists who kicked British ass at Omdurman, it was the whirling dervishes, the Sufis.*

'*There is a great clash of cultures happening here, and if Islam survives, and it will, it will be because it absorbs what we have to teach and goes on.*

'*And if Western Civilization survives, and we will, it will be because we have absorbed what the Near East has to teach us. We have invaded the cradle of civilization, and one of the main things it has to teach, it seems to me, is that before human civilization, it wasn't a desert.*

'*Remember when Carl Reiner used to interview Mel Brooks as the Two-thousand-year-old Man. One of their gags was, "that happened in the Sahara Forest."*

"*You mean the Sahara Desert?*"

"*Sure, now*".'

1   'A Time of Testing' by Dr George Friedman: *The Stratfor Weekly*, April 30, 2003
2   To be published early 2004
3   'Group Says Iran Has Two Undisclosed Nuclear Laboratories' by Sheryl Gay Stolberg, *New York Times*, May 27, 2003
4   Ben Lynfield, *The Jerusalem Post*, March 31, 1999
5   Interview with author
6   'Two Trailers Deemed Biological Labs' by Rowan Scarborough; *The Washington Times*, May 29, 2003
7   'Illicit Arms Kept Till Eve of War, an Iraqi Scientist is Said to Assert' by Judith Miller; *The New York Times*, April 21, 2003
8   'Iraqis: We Were Told to Destroy Bacteria' by Niko Price, The Associated Press: *Seattle Post-Intelligencer*, Seattle, April 23, 2003
9   'Saddam "May Have Destroyed Weapons"': BBC News by Justin Webb, BBC's Washington Correspondent, May 28, 2003
10 'Sarin Ingredients Easy to Buy': BBC News, May 30, 2003
11 'The Proof That Saddam Worked with Bin Laden' by Inigo Gilmore; *The Daily Telegraph*, London, filed April 27, 2003
12 'Iraq's Crude Awakening: It's only a trickle now, but it could become a gusher that rocks the world': by Donald L Barlett and James B Steele: *Time*, May 10, 2003. See also by the same authors, 'The Oily Americans: Why the world does not trust the US about Petroleum: a History of meddling': *Time*, May 12, 2003
13 The Iran Debate: Pentagon Eyes Massive Covert Attack on Iran: ABC News Investigative Legal Unit: May 29, 2003
14 'Paying for Saddam's Sins': *The Economist*, London, May 17, 2003, p 76

EPILOGUE

'When evil men combine, good men must unite, or else they will fall one by one, an unpitied sacrifice in a contemptible struggle.'

Winston S Churchill

In recording contemporary history, time becomes an enemy because of the constant change in world affairs. Each new day brings with it another set of imponderables. In the Arab world, alliances sometimes alter with the weather and today's friends become tomorrow's enemies. Solemn promises are forgotten or cynically subverted.

The only certainty is that the list of casualties – both the innocent and the not-so-innocent - grows longer. It goes without saying that the immediate future would radically alter course if Saddam were killed, or if America suddenly decided to pull out and send its people home. Ultimately, of course, they will all have to go: the US Forces, the British, the Poles, the Italians and the whole slew of other nationalities who have tried to bring stability to a land that has suffered exceedingly.

In a certain sense, the same equation holds for Afghanistan, though there one has a much better idea of who the enemy is. In that benighted land, the Taliban and its cohorts are on the back foot thanks to the policy of vigorous US counter-insurgency. However, were Washington to call it a day, that scenario could also be turned on its head. The bottom line is that taking on what Frederick Forsyth calls 'the world's most blood encrusted dictator' on his home turf was a monumental risk for both the Bush and Blair administrations. Indeed, Operation Iraqi Freedom was arguably one of the biggest military and political gambles since Korea.

Throughout, the media has been vehemently and often vituperatively opposed to any sort of action against an Arab state, Iraq in particular. But then there were those who were powerfully opposed to tackling Hitler when he was doing his worse.

A few random examples: About the time that Dr David Kay returned home from his post-campaign inspection tour of Iraq, London's Guardian published a piece by Tariq Ali, a prominent, sometimes radical Islamic commentator. The thrust of his reasoning can be summed up in this one amazing sentence: 'Few can deny that Iraq under US occupation is in a much worse state than it was under Saddam Hussein.' Really?

A totally contrary view came from Arab News columnist Fawaz Turki who admitted that he had been wrong to initially oppose the liberation of Iraq.

Turki wrote: 'One need offer no apology for saying that the supreme virtue of this war is that Saddam Hussein was gotten rid of. Period. The very man who had established arguably the closest approximation of a genuine fascist state in the Arab world, that sustained itself on fear, repression, genocide, cult of personality and wanton murder - a state whose law was that those who rule are the law.'

Brave man, he went on: 'Washington may not succeed in turning Iraq into a beacon of democracy'. But, he added, 'it will succeed, after all is said and done, in turning it into a society of laws and institutions where citizens, along with high-school kids, are protected against arbitrary arrest, incarceration, torture and execution.'

Just as pertinent were the utterances of Bassem Mroue, an Associated Press writer who reported that the top human rights official in the US-led civilian administration told him that as many as three hundred thousand Iraqis had been killed during Saddam Hussein's twenty-three-year dictatorship. All were believed to have been buried in more than two hundred and fifty mass graves scattered around the country. He disclosed, too, that near the southern town of Mahaweel one of the biggest mass graves had been uncovered the previous May. These contained the remains of more than three thousand bodies, most of them shot in the head.

Shortly afterwards, columnist Barbara Amiel observed in London's Daily Telegraph: 'I've heard Americans gloat over their own casualties in Iraq, as if every death were a stab in Bush's heart alone rather than in American soldiers, so profound is their hatred.' Harsh words, but unfortunately true. There are many Americans who would happily see all the Americans deployed east of Suez go up in a puff of smoke, if only to make the point that Bush was an idiot for getting the country into that mess in the first place. That their incantations sting the ears of their fellow countrymen and women matters not a damn.

Another barb came from a bunch of Democratic Party supporters. Posted late 2003 on <www.democrats.org> the Democratic National Committee's official web site, commented on the deaths of fifteen American servicemen in a Chinook helicopter shot down by a hand-held missile near Baghdad. Gloatingly it declared: 'Morning all. It occurred to me that all the bump that Bush got late last week from the economic figures went up in flames yesterday with that helicopter.'

For the Angry Left, it seems, every dark cloud in this ongoing struggle has a silver lining.

Yet according to The Weekly Standard's Stephen Hayes, the Pentagon had already provided the Senate Intelligence Committee a detailed sixteen-page memorandum that provided solid evidence that Saddam and bin Laden 'had an operational relationship from the early 1990s to 2003'.

According to this document, it was a relationship that involved training in explosives and weapons of mass destruction, logistical support for terrorist attacks, al Qaeda training camps as well as safe haven in Iraq together with Iraqi financial support for al Qaeda, 'perhaps even for Mohamed Atta'. Dated October 27, 2003, the report was sent from Undersecretary of Defense for Policy Douglas J. Feith to Senators Pat Roberts and Jay Rockefeller, chairman and vice chairman of the Senate Intelligence Committee. It was written in response to a request from the committee as part of its investigation into prewar intelligence claims made by the administration and intelligence came from a variety of domestic and foreign agencies, including the FBI, the Defense Intelligence Agency, the Central Intelligence Agency, and the National Security Agency. Much of it was detailed, conclusive, and corroborated by multiple sources. Some was new, obtained in custodial interviews with high-level al Qaeda terrorists and Iraqi officials.

The picture that it presented was one of a history of collaboration between two of America's most determined and dangerous enemies. Iraq and al Qaeda initiated contact in 1990 and the relationship continued through mid-March 2003, only days before Operation Iraqi Freedom was launched. Significantly, most of the contents contained straight, fact-based intelligence reporting which, in some cases, included an evaluation of the credibility of the source.

Hayes quoted at length from the memo, and his article closed with the observation that 'it covers only a fraction of the evidence that will eventually be available to document the relationship between Iraq and al Qaeda'.

As Hayes tells it, CIA and FBI officials methodically reviewed Iraqi intelligence files that survived the initial three-week blitzkrieg of early 2003. He added that the documents involved were in Arabic and would probably cover several miles if laid end-to-end. They revealed not only connections between bin Laden and Saddam, but also revolting details of the regime's long history of brutality. The notion that Saddam was entitled to a presumption of innocence was itself an error, he suggested.

Much more profound were the essentials of the report issued by Dr Kay, former UNSCOM Chief Inspector (Nuclear) when he returned from Baghdad after Operation Iraqi Freedom.

His mandate, late 2003, was to search for Iraq's putatively hidden weapons of mass destruction. It mattered little that the tyrant and his supporters had four long years in which to destroy, secrete or export the huge armory which is detailed in these pages, or that Baghdad claimed that everything that had gone before was a bundle of lies.

Kay quickly went to work and published his findings after reporting to Congress. But according to the majority of newspaper reports in the US, Britain, most European countries - and the Middle East especially - the trip was a waste of time.

For the sake of accuracy, look at the facts. Courtesy of Andrew Sullivan, as well as The Wall Street Journal's 'Best of the Web Today', here are some of the highlights:

Kay said that he and his team had discovered dozens of WMD-related program activities together with significant amounts of equipment that Iraq concealed from the United Nations during the inspections that began in late 2002. He went on to state that the discovery of 'these deliberate concealment efforts had come about both through admissions of Iraqi scientists and officials concerning information they deliberately withheld and through physical evidence of equipment and activities that the ISG (Iraq Survey Group) discovered and that should have been declared to the UN'.

Dr Kay offered examples of these concealment efforts:

- A clandestine network of laboratories and safe houses within the Iraqi Intelligence Service that contained equipment subject to UN monitoring and suitable for continuing chemical and biological weapons research.
- A prison laboratory complex, possibly used in human testing of BW agents, that Iraqi officials preparing to meet United Nations inspections were explicitly ordered not to declare to the UN.
- Reference strains of biological organisms concealed in a scientist's home, one of which could be used to produce biological weapons.
- New research on biowarfare-applicable agents, Brucella and Congo Crimean Hemorrhagic Fever (CCHF), and continuing work on ricin and aflatoxin, all of which were not declared to the UN.
- Documents and equipment, hidden in scientists' homes, that would have been useful in resuming uranium enrichment by centrifuge and electromagnetic isotope separation (EMIS).
- A line of UAVs (unmanned aerial vehicles) not fully declared at an undeclared production facility and an admission that they had tested one of their declared UAVs out to a range of three hundred miles, or roughly two hundred miles beyond the permissible limit.
- Continuing covert capability to manufacture fuel propellant useful only for prohibited SCUD variant missiles, a capability that was maintained at least until the end of 2001 and that cooperating Iraqi scientists have said they were told to conceal from the UN.

- Plans and advanced design work for new long-range missiles with ranges up to at least six hundred miles, well beyond the hundred-mile range limit imposed by the UN.
- Missiles of a six-hundred-mile range would have allowed Iraq to threaten targets throughout the Middle East, including Ankara, Cairo and Abu Dhabi.
- Clandestine attempts between late 1999 and 2002 to obtain from North Korea technology related to eight-hundred-mile-range ballistic missiles - probably the No Dong - together with anti-ship cruise missiles and other prohibited military equipment.

'In addition to the discovery of extensive concealment efforts,' Kay reported, 'we were faced with a systematic sanitization of documentary and computer evidence in a wide range of offices, laboratories, and companies suspected of WMD work. The pattern of these efforts was to erase evidence - hard drives destroyed, specific files burned, equipment cleaned of all traces of use.' These were deliberate rather than random, acts, Dr Kay records.

What is curious is that as a consequence of his revelations, The New York Times ran the headline: 'No Illicit Arms Found in Iraq, U.S. Inspector Tells Congress'. Many other American - as well as British and European - newspapers, including London's Guardian and Independent reached similar conclusions.

President Bush commented after details of the investigation were promulgated that that 'Kay's findings make clear that Saddam Hussein actively deceived the international community, that Saddam Hussein was in clear violation of United Nations Security Council Resolution 1441, and that Saddam Hussein was a danger to the world.'

As the Wall Street Journal subsequently noted, 'no one can argue with that.'

About the time that Kay was giving Congress the facts, the CIA stepped up to the podium with an assessment of its own.

James Clapper Jr., a retired air force lieutenant general who heads the CIA's National Imagery and Mapping Agency, said he believed that material from Iraq's illicit weapons program was transported into Syria and perhaps other countries. 'It was all part of an effort by Iraqis to disperse and destroy evidence immediately before the recent war.' He said. Satellite images showing a heavy flow of traffic from Iraq into Syria just before the American invasion in March had led him to believe unquestionably that illicit weapons material was moved outside Iraq, Clapper declared. He added a personal assessment: 'I think people below the level of Saddam Hussein and his sons saw what was coming and decided the best thing to do was to destroy and disperse.'

He believed that at the level 'below the senior leadership of Iraq' there were officials who 'saw what was coming and went to extraordinary lengths to dispose of the evidence.'

Clapper's agency was responsible in particular for interpreting satellite intelligence. He said the heavy volume of traffic leading from Iraq to Syria before and during the American-led invasion had convinced him 'inferentially' that illicit weapons material had been smuggled outside the country. Countries mentioned in this context included Syria, Iran and Libya.

Gary Samore, director of studies at London's International Institute for Strategic Studies suggested another theory. A former nonproliferation expert on the National Security Council under President Bill Clinton, he suggested that Saddam Hussein ordered the destruction of his weapon stocks well before the war. This was done 'to deprive the United States of a rationale to attack his regime and to hasten the eventual lifting of the United Nations sanctions,' declared Samore. At the same time, he warned, the Iraqi dictator retained the scientists and the technical capacity to resume the production of chemical and biological weapons and, eventually, to develop nuclear arms.

'Mr. Hussein's calculation was that he could restart his weapons programs once the international community lost interest in Iraq and became absorbed with other crises. That would enable him to pursue his dream of making Iraq the dominant power in the Persian Gulf region and make it easier for him to deter enemies at home and abroad.'

With the level of hostilities in Iraq escalating, the specter of al Qaeda involvement has again surfaced. And not for the first time.

Late 2003, the Middle East Media Research Institute translated a report from Al-Yawm Al-Aakher, an independent weekly newspaper in Iraq on Saddam Hussein's ties to al Qaeda. The paper reported that two months before the September 11 attacks (according to an Iraqi officer identified only as "L") about a hundred trainees arrived at the Iraqi military's special forces school. 'They were a mixture of Arabs, Arabs from the Peninsula [Saudi Arabia], Muslim Afghans, and other Muslims from various parts of the world.'

It went on: 'Divided into two groups, the first went to Al-Nahrawan and the second to Salman Pak, and it was this group that was trained to hijack airplanes. The training was under the direct supervision of an Iraqi major general (M. DH. L) [identified only by initials] who, Al Yawm reported, had since achieved the position of a police commander in one of the provinces in post-Saddam Iraq. Upon the completion of the training most of them left Iraq, while the others stayed in the country through the last battle in Baghdad against coalition forces. "L" told the paper that during Iraq's liberation, al Qaeda members 'participated immediately in extremely fierce battles that astonished the Iraqis and the Americans: on April 5, 2003 orders were issued to send these individuals to the battle front immediately. About a hundred of them were sent to the 11th company division in Nasiriya.

'And for the sake of history I will say that this division's endurance was due to some formidable fighters, the commanding officer and members of al Qaeda who fought with intensity and brutality that are seldom matched, while they were praising Allah.'

Steven Stalinsky, a prescient observer of goings-on in Arab lands provides another insight to a problem that persists: that of foreign Islamic radicals who enter Iraq to oppose the Allies. Titled Arab and Muslim Jihan Fighters in Iraq, it was published 'Special Report 19' in 2003 by The Middle East Media Research Institute.

Some of Stalinsky's conclusions are disturbing. He observes for instance, that beginning in March, 2003 the Arab media published a variety of stories of young Arabs traveling to Iraq to carry out an Islamic 'holy war' against the U.S. 'They came from various Arab countries, including Saudi Arabia, Syria, Yemen, Egypt, Lebanon, the Palestinian territories, Algeria, the United Arab Emirates, Libya, as well as from Afghanistan.'

He recalls a report in the Lebanese daily Al-Nahar which told of thirty six Islamists (Lebanese, Palestinians, Egyptians, and Syrians) receiving visas from the Iraqi Embassy in Beirut to volunteer as martyrs.

Syria's Foreign Minister, Farouq Al-Shar, stated that his country would not stop volunteers going to Iraq via Syria, while the Saudi Minister of Interior Prince Nayef bin Abd Al-Aziz claimed that there was no evidence of Saudis volunteering in droves for Jihad in Iraq. Since then, there have been a number of al Qaeda attacks in the Saudi capital, and overnight, that conciliatory approach changed.

'Religious personalities in the Arab world have given a mixed blessing on allowing Arab youth to travel to fight the U.S. In a recent Fatwa (Islamic religious ruling), the Shariah Court in Qatar banned such travel unless it was with the parents' permission: It is considered against Islam to travel to another country for Jihad without permission from one's parents.' The Court also stated that the permission of 'those charged with authority among Muslims' is necessary to initiate Jihad.

'On the other hand, one of the Spiritual leaders of the Muslim Brotherhood movement, Sheikh Yousef Al-Qaradhawi, called for Jihad "to expel foreign troops from Iraq." However, he too qualified his statement, saying that "only governments have the right to organize volunteers for Jihad."

'In Baghdad, Sheik Ahmad al-Kubaysi praised these Arab volunteers: "These young men who came here from other Muslim countries to defend Iraq are very brave. They left their homes and comfortable lives to protect fellow Muslims. That is the most important form of Jihad. These Mujahideen are guaranteed paradise."'

For all the hype and obfuscation that has emerged in this embattled land, there is a fundamental truth that needs to be recognized:

Saddam Hussein was not the first mogul to rule along the great waterways of the Tigris and the Euphrates and who, after terrorizing the nation, was ousted by force. Go back in time and you will find more tyrants who established virtually unassailable seats of power in Baghdad. Yet more came from ancient capitals like Babylon, Sumer and Assyria. History has only repeated itself. The question that now begs is whether this modern-day, convoluted political entity with a penchant for violence can ever be fairly and effectively governed? That issue remains moot.

Part of the answer could come from looking back at a spot of 20th Century history. Here I am indebted once more to The Wall Street Journal when its 'Best of the Web Today' quoted George W. Bush's speech marking the 20th anniversary of the National Endowment for Democracy. The President, said the report, affirmed America's commitment to democracy in the Muslim world. I quote:

'Some skeptics of democracy assert that the traditions of Islam are inhospitable to the representative government. This "cultural condescension," as Ronald Reagan termed it, has a long history.

'After the Japanese surrender in 1945, a so-called Japan expert asserted that democracy in that former empire would "never work". Another observer declared the prospects for democracy in post-Hitler Germany were 'most uncertain at best'. He made that claim in 1957.

'Seventy-four years ago, The London Sunday Times declared nine-tenths of the population of India to be "illiterates not caring a fig for politics." Yet when Indian democracy was imperiled in the 1970s, the Indian people showed their commitment to liberty in a national referendum that saved their form of government.

'Time after time, observers have questioned whether this country, or that people, or this group, [is] "ready" for democracy - as if freedom were a prize you win for meeting our own Western standards of progress. In fact, the daily work of democracy itself is the path of progress. It teaches cooperation, the free exchange of ideas, and the peaceful resolution of differences.

'As men and women are showing, from Bangladesh to Botswana, to Mongolia, it is the practice of democracy that makes a nation ready for democracy, and every nation can start on this path. It should be clear to all that Islam - the faith of one-fifth of humanity - is consistent with democratic rule.

'Democratic progress is found in many predominantly Muslim countries - in Turkey and Indonesia, and Senegal and Albania, Niger and Sierra Leone. Muslim men and women are good citizens of India and South Africa, of the nations of Western Europe, and of the USA.'

'Bush cited a two-decade-old speech by a previous great progressive internationalist: In June 1982, President Ronald Reagan spoke at Westminster Palace and declared that the turning point had arrived in history. He argued that Soviet communism had failed, precisely because it did not respect its own people - their creativity, their genius and their rights. ...A number of critics were dismissive of that speech by the president.

'According to one editorial of the time, "It seems hard to be a sophisticated European and also an admirer of Ronald Reagan." Some observers on both sides of the Atlantic pronounced the speech simplistic and naive, and even dangerous. In fact, Ronald Reagan's words were courageous, optimistic and entirely correct.'

Writing in Britain's Spectator, Max Hastings, an illustrious former editor and war correspondent had his own take on these issues late in 2003. Critical of many aspects of what is going on in Iraq, he wrote:

'A distinguished American writer reported after visiting Iraq: "The troops returning home are worried. "We've lost the peace," men tell you. "We can't make it stick." Friend and foe alike look you accusingly in the face and tell you how bitterly disappointed they are in you as an American.... Instead of coming in with a bold plan of relief and reconstruction, we came in full of evasions and apologies. A great many Iraqis feel that the cure has been worse than the disease.'

Hastings admitted that he had cheated by substituting the word Iraq for Europe in the passage above. John Dos Passos wrote the original for Life magazine in January 1946. An American newspaper, he recalls, resurrected the piece in November, 2003, largely to reassure the modern fainthearted in Iraq. Here was evidence, said the hawks. Even after the United States triumphed in the most honorable war in history, the difficulties of reconstruction proved awesome.

'Yet in Iraq today the pessimists are in the ascendant. Newsweek's front cover that week was headed: "Bush's $87 billion mess. Waste, Chaos and

Cronyism". The great Arthur Schlesinger, at the age of 86, produced a coruscating critique of Bush's foreign policy for the New York Review of Books. "Like Milton's Samson in Gaza", he wrote, "we are eyeless in Iraq.'"

According to Hastings, Iraq today 'is simply a country in which large quantities of munitions are readily available. There are many people, both local and foreign fedayeen, who hate the West for the same reasons as al-Qaeda, or because the fall of the Ba'ath party has stripped them of power and livelihood. The opposition has huge quantities of cash with which to bribe anyone capable of using a shoulder-fired missile to do so. Dissidents can argue that recent history is on their side. Again and again, American patience in difficult situations has proved less durable than the will of local societies who want Americans out.'

Iraq, he points out, is not Vietnam and the scale of guerrilla attacks on the allies is still relatively tiny.

'Yet the British consider that the security situation on the ground is worse than the media convey because many local attacks go unreported, unless the allies suffer casualties. There is already a tension between the US administration, which is leaking hints of early troop withdrawals to meet Bush's electoral requirements, and the urgent military need for more soldiers on the ground.'

Special Report: Jane's *Islamic Affairs Analyst; February, 2003*

ARAB PROGRESS
IN REVERSE GEAR

By Stephen Ulph, Founding Editor, Jane's *Islamic Affairs Analyst*

In a world region that is described as 'richer than it is developed',
the Arab states are alone in demonstrating not only relative
weakness ...
...but concrete signs of economic, intellectual and cultural
regression. If the trend continues unchallenged, the future of the
Arabs will be permanently on hold.

Behind the accusations and counter-accusations, away from the spotlight of the 'war on terrorism' and the campaign against Iraq, the time that has passed since 11 September has been a time of self-examination for Arab societies. For parallel to the chase for Al Qaeda, there is a chase for the answer to the question: "what went wrong?"

Looking broadly, economists mark some positive notes: the standard of living across Arab countries as a whole has advanced; life expectancy is longer than the world average of sixty-seven years; the level of abject poverty is the world's lowest; and money spent on education is higher than anywhere else in the developing world.

Yet despite this, on further examination the Arab countries are alone in bucking the global trend. For all the promise of oil wealth, per capita income growth has shrunk in the last twenty years to a level just above that of sub-Saharan Africa; the maternal mortality rate is double that of Latin America and four times that of East Asia; productivity is declining; science research and development are dormant; Arab intellectual life takes place almost entirely outside the homeland; and whatever the education spending, still half of Arab women cannot read or write.

Since last summer such observations can neither be written off as anecdote nor ill will. For they are the conclusions of a joint United Nations and Arab League sponsored study, *The Arab Human Development Report 2002*, researched and written by Arabs under the direction of Rima Khalaf Hunaidi, director of the United Nations Development Program's Arab Regional Bureau and a former deputy prime minister of Jordan, who is concerned at "some very scary signals that were specific to Arab countries and not other regions".

This genuine introspection is a rare approach for the Arab world, long used to the language of plots and machinations of 'the enemy' – whether that be Zionism, NATO, Islamophobia, neo-Crusadism, atheism or economic globalisation. It left many in the Arab press reeling. Up to then, it was long axiomatic that the woes of the nation were the product of foreign sabotage and the hypocrisy of Western democratic support of anti-democratic forces at home. However, the report pointedly addresses those "who do not fault others for what they see as the deficits in contemporary Arab culture".

The Arab deficit

The authors of the report describe a "severe shortage" of new writing and a dearth of translations of works from outside. The report talks of the Arab world's annual tally of translations from foreign works as about one-fifth the number that Greece translates. "In the 1,000 years since the reign of the Caliph Al-Ma'mun, the Arabs have translated as many books as Spain translates in just one year," the report states.

A lack of intellectual curiosity and a sense of being watched by both the state and religious authorities can be seen at its most glaring in Egypt, the intellectual capital of the Arab world. Artistic experimentation is out; from TV soap operas to the wide screen, the quality of films is in decline, away from the social realism of Yusuf Shahine's *Cairo Station* that challenged society's attitudes at home, to deliberately 'other'-focused films such as *Horseman without a Horse* which is safely controversial only to those outside the country. It is as if there is a desperate effort made to keep Arabs looking outside and away from themselves.

Shattered self-confidence

The above statistics highlight a deep-rooted crisis of confidence and self-esteem. The Arab world's experience of contact with an aggressively accelerating Europe has not been pleasant. The humiliation began with the conquest of Egypt by Napoleon and ended with the colonisation of most Arab lands; the first Arab revolt against the collapsing Ottoman Empire brought about the conditions which eventually lead to the creation of the State of Israel; and the first flexing of the muscles of independence ended with the defeat in the Six-Day War.

A once triumphant and world-dominating culture - the echoes of this persist in the absolutisms of the militant Islamists - has yet to recover from the shock of these defeats, in the way that, for example, the Hindu population of the subcontinent enthusiastically embraced Western learning and still today outstrips their Muslim compatriots.

Japan's experience, in particular, is a major complicating factor for Arab thinkers. "Muhammad Ali began the modernisation project," writes Muhammad Jabir al-Ansari in *al-Majalla*, referring to Egypt's 19th Century dictator. "At that time, he was ahead of the Japanese. The gap between the Egypt of his day was, relatively speaking, not so great. But now the gap has grown huge."

Intolerance

Yet any intellectual investigations into the reasons for this failure - if they touch on first causes - is a more dangerous road to follow today than it was a century ago. In 1992, Egyptian author Farag Foda was gunned down by a fanatical Islamist after an open debate at a Cairo book fair, and authors who are rash enough to include dialogues touching on Arab and Islamic sanctities find themselves as ever so many Salman Rushdies. Even retrospectively: popular novels or academic anthropological studies that have remained for decades on library shelves disappear as soon as there is a whiff of unorthodoxy detected in their pages.

"The 'Inquisition Courts' of the days of Nasser and Sadat have become popular again in Egypt," wrote Hazem Saghiyeh in the pan-Arab *al-Hayat*, "they break into universities, knock on the doors of houses, and interrogate the body and soul.

"Egypt is no longer what it used to be in the first half of the 20th Century. Then, an Arab who was looking for stars in the press, literature, cinema, dance, or poetry, went to Cairo. A visit by Mohammed Abduh or Taha Hussein in any Arab country was an event by itself. Today, the number one export product is Shaykh Yusuf al-Qaradawi [a prominent spiritual leader of the Muslim Brotherhood movement]." Also, the best seller list in present-day Egypt is dominated by inward-looking religious literature. Saghiyeh adds: "Today we look like the Weimar Republic, only without the joy, the freedom, and the creativity."

For Fouad Ajami, director of Middle East Studies at Johns Hopkins University in the US, the decrease in intellectual freedom is due to the growing power of a lower middle class whose members are literate but not broadly educated. They show, he states, "its lack of hospitality to anyone of free spirit, anyone who is a dissident, anyone who is different". Which means that for many Arab intellectuals the only option has been exile. "There is a deep, deep nostalgia today in the Arab world," Ajami says. "Societies looking ahead and feeling a positive movement never succumb to nostalgia."

An appreciating religious currency

The weak self-confidence is compounded by the collapse of the old, rural world as the migration to the cities gains pace. For these dislocated populations, assaulted on all sides by an unfamiliar urban, 'modern' culture, the breadth of the confident, locally nuanced Islam of the village yields to a more abstracted search for fundamental, unchanging, roots. Suffering the contradictory effects of modernisation without benefiting from its positive aspects, and in the absence of political freedoms, it is natural that they clutch at the nearest ideological tool - traditional culture allied to religion. Consequently, the currency of the religious apparatus has increased sharply. However, these too are having to face the challenges of modernism, and for these it is but a small step to drawing up battle lines which confuse modernisation with abandonment of Islamic culture. While the UN report itself steers clear of pointing the finger at Islamic militancy and its effects on intellectual and economic growth, this conclusion is implicit in passages that refer to a less tolerant environment.

It does, of course, have one direct impact on development. The opposition of Islam to the mixing of sexes (seen as a Western phenomenon) provides the Islamists with a readily understandable symbol, and bequeaths the region its most important obstacle to adapting to modern life and maximising productivity.

Confusion of terms

The opposition is acrimonious. "Since the middle of the 20th Century an increasing number of people in Islamic countries have concluded that the only way to escape the domination of the West is to adopt Western culture," writes Mohammad Reza Shalguni.

"For the defenders of Islamic culture who carry the glories of the thousand years and the humiliation of the last three hundred, the distinction between modern Western and Christian culture is blurred. They focus less on the reasons for Western advance as on the reasons for the backwardness of the Islamic people," he adds. This confusion between Westernism and modernism, and the distaste for what the Iranians call *gharbzâdegî*, 'Westoxication', is lent all the more permanent a footing through its reflection in the rift of the 'two-speed' culture of the Islamic societies. "The magnitude of this rift," according to Shalguni, "is such that dialogue on cultural and value systems have become all but impossible. Furthermore, this social schism is vertical: that is the traditional layers of both the classes above and the classes below confront their modern counterparts."

Limping modernisation

However, the problem of the Arab world is not so much a too rapid modernisation, as an unequal modernisation, one conducted at a rate below the region's current needs. While the process of integration into the global market has been faster in the Arab world than anywhere else, the level of economic and cultural modernisation has been the most uneven. The effect of this is that the traditional economic, social, political, and cultural structures are being torn down without any modern institutions taking their place. Developments are being made to live side by side, which belong to historically different eras and which repel each other's reason for existence. The 'battles' with the West are reflections of internal conflicts.

The state of political activity is symptomatic of this lack of institutions. Egypt is again a good example. Here political life, according to Saghiyeh, simply has no meaning. He states: "Elections? Yes, but the results are known in advance. Political parties? Yes, but let us examine the age of their leaders: Nu'man Gum'a, leader of the Al-Wafd party, is the youngest. He was born in 1934. Mustafa Mashhur, of the Muslim Brotherhood, was born in 1921. Ibrahim Shukri of the Labour party, in 1916. Khalid Muhyi al-Din of the Tagammu' party, in 1922, Diya' al-Din Da'ud of the Nasserist party, in 1926. And President Mubarak, head of the ruling national party, was born in 1928. The dead are sitting on the chests of the living."

A failed 'awakening'

The result is that at a time of unprecedented technological and communications revolutions over the globe, the Arab world is still wrestling with questions that seem to be from a former age: the Cold War era or the time of the creation of independent Arab states in the 1940s, or the first encounter with the West in the 19th Century. The 'outside' was prioritised over the 'inside'.

"We gave priority to a policy of confrontation [with Israel] while postponing progress in the hope of completely achieving our rights," writes Saghiyeh. "In order to justify this approach we said that progress is against us and is intended to plunder our treasures. Since then the treasures have diminished and so did progress, as well as our rights. Only dictatorship is spreading."

The language of Arab intellectuals now openly speaks of the failure of Al-Nahda, the 'awakening' project that at the end of the 19th Century seemed an exhilarating possibility. "The Al-Nahda project," al-Ansari warns, "was not some project for growth like some Marshall Plan to awaken Japan after Hiroshima, for Japan realised its awakening project since the 19th Century, and Europe began it in 14th Century Italy.

"The Japanese experience ended in defeat in 1945. We have and are still being defeated. But the Japan, defeated yesterday has arisen from the débris to become a major world economic power. What befell the Japanese was worse than anything inflicted on Arabs. Since then all we have achieved is to make everyone enemies of us. Our problem as Arabs is that we have started to confuse the civilisation war with the imperialism war."

Delusion culture
The misconception underpins a widespread culture based on delusion. Part and parcel of this is the titanic struggle 'to defend ourselves against a new imperial conspiracy constantly reinventing itself', a position lampooned by Saghiyeh. He states: "Whoever follows the news coming from Egypt – and the positions of most of Egypt's intellectuals, journalists, and politicians – begins to think the world wakes up every morning, rubs its eyes, and exclaims: 'Oh my Goodness, it's seven, I'm late, I have to start immediately to conspire against Egypt!'" The political culture has been reduced to an idle-duality: greatness versus treason; nationalism versus normalisation; fundamentalism versus globalisation. Saghiyeh states: "These express the intelligence of a simple mind. Egypt is too great to be limited to such a simplistic duality."

Nor is it harmlessly simple, since it directly impacts upon foreign relations, particularly when governments that do not have a delusional culture find themselves having to react to its contradictions. For example, an overwhelming majority of Egyptians prefer the severing of relations with the US, but American aid to Egypt has reached US$50 billion since Camp David in 1979. More ominously, it devours anything that might weaken its hold. For instance, by pressing the 'Arab dignity' and 'foreign conspiracy' buttons, the Egyptian government was able to silence most of the population, and even the thinking classes on the issue of Sa'ad al-Din Ibrahim, the human rights campaigner arrested for speaking out on legal, communitarian and electoral abuses. As al-Ansari warns: "The Arab mind is only deceiving and destroying itself, no one else."

A future permanently on hold
"The West is exploiting our backwardness and our differences," states al-Ansari. "There are bills to pay in the general sense for this Arab position, politically, religiously, economically." As late-comers to the issue of modernisation, and as people still to place a full trust in the intellectual revolution 'wherever the chips may fall', Arabs, al-Ansari warns, must start to direct their censure at themselves and address the causes of defeat. There are still few signs that these calls are being taken seriously enough to effect

a change. During last October there took place the somewhat oddly titled 'First Arab Thought Conference', organised by the Arab Thought Institute, brainchild of Saudi Prince Khaled Al-Faisal, to address this problem. Its purpose "to contribute to the development of the nation and rise to its expectations" was, however, belied by the non-controversial, PR-oriented lecture programme, with papers such as *Towards a fair relationship between the Arabs and the West; Monotheistic religions and Arab identity;* and *The media and Arab problems.* Many of the more respected Arab scholars and independent intellectuals stayed at home.

The reality is that delusion and defeat have been an effective tool in both foreign and domestic affairs and there is little official impetus to give them up. As B.A. Wardam laments in the Jordanian daily *al-Dustour:* "For more than 50 years democracy in the Arab world has remained on hold because of the pretext of the conflict with Israel. This conflict, however, is now merely verbal... a battle that has never happened, and will never happen."

Similarly for the official guardians of social mores. While religious reform in Europe antedated modernism, in the Arab world it is the reverse. Most Islamic reform movements began as a reaction to modernisation and therefore reform, with this label attached to it still proves easy to brush aside. The failure of the Arab intellectual is nowhere more apparent than in the present crisis over the war with Iraq.

"It is embarrassing for Arabs," writes Abd al-Wahhab al-Affendi in the pan-Arab daily *al-Quds al-'Arabi,* "to see mighty demonstrations take to the streets of Washington, Tokyo, London and Paris, while their own capitals remain silent... Is that not proof enough that the root of the problem lies not in Washington but in the lands of the Arabs? Why not call on Bush to occupy the entire Arab world? At least then we would have the right to demonstrate freely against his policies."

However the rulers, al-Affendi caustically points out, are not the principal ones to blame: "Those rulers would never have been able to survive in power for as long as they have, had it not been for the armies of sycophantic intellectuals, journalists, clerics and others who do their bidding.

"Where are the signs of life in the vast graveyard that is the Arab world? We are already lamenting a future occupation of Iraq, yet we ignore the far greater - and present - catastrophe manifested in the oppression and slavery we are living under."

"We are under the illusion that the world waits for us," Hazem Saghiyeh regrets. "We are still confident that our future is ahead of us and is a glorious future. But this future will remain ahead of us forever."

CIA FACT FILE ON IRAQ

INTRODUCTION

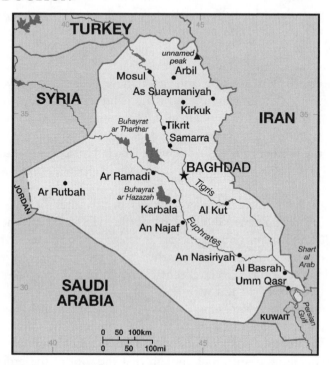

Background:

Formerly part of the Ottoman Empire, Iraq became an independent kingdom in 1932. A "republic" was proclaimed in 1958, but in actuality a series of military strongmen have ruled the country since then, the latest being Saddam Hussein. Territorial disputes with Iran led to an inconclusive and costly eight-year war (1980-88). In August 1990 Iraq seized Kuwait, but was expelled by US-led, UN Coalition Forces during the Gulf War of January-February 1991. Following Kuwait's liberation, the UN Security Council (UNSC) required Iraq to scrap all weapons of mass destruction and long-range missiles and to allow UN verification inspections. Continued Iraqi noncompliance with UNSC resolutions during the past twelve years resulted in the US-led invasion of Iraq in March 2003 and the ousting of the Saddam Hussein regime. Coalition Forces remain in Iraq, helping to restore degraded infrastructure and facilitating the establishment of a freely elected government.

GEOGRAPHY

Location:
Middle East, bordering the Persian Gulf, between Iran and Kuwait

Geographic coordinates:
33 00 N, 44 00 E

Map references:
Middle East

Area:
total: 437,072 sq km
water: 4,910 sq km
land: 432,162 sq km

Area - comparative:
slightly more than twice the size of Idaho

Land boundaries:
total: 3,650 km
border countries: Iran 1,458 km, Jordan 181 km, Kuwait 240 km, Saudi Arabia 814 km, Syria 605 km, Turkey 352 km

Coastline:
58 km

Maritime claims:
continental shelf: not specified
territorial sea: 12 NM

Climate:
mostly desert; mild to cool winters with dry, hot, cloudless summers; northern mountainous regions along Iranian and Turkish borders experience cold winters with occasionally heavy snows that melt in early spring, sometimes causing extensive flooding in central and southern Iraq

Terrain:
mostly broad plains; reedy marshes along Iranian border in south with large flooded areas; mountains along borders with Iran and Turkey

Elevation extremes:
lowest point: Persian Gulf 0 m
highest point: Haji Ibrahim 3,600 m

Natural resources:
petroleum, natural gas, phosphates, sulfur

Land use:
arable land: 11.89%
permanent crops: 0.78%
other: 87.33% (1998 est.)

Irrigated land:

35,250 sq km (1998 est.)

Natural hazards:

dust storms, sandstorms, floods

Environment - current issues:

government water control projects have drained most of the inhabited marsh areas east of An Nasiriyah by drying up or diverting the feeder streams and rivers; a once sizable population of Marsh Arabs, who inhabited these areas for thousands of years, has been displaced; furthermore, the destruction of the natural habitat poses serious threats to the area's wildlife populations; inadequate supplies of potable water; development of Tigris-Euphrates Rivers system contingent upon agreements with upstream riparian Turkey; air and water pollution; soil degradation (salination) and erosion; desertification

Environment - international agreements:

party to: Law of the Sea, Nuclear Test Ban

signed, but not ratified: Environmental Modification

Geography - note:

strategic location on Shatt al Arab waterway and at the head of the Persian Gulf

PEOPLE

Population:

24,001,816 (July 2002 est.)

Age structure:

0-14 years: 41.1% (male 5,003,755; female 4,849,238)

15-64 years: 55.9% (male 6,794,265; female 6,624,662)

65 years and over: 3% (male 341,520; female 388,376) (2002 est.)

Population growth rate:

2.82% (2002 est.)

Birth rate:

34.2 births/1,000 population (2002 est.)

Death rate:

6.02 deaths/1,000 population (2002 est.)

Net migration rate:

0 migrant(s)/1,000 population (2002 est.)

Sex ratio:

at birth: 1.05 male(s)/female

under 15 years: 1.03 male(s)/female

15-64 years: 1.03 male(s)/female
65 years and over: 0.88 male(s)/female
total population: 1.02 male(s)/female (2002 est.)

Infant mortality rate:
57.61 deaths/1,000 live births (2002 est.)

Life expectancy at birth:
total population: 67.38 years
female: 68.5 years (2002 est.)
male: 66.31 years

Total fertility rate:
4.63 children born/woman (2002 est.)

HIV/AIDS - adult prevalence rate:
less than 0.01% (1999 est.)

HIV/AIDS - people living with HIV/AIDS:
NA

HIV/AIDS - deaths:
NA

Nationality:
noun: Iraqi(s)
adjective: Iraqi

Ethnic groups:
Arab 75%-80%, Kurdish 15%-20%, Turkoman, Assyrian or other 5%

Religions:
Muslim 97% (Shi'a 60%-65%, Sunni 32%-37%), Christian or other 3%

Languages:
Arabic, Kurdish (official in Kurdish regions), Assyrian, Armenian

Literacy:
definition: age 15 and over can read and write
total population: 58%
male: 70.7%
female: 45% (1995 est.)

GOVERNMENT

Country name:
conventional long form: Republic of Iraq
conventional short form: Iraq
local short form: Al Iraq
local long form: Al Jumhuriyah al Iraqiyah

Government type:
in transition following April 2003 defeat of Saddam Hussein regime by US-led Coalition

Capital:
Baghdad

Administrative divisions:
18 governorates (muhafazat, singular - muhafazah); Al Anbar, Al Basrah, Al Muthanna, Al Qadisiyah, An Najaf, Arbil, As Sulaymaniyah, At Ta'mim, Babil, Baghdad, Dahuk, Dhi Qar, Diyala, Karbala, Maysan, Ninawa, Salah ad Din, Wasit

Independence:
3 October 1932 (from League of Nations mandate under British Administration)

National holiday:
Revolution Day, 17 July (1968)

Constitution:
in transition following April 2003 defeat of Saddam Hussein regime by US-led Coalition

Legal system:
in transition following April 2003 defeat of Saddam Hussein regime by US-led Coalition

Suffrage:
formerly 18 years of age; universal; in transition following April 2003 defeat of Saddam Hussein regime by US-led Coalition

Executive branch:
chief of state: in transition following April 2003 defeat of Saddam Hussein regime by US-led Coalition

Legislative branch:
in transition following April 2003 defeat of Saddam Hussein regime by US-led Coalition

Judicial branch:
in transition following April 2003 defeat of Saddam Hussein regime by US-led Coalition

Political parties and leaders:
in transition following April 2003 defeat of Saddam Hussein regime by US-led Coalition

Political pressure groups and leaders:
in transition following April 2003 defeat of Saddam Hussein regime by US-led Coalition

International organization participation:

ABEDA, ACC, AFESD, AL, AMF, CAEU, CCC, EAPC, ESCWA, FAO, G-19, G-77, IAEA, IBRD, ICAO, ICRM, IDA, IDB, IFAD, IFC, IFRCS, ILO, IMF, IMO, Interpol, IOC, ISO, ITU, NAM, OAPEC, OIC, OPEC, PCA, UN, UNCTAD, UNESCO, UNIDO, UPU, WFTU, WHO, WIPO, WMO, WToO

Diplomatic representation in the US:

in transition following April 2003 defeat of Saddam Hussein regime by US-led Coalition

Diplomatic representation from the US:

in transition following April 2003 defeat of Saddam Hussein regime by US-led Coalition

Flag description:

three equal horizontal bands of red (top), white, and black with three green five-pointed stars in a horizontal line centered in the white band; the phrase ALLAHU AKBAR (God is Great) in green Arabic script - Allahu to the right of the middle star and Akbar to the left of the middle star - was added in January 1991 during the Persian Gulf crisis; similar to the flag of Syria which has two stars but no script and the flag of Yemen which has a plain white band; also similar to the flag of Egypt which has a symbolic eagle centered in the white band

ECONOMY

Economy - overview:

Iraq's economy is dominated by the oil sector, which has traditionally provided about 95% of foreign exchange earnings. In the 1980s financial problems caused by massive expenditures in the eight-year war with Iran and damage to oil export facilities by Iran led the government to implement austerity measures, borrow heavily, and later reschedule foreign debt payments; Iraq suffered economic losses from the war of at least $100 billion. After hostilities ended in 1988, oil exports gradually increased with the construction of new pipelines and restoration of damaged facilities. Iraq's seizure of Kuwait in August 1990, subsequent international economic sanctions, and damage from military action by an international Coalition beginning in January 1991 drastically reduced economic activity. Although government policies supporting large military and internal security forces and allocating resources to key supporters of the regime have hurt the economy, implementation of the UN's Oil-For-Food program beginning in December 1996 helped improve conditions for the average Iraqi citizen. Iraq was allowed to export limited amounts of oil in exchange for food, medicine, and some infrastructure spare parts. In December 1999 the UN Security Council authorized Iraq to export under the program as much oil as required to meet humanitarian needs. Oil exports have recently been more than three-quarters pre-war level. However, 28% of Iraq's export revenues under the program have been deducted to meet UN Compensation Fund and UN administrative expenses. The drop in GDP in 2001-02 was largely the result of the global economic slowdown and lower oil prices. Per capita food imports increased significantly, while medical supplies and health care services steadily improved. Per capita output and living standards were still well below the pre-war level, but any estimates have a wide range of error. The military victory of the US-led Coalition in March-April 2003 resulted in the shutdown of much of the central economic administrative structure and the loss of a comparatively small amount of capital plant.

GDP:
purchasing power parity - $59 billion (2001 est.)

GDP - real growth rate:
-5.7% (2001 est.)

GDP - per capita:
purchasing power parity - $2,500 (2001 est.)

GDP - composition by sector:
agriculture: 6%
industry: 13%
services: 81% (1993 est.)

Population below poverty line:
NA

Household income or consumption by percentage share:
lowest 10%: NA
highest 10%: NA

Inflation rate (consumer prices):
60% (2001 est.)

Labor force:
6.5 million (2002 est.)

Labor force - by occupation:
agriculture NA, industry NA, services NA

Unemployment rate:
NA

Budget:
revenues: NA
expenditures: NA, including capital expenditures NA

Industries:
petroleum, chemicals, textiles, construction materials, food processing

Industrial production growth rate:
NA

Electricity - production:
27.3 billion kWh (2000)

Electricity - production by source:
fossil fuel: 98%
hydro: 2%
other: 0% (2000)
nuclear: 0%

Electricity - consumption:
25.389 billion kWh (2000)

Electricity - exports:
0 kWh (2000)

Electricity - imports:
0 kWh (2000)

Agriculture - products:
wheat, barley, rice, vegetables, dates, cotton; cattle, sheep

Exports:
$15.8 billion f.o.b. (2001 est.)

Exports - commodities:
crude oil

Exports - partners:
US 46.2%, Italy 12.2%, France 9.6%, Spain 8.6% (2000)

Imports:
$11 billion f.o.b. (2001 est.)

Imports - commodities:
food, medicine, manufactures

Imports - partners:
France 22.5%, Australia 22%, China 5.8%, Russia 5.8% (2000)

Debt - external:
$120 billion (2002 est.)

Economic aid - recipient:
$327.5 million (1995) (1995)

Currency:
Iraqi dinar (IQD)

Currency code:
IQD

Exchange rates:
Iraqi dinars per US dollar - 0.3109 (fixed official rate since 1982); black market rate - Iraqi dinars per US dollar - 2,000 (December 2001), 1,910 (December 1999), 1,815 (December 1998), 1,530 (December 1997), 910 (December 1996); note - subject to wide fluctuations

Fiscal year:
calendar year

COMMUNICATIONS

Telephones - main lines in use:
675,000 (1997)

Telephones - mobile cellular:
NA; service available in northern Iraq (2001)

Telephone system:
general assessment: an unknown number of telecommunication facilities were damaged during the March-April 2003 war
domestic: the network consists of coaxial cables and microwave radio relay links
international: satellite earth stations - 2 Intelsat (1 Atlantic Ocean and 1 Indian Ocean), 1 Intersputnik (Atlantic Ocean region), and 1 Arabsat (inoperative); coaxial cable and microwave radio relay to Jordan, Kuwait, Syria, and Turkey; Kuwait line is probably nonoperational

Radio broadcast stations:
AM 19 (5 are inactive), FM 51, shortwave 4 (1998)

Radios:
4.85 million (1997)

Television broadcast stations:
13 (1997)

Televisions:
1.75 million (1997)

Internet country code:
.iq

Internet Service Providers (ISPs):
1 (2000)

Internet users:
　12,500 (2001)

TRANSPORTATION
Railways:
　total: 2,339 km
　standard gauge: 2,339 km 1.435-m gauge (2001)
Highways:
　total: 45,550 km
　paved: 38,400 km
　unpaved: 7,150 km (1996 est.)
Waterways:
　1,015 km
　note: Shatt al Arab is usually navigable by maritime traffic for about 130 km; channel has been dredged to 3 m and is in use; Tigris and Euphrates Rivers have navigable sections for shallow-draft boats; Shatt al Basrah canal was navigable by shallow-draft craft before closing in 1991 because of the Gulf War
Pipelines:
　crude oil 4,350 km; petroleum products 725 km; natural gas 1,360 km
Ports and harbors:
　Umm Qasr, Khawr az Zubayr, and Al Basra have limited functionality
Merchant marine:
　total: 25 ships (1,000 GRT or over) totaling 186,709 GRT/278,575 DWT
　ships by type: cargo 14, passenger 1, passenger/cargo 1, petroleum tanker 8, roll on/roll off 1 (2002 est.)
Airports:
　150 (2002); note - unknown number were damaged during the March-April 2003 war
Airports - with paved runways:
　total: 77
　over 3,047 m: 21
　2,438 to 3,047 m: 36
　1,524 to 2,437 m: 5
　914 to 1,523 m: 6
　under 914 m: 9 (2002)
Airports - with unpaved runways:
　total: 73

over 3,047 m: 5
2,438 to 3,047 m: 5
1,524 to 2,437 m: 24
914 to 1,523 m: 28
under 914 m: 11 (2002)

Heliports:
5 (2002)

MILITARY

Military branches:
Army, Republican Guard, Navy, Air Force, Air Defense Force, Border Guard Force, Fedayeen Saddam; note - with the defeat of Saddam Hussein's regime in 2003, the data listed in the following entries for Iraq is invalid, but is retained here for historical purposes and until replaced by valid information related to the future Iraqi Government (April 2003)

Military manpower - military age:
18 years of age (2002 est.)

Military manpower - availability:
males age 15-49: 6,135,847 (2002 est.)

Military manpower - fit for military service:
males age 15-49: 3,430,819 (2002 est.)

Military manpower - reaching military age annually:
males: 274,035 (2002 est.)

Military expenditures - dollar figure:
$1.3 billion (FY00)

Military expenditures - per cent of GDP:
NA

TRANSNATIONAL ISSUES

Disputes - international:
despite restored diplomatic relations in 1990, disputes with Iran over maritime and land boundaries, navigation channels, and other issues from the eight-year war persist; land and Shatt al Arab boundary demarcation put an end to claims to Kuwait and to Bubiyan and Warbah Islands, but no maritime boundary exists with Kuwait in the Persian Gulf; Iraq protests Turkey's hydrological projects to regulate the Tigris and Euphrates rivers upstream

WHY ARABS LOSE WARS

Courtesy of *American Diplomacy:* http://americandiplomacy.org
By Norvell B. de Atkine[1]

The author, a retired U.S. Army colonel, draws upon many
years of firsthand observation of Arabs in training to reach
conclusions about the ways in which they go into combat.
His findings derive from personal experience with Arab
military establishments in the capacity of U.S. military
attache and security assistance officer, observer officer with
the British-officered Trucial Oman Scouts (the security force
in the emirates prior to the establishment of the UAE), as
well as some thirty years of study of the Middle East.

ARABIC-SPEAKING ARMIES have been generally ineffective in the
modern era. Egyptian regular forces did poorly against Yemeni irregulars in
the 1960s. Syrians could only impose their will in Lebanon during the mid-
1970s by the use of overwhelming weaponry and numbers. Iraqis showed
ineptness against an Iranian military ripped apart by revolutionary turmoil
in the 1980s and could not win a three-decades-long war against the Kurds.
The Arab military performance on both sides of the 1990 Kuwait war was
mediocre. And the Arabs have done poorly in nearly all the military
confrontations with Israel. Why this unimpressive record? There are many
factors - economic, ideological, technical - but perhaps the most important
has to do with culture and certain societal attributes which inhibit Arabs
from producing an effective military force.

False Starts

Including culture in strategic assessments has a poor legacy, for it has often
been spun from an ugly brew of ignorance, wishful thinking, and
mythology. Thus, the U.S. Army in the 1930s evaluated the Japanese
national character as lacking originality and drew the unwarranted
conclusion that that country would be permanently disadvantaged in
technology. Hitler dismissed the United States as a mongrel society and
consequently underestimated the impact of America's entry into the war.
American strategists assumed that the pain threshold of the North
Vietnamese approximated our own and that the air bombardment of the

North would bring it to its knees. Three days of aerial attacks were thought to be all the Serbs could withstand; in fact, seventy-eight days were needed.

As these examples suggest, when culture is considered in calculating the relative strengths and weaknesses of opposing forces, it tends to lead to wild distortions, especially when it is a matter of understanding why states unprepared for war enter into combat flushed with confidence. The temptation is to impute cultural attributes to the enemy state that negate its superior numbers or weaponry. Or the opposite: to view the potential enemy through the prism of one's own cultural norms.

It is particularly dangerous to make facile assumptions about abilities in warfare based on past performance, for societies evolve and so does the military subculture with it. The dismal French performance in the 1870 Franco-Prussian war led the German high command to an overly optimistic assessment prior to World War 1. Then tenacity and courage of French soldiers in World War I lead everyone from Winston Churchill to the German high command vastly to overestimate the French army's fighting abilities. Israeli generals underestimated the Egyptian army of 1973 based on Egypt's hapless performance in the 1967 war.

Culture is difficult to pin down. It is not synonymous with an individual's race nor ethnic identity. The history of warfare makes a mockery of attempts to assign rigid cultural attributes to individuals - as the military histories of the Ottoman and Roman empires illustrate. In both cases it was training, discipline, esprit, and élan which made the difference, not the individual soldiers' origin. The highly disciplined and effective Roman legions, for example, recruited from throughout the Roman Empire, and the elite Ottoman Janissaries (slave soldiers) were Christians forcibly recruited as boys from the Balkans.

The Role of Culture

These problems notwithstanding, culture does need to be taken into account. Indeed, awareness of prior mistakes should make it possible to assess the role of cultural factors in warfare. John Keegan, the eminent historian of warfare, argues that culture is a prime determinant of the nature of warfare. In contrast to the usual manner of European warfare, which he terms "face to face," Keegan depicts the early Arab armies in the Islamic era as masters of evasion, delay, and indirection. Examining Arab warfare in this century leads to the conclusion that the Arabs remain more successful in insurgent, or political, warfare - what T. E. Lawrence termed "winning wars without battles." Even the much-lauded Egyptian crossing of the Suez in 1973 at its core entailed a masterful deception plan. It may well be that these seemingly permanent attributes result from a culture that engenders subtlety, indirection, and dissimulation in personal relationships.

Along these lines, Kenneth Pollock concludes his exhaustive study of Arab military effectiveness by noting that "certain patterns of behavior fostered by the dominant Arab culture were the most important factors contributing to the limited military effectiveness of Arab armies and air forces from 1945 to 1991." These attributes included over-centralization, discouraging initiative, lack of flexibility, manipulation of information, and the discouragement of leadership at the junior officer level. The barrage of criticism leveled at Samuel Huntington's notion of a "clash of civilizations" in no way lessens the vital point he made - that however much the grouping of peoples by religion and culture rather than political or economic divisions offends academics who propound a world defined by class, race, and gender, it is a reality, one not diminished by modern communications.

But how does one integrate the study of culture into military training? At present, it has hardly any role. Paul M. Belbutowski, a scholar and former member of the U.S. Delta Force, succinctly stated a deficiency in our own military education system: "Culture, comprised of all that is vague and intangible, is not generally integrated into strategic planning except at the most superficial level." And yet it is precisely "all that is vague and intangible" that defines low-intensity conflicts. The Vietnamese communists did not fight the war the United States had trained for, nor did the Chechens and Afghans fight the war the Russians prepared for. This entails far more than simply retooling weaponry and retraining soldiers. It requires an understanding of the cultural mythology, history, attitude toward time, etc.; and it demands a more substantial investment in time and money than a bureaucratic organization is likely to authorize.

Mindful of walking through a minefield of past errors and present cultural sensibilities, I offer some assessments of the role of culture in the military training of Arabic-speaking officers. I confine myself principally to training for two reasons:

- First, I observed much training but only one combat campaign (the Jordanian Army against the Palestine Liberation Organization in 1970).
- Secondly, armies fight as they train. Troops are conditioned by peacetime habits, policies, and procedures; they do not undergo a sudden metamorphosis that transforms civilians in uniform into warriors. General George Patton was fond of relating the story about Julius Caesar, who "in the winter time... so trained his legions in all that became soldiers and so habituated them to the proper

performance of their duties, that when in the spring he committed them to battle against the Gauls, it was not necessary to give them orders, for they knew what to do and how to do it."

Information as Power

In every society information is a means of making a living or wielding power, but Arabs husband information and hold it especially tightly. U.S. trainers have often been surprised over the years by the fact that information provided to key personnel does not get much further than them. Having learned to perform some complicated procedure, an Arab technician knows that he is invaluable so long as he is the only one in a unit to have that knowledge; once he dispenses it to others he no longer is the only font of knowledge and his power dissipates. This explains the commonplace hoarding of manuals, books, training pamphlets, and other training or logistics literature.

On one occasion, an American mobile training team working with armor in Egypt at long last received the operators' manuals that had laboriously been translated into Arabic. The American trainers took the newly minted manuals straight to the tank park and distributed them to the tank crews. Right behind them, the company commander, a graduate of the armor school at Fort Knox and specialized courses at the Aberdeen Proving Grounds ordnance school, promptly collected the manuals from those crews. Questioned why he did this, the commander said that there was no point in giving them to the drivers because enlisted men could not read. In point of fact, he did not want enlisted men to have an independent source of knowledge. Being the only person who could explain the fire control instrumentation or bore sight artillery weapons brought prestige and attention.

In military terms this means that very little cross-training is accomplished and that, for instance in a tank crew, the gunners, loaders and drivers might be proficient in their jobs but are not prepared to fill in should one become a casualty. Not understanding one another's jobs also inhibits a smoothly functioning crew. At a higher level it means that there is no depth in technical proficiency.

Education Problems

Training tends to be unimaginative, cut and dried, and not challenging. Because the Arab educational system is predicated on rote memorization, officers have a phenomenal ability to commit vast amounts of knowledge to memory. The learning system tends to consist of on-high lectures, with students taking voluminous notes and being examined on what they were told. (It also has interesting implications for a foreign instructor, whose credibility, for example, is diminished if he must resort to a book.) The emphasis on memorization has a price, and that is in diminished ability to reason or engage in analysis based upon general principles. Thinking outside the box is not encouraged; doing so in public can damage a career. Instructors are not challenged and neither, in the end, are students.

Head-to-head competition among individuals is generally avoided, at least openly, for it means that someone wins and someone else loses, with the loser humiliated. This taboo has particular import when a class contains mixed ranks. Education is in good part sought as a matter of personal prestige, so Arabs in U.S. military schools take pains to ensure that the ranking member, according to military position or social class, scores the highest marks in the class. Often this leads to "sharing answers" in class - often in a rather overt manner or in junior officers concealing scores higher than those of their superiors.

American military instructors dealing with Middle Eastern students learn to ensure that, before directing any question to a student in a classroom situation, particularly if he is an officer, the student does possess the correct answer. If this is not assured, the officer may feel he has been deliberately set up for public humiliation. In the often-paranoid environment of Arab political culture, he may then become an enemy of the instructor, and his classmates will become apprehensive about their also being singled out for humiliation - and learning becomes impossible.

Officers vs. Soldiers

Arab junior officers are well trained on the technical aspects of their weapons and tactical know-how, but not in leadership, a subject given little attention. For example, as General Sa`d ash-Shazli, the Egyptian chief of staff, noted in his assessment of the army he inherited prior to the 1973 war, they were not trained to seize the initiative or volunteer original concepts or new ideas. Indeed, leadership may be the greatest weakness of Arab training systems. This problem results from two main factors: a highly accentuated class system bordering on a caste system, and lack of a non-commissioned-officer development program.

Most Arab armies treat enlisted soldiers like sub-humans. When the winds in Egypt one day carried biting sand particles from the desert during a demonstration for visiting U.S. dignitaries, I watched as a contingent of soldiers marched in and formed a single rank to shield the Americans; Egyptian soldiers, in other words, are used on occasion as nothing more than a windbreak. The idea of taking care of one's men is found only among the most elite units in the Egyptian military. On a typical weekend, officers in units stationed outside Cairo will get in their cars and drive off to their homes, leaving the enlisted men to fend for themselves by trekking across the desert to a highway and flag down busses or trucks to get to the Cairo rail system. Garrison cantonments have no amenities for soldiers. The same situation, in various degrees, exists elsewhere in the Arabic-speaking countries - less so in Jordan, even more so in Iraq and Syria. The young draftees who make up the vast bulk of the Egyptian army hate military service for good reason and will do almost anything, including self-mutilation, to avoid it. In Syria the wealthy buy exemptions or, failing that, are assigned to noncombatant organizations. As a young Syrian told me, his musical skills came from his assignment to a Syrian army band where he learned to play an instrument. In general, the militaries of the Fertile Crescent enforce discipline by fear; in countries where a tribal system still is in force, such as Saudi Arabia, the innate egalitarianism of the society mitigates against fear as the prime mover, so a general lack of discipline pervades.

The social and professional gap between officers and enlisted men is present in all armies, but in the United States and other Western forces, the non-commissioned officer (NCO) corps bridges it. Indeed, a professional NCO corps has been critical for the American military to work at its best; as the primary trainers in a professional army, NCOs are critical to training programs and to the enlisted men's sense of unit esprit. Most of the Arab world either has no NCO corps or it is non-functional, severely handicapping the military's effectiveness. With some exceptions, NCOs are considered in the same low category as enlisted men and so do not serve as a bridge between enlisted men and officers. Officers instruct but the wide social gap between enlisted man and officer tends to make the learning process perfunctory, formalized, and ineffective. The show-and-tell aspects of training are frequently missing because officers refuse to get their hands dirty and prefer to ignore the more practical aspects of their subject matter, believing this below their social station. A dramatic example of this occurred during the Gulf War when a severe windstorm blew down the tents of Iraqi officer prisoners of war. For three days they stayed in the wind and rain rather than be observed by enlisted prisoners in a nearby camp working with their hands.

The military price for this is very great. Without the cohesion supplied by NCOs, units tend to disintegrate in the stress of combat. This is primarily a function of the fact that the enlisted soldiers simply do not have trust in their officers. Once officers depart the training areas, training begins to fall apart as soldiers begin drifting off. An Egyptian officer once explained to me that the Egyptian army's catastrophic defeat in 1967 resulted from of a lack of cohesion within units. The situation, he said, had only marginally improved in 1973. Iraqi prisoners in 1991 showed a remarkable fear of and enmity toward their officers.

Decision-Making and Responsibility

Decisions are highly centralized, made at a very high level and rarely delegated. Rarely does an officer make a critical decision on his own; instead, he prefers the safe course of being identified as industrious, intelligent, loyal - and compliant. Bringing attention to oneself as an innovator or someone prone to making unilateral decisions is a recipe for trouble. As in civilian life, conforming is the overwhelming societal norm; the nail that stands up gets hammered down. Decisions are made and delivered from on high, with very little lateral communication. Orders and information flow from top to bottom; they are not to be reinterpreted, amended, or modified in any way.

U.S. trainers often experience frustration obtaining a decision from a counterpart, not realizing that the Arab officer lacks the authority to make the decision - a frustration amplified by the Arab's understandable reluctance to admit that he lacks that authority. This author has several times seen decisions that could have been made at the battalion level concerning such matters as class meeting times and locations referred for approval to the ministry of defense. All of which has led American trainers to develop a rule of thumb: a sergeant first class in the U.S. Army has as much authority as a colonel in an Arab army.

Methods of instruction and subject matter are dictated by higher authorities. Unit commanders have very little to say about these affairs. The politicized nature of the Arab militaries means that political factors weigh heavily and frequently override military considerations. Officers with initiative and a predilection for unilateral action pose a threat to the regime. This can be seen not just at the level of national strategy but in every aspect of military operations and training. If Arab militaries became less politicized and more professional in preparation for the 1973 war with Israel, once the fighting ended, old habits returned. Now, an increasingly bureaucratized military establishment weighs in as well. A veteran of the Pentagon turf wars will feel like a kindergartner when he encounters the rivalries that exist in the Arab military headquarters.

Taking responsibility for a policy, operation, status, or training program rarely occurs. U.S. trainers can find it very frustrating when they repeatedly encounter Arab officers placing blame for unsuccessful operations or programs on the U.S. equipment or some other outside source. A high rate of non-operational U.S. equipment is blamed on a "lack of spare parts" - pointing a finger at an unresponsive U.S. supply system despite the fact that American trainers can document ample supplies arriving in country and disappearing in a moribund supply system. (It should be added, and is important to do so, that this criticism was never caustic or personal and was often so indirect and politely delivered that it wasn't until after a meeting that oblique references were understood.) This imperative works even at the most exalted levels. During the Kuwait war, Iraqi forces took over the town of Khafji in northeast Saudi Arabia after the Saudis had evacuated the place. General Khalid bin Sultan, the Saudi ground forces commander, requested a letter from General Norman Schwarzkopf, stating it was the U.S. general who ordered an evacuation from the Saudi town. And in his account of the Khafji battle, General Bin Sultan predictably blames the Americans for the Iraqi occupation of the town. In reality the problem was that the light Saudi forces in the area left the battlefield. The Saudis were in fact outgunned and outnumbered by the Iraqi unit approaching Khafji but Saudi pride required that foreigners be blamed.

As for equipment, a vast cultural gap exists between the U.S. and Arab maintenance and logistics systems. The Arab difficulties with U.S. equipment is not, as sometimes simplistically believed, a matter of "Arabs don't do maintenance," but a vast cultural gap. The American concept of a weapons system does not convey easily. A weapons system brings with it specific maintenance and logistics procedures, policies, and even a philosophy, all of them based on U.S. culture, with its expectations of a certain educational level, sense of small unit responsibility, tool allocation, and doctrine. The U.S. equipment and its maintenance are predicated on a concept of repair at the lowest level and therefore require delegation of authority. Tools that would be allocated to a U.S. battalion (a unit of some 600-800 personnel) would most likely be found at a much higher level – probably two or three echelons higher – in an Arab army. The expertise, initiative and, most importantly, the trust indicated by delegation of responsibility to a lower level are rare. Without the needed tools, spare parts, or expertise available to keep equipment running, and loathe to report bad news to his superiors, the unit commander looks for scapegoats.

All this explains why I many times heard in Egypt that U.S. weaponry is "too delicate." I have observed many in-country U.S. survey teams: invariably, hosts make the case for acquiring the most modern of military hardware and do everything to avoid issues of maintenance, logistics, and training. They obfuscate and mislead to such an extent that U.S. teams, no matter how earnest their sense of mission, find it nearly impossible to help. More generally, Arab reluctance to be candid about training deficiencies makes it extremely difficult for foreign advisors properly to support instruction or assess training needs.

Combined Arms Operations

A lack of cooperation is most apparent in the failure of all Arab armies to succeed at combined arms operations. A regular Jordanian army infantry company, for example is man-for-man as good as a comparable Israeli company; at battalion level, however, the coordination required for combined arms operations, with artillery, air, and logistics support, is simply absent. Indeed, the higher the echelon, the greater the disparity. This results from infrequent combined arms training; when it does take place, it is intended to impress visitors (which it does - the dog-and-pony show is usually done with uncommon gusto and theatrical talent) rather than provide real training.

Three underlying factors further impede coordination necessary for combined operations.

- First, the well-known lack of trust among Arabs in anyone outside their own families adversely affects offensive operations. In a culture in which almost every sphere of human endeavor, including business and social relationships, is based on a family structure, this basic mistrust of others is particularly costly in the stress of battle. Offensive action, at base, consists of fire and maneuver. The maneuver element must be confident that supporting units or arms are providing covering fire. If there is a lack of trust in that support, getting troops moving forward against dug-in defenders is possible only by officers getting out front and leading, something that has not been a characteristic of Arab leadership. (Exceptions to this pattern are limited to elite units, which throughout the Arab world have the same duty - to protect the regime rather than the country.)

- Second, the complex mosaic system of peoples creates additional problems for training, as rulers in the Middle East make use of the sectarian and tribal loyalties to maintain power. The `Alawi minority controls Syria, east bankers control Jordan, Sunnis control Iraq, and Nejdis control Saudi Arabia. This has direct implications for the military, where sectarian considerations affect assignments and promotions. Some minorities (such the Circassians in Jordan or the Druze in Syria) tie their well-being to the ruling elite and perform critical protection roles; others (such as the Shi`a of Iraq) are excluded from the officer corps. In any case, the careful assignment of officers based on sectarian considerations works against assignments based on merit. The same lack of trust operates at the inter-state level, where Arab armies exhibit very little trust of each other, and with good reason. The blatant lie Gamal Abdel Nasser told King Husayn in June 1967 to get him into the war against Israel – that the Egyptian air force was over Tel Aviv (when the vast majority of planes had been destroyed) – was a classic example of deceit. Sadat's disingenuous approach to the Syrians to entice them to enter the war in October 1973 was another (he told them that the Egyptians were planning total war, a deception that included using a second set of operational plans intended only for Syrian eyes). With this sort of history, it is no wonder that there is very little cross or joint training among Arab armies and very few command exercises. During the 1967 war, for example, not a single Jordanian liaison officer was stationed in Egypt, nor were the Jordanians forthcoming with the Egyptian command.

- Third, Middle Eastern rulers routinely rely on balance-of-power techniques to maintain their authority. They use competing organizations, duplicate agencies, and coercive structures dependent upon the ruler's whim. This makes building any form of personal power base difficult, if not impossible, and keeps the leadership apprehensive and off-balance, never secure in its careers or social position. The same applies within the military; a powerful chairman of the joint chiefs is inconceivable. Joint commands are paper constructs that have little actual function. Leaders look at joint commands, joint exercises, combined arms, and integrated staffs very cautiously for all Arab armies are double-edged swords. One edge points toward the external enemy and the other toward the capital. Land forces are at once a regime-maintenance force and threat to the same regime. This situation is most clearly seen in Saudi Arabia, where the land forces and aviation are under the minister of defense, Prince Sultan, while the National Guard is under Prince Abdullah, the deputy prime minister and crown prince. In Egypt, the Central Security Forces balance the army. In Iraq and Syria, the Republican Guard does the balancing.

No Arab ruler will allow combined operations or training to become routine, for these create familiarity, soften rivalries, erase suspicions, and eliminate the fragmented, competing organizations that enable rulers to play off rivals against one another. Politicians actually create obstacles to maintain fragmentation. For example, obtaining aircraft from the air force for army airborne training, whether it is a joint exercise or a simple administrative request for support of training, must generally be coordinated by the heads of services at the ministry of defense; if a large number of aircraft are involved, this probably requires presidential approval. Military coups may have gone out of style for now, but the fear of them remains strong. Any large-scale exercise of land forces is always a matter of concern to the government and is closely observed, particularly if live ammunition is being used. In Saudi Arabia a complex system of clearances required from area military commanders and provincial governors, all of whom have differing command channels to secure road convoy permission, obtaining ammunition, and conducting exercises, means that in order for a coup to work it would require a massive amount of loyal conspirators. The system has proven to be coup-proof, and there is no reason to believe it will not work well into the future.

Security and Paranoia

Arab regimes classify virtually everything vaguely military. Information the U.S. military routinely publishes (about promotions, transfers, names of unit commanders, and unit designations) is top secret in Arabic-speaking countries. To be sure, this does make it more difficult for the enemy to construct an accurate order of battle, but it also feeds the divisive and compartmentalized nature of the military forces. The obsession with security can reach ludicrous lengths. Prior to the 1973 war, Sadat was surprised to find that within two weeks of the date he had ordered the armed forces be ready for war, his minister of war, General Muhammad Sadiq, had failed to inform his immediate staff of the order. Should a war, Sadat wondered, be kept secret from the very people expected to fight it?

One can expect to have an Arab counterpart or key contact changed without warning and with no explanation as to his sudden absence. This might well be simply a transfer a few doors away, but the vagueness of it all leaves foreigners imagining dire scenarios - that could be true. And it is best not to inquire too much; advisors or trainers who seem overly inquisitive may find their access to host military information or facilities limited. The presumed close U.S.-Israel relationship, thought to be operative at all levels, aggravates and complicates this penchant for secrecy. Arabs believe that the most mundane details about them are somehow transmitted to the Mossad via a secret hotline. This explains why an U.S. advisor with Arab forces is likely to be asked early and often about his opinion on the "Palestine problem," then subjected to monologues on the assumed Jewish domination of the United States.

Indifference to Safety

There is a general laxness with respect to safety measures and a seeming carelessness and indifference to training accidents, many of which could have been prevented by minimal safety precautions. To the (perhaps overly) safety-conscious Americans, Arab societies appear indifferent to casualties and to the importance of training safety. There are a number of explanations for this. Some would point to the inherent fatalism within Islam, and certainly anyone who has spent considerable time in Arab taxis would lend credence to that theory; but perhaps the reason has less to do with religion than with political culture. As any military veteran knows, the ethos of a unit is set at the top; or, as the old saying has it, units do those things well that the boss cares about. When the top political leadership displays a complete lack of concern for the welfare of its soldiers, such attitudes percolate down through the ranks. Exhibit A was the betrayal of Syrian troops fighting Israel in the Golan in 1967: having withdrawn its elite units, the Syrian government knowingly broadcast the falsehood that Israeli troops had captured the town of Kuneitra, which would have put them behind the largely conscript Syrian army still in position. The leadership took this step to pressure the great powers to impose a truce, though it led to a panic by the Syrian troops and the loss of the Golan Heights.

Conclusion

It would be difficult to exaggerate the cultural gulf separating American and Arab military cultures. In every significant area, American military advisors find students who enthusiastically take in their lessons and then resolutely fail to apply them. The culture they return to – the culture of their own armies in their own countries – defeats the intentions with which they took leave of their American instructors. Arab officers are not concerned about the welfare and safety of their men. The Arab military mind does not encourage initiative on the part of junior officers, or any officers for that matter. Responsibility is avoided and deflected, not sought and assumed. Political paranoia and operational hermeticism, rather than openness and team effort, are the rules of advancement (and survival) in the Arab military establishments. These are not issues of genetics, of course, but matters of historical and political culture.

When they had an influence on certain Arab military establishments, the Soviets strongly reinforced their clients' own cultural traits. Like that of the Arabs, the Soviets' military culture was driven by political fears bordering on paranoia. The steps taken to control the sources (real or imagined) of these fears, such as a rigidly centralized command structure, were readily understood by Arab political and military elites. The Arabs, too, felt an affinity for the Soviet officer class's contempt for ordinary soldiers and its distrust of a well-developed, well-appreciated, well-rewarded NCO corps.

Arab political culture is based on a high degree of social stratification, very much like that of the defunct Soviet Union and very much unlike the upwardly mobile, meritocratic, democratic United States. Arab officers do not see any value in sharing information among themselves, let alone with their men. In this they follow the example of their political leaders, who not only withhold information from their own allies, but routinely deceive them. Training in Arab armies reflects this: rather than prepare as much as possible for the multitude of improvised responsibilities that are thrown up in the chaos of battle, Arab soldiers, and their officers, are bound in the narrow functions assigned them by their hierarchy. That this renders them less effective on the battlefield, let alone that it places their lives at greater risk, is scarcely of concern, whereas, of course, these two issues are dominant in the American military culture and are reflected in American military training.

Change is unlikely to come until it occurs in the larger Arab political culture, although the experience of other societies (including our own) suggests that the military can have a democratizing influence on the larger political culture, as officers bring the lessons of their training first into their professional environment, then into the larger society. It obviously makes a big difference, however, when the surrounding political culture is not only avowedly democratic (as was the Soviet Union's), but functionally so.

Until Arab politics begin to change at fundamental levels, Arab armies, whatever the courage or proficiency of individual officers and men, are unlikely to acquire the range of qualities which modern fighting forces require for success on the battlefield. For these qualities depend on inculcating respect, trust, and openness among the members of the armed forces at all levels, and this is the marching music of modern warfare that Arab armies, no matter how much they emulate the corresponding steps, do not want to hear.

First printed in *Middle East Quarterly* December 1999, Vol. 6, No. 2. Republished by permission. The author notes that the opinions expressed in this article are strictly his own.

1   Norvell "Tex" de Atkine served eight years in Lebanon, Jordan, and Egypt (in addition to extensive combat service in Vietnam). A West Pointer, he holds a graduate degree in Arab studies from the American University of Beirut. Currently he teaches at the JFK Special Warfare School at Ft. Bragg, North Carolina. See also his 'The Political-Military Officer: Soldier Scholar or Cocktail Commando?' in *American Diplomacy* Vol. IV, No. 1 (Winter 1999)

INDEX